FOLLOWING THE LIGHT

TEACHINGS, TESTIMONIES, TRIALS, AND TRIUMPHS OF THE

CHURCH OF GOD MOVEMENT
(ANDERSON)

A DOCUMENTARY HISTORY

BARRY L. CALLEN
COMPILER AND EDITOR

Arthur Kelly, Publishing Coodinator
Barry L. Callen, Compiler and Editor
Cover and Layout by
Curtis D. Corzine and Virginia L. Wachenschwanz

CONTENTS

Part Three: Implementing the Light
The General Assembly,
United States and Canada, 1917-2000

9

Part Four: Honoring the Light
Ecumenical and Cross-Cultural
Vision, Initiatives, Partnerships

**Part Five: Spreading the Lighjt
International Vision,
Initiatives, and Partnerships**

Foreword

Following the Light is a substantial documentary history of the teachings, testimonies, trials, and triumphs of the Church of God movement (Anderson) from 1880 through the year 2000. Church of God Ministries commissioned the compiler and editor, Dr. Barry L. Callen, to prepare this volume in a way that both chronicles the historic tradition of this movement and provides detail and perspective on the monumental changes that recently have taken place in the life of the Church of God in North America. The result, this truly significant publication, includes all of the material previously published in Dr. Callen's books *The Assembly Speaks* (1985), *Thinking and Acting Together* (1992), and *Journeying Together* (1996). Also included are some of the often-sought materials available only in his earlier *The First Century* volumes (1979), with everything brought fully up to date and much new material added.

Found here are numerous sermons, essays, resolutions, testimonies, histories, and photographs that could only be found in the Archives of the Church of God housed on the campus of Anderson University. There is the largest bibliography of the publications of this movement ever assembled. An extensive index and internal numbering system enables a reader to find quickly whatever is of particular interest. Of special note is Dr. Callen's insightful and orienting overview essay, "A Developmental Profile of the Church of God Movement:" Realizing the Ideal. The book provides the reader with important primary materials that will augment a proposed new narrative history of the Church of God by Dr. Merle Strege. The Church of God is indebted to Dr. Callen for faithfully and efficiently executing this important compiling, editing, and interpretive work. It is a prominent milestone in our history.

Following the Light will serve for years to come as a major reference book for Church of God leaders and students and for many others in the larger Christian community who can benefit from a better understanding of the witness to God's work through this movement. May a copy of this book soon be found in every pastor's library, in every congregational resource center, and in the hands of every student who is interested in the history, theology, people, and worldwide ministries of the Church of God movement. A thorough understanding of the wonderful heritage of this movement is critical as it prepares to embrace the opportunities of a new century and millennium.

Church of God Ministries was formed by the General Assembly of the Church of God in the United States and Canada through successive actions in 1996 and 1997 (this story and the historic actions are all found in these pages). Its creation followed a ten-year period of examination regarding the organizational structures of the Church of God in North America. Today, Church of God Ministries includes the ministries previously assigned by the Assembly to the following entities: the Leadership Council of the Church of God and its two divisions, Church and Ministry Service and World Service; the Board of Christian Education; the Mass Communications Board; the Missionary Board; Vision-2-Grow; the Departments of Home Missions and Church Growth (from the Board of Church Extension); and curriculum, books, and periodicals (from Warner Press). Warner Press continues to function as a subsidiary organization under the umbrella of Church of God Ministries and its governing board, the Ministries Council.

May that which God has done in the past bring joy and new resolve into the present, all for the sake of what God is yet to do in the future that lies just ahead!

Robert W. Pearson,
General Director,
Church of God Ministries

PREFACE

This book is meant to be more than a trip down memory lane, although it provides everything necessary for quite a nostalgic journey. It is intended primarily to be a significant sampling of the people, beliefs, and actions of a modern reform movement in the church. It is a "documentary" history of one body of believers whose heritage holds potential wisdom for the future of the whole Christian community. Thus, reaching into the past is done as a service to the future.

Most bodies of Christians establish for themselves a pattern of formal church authority (their "polity") which defines in detail accepted doctrines and regulates carefully the group's life. Sometimes the power inherent in this pattern centers in a pope or council of bishops, sometimes in synods, conferences, or superintendents. Such centralizing typically is justified either by claiming that God established things that way in the church (a Roman Catholic stance) or by assuming that biblical principles and practical necessity join in given circumstances to evolve a pattern that is transitional, always to be reviewed, and subject to change in changing circumstances (a central principle of Protestantism). The Church of God movement is clearly Protestant in the sense of its commitment to ongoing reformation, but it also is "catholic" in its vision of the whole people of God. To date, this movement has been an exercise in great caution about human things like fixed creeds and powerful institutions in the church's life.

The usual pattern of formalized church authority has led to many distortions in church life. This tendency to distortion has been resisted since the nineteenth century by a reformation movement known simply as the "Church of God" (Anderson, Indiana). From its beginnings in the 1880s, this movement have longed to return to the truths, simplicities, and Spirit-directedness of the apostolic church. This longing has resulted in an unwillingness to accept and an attempt not to perpetuate what has been judged the centuries of corruption and humanization that have burdened the life of the Christian community—and thus hindered the church in its mission to the world.

In the face of a maze of brittle and binding church creeds and a bewildering variety of complex and often coercive church organizations scattered across the Christian community, this movement of the Church of God has attempted to remain open to the fresh and freeing moves of the Spirit of God. It's polity, or chosen way of being together, has sought a dynamic flexibility featuring an open Bible and the constant guidance of the Spirit. While much of traditional church life has tended to function in mechanical and manipulative ways more related to the non-church world than to what the New Testament teaches, there has been a persistent determination in the Church of God. Such is not to be so among us!

14

Once only a vision burning in the hearts of a few, such as Daniel S. Warner (1842-1895) who was the movement's primary pioneer, the Church of God now has emerged as a worldwide phenomenon sponsoring gospel proclamation, ministerial education, and human service in about ninety countries. It began when laypersons and ministers, initially isolated from each another, soon found themselves with common reformation perspectives and desirous of fellowship, inspiration, and a coordination of activity. A crucial publication the *Gospel Trumpet* developed, and helped greatly to meet the communication need. So did camp meetings and assemblies of leaders that eventually came to assume business as well as strictly "spiritual" roles in the movement's emerging life. Leaders were intent on spreading good news and strategizing for effective church mission, but without laying controlling human hands on the essence of the church itself (thus forming another denomination and adding to the divisive confusion already judged intolerable).

By 1917 the most prominent of the assemblies of the Church of God in North America was meeting annually in Anderson, Indiana [see Entry 42]. Since then this General Assembly has formalized its identity and functions and created a coordinating body and legal arm (known since 1997 as Church of God Ministries, Inc."). This body, directed by a Ministries Council elected by leaders from across Canada and the United States, has become influential in the oversight of most of the movement's cooperative ministries which are based in North America [see Entries 71, 203]. "Oversight," however, does not center in the flow of power, but in the nurturing of fellowship and the sharing of ministry resources. Oversight also is accomplished by the influence of the General Assembly's united voice when a consensus can be reached on issues of common concern. Even then, the Assembly speaks "to" and not "for" the church. All of the Assembly's significant actions since its beginning are found in this volume.

Through the years the General Assembly has sought to avoid "exercising ecclesiastical authority" in the process of its work. After all, it is not the church sitting in control of local congregations or of state/provincial assemblies. Being the most representative body of the Church of God movement in North America, however, on many occasions the General Assembly has spoken its corporate opinion and even expectation to Church of God congregations, the national ministry agencies, and even to the church and society at large. The Assembly has announced convictions and sounded warnings. It has attempted to encourage vision, influence opinion, gather resources, and mobilize effort. While abhorring the very idea of organizing and controlling the church itself, because God's family is answerable only to God's Word and Spirit, it certainly has sought to coordinate, direct, and energize the work of the church. The challenge has been to be active and effective in common ministry and mission without being guilty of manipulating and denominationalizing the life of the church. Freedom in the Spirit and accountability to each other have been twin values, each cherished and sometimes found to be in conflict.

This volume begins with a major overview essay, a "developmental profile" of the Church of God movement. It then is organized into five sections of material, each using the "light" theme often employed by the movement. The sections are

Part One: "Seeing the Light," focuses on teachings and personal testimonies. What did these people see and why did they dedicate themselves to this cause?

Part Two: "Clarifying the Light," recalls a series of persons, documents, and events that brought the movement's self-identity into sharp focus. What have been some of the central issues, questions, and crises in the movement's life?

Part Three: "Implementing the Light," highlights the General Assembly in North America, including the fruit of its life together since its beginning in 1917. What has this Assembly done and said that was and still might be significant?

Part Four: "Honoring the Light," seeks to review a range of statements and actions related to the vision of Christian unity that lies at the heart of this Church of God movement. What has been said and done to further the vision of reuniting of God's people?

Part Five: "Spreading the Light," traces the increasing multi-culturalism and internationalization of the Church of God movement. How and to whom has the light now spread across the world? What new mission challenges are being faced?

Together, this beginning essay and these five large blocks of heritage materials provide a good orientation to and documentary sampling of the people, contexts, teaching tradition, and cooperative life of a church movement that, since the nineteenth century, has sought to be a prophetic voice to and a unifying force in the church worldwide. All units of material are numbered in sequence and also are placed in chronological order where appropriate. Included at the end of the volume is an extensive bibliography of published materials by this movement and an extensive index to allow ready access to the specific material of interest to the reader.

As the compiler and editor of the materials of this reforming Christian tradition, I am in debt to eight senior leaders of the Church of God movement who took the time to review the first draft of this work and suggest a few important refinements to what I originally had envisioned. While no collection such as this could ever be complete, this one is better than it would have been because of the shared wisdom of these historically sensitive consultants. I am in debt to Wilfred Jordan, Arlo F. Newell, Robert W. Pearson, Robert H. Reardon, Fredrick K. Shively, L. Spencer Spaulding, Merle D. Strege, and Douglas E. Welch. Across my years of ministry within the Church of God movement, I also have been nurtured and informed significantly by Lillie S. McCutcheon, Austin Sowers, Gene W. Newberry, Boyce W. Blackwelder, John W. V. Smith, James Earl Massey, and many others! I have been blessed richly and I hope that their influences are reflected adequately in these pages.

We seek in these pages to remember the milestones of the past and celebrate what God already has done as one body of Christians has sought to follow God's light and journey together for the sake of the divine mission in the world. It is inevitable that history will remain with us, even if we are unaware; it is not inevitable that the best of that history will be remembered and translated in ways that will enlighten the challenges of today and enable God's intended tomorrow. So, let us remember yesterday. Let us translate for today. Let us be what God wants us to be. Let us continue to follow God's light!

—Barry L. Callen

OVERVIEW ESSAY

A DEVELOPMENTAL PROFILE OF THE CHURCH OF GOD MOVEMENT

"REALIZING THE IDEAL"

BY BARRY L. CALLEN

God said to Moses: "Speak to all the congregation of the people of Israel and say to them: You shall be holy, for I the Lord your God am holy" (Lev. 19:2). Paul said to the Thessalonians: "May the God of peace himself sanctify you entirely; and may your spirit and soul and body be kept sound and blameless at the coming of our Lord Jesus Christ" (1 Thess. 5:23).

Jesus prayed: ". . .that they may *all be one*. As you, Father, are in me and I am in you, may they also be in us, so that the world may believe that you have sent me. The glory that you have given me I have given them, so that they *may be one, as we are one*, I in them and you in me, that they may become *completely one*, so that the world may know that you have sent me and have loved them even as you have loved me." (John 17:21-23)

Barry L. Callen
Anderson University

The above biblical verses illustrate well both central divine intentions and thus central burdens which lie at the foundation of the ideals of the "reformation movement" of the Church of God (Anderson, Indiana). The holiness of God should be reflected in God's people. A distinctive aspect of this reflection is intended by God to be a unifying bond of love among God's people, a love that should shape the corporate life of Christians and strengthen the credibility of their witness in the world. Good perspective is provided by Robert Reardon:

The reformation movement [of the Church of God] was a great outburst of idealism. It was a call to return to the "early morning time"—to a church "without spot or wrinkle"—to a life of perfection and holiness, to a union of the saved and sanctified, drawn out of sin and the confusion of sectism. In many ways, Anderson [Indiana, the eventual North American home of the movement's cooperative ministries]. . .was expected to be a reflection of these great ideals, and when the ideal met the real the discrepancies were hard to handle and difficult to explain.[1]

---

1. Robert H. Reardon, *This is the Way It Was: Growing Up in the Church of God* (Anderson, Ind.: Warner Press, 1991), 16.

18

This essay uses for perspective the concept of the *ideal* in tension with the *real*. The Church of God movement has envisioned the ideal for the church and has sought to approach realizing it in the midst of the sometimes hard realities of church life in this world.

I first explored the concept of "realizing the ideal" in my master's thesis in 1969 at Asbury Theological Seminary. In the decades since, both I and the Church of God have matured and persisted in pursuit of the ideal of God's highest for the church. These pages seek to explore the distinctive reformation concerns and goals of the Church of God movement that center around the related concerns of realizing *holiness* and *unity*. This is done by following this particular church body's quest for twelve decades (1880-2000) to teach and bring this holiness-unity renewal vision to functioning reality in its own life and in the church generally.

At issue is a difficult and dynamic process similar to the one operating in much of Eastern Europe in the 1990s after the Iron Curtain had been drawn back and the tragic social and economic failures of Marxism had been exposed. Democracy burst on the scene as a liberating and exhilarating concept to those burdened by decades of totalitarianism. Tens of millions of people were now free! However, making democratic social theory understood, operational, and socially productive would prove to be a much more challenging task than merely being able to voice freely in public its enticing rhetoric. The hard work is always to move from merely announcing the ideal to actually achieving it in practical terms.

The inspired teaching about Christian holiness and unity was exhilarating indeed for many Christians of the late nineteenth and early twentieth centuries who felt locked behind a rigid ecclesiastical curtain of denominational arrogance and division. With an idealistic vision of what God really intended for the church, these wall-smashing and liberty-hungry believers "came out" with a call that soon became the heart of the Church of God reformation movement. That was the revolutionary beginning; but the really demanding quest ever since 1880[2] has been to operationalize effectively this distinctive vision. This Church of God movement has sought over the decades to adjust effectively within its own shifting self-images[3] and to act faithfully through the ministry structures that it has developed with great

---

2. This dating is approximate since the movement emerged almost simultaneously in several places in the United States, was resistant to the thought of any new "church" (denomination) being "founded," and soon was carried along by a new publication, the *Gospel Trumpet*, that began publication in 1881.

3. This movement's self-images have included: "The Saints," the "Come-Outers," the "Last Reformation," and particularly the "Church of God Reformation Movement." Slogans often used have been "A United Church for a Divided World" and "Where Christian Experience Makes You a Member."

caution and self-imposed limitations[4] (wanting not to become more of the divisive denominational problem).

The following pages describe briefly the idealism at the heart of this particular movement as it exists within today's larger Christian community. They also assess subjects which this movement has stressed and around which it has changed over the twelve decades of its existence to date. Consequently, there is a brief review of (1) the relation of *idealism* and *realism* in ancient Israel and in the Church of God movement; (2) the history of affirming and then questioning a validation of the movement by use of select portions of the Bible's prophetic literature; (3) the issue of historical illusion and innocence sometimes experienced by the movement; (4) select accommodations which this movement has made in the process of seeking to implement its vision; (5) a recommended stance toward church tradition consistent with the movement's mission (if not always with its self-understanding); (6) a fresh view of how movements such as the Church of God can/should relate to the church's intended oneness; and (7) a resulting agenda for the future of the Church of God movement.

While final answers rarely are available, I am hopeful that this reform movement at least has been asking the right questions and pursuing responsibly God's intended answers. The important thing is to know where one fits in the Body of Christ so that the right gifts are shared and lessons learned for the benefit of the whole of God's people.

IDEALISM AND REALISM IN ANCIENT ISRAEL

An analysis of the biblical book of First Samuel reveals the record of two apparently competing viewpoints within the ancient Israelite community. These viewpoints are insightful for the Church of God movement. At issue in Israel was the wisdom of establishing a monarchy among God's chosen people. Would God be pleased—or at least tolerate—the chosen people having their own human king? The contrasting viewpoints are instructive for an analysis of the traditional approach of the Church of God movement to the issue of Christian unity. One viewpoint in ancient Israel, held by idealistic conservatives, argued that God alone was their king. Success for God's people would be found only in covenant faithfulness and unwavering

---

4. Such limitations are to be seen clearly in the movement's early concern about institutionalizing and "humanizing" the preparation of its ministers. See Barry Callen, *Preparing For Service: A History of Higher Education in the Church of God* (1988), and *Guide of Soul and Mind: The Story of Anderson University* (1992). The movement's first "institution," its publishing house (Gospel Trumpet Company), is another good case study (see Harold Phillips, *Miracle of Survival*, Warner Press, 1979). The commitment was certainly not to anti-education as such, but to a renewed focus on the necessity, even primacy of the Spirit's calling and gifting for Christian ministry.

trust in divine power, not in some desperate accommodation to human ways of organizing, governing, and surviving as the people of God. Hope lay only in championing divine principle rather than in leaning on traditional human arrangements. The challenge was to be the distinctive people of God who always should resist the temptation to accept human standards and structures, and thus to become "like the nations."

Increasingly, however, this idealistic conservative argument lost ground to the persistent voices of people who might be called progressive realists. This counter crowd began its persuasive argument by calling attention to the harsh realities being experienced by God's people in a less-than-ideal world. Certain selected ventures into "worldly ways," therefore, were said to be timely and justifiable. In this view, innovations, such as introducing a monarchy to enable God's people to function more effectively together, were the only reasonable and responsible ways of dealing with things as they then were. Surely God wants progressive, practical, adaptive people who always are finding fresh ways to be faithful and effective in their covenant relationship with God.

Shifting to the world of Christianity, itself an outgrowth of this Hebrew heritage, there has evolved a long tradition of both "practical" monarchists and "radical" dissenters. The Church of God (Anderson) is a body of conservative Christians representing one contemporary expression of this dissenting "radical" tradition.[5] Placed in the setting of states like Indiana and Michigan about 1880 A.D., the fear of many conservative and idealistic Christians was of a human usurping of divine prerogatives, then appearing in the form of the temptation to be like the arrogant, compromising, and divisive denominations. Denominations within the body of Christian people were perceived to be a form of the old temptation to be dominated by human goals, rulers, and gods "like the nations." The progressive realists of nineteenth-century American Protestantism long since had accepted the apparent necessity of denominational structures to govern the life of the church in a less-than-ideal world. But now a contrary and idealistic voice emerged again, announcing that God's will was otherwise. What God willed for the church surely was in the range of practical possibility—at least with divine help. Daniel S. Warner, then an evangelist of the Northern Indiana Eldership of the Churches of God (Winebrennarian), stood up in a meeting in October, 1880, and announced his separation from all sectarian expressions of Christianity (see Entries 1-3).[6] The movement of the Church of God had begun.

---

5. For an extended discussion of the history and theological distinctives of this "radical" or "believers church" tradition, see Barry Callen, *Radical Christianity: The Believers Church in Christianity's History and Future* (Nappanee, Ind.: Evangel Publishing House, 1999).

6. For an account of this and subsequent events that launched the movement of the Church of God, see Barry Callen, *It's God's Church!: Life and Legacy of Daniel Sidney Warner* (Anderson, Ind.: Warner Press, 1995), chapters 5-7.

FOLLOWING THE LIGHT

The imaginations and aspirations of these organizationally beleaguered and newly Spirit-filled believers were fired with fresh hope and resolve. Often they were involved deeply in the Holiness Movement of the time.[7] The presumed simplicity and Spirit-led nature of the apostolic church became for them a model for their renewed vision of God's will for the church on earth. These Christians began to find each other, encourage each other, and write and sing songs that set them marching joyously to a divine and not a human drummer. There was no official founder, single authoritative leader, or claimed extra-biblical revelation. Rather, the Spirit of Jesus was to be in full control of the church. A marching song for this young movement reported this: "And gladly to His [God's] blessed will submissive we shall be, And from the yokes of Babel's lords from hence-forth we are free."[8] "There's a mighty reformation sweeping o'er the land," this movement has sung for generations. "God is gathering His people by His mighty hand; for the cloudy day is ending and the evening sun is bright, With a shout of joy we hail the light."[9]

No longer acceptable as the visible signs of the unity of God's people would be common allegiance to any churchly structure, pope, bishop, super-intendent, or set of liturgical practices. No longer tolerated by these "come-outers" would be the coercive control of humanly written creeds and human-ly conditioned church standards. Particularly through wide circulation of the *Gospel Trumpet* periodical and the preaching and singing of traveling groups of "the saints," pioneers of this new movement announced that nothing should be permitted to choke the God-given unity present among all those persons who find new life in Christ, new power and freedom in Christ's Spirit, and thus also find each other as members of God's one body, the church. The Bible was to be considered authoritative, although its interpretation was not to be prematurely fixed and finalized, with such interpretations then used as divisive creeds (see Entry 75).

These holiness-enthused and unity-minded Christians gladly followed the lead of Daniel Warner, the movement's primary pioneer, who had announced that "we wish to cooperate with all Christians, as such, in saving souls—but forever withdraw from all organisms that uphold and endorse sects and denominations in the body of Christ."[10] On the fiftieth anniversary of the Gospel Trumpet Company in 1931, Robert L. Berry recalled the sadly divided state of the church in Warner's day (1842-1895). Those final decades

---

7. See Melvin Dieter, *The Holiness Revival of the Nineteenth Century* (Metuchen, N.J.: The Scarecrow Press, 1980).

8. A portion of verse four of "The Church's Jubilee," a prominent gospel song of the Church of God by Charles Naylor and Andrew Byers (appears as song 312 in the current hymnal of the Church of God—*Worship the Lord*, Warner Press, 1989).

9. Charles Naylor, Andrew Byers, *Worship the Lord*, 311.

10. Daniel Warner, editorial, *Gospel Trumpet*, June 1, 1881.

of the nineteenth century often witnessed bitter doctrinal debates and denominational competition so vigorous that often no one was thought to be a Christian unless belonging to the "right" denomination. Therefore, reported Berry, Warner and others had "severed their connection with humanly organized churches and boldly maintained that Christ had built a church and that membership in it was the only essential thing to consider." Warner and his ministerial colleagues made no effort to organize a church along denominational lines, but made their appeal to the Scripture itself. They contended that spiritual fellowship with Christ and with one another, and devotion to Scriptural ideals and practices, were all the bonds that Christians needed.[11]

This come-out call was an impassioned and idealistic crusade to lead Christians back to the holiness, freedom, and unity presumed to characterize the apostolic church. One way to get back, movement leaders assumed, was to drop all official creeds, insofar as they were considered official, authoritative, and binding definitions of denominational belief, refusing to receive them as verbal walls isolating true Christians from each other. The result was expected to be substantial and radical. All denominational divisions among Christian people were to be abolished. God was in this, gathering his people from their scattered divisions into one dynamic, whole, and holy body before the soon return of Christ (see Entries 5-6). This ecumenical idealism was based on the central role assumed to be played by the experience of Christian holiness as taught by John Wesley and then as later popularized in America's Midwest holiness revivals.

On March 7, 1878, Daniel Warner wrote the following in his private journal about a "new commission" he had received from God:

> The Lord showed me that holiness could never prosper upon sectarian soil encumbered by human creeds and party names, and he gave me a new commission to join holiness and all truth together and build up the apostolic church of the living God.

Here were clear marching orders for a renewal movement, an idealistic effort on behalf of the whole church of God. Visions of achieving a greater presence of real Christian unity were said to be of no more value than the spiritual reality upon which they were based. If a cleansing by the Spirit of God, the purging enabled only by divine love, became reality for individual believers, then a united fellowship of love and service would be the natural consequence, the fulfillment of a properly founded unity idealism (see Entry 178). Diversity might remain, but division would not! As one of the

---

11. Robert L. Berry, *Golden Jubilee Book* (Anderson, Ind.: Gospel Trumpet Company, 1931), 8.

movement's songs puts it: "Beloved how this perfect love, Unites us all in Jesus! One heart, and soul, and mind: we prove, The union heaven gave us."[12]

From the beginning of this movement of the Church of God there has been the insistence that its "come-outism" emphasis was not a call for newly liberated believers to leave sectism only to form another sect. Rather, there was a vision of a free fellowship of the Spirit that should and could function outside sectarian division (see Entry 10). The only way to escape to the outside, to "see the church" and really "be" the church, according to Warner and others, was the way of holiness. Thus, one published history of the Church of God movement not surprisingly is titled *The Quest for Holiness and Unity* (John Smith, 1980). The envisioned ideal of a united church necessarily was premised on an experience of the cleansing, empowering, and unifying Spirit of God.

There has been a persistent paradox, however, ever since the emergence of this reformation movement. Participants in the Church of God movement have functioned together with a rather clear set of goals and, for the most part, basic theological agreement.[13] At the same time, they have been committed in principle to resisting the narrowing effects of traditional denominationalism. Living with this paradox has been judged hypocritical by some Christians who continue to see denominationalism as unavoidable and not altogether negative. They have seen the movement's substantial consensus of theological thought as clearly denominational in character (see Entries 30-32). Other Christians have studied the movement's vision and life and have used words like *admirable* and *idealistic.* They have judged it to be most commendable, even if destined to inevitable frustration.[14]

Admiration is elicited by a vision of the church (1) that is divinely oriented, (2) that by intent is inclusive of all true Christians without regard to affiliation, nationality, race, gender, or current biblical understanding, (3) that always is open to more of the truth, and (4) that refuses to recognize human standards and organizations as legitimate fences that too often are allowed to divide Christians from each other. But it is this very admirable vision that has made the Church of God movement unusually vulnerable to

12. Chorus of "The Bond of Perfectness," by Daniel Warner and Barney Warren, as in *Worship the Lord: Hymnal of the Church of God* (Anderson, Ind.: Warner Press, 1989), 330.

13. For an anthology of the teachings of the Church of God movement, including key selections from a wide range of its writers and institutions, see Barry L. Callen, *The First Century*, vol. 1 (Anderson, Ind.: Warner Press, 1979), 241-456.

14. Note, e. g., Melvin Dieter, *The Holiness Revival of the Nineteenth Century* (The Scarecrow Press, 1980), 245-257. While the "come-outers" were said to be "a source of embarrassment to the leaders of the mainstream Methodist holiness movement," Dieter nonetheless concludes that "the significance of this radical movement. . .should no longer be relegated so completely to so negative a context." After all, here was an idealistic movement insisting that "the individual, after being challenged by his respective church on the issue of holiness evangelism, sought to apply the logic of Christian perfectionism, with all the ultraistic inclinations of the perfectionist mentality, to the church question" (245-46).

L. to R. Barney Warren, Daniel Warner, Nannie Kigar, Sarah Smith, Frankie Miller

criticism when the movement's own functioning has proven to be less than the ideal for which it stands and toward which it strives. Even so, this vision is vigorously maintained because it continues to commend itself to this movement as God's will for the church.

Daniel S. Warner (1842-1895), primary pioneer of the Church of God movement, was a poet, dreamer, idealist, "a lion roaring mightily against what he understood to be wrong in God's church."[15] In assessing him and the movement's subsequent life, a distinction should be drawn between a *reformer* and a *prophet*. According to one of this movement's church sociologists:

> A reformer would have cut the problem up into smaller pieces and tackled them one at a time. But the prophet sees only the vision of the complete ideal which he seeks and he will accept no half-way measures. So Warner preached the elimination of the entire structure of organized Christianity. Since formal organization served as a harness holding in rein the Holy Spirit, it was a man-made obstacle to grace. It must go, and all God's children would then worship freely together in an undivided Zion. On several occasions Warner indicated that he expected to see this happen within a generation, perhaps within his own lifetime.[16]

Formal church organizations, however, did not disappear in Warner's lifetime and still have not a century later.

What has improved since the late nineteenth century is the tendency of churches (denominations) to assume the prerogatives of the church universal. While Warner's prophetic voice continues to speak, responding today to this vision requires practical reforming activity, not just the excitement of a grand vision. By 1921 Andrew Byers already was noting Warner's "pioneer position" from which he had denounced "all things sectarian." Warner's work was said to have been "the initial or birth stage of the reform." The task by 1921 had moved to the "constructive" stage in which, rather than constantly denouncing the failures of the sects, the challenge was to manifest "those essential principles that characterize the church in her purity and entirety."[17] The act of somehow making the vision concrete actuality is the

15. Barry L. Callen, *It's God's Church! The Life and Legacy of Daniel S. Warner* (Anderson, Ind.: Warner Press, 1995), 152.

16. Val B. Clear, *Where the Saints Have Trod* (Chesterfield, Ind.: Midwest Publications, 1977), 41.

17. Andrew L. Byers, *Birth of a Reformation: Life and Labors of D. S. Warner* (Anderson, Ind.: Gospel Trumpet Company, 1921), 31-32.

difficult move from the envisioned ideal to the implemented real. To do so requires a coming to terms with several pivotal issues that have been prominent in the actual teaching tradition and life of the Church of God movement.

A PROPHETIC VALIDATION

In the early ministry of Daniel Warner, the primary theme (beyond salvation itself) was Christian unity. Then the burden evolved into holiness and unity, and finally it became unity and holiness in light of biblical prophecy. Thus, Warner was involved in two different interpretations of the reason for being of the Church of God movement.[18] First it was to spread the news of the divinely intended unity of Christians that is enabled by the sanctifying power of God. Later there was added a specialized context of movement self-understanding, a "church-historical" interpretation of the Bible's prophetic literature, especially the Book of Revelation. The movement of the Church of God came to be seen as a special instrument called of God in the last days to help regather from divided Romanism and Protestantism the one church comprised of all God's children (see Entry 5).

Soon after 1878 Warner's spiritual experience and related theological insights moved toward at least minimal corporate expression. It was essentially a spontaneous, generally uncoordinated, non-denominational "movement." This Church of God movement, while resisting any denominational identity or intent of its own, nonetheless began evolving the consciousness of a distinctive group identity and mission, a special cause understood to be on center stage as God was working out a plan for reforming and reuniting the one true Church. This developing sense of group destiny soon found something that vividly identified the movement for its adherents. It placed the movement within the whole context of Christian church history, gave increased incentive to proclaim the original concepts of the movement's pioneers, and provided a dramatic, colorful, and compelling way to package and proclaim these concepts widely. This "something" was a fresh adaptation and then adoption of the church-historical method of interpreting the biblical books of Daniel and Revelation.

Warner became aware of such a method in the work of Seventh-Day Adventist scholar Uriah Smith, although he disputed many details of Smith's interpretation.[19] By 1887 Warner himself was publishing in the *Gospel*

---

18. It should be noted that Warner had no intent of launching a new "movement" in the sense of a fresh organizational reality in church life. The chapter titled "A Developing Reformation Consciousness" in John Smith's history of the movement (1980) covers the time period 1880-1895. Warner died in 1895. Says Smith: "these early leaders were preoccupied with their doing and never really took the time to be analytical as to the why of their activity beyond the point of convincement that what they were doing was God's will.... They were themselves reluctant to formalize either a statement of their beliefs or declaration of their objectives" (82).

Trumpet his own articles using prophetic biblical literature to explain church history and lay out a chronological timetable for a radical reformation of the church in the "evening time." Later, this reformation scenario, "restorationist" in many ways, was called "a cleansing of the sanctuary" in a book by that title begun by Warner and completed by Herbert M. Riggle in 1903 after Warner's death. By 1908 the Gospel Trumpet Company also had published Frederick G. Smith's *The Revelation Explained*. Smith, a gifted writer, public speaker, and later editor of the Gospel Trumpet Company, soon became the chief spokesperson in the Church of God movement for this interpretive scheme.[20] What the scheme did, according to church historian John W. V. Smith, was "to solidify this framework for validating the group's self-consciousness and to make it the generally accepted rationale for the movement's existence for at least half of its history" (1980, 100).

In brief, this prophetic scheme was developed as follows. Babylon, a place of exile for the ancient Israelites, was seen pictured in the prophecies of the Book of Revelation as a powerful symbol of the exile of the Christian church for much of its history. "All the evils inherent in the false, unscriptural systems of so-called Christianity," wrote Smith, "are summed up under the one word Babylon..." (1919, 226). Also seen by Smith was a dramatic prophecy of a "coming out" of this more modern Babylonian captivity so that before the end of time there would be "a revival of pure, apostolic Christianity, a reformation in which the true people of God will take their stand outside of all forms of the apostasy and carry the full gospel of the Son of God to 'every nation, and kindred, and tongue and people'" (227).

Just as God enabled the chosen people of old to be released from Babylon and return to their promised land, so there was seen promised in the biblical prophecies a "last reformation" in which freedom would be gained from the Babylon of denominationally imprisoned and therefore apostate and crippled Christianity. This redeemed company would be a reappearance of the "primitive church" pictured as a pure woman (Rev. 12:1). The church would end its scattered condition (divided in sect confusion), bear only the Father's name (Rev. 14:1-5), and, as the Bride of Christ, await with anticipation the early return of the Lord.

Since the apostasy was understood to have been twofold in its nature, including a corruption of the substance of the faith and the intrusion of ecclesiasticism into the life of the church, the evidence of the cleansing of the apostasy would include a restoring of the full truth and an elimination of the ecclesiasticism. This was to be accomplished "by literally forsaking the

---

19. Uriah Smith, *Thoughts on the Prophecies of Daniel and the Revelation* (Battle Creek, Mich.: Review and Herald Publishing Co., 1897). This is his major work. Earlier writings of his on the subject were also available and known to Warner.

20. Note, e.g., F. G. Smith's 1919 volume titled *The Last Reformation* (Anderson, Ind.: Gospel Trumpet Co.).

systems of man-rule just as ancient Israel was restored home to Zion" (Smith, 1919, 249). The goal was to "reestablish in power and glory the simple, primitive theocracy, where Christ shall be exalted as the true and only ruler of his people" (Smith, 1919, 253). There would be, in the terms of 1 Samuel, a dramatic reversal of all vestiges of human monarchy in the household of faith.[21]

The Church of God movement (named consciously to convey its being *of* God and being *only* God's church) soon was being seen through the lens of this prophetic validation, and thus often understood itself as the "final reformation" because its goal was to leave nothing to be restored in doctrine, practice, or spirit (see Entry 5). As F. G. Smith put it, the movement stands "committed to the restoration of apostolic Christianity in its entirety—its doctrines, its ordinances, its personal regenerating and sanctifying experiences, its spiritual life, its holiness, its power, its purity, its gifts of the Spirit, its unity of believers, and its fruits" (Smith, 1919, 254-255). Full accomplishment of this restoration was not being claimed, but a reaching for this comprehensive goal was the commitment.

Persons caught up in such a movement of God would be especially open to the sanctifying work of God and a discerning of God's holiness-related plan for effecting Christian unity. They would, in short, ignore all lines of human ecclesiasticism, recognize as the church nothing short of *all* those and *only* those belonging to Christ through salvation grace, and accept as church authority nothing other than the dominion of Christ administered by the work of the Holy Spirit. Thought and imagery commonly used in the Church of God movement typically announced that it was time in the "evening" of church history to be again like it was in the fresh innocence of the "morning" of the church.[22] Holiness was the key. "Seeing the church" was the privilege of those whose spiritual eyes had been opened. It all was the fulfillment of biblical prophecy. It was believed that "light on the church" had been revealed—and the faithful will always gladly follow God's light.

ILLUSION AND INNOCENCE

The reformation movement of the Church of God now has grown from small numbers of "scattered saints" in the 1880s to about 234,300 constituents in the United States and Canada and 417,000 more scattered among eighty-seven other countries.[23] Thinking only of the movement in the United

21. See especially Daniel Warner and Herbert Riggle, *The Cleansing of the Sanctuary, Or, The Church of God in Type and Antitype, and in Prophecy and Revelation* (Moundsville, W.Va.: Gospel Trumpet Publishing Co., 1903).

22. Note, e.g., John Smith's *Heralds of a Brighter Day* (Anderson, Ind.: Gospel Trumpet Co., 1955) and Robert Reardon's *The Early Morning Light* (Anderson, Ind.: Warner Press, 1979).

States, much beyond size of constituency has changed over the decades since 1880. Cooperative ministries and educational institutions have emerged, some substantial in degree of organization and range of mission. Each was begun out of the urgency of felt need, usually with reluctance rather than movement-wide enthusiasm, in part because of the anti-organizational concerns of this reforming tradition (see Entry 42). For instance, as Barry L. Callen concluded about the arena of higher education within the movement, "the emphasis on local autonomy and the bias against the controlling ability of central organizations or persons has meant that colleges have had maverick-like beginnings. . .and have benefited from very little effective coordination of their efforts or the available resources."[24]

The commitments that have tended to shape the movement's congregational and larger corporate lives have included local church autonomy and democratic procedures, typically clergy dominated, especially at the national level until more recent years (see Entries 46, 56, 59, 64). A simple logic has been used widely since the 1920s to justify the creation of a series of church-related ministry structures at the state, province, and national levels, and now somewhat at the international level (see Entries 28, 205-206). According to this logic, while it is inappropriate and actually impossible for humans to organize God's church, it is appropriate, possible, and expedient for Christians, under the Spirit's direction and empowerment, to organize the *work* of the church. Such organization does not control membership in the church, dictate restrictive belief expectations, or stop local congregational bodies from pursuing their lives and ministries as they feel God intends. The movement's General Assembly in North America has in its constitution a formal statement of its own limitations (see Entry 43).

The movement's pioneers rejected the convenient concept of the "invisible" church, a concept popular with the classic Protestant reformers and dating back to St. Augustine. This concept was judged to have no biblical base and to allow an easy accommodation to the imperfection, division, and failures of the "visible" church. Leaders of the Church of God movement envisioned the visible-invisible church as one, ideally and by divine intention, and they committed themselves to realizing functionally that oneness by the power of sanctifying and gathering (unifying) grace. While proceeding with a strong prejudice against any humanly devised and controlled administration of the invisible-visible church, movement pioneers were hardly anarchists advocating no organization at all. Even before the "work of the church" rationale was verbalized and generally accepted (1940s),[25] always strongly advocated has been the reality of divine organizational ini-

---

23. These statistics are from the 1999 edition of the *Yearbook of the Church of God*.

24. Barry L. Callen, *Preparing for Service: A History of Higher Education in the Church of God* (Anderson, Ind.: Warner Press, 1988), 189.

25. Charles E. Brown, "The Visible and Invisible Church," *Gospel Trumpet*, February 9, 1946.

29

tiative and the gifting and guiding control of God's Spirit over the actual life of the church.

This focus on the singularity of divine control has necessitated a long and continuing quest to discover how church members can come to know and participate effectively in the governance activity of the Holy Spirit. As historian John W. V. Smith concluded in the movement's centennial year of 1980, "the first category of unfinished business is that of harmonizing methodology with theology in regard to functional procedures in the church. Organization has been the most persistent problem the movement has faced" (1980, 436). Earlier Smith had identified six periods within the movement's history that reflect differing general interpretations by the movement of the manner by which government of the Spirit was understood to be realized. These are (1) Spirit governance through charismatic individuals (1880-1900); (2) expedient procedures (1900-1917); (3) national agencies (1917-1930); (4) state structures (1930-1950); (5) planned coordination (1950-1970); and (6) a developing spiritual democracy.[26] Of course, emphases and time periods have intertwined in complex ways. Nonetheless, the general direction of interpretive change is rather clear.

Recently, through the work of the multi-year Task Force On Governance and Polity named by the General Assembly of the Church of God, there was a very visible and intense effort by the movement in North America to address the continuing challenges and persisting dilemmas of church organization (see Entry 173). How, in a now large and diverse body of Christians with more than a century of its own history and institutions, can there be maximum faithfulness to the ideals of this theological tradition and, at the same time, how can the movement function as a cohesive body with mutual accountability and effectiveness in cooperative ministry? (See Entries 166, 171, 176, 177.) A sometimes painful paradox is now being faced. There is both the fellowship's hope of freedom from Spirit-stifling human organizational machinery and the seemingly necessary development of denomination-like structures. Pragmatic realities often have tended to resist the consistent maintenance of theological ideals. Thus this writer's earlier thesis characterized the movement's whole history as a study in "ecumenical idealism" (Callen, 1969).

That Task Force on Governance and Polity made its final report to the General Assembly of the Church of God in June, 1992. After five years of labor, it affirmed a series of "strong convictions," including these:

---

26. Final report of the Consultation On Doctrine, convened by the Executive Council of the Church of God, 1974 (see Entry 7). Aubrey Forrest had suggested a similar set of developmental periods in his earlier sociological study (Forrest, 1948).

- That the Holy Spirit is still in charge of the Church....
- That the solution to the conflict between autonomy and authority is not rejection of either one, but rather their proper balance.
- That authority should be more relationally-based than positionally based.
- Our strong desire to be movemental rather than primarily denominational. We admit that this aspiration is neither simple nor easy... (p. 2).

The argument certainly now could be made that the pioneer thinkers of the Church of God movement, to draw on the provocative picture painted by C. Leonard Allen and Richard T. Hughes (1988), participated heavily in the general American "innocence" of looking longingly back to an earlier time (the apostolic church) when all was thought well, when things once were as they always should be and again now will be. History has brought its share of forced humility (see Entry 195), but without eliminating the enduring idealism.

This backward "restorationist" look led some well-intentioned Church of God people to share a common illusion of the possibility of themselves escaping the accumulated guilt of church history by restoring a purer order that somehow itself could be immune from new historical guilt.[27] This longing look was and, to a significant degree still is, a fundamental factor in this movement's understanding of its own identity and mission. Just as Allen and Hughes wrote of a central irony in the American experience—that of affirming the freedom of all persons to determine their own cultures while at the same time the new nation was judging and even enforcing its own culture as the destiny of the world (Allen, Hughes, 205)—so the Church of God movement has struggled over the decades to champion a vision of non-sectarian Christianity without losing its own innocence by sectarianizing and inappropriately institutionalizing its own expression of that non-sectarian vision.

ASSESSING ACCOMMODATIONS

The religious worlds of the 1880s and the year 2000 are very different. The ecumenical scene in the larger Christian community, for instance, has changed radically. The Church of God movement, at least in its formal statements at the national level, has softened its "come-outism" emphasis accordingly (see Entry 192), questioned its early pattern of prophetic self-validation,[28] and developed many church-related organizations and with

---

27. It should be noted that in the earliest years of this movement there was strong expectation of the soon return of the Lord. Thus, there was no intent of establishing a new set of long-term church institutions, which might themselves become susceptible later to such historical guilt.

them the rationale for their functional necessity and limited legitimacy. It also has accommodated to various standards and styles of the cultures in which it has found itself, sometimes for the sake of relevant ministry and often times, unfortunately, more for the sake of a convenience and comfort in conflict with its mission. A series of historical, theological, and sociological studies have sought to describe, analyze, and influence these changes and accommodations.[29] Following is a brief review of these in four general categories.

1. Prophetic Self-Understanding of the Movement. A first area of such study has been a fresh assessment of the continuing legitimacy of the prophetic understanding and validation of the movement itself. Otto F. Linn's three-volume publication in New Testament interpretation (1941-1942), for instance, provided an alternative to the movement's early and influential church-historical pattern of interpreting the Book of Revelation that had yielded a prophetic validation of the movement (see Entry 38).[30] More recently that traditional interpretative pattern has been reaffirmed with only minor alterations by some church leaders who are calling the movement back to its earlier sense of certainty about itself and many other things (e.g., McCutcheon, 1964, rev. 1999, see Entry 35). But this pattern also has been questioned vigorously by numerous contemporary scholars in the movement, including Kenneth Jones (in Callen, 1990, 133-150) and Marie Strong (1980, rev. 1996). Something of an alternative was provided by historian-theologian Charles E. Brown, who went beyond questioning the church-historical interpretative approach to the Book of Revelation. He found validation for the movement in its being a continuation of the "radical" approach to Christianity which always looked to the original or root of the faith as its defining basis (Brown, 1954). In recent years the Church of God movement has made efforts to renew an understanding of its historical roots and present affinities with both the Believers' Church[31] and Wesleyan[32] theological traditions.

28. For an extensive treatment, see John E. Stanley, "Unity Amid Diversity: Interpreting the Book of Revelation in the Church of God (Anderson)," in *Wesleyan Theological Journal*, Fall, 1990, pp. 74-98.

29. For a partial listing of these studies, mostly master's theses and doctoral dissertations, see Barry L. Callen, *The First Century*, vol. 2, Warner Press, 1979, pp. 673-676. See also the bibliography in this volume which identifies many of them.

30. Russell R. Byrum, in his teaching in the 1920s at Anderson Bible Training School (now Anderson University), at least had been open to fresh thinking in this area, something which caused considerable political difficulty for him and the school at the time (see Entries 31, 33).

31. See, e.g., Merle Strege, ed., *Baptism and Church: A Believers' Church Vision*, 1986, a book resulting from a Believers Church conference convened on the Anderson University campus. Also, see Barry L. Callen, *Radical Christianity: The Believers Church Tradition in Christianity's History and Future* (Nappanee, Ind.: Evangel Publishing House, 1999).

32. For instance, since 1993 Barry Callen of the Church of God has been Editor of the *Wesleyan Theological Journal* and in his books, he has highlighted the Wesleyan rootage of the Church of God movement (especially *Contours of a Cause*, 1995, and *God As Loving Grace*, 1996).

The distinctive nature and role of the Church of God movement in God's plan for the unifying of all true believers has become less evident and thus less motivating for many of the movement's contemporary adherents (see Entries 181-182). The questioning of the prophetic validation and the lack of consensus on a clear and compelling alternative are certainly two reasons for this lessening motivation.[33] Another is a matter of the reasons for current patterns of church affiliation in general. In local congregations of the movement today, one typically finds significant numbers of laypersons who have no personal background in this particular movement and who often have associated recently with these congregations for reasons other than theological ones. If, then, the movement is still dynamic, still moving today, there appears to be less of a distinctive driving force, and the direction of motion is not easily distinguishable from that of conservative Protestantism in general.

What has diminished over the years is the dramatic sense of a reformationist or restorationist cause for which all should be sacrificed, a powerful and preachable biblical mandate like the one that inspired several earlier generations of the movement. As President-Emeritus Robert Reardon summarized the situation in his annual report to the Board of Trustees of Anderson University in 1979, just as the movement was about to celebrate its centennial in 1980: "Unfortunately, our historic antagonism to anything creedal in nature has left the Church of God drifting too much at the mercy of current winds of doctrine, and new people among us have had a hard time finding out who we are and what kind of theological cement holds us together."[34] There was clear concern that too little "cement" remained. Reardon's 1979 concern was only magnified for many in the movement when the publication of *Vital Christianity* was suspended in 1996 for financial reasons (see Entries 61, 71). This periodical, earlier known as the *Gospel Trumpet*, had been so significant in the movement's history.

---

33. According to Robert Reardon, *The Early Morning Light* (1979): ". . .our most serious problem has been to redefine our mission and identity. Consider the chief pillar in the house, a prophetic calculation that identified us in Scripture with a great reformation beginning in 1880, destined to restore the Church and herald the end of the age.... An open, honest, scholarly look at the Book of Revelation simply would not support the previous conclusions expounded by F. G. Smith and others.... This writer holds that the collapse of 'last reformationism' which began to appear among us in the twenties and thirties left a central theological vacuum, an identity crisis, which cannot be underestimated in the traumatic effect it has had on the movement" (86-87).

34. In response to President Reardon's concern, the faculty and administration of Anderson University's School of Theology developed a "WE BELIEVE" booklet that was distributed widely by Warner Press (see Entry 9). More recently, Merle Strege, current historian of the movement, has sought to address this problem in a "narrative theology" style. See his book *Tell Me the Tale* (1991).

2. Sociological Analysis. In addition to the reworking of the early prophetic validation for the movement, a second arena of reassessment has been sociological. Lyle E. Schaller, church planner and consultant who has worked closely with several Church of God congregations and national agencies in recent years, pointed out that religious organizations tend to behave like other organizations rather than displaying a distinctively *religious* emphasis in making decisions. Thus, their behavior and developmental patterns are predictable, a most disconcerting thought for a movement attempting to resist the encroachment of human institutionalizing on the divine Body of Christ. What if the Church of God movement's own ministry programs and institutions were to be assessed as exhibiting such a typical tendency? Valorous Clear did just such a sociological assessment of the development of the Church of God movement and documented a typical path from "sect" to "denomination" (Clear, 1953). He lamented the relative loss of prophetic witness that inevitably accompanies such cultural accommodation and institutional development.

In more recent years Clear has offered the judgment that the movement, living now in a much less polemical environment than in the years of its beginning, has tended to present its understandings of the goal, the evidences, and the processes toward Christian unity in non-judgmental terms not likely to be offensive to other Christians who yet remain in their denominationalized settings. He concluded that this more non-judgmental approach goes beyond the movement's desire to maximize constructive relationships with all Christians and its need to involve allies to support its own institutions. At points it has deteriorated, argues Clear, into a quiet quest for the movement to gain recognition from and acceptance by mainstream Christianity (Clear, 1977, 6). This tendency to blend into the establishment Protestant landscape, to the degree that it is real, is clearly abortive of the original movement's idealism and mission. A similar study of the Church of God movement by Aubrey Leland Forrest, however, concluded that the obvious shift need not be seen so negatively:

> [The Church of God movement] has been found to have wide areas of accommodation, especially as regards its place in the scheme of religious life and its attitude toward other church bodies.... The religious truth held by the Church of God. . .is now being presented in more universal terms in the literature of the body. At present. . .it appears to be taking its place as one of the contributing and permanent religious bodies (1948, 310-311).

In 1996, after a year of research initiated by the Leadership Council of the Church of God, consultant Leith Anderson made this discomforting observation about the Church of God movement of the mid-1990s: "There is a very strong desire to be described and identified as a *movement* and not as

34

a *denomination*. However, the Church of God retains few characteristics of a movement and many characteristics of an aging denomination."[35] The General Assembly proceeded to affirm in principle Anderson's series of recommended organizational changes in national ministry structures. It then set in motion an implementation study intended to facilitate significant changes. The intent in part was to "downsize" the time and expense invested in national ministry structures and increase effective ministry that is vision-driven. Some voices feared that the result could actually increase the control of a few leaders and undercut grassroots commitment to cooperative ministries through the national agencies based in Anderson, Indiana. While only time will tell, by the year 2000 the changes were fully in place and optimism was running high in most quarters (see Entries 71, 77, 203).

Beyond the dilemmas that seem inevitable in the area of organized ministry structures, there are two examples of some degree of unfortunate accommodation by this movement to non-church cultural standards not in accord with the movement's early history or theological ideals. These lie in the areas of race relations and women in ministry. The ideals and earlier practices of the movement are a matter of some group pride. The movement was inclusive in emphasis and welcomed large numbers of African-Americans and women into fellowship and leadership, often setting the pace in these regards among Wesleyan/Holiness and other church bodies. Possibly in part because of its ecumenical idealism and the relatively significant presence of African-American and female leaders available to function as inside critics, the movement has been particularly sensitive to and articulate about its own failures over the decades as society's standards of church domination by males and racial discrimination have managed to leave their marks even on the life of this movement (see Entries 119-121, 123, 144, 185, 187).

In 1956 about 14,000 of the 126,000 then persons affiliated with the Church of God movement in the United States and Canada were African-American and about 400 of the 2,200 congregations were primarily African-American in membership. The civil rights movement was underway and young African-American pastor James Earl Massey highlighted the movement's successes and failures and called for the movement to "re-study our policies and practices as they relate to race and correlate them with the tenets of the gospel we preach" (Massey, 1957, 66). Especially during the 1960s this challenge was addressed in part by a series of strong statements on racial equality, an "open door" policy, and so on, all endorsed by the movement's General Assembly meeting annually in Anderson, Indiana (see Entries 119-121). Today, although many challenges remain, several of the more prominent leadership positions in the movement's life at the national level are staffed by highly qualified African-American leaders, and the African-

---

35. See page 9 of the Leith Anderson report to the Leadership Council, April 23, 1996 (then presented to the General Assembly in June, 1996). It was titled: "Movement for the 21st Century: Structuring the Church of God for Future Mission and Ministry."

American community within the movement is experiencing relatively vigorous life and growth.[36] In addition, a significant African-American organization—the National Association of the Church of God (see Entry 187)—has existed since 1917.[37]

In 1989, in conjunction with the first National Consultation on Women in Ministry and Missions of the Church of God. convened on the Anderson University campus, a volume was published to celebrate representative women who have provided outstanding leadership in the history of the Church of God movement. This publication provided a platform to a range of current female leaders and scholars in the movement's life for exploring candidly several related issues. Comments ranged from Juanita Leonard giving thanks for "our foremothers (who) have woven a tapestry with a rich pattern" to Cheryl Sanders who, while giving thanks for notable exceptions, nonetheless reported that "sexist and racial practices within the Church of God are not only in evidence in the pulpits and agency offices, but in the local congregations as well…. While women may be gladly received into the fellowship, their ministries are often regarded as subordinate and auxiliary to the ministry of males" (Leonard, xv, 142). Virtually no one in the movement's leadership would argue openly on behalf of such subordination, but sometimes attitudes function without the presence of any public rationale.

A recent case study features the unusual story of the life and pastoral ministry of one prominent woman in the Church of God, Rev. Lillie S. McCutcheon (Callen, *She Came Preaching*, 1992). One Church of God scholar, Susie Cunningham Stanley, functioned as president of the Wesleyan Theological Society and another, Sharon Clark Pearson, will soon be doing likewise. Pearson published an oft-quoted scholarly article titled "Women in Ministry: A Biblical Vision."[38] Nonetheless, the proportion of women in major church leadership positions in the movement has lessened in recent years, and the percentage of women in the student body of the movement's seminary in Anderson, Indiana, is not equal to what is now typical in seminaries generally.[39] There are various practical reasons, of course, but there also is concern, even embarrassment that one reason may well be accommodation to gender role stereotypes of the dominant culture. Even so, active

---

36. James Earl Massey is Dean Emeritus of the School of Theology of Anderson University, the seminary of the Church of God movement, and Edward Foggs, another gifted African-American, retired in 1999 from many years as the elected General Secretary of the movement's Leadership Council at the national level (now Church of God Ministries, Inc., with Robert Pearson serving as General Director). Included among contemporary African-American leaders are Robert Culp, Chair of the General Assembly, and Michael Curry, Director of Outreach Ministries.

37. See Wilfred Jordan and Richard Willowby, eds., *Diamond Jubilee: National Association of the Church of God* (Anderson, Ind.: Warner Press, 1991).

38. *Wesleyan Theological Journal*, 31:1 (Spring 1996), 141-170.

39. For detail, see Juanita Evans Leonard, ed., *Called to Minister, Empowered to Serve* (Anderson, Ind.: Warner Press), 151-167.

support for women in church leadership has been a hallmark of this movement from its beginning.

3. Theological Perspective. The Church of God movement is a reforming tradition especially indebted to the "Radical" Reformation[40] and the Wesleyan reforming tradition from England. The Stone-Campbell movement (the Disciples or "Christian" tradition) from early in the nineteenth century had perceived most of the same dilemmas and proposed some of the same solutions that later would characterize the Church of God movement.[41] Only in recent years has the Church of God become closely aware of this parallel tradition.[42] A more immediate reforming tradition very influential on the Church of God was the one launched by John Winebrenner (1797-1860)[43] (see Entry 3). Winebrenner and the reforming movement he spawned held its first General Eldership meeting in 1849. This new body, later to be related directly to the beginnings of the Church of God movement through its relationship to Daniel Warner,[44] had "abandoned the Calvinist stance of the German Reformed Church and declared themselves to be Arminian. Intensely biblical, they adopted no written creed but affirmed that the Word of God was their only rule of faith."[45] Winebrenner had become involved in revivalism and interacted with leaders of groups like the United Brethren in Christ that reflected roots in German Pietism and other "radical" elements of the Protestant Reformation, by then transplanted to America. He came to believe that there is only one true church, the church of God, and that it is the duty of God's people to belong to it and to none else.

John Howard Yoder, prominent Mennonite theologian, reflects helpfully on this "radical" Christian tradition. He identifies an approach referred to variously as free church, believer's church, and radical reformation. These phrases seek to describe a common view of Christian faith and life that differs significantly from much usually referred to as the Protestant

40. Callen, *Radical Christianity*.

41. For broad perspective on the Stone-Campbell movement that spanned almost all of the nineteenth century and remains significant yet today, see Louis and Bess White Cochran, *Captives of the Word* (Joplin, Mo.: College Press Pub. Co., 1987, original 1969); Henry Webb, *In Search of Christian Unity* (Cincinnati: Standard Publishing, 1990); Mark Toulouse, *Joined in Discipleship* (St. Louis: Chalice Press, 1992), and James North, *Union in Truth* (Cincinnati: Standard Publishing, 1994).

42. See Barry L. Callen and James North, *Coming Together in Christ* (Joplin, Mo.: College Press, 1997).

43. See Richard Kern, *John Winebrenner, Nineteenth-Century Reformer* (Harrisburg, Pa.: Central Publishing House, 1974).

44. Callen, *It's God's Church!*

45. Smith, *The Quest for Holiness,* 38.

Reformation, and what more recently has become known as "evangelical-ism." "Reformation," explains Yoder, "means standing in judgment on what has come of Christianity over time."[46] Poor "forms" have evolved, whether of lifestyle, organization, or doctrinal formulations. The needed re-formation should be "radical," should go to the root and avoid superficial analyses and corrections. Emphasis on "believers" makes plain that the biggest correction needed is to reverse the "Constantinian" compromise of inclusivism in the constituency of the visible church.[47] The church should be reformed on the basis of consciously committed adult believers. "Free" focuses on liberation from state control so that the church again can be God's and God's alone, not coterminius with, but "resident aliens" within any nation or culture.

The critiquing, liberating, radical (not superficial corrections, but back-to-the-root) elements of this free-church stance entered directly into the the-ological bloodstream of the Church of God movement. The result has been an unrelenting commitment to truth, God's truth, truth released from com-promise, establishment control, and uncommitted adherents. The Believers Church tradition asks if the only options for pursuing truth are coercive uni-formity and tolerant inclusivism. Yoder says that the free church responds with this claim: "There are ways to disavow coercion without giving up on the truth; namely, through binding dialogue under the rule of Scripture."[48]

To summarize, the Church of God movement has been shaped signifi-cantly by (1) Martin Luther and other "magesterial"[49] reformation leaders; (2) the "restorationist" and "Anabaptist" free-church traditions[50] which sharply criticize aspects of the mainstream Protestant Reformation; and (3) the "holiness" heritage going back especially to the work of John Wesley in eighteenth-century England[51] and appearing prominently in the American

46. John Howard Yoder, "Thinking Theologically From a Free Church Perspective," in J. Woodbridge, T. McComiskey, eds., *Doing Theology in Today's World* (Grand Rapids: Zondervan, 1991), 251.

47. See Stanley Hauerwas and William Willimon, *Resident Aliens* (Nashville: Abingdon Press, 1989), 17-18. When the Roman Emperor Constantine embraced Christianity and even established it as "official" in the Empire (c315 C.E.), the faith is said then to have "fallen."

48. John Howard Yoder, in his Introduction to Merle Strege, ed., *Baptism & Church* (Grand Rapids: Sagamore Books, 1986), 7.

49. Leaders like Martin Luther, Huldrych Zwingli, and John Calvin sometimes are called "magesterial" because their reform movements were endorsed, even established by ruling civil authorities. By contrast, Menno Simons ("Mennonites"), an Anabaptist and more "radical" ref-ormation leader, was a non-establishment reformer often at odds with civil authorities.

50. Timothy George, *Theology of the Reformers* (Nashville: Broadman Press, 1988), serves as a good introduction to the thought of the "magisterial" reformers. See Henry Webb, *In Search of Christian Unity: A History of the Restoration Movement* (Cincinnati: Standard Publishing, 1990), and James North, *Union In Truth* (Cincinnati: Standard Publishing, 1994), for recent histories of the restorationist (Disciples) tradition. A classic work on the Anabaptist tradition is Donald Durnbaugh, *The Believers' Church*, 1985 ed. (Scottdale, Pa: Herald Press). A recent work on the "Radical Reformation" stream of Christianity is Callen, *Radical Christianity*.

Holiness movement of the latter decades of the nineteenth century. The teachings of John Wesley seldom have been examined from the perspective of the Anabaptist or Radical Protestant tradition. Because that tradition is providing one of the "primary paradigms" for church renewal today, and because the crucial events in Wesley's life from 1738 to 1740 "pushed him in directions parallel to Radical Protestantism," such examination can yield valuable insight into the vision that has motivated the Church of God movement.[52]

Being radically apostolic and sensitive to the Believers Church tradition, especially when filtered through key aspects of a Wesleyan lens, is important historical perspective on theology as generally understood and taught in the Church of God movement. The resulting mix (reformation-ist/restorationist/holiness/free-church) is a theological model that is biblical and dynamic, traditional and contemporary, both pointedly apostolic and potentially authentic in any present. It is "radical" and "orthodox," "protestant" and "catholic," and deeply "pentecostal" (in the non-tongues, New Testament sense).[53]

This perspective highlights the experiential, practical, and dialogical (see Entry 7). It tends to focus on genuine personal transformation, to insist on Christ-like discipleship, and to initiate fundamental church renewal in the life of the Spirit. It calls for an abrupt departure from the status-quo of the institutional church, highlighting (1) the root, the radical, the apostolic Christian past; (2) the mainstream, the orthodox, the classic church tradition; and (3) the incarnational present, the mission, the radical in the sense of being distinct from any civil authority or human establishment seeking to supplant the church *of the Spirit* (see Entry 11). It stands on two "reformation principles" of the Church of God: the lordship of Jesus Christ and the authority of the Bible (see Entry 13).

4. Relational Analysis. A fourth area of assessment, beyond the prophetic, sociological, and theological, has been the relational. There is irony in a movement that both is committed to Christian unity and at the same time has placed itself in substantial isolation from the larger Christian

---

51. For substantive presentations of Wesleyan theology, see H. Ray Dunning, *Grace, Faith & Holiness* (Kansas City: Beacon Hill Press of Kansas City, 1988) and Randy Maddox, *Responsible Grace: The Practical Theology of John Wesley* (Nashville: Kingswood Books, Abingdon Press, 1994).

52. Howard Snyder, *The Radical Wesley* (Downers Grove, Ill.: InterVarsity Press, 1980), 110. Snyder explains how John Wesley was himself a "restorationist radical" in the midst of his high-church Anglicanism. Also see Luke Keefer, Jr., "John Wesley: Disciple of Early Christianity," *Wesleyan Theological Journal* (Spring, 1984), 23-32.

53. Note Frederick Norris, *The Apostolic Faith* (Collegeville, Minn.: The Liturgical Press, 1992). Norris suggests that a tradition similar to the Church of God movement is described well as "free-church catholic" (xxvii). This phrase probably was originated by Alfred DeGroot, *Disciple Thought: A History* (Fort Worth: Texas Christian University, 1965).

community (the Church of God movement has been a "non-joiner" in most formalized ecumenical settings). The Church of God movement originated in a very polemic atmosphere. "Unity as a doctrine or an ideal for the church was itself a source of conflict," recalled John W. V. Smith, "because it was opposed by loyal 'sectarians' who were offended by the call to 'come out' of their denominations and stand together in an open fellowship of the Spirit" (1980, 439). When the larger Christian community also began espousing an ecumenical ideal in the twentieth century (with little direct influence from the Church of God movement, which remained aloof from most inter-church ecumenical discussions), the polemical atmosphere was altered significantly. But the Church of God did not rejoice in such an apparently positive change. Rather, it remained apart from this general unity quest, tending to critique popular ecumenism as a misguided search for a humanly contrived union of church structures more than a longing for a true Christian unity of the Spirit (see Entry 63).

The Church of God movement began reflecting on itself and its continuing mission in these changing circumstances. If a protest movement gains self-identity by the presence of clearly defined issues and adversaries, this one appears to have developed a weakened self-identity as the twentieth century progressed. Traditional adversaries became common users of at least the language of the ecumenical ideals of the Church of God. To compound the relative aloneness of the movement in the Christian world, John W. V. Smith pointed out that "at the same time that the movement was losing its enemies it was not cultivating many close friends" (1980, 440). A relatively unstructured fellowship critiquing structural merging and creedal compromises as unity blind alleys was hardly a body of believers organized for or committed to any systematic building of relationships outside its own tradition. Movement leaders sometimes have reflected on how the movement has managed to keep its presence and potential contribution to the larger church a rather well-hidden and therefore relatively ineffectual secret.

Not until 1965 was a Committee on Christian Unity authorized by the movement at the national level (see Entry 52) and not until 1975 was it recast as a more permanent Commission on Christian Unity intended to facilitate cooperative work among Christians for witness and evangelism and to be "a representative group to make contacts, hold conversations, and develop lines of cooperation with other church bodies of similar spirit and concern." Various national agencies of the movement have maintained for many years modest working relationships with several units of the National Council of Churches for the sharing of ministry-oriented resources and expertise. These relationships have been cautioned and guided since 1985 by a stance taken by the General Assembly (see Entry 63). A significant emerging educational relationship between the seminary of the Church of God (USA) and an ecumenical consortium of seminaries was blocked by the General Assembly in the 1970s (see Entry 36). Responsible relationships are encouraged for the sake of effective Christian mission, as long as the lordship of Christ is honored and biblical authority is respected by all partners. Interdependence is necessary for ministry goals and as a fulfillment of the Church of God movement's burden for Christian unity (see Entry 171).

The most in-depth and sustained dialogue involving the Church of God and a sister Christian body has been the "Open Forum" with the Independent Christian Churches/Churches of Christ (see Entries 194-195). A committed group of leaders from each body met periodically from 1989 to 1998 to explore together their two traditions, key theological issues, and possible joint ministry efforts (not church mergers). The story of this extensive initiative can be found in *Coming Together in Christ* (Barry Callen and James North, 1997). The effort, significant to those involved, did not capture widespread attention and priority consideration in these two bodies. Even so, it was a meaningful effort, a worthy model for other Christian bodies committed to biblical Christianity and concerned about the dividedness of Christ's church.[54] The Church of God in North America convened in 1984 a major Consultation on Mission and Ministry that called for daring experimentation and risking on behalf of Christian unity for the sake of effective mission (see Entry 171). Gilbert W. Stafford has attempted to fulfilled this call by his long participation in the Faith and Order Movement of the National Council of Churches (USA) (see Entry 196).

THE LIVING AMONG THE DEAD

The Church of God movement began by living from the exhilaration of an ideal, a vision of God's perfect will that encouraged harsh judgment of many of the traditions which had evolved in various Christian communities over the centuries. Today the movement itself has existed long enough to have evolved a few of its own traditions and to have found it necessary to begin facing how to regard them and sometimes even how to defend, alter, or eliminate them in the face of its own vision.

Jaroslav Pelikan has identified two possible attitudes toward the past. One is a negative traditionalism, a "dead faith of the living" that regards continuity with an embalmed past a priority—if only an artificial present reality. The other is a healthy respect for enduring tradition, the "living faith of the dead" which is open to both continuity and change and for which time manages to be transcended for the sake of dynamic meaning and current relevance. Given the concerns and emphases of the Church of God heritage,

---

54. The book resulting from this dialogue (Callen/North, *Coming Together in Christ*, 1997) was highlighted with appreciation by Elizabeth Mellen of the Graymoor Ecumenical & Interreligious Institute of New York City ("An Ecumenical Vocation for the Wesleyan/Holiness Tradition?", *Wesleyan Theological Journal*, Spring 1999, 101-125).

Charles E. Brown	John W. V. Smith	Merle D. Strege
Church Historian	Church Historian	Church Historian

one would assume a heavy concentration on the latter of Pelikan's options. Movement historian Merle D. Strege has affirmed that "in our better moments we. . .have been people of tradition rather than traditionalism.... We respect the work of previous authors in the movement without elevating it to the status of a creed" (1991, 121-22). There, of course, have been moments other than the better ones (see Entries 27, 30, 34)..

Beyond living in a creative tension with the many church traditions that have a long past and make authoritative claims on the present, the movement always has gone "back to the blessed old Bible" as the place of legitimate authority for Christian life. But even here a similar tension arises. In what way is the Bible to be received as authoritative? The movement arose primarily in a Wesleyan-Holiness revivalist environment and was nurtured by the belief that the present ministry of the Holy Spirit and the necessity of life-changing spiritual experience are critical components of the Christian's pattern of authority. This combination has shielded the movement from a rigid fundamentalist mentality, away from a stance that features creedal fixity or biblical "inerrancy"—that is, seeing revelation as finished verbal propositions that deserve mandatory adherence.[55] See Entry 75 where the rigidity of "inerrancy" teaching is carefully avoided.

How then should today's Christian community proceed, recognizing the limitations of the all-too-human church traditions, the essential centrality of Jesus Christ, the contemporary ministry of the Holy Spirit, and the abiding authority of the Bible when interpreted with care in the light of Christ and with the aid of the Spirit? Merle Strege has pointed to a helpful distinction involving the idea of authority in the church. One type of authority finds the living community members relying on the founders of the past for that which always will remain normative. The other, probably more compatible with the Bible's own apparent assumption about itself, locates legitimate authority in "that which gives life" (1991, 124).

If the church is conceived as an institution to be managed, a normative

---

55. See Barry L. Callen, *Contours of a Cause*, chapters 2 and 5, and *God As Loving Grace,* chapters 6 and 7.

tradition to be preserved and perpetuated, then a power politics that manipulates the necessary elements of the tradition becomes typical and justifiable in church life. If, however, the church is conceived more as a living organism and truth is understood to have a personal dimension, even an undefinable dimension only partially perceived to date, then authority becomes more a process of enablement where power resides in divine gifts recognized and exercised in community. The difference is between a controlling manager and a wise and loving sage, a power broker and a community creator and individual enabler. The Church of God movement has certainly been biblically convictional, but primarily in the creative, personal, and enabling sense. The Bible is the essential and faithful witness to those events that make the church distinctively Christian. Even so, it is less a sterile set of unchanging rules and creeds and more that fertile apostolic soil in which each new generation of Christians can grow when the light of Christ and the water of the Spirit are added in the changing seasons and cultures of our human history.

Mennonite theologian John Howard Yoder has spoken helpfully in relation to the heart of the "radical" reformation stream in which Charles E. Brown (1954), John W. V. Smith (1954), and Barry L. Callen (1999) have placed the Church of God movement historically. The church, understood as a voluntary community gathered around Christ, "can affirm individual dignity. . .without enshrining individualism." It likewise "can realize community without authoring lordship or establishment."[56] This view describes well the central challenge now before the Church of God movement so far as understanding and ordering its own life is concerned. In Pelikan's terms, the goal always is discovering and practicing the "living faith of the dead." Regarding the concept of authority, the goal is individual growth and community enablement, not exercising power and building an ecclesiastical empire in Christ's name—the destructive "denominational" mentality.

The Church of God movement certainly has been opposed to ecclesiastical empire building and denominational mentalities—things it has opposed vigorously from its beginning. Even so, there have been times when some movement leaders have feared the rise of these very things in the midst of the movement's own life (see Entries 34, 180). An example occurred in the 1920s when George Tasker, Canadian Church of God missionary in India, found himself in conflict with the relatively new Missionary Board of the Church of God in Anderson, Indiana (Entries 28, 30).[57] The Board took action in 1924 to disassociate itself from Tasker's work, saying that he had "grown out of sympathy with the work which this Board seeks to do in India. . .

56. John Howard Yoder, *The Priestly Kingdom* (Notre Dame, Ind.: University of Notre Dame Press, 1984), 24.

57. For more detail on the George Tasker incident, see Strege, *Tell Me the Tale* chapter 1.

[and was] working at cross purposes with the vast majority of the brethren in the home land." He was judged to be no longer faithfully representing the thought of the people whom he professed to represent in India. Tasker responded, saying that the key issue was "ecclesiasticism" and "a betrayal of the Divine principle of this movement as it came to birth in the soul of D. S. Warner." To him, there had developed in the movement a come-to-us attitude that assumed for the Anderson-based body the exalted status of being God's rendezvous point for the regathering of God's divided people. This sounded to Tasker like the "language of the apostasy." At issue was the self-identity of the movement itself. See Entries 31-33.

In more recent years, a test case for internal unity in the Church of God movement has been the development in the 1970s of the Pastors' Fellowship within the larger life of the Church of God movement (see Entries 35, 169, 170). This annual series of regional gatherings of interested pastors and laypersons has shown strong commitment to the renewal of vigorous preaching and publishing of the truths traditionally affirmed in the Church of God movement, and especially as understood in earlier generations (often including the earlier prophetic validation of the movement). At times the Pastors' Fellowship has functioned as an ad hoc political block on behalf of "conservative" causes in the life of the movement. Most of its leaders, however, are anxious that this movement within the larger Church of God movement be a constructive and essentially non-political force, an opportunity for leaders to be refreshed, inspired, and better equipped, and for "Church of God doctrine" to be proclaimed.[58] There now is a separate periodical, the *Reformation Witness,* claiming a circulation of some 34,000.[59] Clearly there have been a variety of agendas at work over the last two decades, but the Pastors' Fellowship movement has been one source for providing the Church of God movement in the United States with new settings to refine and practice its own ecumenical idealism, at least within its own group boundaries. This movement within the movement has not resulted in a "split," but has presented the opportunity for remembering and reassessing the continuing relevancy of some of the movement's previous teaching emphases.

Which prophetic, sociological, theological, and relational accommodations over the decades have been timely and right and which have been unnecessarily costly to the distinctive message and mission of the Church of God movement? Such a question persists while even more testing continues.

---

58. Its founding leader, Rev. Lillie S. McCutcheon, was uncomfortable with the political posturing and power plays occasionally made by a few of the participants in its early years (see Callen, *She Came Preaching).*

59. The North American periodical of the Church of God movement, in existence since the movement's beginning, was known as the *Gospel Trumpet* beginning in 1881. More recently known as *Vital Christianity,* it suddenly ceased publication in September, 1996, for economic reasons. This demise raised the question of how effective communication and tradition maintenance will be accomplished in the future.

Dialogue is the way of life in a true movement. The settings usually are ad hoc retreats, emergency dialogues, and occasionally well-planned but one-time strategy gatherings of various kinds. Twelve such events have convened since 1963 (see Entries 166-177), including the Consultation on Mission and Ministry (1984) that sought to set ministry goals for the movement in North America to the end of the twentieth century. A new pattern of periodic "Visioning Conferences" began with the first convened in Colorado in 1998 (see Entry 177).

This testing and dialogue within the Church of God movement now has expanded to include significant ecumenical and international arenas. Of particular note is the multi-year ecumenical dialogue with the Christian Churches/Churches of Christ (see Entries 194-195)[60] and, since 1980, the international networking of the Church of God through its World Forums and International Dialogues on Doctrine (see Entries 205-206).[61] Not "ecclesiastical" or legislative in nature, these venues are convened each four years to focus on increasing acquaintance, mutual appreciation, and meaningful cooperation in ministry. Given the dramatic internationalism of the Church of God movement today (see Entries 211-212), the new challenges are to affirm the diversity and build a truly international partnership in mission (see Entries 207-208).

MOVEMENTS AND THE CHURCH'S ONENESS

A current challenge facing the Church of God movement is to understand more carefully and creatively the relationship between a "denominated" tradition and the goal of the unity of the whole church. There appears to be an awkward paradox in a movement, itself now a very identifiable Christian tradition, having as a key aspect of its mission the call to speak prophetically against such traditioning because of associated human and divisive tendencies. A good way to reapproach this paradox is with the realization that, while Christian unity is a gift from God through the Spirit, it also is realized only as Christians intentionally open themselves to be in community with other believers. "Unity is given," according to James Earl Massey, "but our experience of it must be gained." The givenness roots in the fact that "the church is the community of those who honor Jesus Christ, sharing his life, teachings, and work. Belonging to him makes every believer belong to all other believers."[62] Gaining operational meaningfulness for this

---

60. Callen and North, *Coming Together In Christ*.
61. Callen, *Journeying Together*, 185-196, 202-215.

givenness, however, requires inspired and risking involvement in gaining what is divinely given—both seeing and actively following the light.

But what of the persistent dividedness among Christ's people? Believers typically experience the fellowship of God's people in connection with some denominational body. Is this fact division by definition? There appears to exist a perplexing paradox: the multiplicity of Christian traditions is due in part to human sin (Gal. 5:19-21) and in part to the inevitable varieties of human cultures, symbol systems, and historical circumstances that are not sinful in themselves. So some level of associational separation among Christians, while less than ideal, probably is inevitable.[63] Further, if indeed the church is fundamentally "charismatic" in nature (the origin and func-tioning of its life deriving principally from the presence, grace, and gifting of God's Spirit), then there always will be some tension between the charis-matic nature and the institutionalized expressions of the church. Whenever the Spirit moves mysteriously like the wind, there is the real potential of ten-sion between "wine" and "wineskins." Established patterns of church order can easily come into conflict with the immediacy and varieties of the Spirit's work.

The question must be asked and has become crucial for the Church of God movement: "How may a people who exist as a distinct community within the Church, for the sake of witness unto the unity of the Church, avoid the negation of their witness by their very existence?"[64] To avoid such a negation, in 1804 there was published *The Last Will and Testament of the Springfield Presbytery* to explain why a reforming Christian group would dissolve its own interim "church" body, would "die the death" organization-

---

62. James Earl Massey, *Concerning Christian Unity* (Anderson, Ind.: Warner Press, 1979), 8, 11, 20. Clark Williamson adds that "unity in the church, fragmentarily but really, is where the diverse members of the body of Christ are aware of and appreciate their essential related-ness to each other, where they love one another with the kind of love with which they have been loved" (*A Guest in the House of Israel*, Louisville: Westminster/John Knox Press, 1993, 262). James Evans, Jr., says that "the solidarity of that community (koinonia of the church). . .is strong enough to render all other stratifications among human beings of only secondary impor-tance. Thus in the holy community 'there is no Greek nor Jew, slave nor free, male nor female'" (*We Have Been Believers: An African-American Systematic Theology*, Minneapolis: Augsburg Fortress, 1992, 136). These are classic Church of God perspectives.

63. What constitutes true and viable Christian unity? Must there be full agreement on beliefs, or a single organizational network, or is the goal more in the area of attitudes? Early leaders of the Church of God movement envisioned denominational structures collapsing (not merging). For the most part that has not happened. Consideration now should be given to this judgment of Emil Brunner: "Certain as is the fact that a number of competing churches represents a scan-dal, equally certain is it on the other hand that a variety of forms of Christian fellowship is a necessity.... Far more important than organizational reunion of the historical churches is the readiness of individual Christians. . .to cooperate in a spirit of brotherliness" (*The Misunderstanding of the Church*, Philadelphia: Westminster Press, 1953, 112). See Entries 27, 39-40.

64. Robert Fife, "The Neglected Alternative" in *Celebration of Heritage* (Los Angeles: Westwood Christian Foundation, 1992), 265.

ally as a witness to Christian unity. "We will," it boldly announced, "that this body die, be dissolved, and sink into union with the Body of Christ at large; for there is but one Body and one Spirit, even as we are called in one hope of our calling."[65]

Questions persist, however. Can an identifiable Christian body successfully "sink" into the whole of God's people as a unity witness without disappearing and thus forfeiting any real base from which to witness to and help realize Christian unity? Is the divisiveness of the denominationalized Christian community so assumed and entrenched, so sociologically inevitable, that there is no alternative? Because of the hurtfulness of division to the church's mission and because the New Testament witness highlights the goal of Christian unity, even presents it as the personal prayer of Jesus on behalf of all his disciples in all times (John 17), many Christians over the centuries have affirmed that there must be an alternative to rampant division.[66] The Church of God movement is coming to understand that a movement that serves to upbuild the church, not divide and tear down, may be seen as a gift of the Spirit to the church and not merely more division by definition. The Church of God movement, while commonly assumed to be a "denomination" by Christians generally, does not choose to accept such a designation—to accept would seem to undercut the originating vision of the movement. Even so, a large majority of the 1996 and 1997 General Assemblies (USA and Canada) supported a major restructuring of the national ministries in North America even though the restructuring plan was characterized by some as a denomination-like centralizing of power in the church. Without violating the autonomy of local churches or regional assemblies, the plan was judged to offer a new level of efficiency and accountability, an opportunity to put "move" back into the movement.

There is precedent for such thinking in the Methodist experience in eighteenth-century England. John Wesley regarded his evolving network of Methodist "societies" as comprising together a movement of authentic Christianity within the larger church that was judged largely decadent. Being himself an ordained minister of the Church of England (Anglican), he at first meant by "the larger church" the Church of England. The renewal societies were in effect little churches within this large church (*ecclesiola* within the *ecclesia*). Increasingly, however, Wesley decided that he should allow non-Anglican Dissenters into the Methodist societies, thus acknowledging that the Methodist movement had become more than a renewal movement within the Church of England. Increasingly it was an "evangelical order" within the universal church, the body of all true believers in Jesus Christ.

For early nineteenth-century Christians in the United States (Kentucky)

---

65. This document, written by Barton W. Stone, is a classic in the "Restorationist" movement.

66. Theodore Jennings insists that "division is a problem for the identity of the church. Division is a sign of the power of the world and sin. Division is then the anti-sign (the countersign) to the reign of God" (*Loyalty To God*, Nashville: Abingdon Press, 1992, 188).

led by Barton Stone and his colleagues, *The Last Will and Testament* declared an intentional "sinking" by no longer defining Christian fellowship in terms of a particular institution to which all Christians could not belong. These visionary reformers sought to become a microcosm of the whole church, with no other criteria of unity except those which can be the bond of unity for the whole church. There would be no restrictive creed mandated on all members. Evangelizing would be done *as the church* (the whole body of Christ) and for the church. Baptizing would be into the church, not into a given segment of it. The invitation to the Lord's Supper would be issued as representatives of the whole body to any in the body wishing to participate (it is, after all, the *Lord's* table, not *ours*).

How, then, should one describe groupings of Christians that are burdened about the church's disunity, but also seek to represent and serve the whole church in distinctive ways, without claiming for themselves those characteristics belonging only to the whole body? One helpful distinction is that between the church and "movements" within it. Affirming that the church is one and that such oneness is obscured when denominations divide the church into "churches," Robert Fife defines a "movement" as "a community of understanding and concern which exists and serves within the Church, and for its edification."[67]

Sometimes particular groupings of Christians come into being because their members share certain understandings and concerns about the faith.[68] Such distinctive communities *within* the church (not *as* the church) can—if they choose—help facilitate the internal dialogue of the church as the whole body of believers seeks its maturity and unity for the sake of its mission.[69] Movements, therefore, are "characteristic of the church as a living organism." They are actions of the body of Christ rather than separations from or usurpations of the body. While a properly motivated renewal movement is not the church and seeks to keep that very clear, it is a vital part of the church and functions in order to make the church more whole and more effective.[70] Movements so defined may be thought of as "renewal orders" within the uni-

---

67. Robert Fife, *op. cit.*, 276.

68. Within the New Testament we already see early approaches to understanding the church's unity in plurality (diversity of spiritual gifts, the Christian conscience and "gray areas," cultural diversity implied in the reality of multiple congregations, their differing settings and range of approaches to problems). In each case, unity left room for some diversity. See Rex Koivisto, *One Lord, One Faith* (Wheaton, Ill.: Victor Books, 1993), 37-42.

69. Robert Fife, *op. cit.*, 265-271. Fife calls for denominations to cease calling themselves "churches" and thus appearing to assume for themselves the dignity and prerogatives belonging only to the church (274). In this regard, note C. C. Morrison when editor of the *Christian Century*, 77:10 (March 9, 1960), 281.

70. Rex Koivisto attributes such wholesome characteristics to "denominations" (*One Lord, One Faith*, 102ff). Such groupings, he says, are inevitable sociologically. Even people uniting around a non-denominational platform are not thereby kept from potentially being at least part of what they oppose (102). This has been a consistent concern for Church of God leaders.

versal church, Christian communities of commitment and concern that are both inevitable and needful.

Much like the restorationist movement represented by Robert Fife, the Church of God movement has been sensitive to the damage done to the church and its mission by denominational divisions when such divisions take to themselves the prerogatives belonging only to the whole body. It has thought of itself as a "movement" in Fife's terms, functioning at God's call *within* the body and *for* the body. Too often, however, even this unity movement has managed to facilitate awkward separations, in spite of itself (see Entry 180). The "we mentality" is a constant danger, as are the inevitable effects of a movement isolating itself from the larger Christian world by featuring an "over against" and "come out" attitude and rhetoric.[71] A movement can facilitate the internal dialogue of the church only as it engages actively with the church, not when it retreats within its own confines out of self-preoccupation or fear of contamination by the beliefs and practices of other Christian traditions. A "movement" can destroy its own genius by failing to move creatively within the larger body.

Denominated bodies can be honorable and effective if they are not honored as ends in themselves, if they function cooperatively as patterns of partnership in relation to the whole body, and if they function as "movements" seeking to facilitate the health of the whole church, aggressively, but not arrogantly. There is, then, nothing inherently divisive in a group of Christians following the natural sociological process of "denominating" itself. In fact, Massey adds this:

> ...no one form should be judged divisive just because it is a form.... Diversity is not division when the spirit of relating to those beyond the group is kept alive.... Diversity is one thing, while a *spirit* of division is quite another.... Every Christian has a legacy in every other Christian. We experience that legacy only as we receive each other and relate, moving eagerly beyond group boundaries.[72]

A helpful analogy was shared at the 1980 centennial consultation on the heritage of the Church of God movement.[73] The Gulf Stream is a marvelous

---

71. Such isolationism was very characteristic of the Church of God movement in its earliest decades. More recently this has changed for the most part, but with the change has come a growing confusion over group identity without any general joining of the larger conversations in the church about the nature and means of enhancing Christian unity. An exception is the precedent of ecumenical involvement by John W. V. Smith that now is followed by Gilbert W. Stafford (see Entry 196).

72. James Earl Massey, *Concerning Christian Unity*, 75, 78, 82.

movement of water that leaves the Gulf of Mexico and flows as a warming river across the vast expanse of the Atlantic Ocean to the European continent. The general path of the warmer water is obvious. Its influence on the ocean environment is definite as it moves along. But its boundaries are imprecise. It is open to all the surrounding ocean, influencing and being influenced. T. Franklin Miller judged this an appropriate image of what a movement should be like within the larger body of Christ. The opposite of such a warming movement, by whatever name, tries delivering its water to Europe in a sealed pipeline, neither warming nor being enriched by the much larger body on the way. The opposite of a movement (an isolated "sect") thinks it knows itself to be the true water without need of enrichment and not wishing to risk being chilled by outside contact (see Entries 188-192).

Christian unity is both a gift of God and the achievement of those committed to its fullest realization. Diversity can be a source of freedom and creativity in the church, the opposite of a regimented and premature uniformity. The diamond of Christian truth has many facets. Difference is not bad unless it hardens into an arrogant, anti-catholic exclusiveness, or deviates from the biblical revelation that is to form the church in all of its expressions. Groupings of Christians need not represent an evil just because they exist as distinct groupings. The question is whether they are in conflict or communion, whether they are contributing to or detracting from the whole body of Christ. Bodies that cut themselves off are acting against the church, even if their divisive platforms include the call for Christian unity (an accusation sometimes leveled at the Church of God movement, particularly in its earliest decades).[74]

Organizational variety in the church appears inevitable as Christians of varying backgrounds focus their lives around differing concerns in order to advance varying understandings of the gospel in multiple cultures. The problem is not the variety as such, but rigid spirits of exclusiveness that act *against* and not *with* and *for* the whole church. The problem of division is its unjustified exclusivism (a sign to the world that is injurious to Christ's

---

73. Convened in February, 1980, at the School of Theology of Anderson University, Anderson, Indiana. Note also the centennial celebration of the Church of God movement in Germany that occured in Hamburg, Germany, September, 1994. A featured guest speaker was the director of the German Evangelical Alliance, an interdenominational Christian organization with which the Church of God movement in Germany had recently affiliated. Such affiliation expressed the desire to cooperate with, contribute to, and benefit from the larger church.

74. In one sense the church is called to be "sectarian." When it is the eschatological church born of the Pentecostal vision, carrying the distinctive marks, and exercising the distinctive gifts of the Spirit, the church moves toward the "sect" type of ecclesiology described by Troeltsch (*The Social Teaching of the Christian Churches*, 1912). He describes Christianity as having three organizational orientations, church, sect, and mysticism. Books like Stanley Hauerwas and William Willimon, *Resident Aliens* (Nashville: Abingdon, 1989) and the whole Believers Church tradition call for a distinctive, counter-cultural identity as the authentic way of really being the church in our kind of world.

mission). Ignoring the necessary mark of catholicity, a divisive body falsely expands some insight, gift, or group tradition into a restricting dominance, failing to hear that "the eye cannot say to the hand, 'I have no need of you.' ... If the whole body were an eye, where would the hearing be?" (1 Cor. 12:21, 17). True division makes human experience normative, even when insisting on Scriptural authority, since only the official and humanly conditioned reading of the particular "tribe" is judged acceptable by that tribe.

The goal of Christian unity is not for a uniformity, with all distinctives somehow eliminated. Christians are to be reconciled *in their diversity*. Realizing that real differences already existed even in the early church, we should insist that genuine unity in the whole body of Christ is not merely a matter of improved organizational management. It is a unity enabled only by the Spirit, who channels diversity without imposing premature uniformity. Being together in Christ by the Spirit is to be "catholic." The task is to be in touch with one's own traditional distinctives within the Christian family, while remaining open to the wisdom resident in the larger reality of the church. The Church of God movement has hoped in this way to be "free-church catholic," a "reforming order" or "renewal movement," a healing and uniting force within the whole body of Christ speaking for a Christian unity enabled uniquely *by the Spirit*.

FINDING A FUTURE AGENDA

There is no end to the quest to truly be God's people in given times and places. The goal is fixed, but the perspectives of believers remain fragile and their strategies always shifting. The church knows herself to be on a journey of realizing in practice God's ideal intent for the church in the world.

Reviewing the Church of God movement's history as a whole, one notes that some cherished perspectives common at various times in the past have not stood well the test of time, while others have. There never has been full consensus on a range of issues, even on how the movement itself should best be understood. Nonetheless, there has persisted a cohesive togetherness of vision and commitment adequate to retain group identity without stagnating the group's essential dynamic as a "non-denominational movement." This persisting cohesion, however, now is under considerable pressure as a "Baby Boomer" culture influences church priorities and programs[75] and as national church structures face economic downturns and significant realignments.

---

75. A shock to many in the Church of God was the unexpected announcement by Warner Press that the September 1996 issue of *Vital Christianity* would be the last. As successor to the *Gospel Trumpet*, the central vehicle for launching the movement beginning in 1881, the loss of this periodical seemed a disturbing loss of movement continuity and togetherness. The reason for stopping publication was said to be economic. Younger generations in the movement either are not committed readers or are distracted by the multitude of reading alternatives.

Without question, the movement is having to re-evaluate its identity and role within the larger Christian community as the twentieth century closes.

To champion real freedom in the Spirit without encouraging rampant individualism has not proven easy. Structuring church ministry without violating the vision of an end to the human usurping of divine prerogative in church life has amounted to a series of cautious experiments. Being critiqued by many reassessments of the movement, often by sympathetic persons from within its own life, has brought discomfort and sometimes appropriately disciplined change. The motion of this prophetic and idealistic movement, if it is to continue without reverting to a standard denominational pattern or disintegrating altogether, must remain rooted in but not limited by its own tentative and experimental past.

There appears to remain a rather firm consensus within the movement about a few enduring concepts, anchors from this tradition's past which are regarded widely as valuable building blocks for its future. They include beliefs that true Christian unity

- Is crucial to the effective witness of the church in the world and, thus, is the Lord's expressed will (John 17);

- Is based on God-initiated Christian fellowship, not on creedal or intellectual uniformity;

- Is controlled by the unquestioned authority of the Bible, an essential "authoring" source of Christian identity that avoids rampant individualism in an open, non-creedal fellowship;

- Highlights that which is God-given in vital Christian experience as the path to true unity, rather than the seeking of any humanly devised structural or theological arrangements;

- Remains linked closely to and genuinely rooted in the Wesleyan teaching of a holiness experience in the lives of individual believers;

- Affirms that unity includes a removal of gender and racial barriers to full incorporation of all God's children into the fellowship and ministries of the church;

- Avoids the potential tyranny of one's own church institutions, traditions, and strong personalities;

- Knows that unity is hardly an end in itself, but is intended to contribute to the evangelistic mission of the church;

- Refuses to settle for the idea of the "invisibility" of the true and united church, an easy way to abort the whole quest for a real and present unity.

These affirmations are similar to conclusions of John W. V. Smith when earlier he had reviewed the "radical" reformation stream of church history. He identified characteristics among related groups, including the Church of God movement, some compatible with and some not in relation to the principle of universalism and the goal of achieving unity among divided Christians. Smith discovered four characteristics to be incompatible, including "a tendency to define 'truth' in terms of the particular emphases which distinguish the group rather than on the basis of the totality of Christian doctrine and human knowledge," and ten compatible, beginning with this: "... the basis of religious authority is defined ... as resting *both* on the Scriptures and in the continuing revelation of the Holy Spirit. This allows for progress and growth and also provides a check against anarchy" (1954, 581-584).

These characteristics listed by Smith, as well as the above nine aspects of the enduring vision of Christian unity, deserve renewed consideration as the Church of God movement and the whole Christian community face a troubled future. The Church of God movement has lived in a tension between its vision of the universal, its focus on holiness and ecumenical idealism, and its particular set of group perspectives, practices, and now structures. These sometimes changing group distinctives and structures have been conditioned by the surrounding cultures of church and society and thus have not always been fully compatible with the movement's own vision and idealism. Even so, there remains in the movement a commitment to somehow realize the ideal (see Entries 37, 40). And what is that ideal? Here is what God wills, as stated by a Lutheran theologian:

> ... we long for a Church which will be both evangelical and catholic, continuous with the faith of the apostles, and coterminous with all that is universally valid in the experience of Christ's body on earth. We long for a Church which will be unified and in which the one bread and the one cup may be shared by all, without regard to class, race, or denomination. We long for a Church in which all the members will be one with Christ and one with one another, even as the Son is one with the Father and the Spirit is one with both. We long for a Church which will be one and catholic, so that the mission of Christ through his Church to all the nations might be accomplished; for unity and mission belong together.[76]

Even more urgently than in the 1880s, God wills today that the church be open at the top, that God's people be free to follow the Spirit's leading unencumbered by institutionalism and human arrogance. God wants faithful

---

76. Carl Braaten, "Rome, Reformation, and Reunion," *Una Sancta* 23:2 (1967), 6.

persons to respond with dedication and vigor to the Spirit's persistent call to renewal and to mission in light of the urgent needs of our world. The Spirit is calling believers to accept their oneness with all true Christians everywhere, and to take upon themselves the responsibility of working out appropriate means of cooperation in the context of common commitment. The will of God has not changed since the perceptions of the earliest days of the movement. God wants to make the whole church of God *visible* and *effective*.[77]

In the early years of the Methodist movement in England, Thomas Maxfield often was left in charge of the gatherings of Bands and Societies at the "Foundery" in London when John and Charles Wesley were gone on evangelistic missions. But he was never allowed to preach because he was not an ordained clergyman—the law of the established church. Once Maxfield's gospel zeal got the best of him and he did preach. John Wesley heard of it and rushed home to exact discipline. His mother Susanna cautioned him, however, since she had heard the preaching and thought it inspired by God despite the prevailing legal restriction. She asked only that the fruits of this preaching be examined before judgment was reached. After patiently hearing Maxfield himself, Wesley declared: "It is the Lord! What am I that I should withstand God!" This decision affected the whole course of Methodism.[78]

The decision of Wesley, giving preference to divine initiative and gifting over denominational law, was the same decision that prevailed at the beginning of the Church of God movement in the nineteenth century. It is the decision that should still prevail in the twenty-first. Wesley once wrote:

> Would to God that all the party names, the unscriptural phrases and forms which have divided the Christian world were forgot; and that we might all agree to sit down together, as humble, loving disciples, at the feet of our common Master, to hear his word, imbibe his Spirit, and to transcribe his in our own.[79]

We who believe are privileged to be members of the church only by God's grace. Our life is in Christ. Our power is only by the Spirit. Our hope lies only in knowing and doing the will of God. What is that will? We are to be Christ's one family, intended to be separated unto God—made holy—and

---

77. See John W. V. Smith, in Barry Callen, *A Time To Remember: Evaluations* (Anderson, Ind.: Warner Press, 1978), 34.

78. Rebecca Harmon, *Susanna: Mother of the Wesleys* (N.Y.: Abingdon Press, 1968), 160-161.

79. John Wesley, *Explanatory Notes Upon the New Testament* (Kansas City: Beacon Hill Press of Kansas City, 1981), preface. For an excellent presentation of the thought of the early Wesleyan movement on the issue of Christian unity, see David L. Cubie, "A Wesleyan Perspective on Christian Unity," *Wesleyan Theological Journal* (Fall 1998), 198-229.

united together in love, so that the world may know the good news of God in Christ. The Church of God movement should now follow the model of its primary pioneer, Daniel S. Warner. The enduring model is this:

> Warner was not an innovator in the sense that he claimed to invent or discover truth previously unknown to the church. Rather, he was a rediscoverer, reaffirmer, re-experiencer, one who took seriously what had been basic all along. He listened to God, believed God, wanted God's word and will to be all in all. It's God's church![80]

---

80. Barry L. Callen, *It's God's Church!*, 161.

Part One:
SEEING THE LIGHT
TEACHINGS AND TESTIMONIES
OF THE TRADITION

Editor's Note: This section includes twenty-five entries, eleven units of the teaching tradition of the Church of God movement and fourteen testimonies of prominent persons who were impacted by this teaching and chose to carry it forward in their own times, places, and ways.

TEACHINGS

Editor's Note: The teaching tradition of the Church of God movement is not formalized in any official and mandatory creed. "Back to the Bible" has been a central principle, with constant resistance to the typical tyranny of humanly devised and denominationally employed creeds and church structures. Barry L. Callen's 1995 book on the teaching tradition of this movement is titled *Contours of a Cause*—emphasizing that the movement's history has been a reforming *cause* with discernable *contours*, but it is not a history with definitive teaching boundaries beyond the essentials of clear biblical teaching. In the teaching samples below, therefore, one will find contexts, usual emphases, and only two "reformation principles" affirmed by the movement's General Assembly—these having to do with the authority of the Bible and the lordship of Jesus Christ. These are judged essential for being a Christian and thus are not viewed as "denominational distinctives" that would divide Christians.

The Church of God is a biblically convictional, but not a creedally restrictive, tradition. Merle Strege, the movement's current church historian, summarizes:

Few questions are of more pressing importance to those who name Jesus as their Master than this: What kind of people is God calling us to be in a world that knows not Jesus as its Lord? Peel away the layers of secondary concern and discussion and one finds Church of God preachers and writers constantly addressing that question in one fashion or another.... The struggle to see the church and then live up to that vision is the concept at the center of that conversation called the Church of God (*Tell Me Another Tale,* 1993, 20, 19).

What kind of people is God calling? According to the early teaching tradition of the Church of God movement, God wants people who see and follow the divine light on the church. For instance, in *The Evening Light,* the 1897 songbook published in Moundsville, West Virginia by the Gospel Trumpet Company, song number one (a movement "theme song") is titled "The Evening Light." Here are the lyrics written by Daniel S. Warner:

Stanzas:
1. Brighter days are sweetly dawning. Oh, the glory looms in sight!
   For the cloudy day is waning, And the evening shall be light.
2. Misty fogs, so long concealing, All the hills of mingled night,
   Vanish, all their sin revealing, For the evening shall be light.
3. Lo! the ransomed are returning, Robed in shining crystal white,
   Leaping, shouting home to Zion, Happy in the evening light.
4. Free from Babel, in the Spirit, Free to worship God aright,
   Joy and gladness we're receiving, Oh, how sweet this evening light.
5. Hallelujah! Saints are singing, Victory in Jehovah's might;
   Glory! Glory! Keep it ringing, We are saved in evening light.

Chorus:
Oh, what golden glory streaming! Purer light is coming fast;
Now in Christ we've found a freedom, Which eternally shall last.

A major vehicle for the early teaching and evangelism of the Church of God movement was the periodical the *Gospel Trumpet,* which first appeared in Rome City, Indiana, in January, 1881, the result of the merger of two other periodicals, *The Herald of Gospel Freedom* and *The Pilgrim.* Daniel Warner was the editor and he put on the masthead the affirmation that the new periodical was being published for "the glory of God in the salvation of men from all sin, and the union of all saints on the Bible." The *Gospel Trumpet* became a fiery proclamation for the "evening light" reformation on behalf of the "morningtime" church.

1. A Journey Toward the Light

Excerpts from Barry L. Callen, *Contours of a Cause*
(Anderson University School of Theology, 1995), 47, 64-69.

Daniel S. Warner (1842-1895) increasingly understood himself in the 1880-1895 period to be a pioneering part of a company of faithful Christian "saints" being raised up by God. Their divinely given mission was understood to center in the courage to stand on the platform of "all truth" as it is in Christ Jesus, free of the entanglements of things of human origin.[1] Warner's understanding was based on a powerful Christian vision, key aspects of which are crucial for all Christians in all times. These aspects are responses to a particular reading of God's revelation. They form elements of any adequate construction of Christian theology in these "latter days."[2] Christian people are to be carriers of good news initiated by God's action. This news is known best in Jesus Christ, spawns a faithful church formed by the news, and nourishes a commitment to "the truth" as it is in Christ, is biblically recorded, and is discerned by the ministry of the Spirit of God. Generating this commitment is a vision that "calls for the renunciation of [human] creeds and dogmas so that all Christians may be free to believe and obey all of the Bible."[3]

1. As quoted in Barry L. Callen, *A Time To Remember: Teachings* (Anderson, Ind.: Warner Press, 1978), 22. Also see Callen, *It's God's Church! Life and Legacy of Daniel Warner* (Anderson, Ind.: Warner Press, 1995).

2. Warner and others in the new Church of God movement used this phrase and, on a rare occasion, even were confused with the Latter-day Saints and the Book of Mormon. In 1898, A. T. Rowe clarified such a total misidentification (*Gospel Trumpet*, January 6, 1898).

3. Albert F. Gray, "Distinctive Features of the Present Reformation," *Gospel Trumpet* (February 23, 1922).

The reform movement associated with Warner is a visionary people hoping to assist the wider Christian community to be at its best as God's people in today's world. The concern is for present realization of what is authentic and enduring in the Christian tradition and mission. This movement of the Church of God stands committed to whatever is true, whatever possesses the stamp of God's will and way, and whatever yields the life of the Spirit and propels forward the Spirit's mission. In short, here is a people seeking to be in love with God's truth, whatever it is, costs, or demands....

There was a public announcement for the Church of God campmeeting in Moundsville, West Virginia, scheduled for June, 1902. It began by saying: "A cordial invitation is given to all lovers of the truth to this general convocation of the children of God, on the campground at the Trumpet Home in the northeast part of the city." "Truth" was a central preoccupation of this community of believers. Many of this movement's adherents read closely what was being published by the Gospel Trumpet Company that was located in Moundsville at the turn of the century.[4] Surely, they believed, God had spoken and divine speech always is to be taken as prior to all other claims to wisdom. In Jesus Christ we humans have been encountered by God, and by God's fullest truth.

Often quoted among these "saints" was the New Testament verse, "Sanctify them in the truth; your word is truth" (John 17:17). This verse was not seen as a pretext for casting God's truth in another set of propositional theological statements that then could be claimed to have captured in so many words a full understanding of divine truth. Truth certainly was understood to point to objective reality; it also was judged to be personal, relational, dynamic, and contextual. Christian truth is restricted by the limits of human understanding and too often is distorted by the distracting weight of intellectualized and mandated human traditions.

Responding to "the truth" was believed by these sincere Christians to represent the potential of a new day for the whole church. God's light was beginning to shine again, and lovers of truth were being called and privileged to "walk in the light" as God enables believers to see it. Soon these "saints" would come to sing these words, vigorously and with joy and deep commitment:

> When the voice from heaven sounded, warning all to flee
> From the darksome courts of Babel back to Zion free;
> Glad my heart to hear the message, and I hastened to obey,
> And I'm standing *in the truth* today.[5]

---

4. This publishing company is now Warner Press. It moved to its present location in Anderson, Indiana, in 1906.

5. "The Reformation Glory," verse 2 (emphasis added), by Charles Naylor and Andrew Byers, in *Worship the Lord* (Anderson, Ind.: Warner Press, 1989), 311.

One published summary of the history of the Church of God movement is titled *Truth Marches On,*[6] an appropriate way of characterizing a central burden of this movement. There has been a questing for the full truth as it is in Christ, not a crusading for any theological finality. Historian Merle Strege identifies helpfully key theological assumptions of the Church of God movement. They tend to be imbedded in the simple, yet profound phrase "lovers of truth,"[7] and they have much wisdom to share as followers of Christ from all traditions move into the twenty-first century. Two of these assumptions are that Christian truth is to be *experienced* and it is *progressive.*

Leaders of this movement did not reduce Christianity "to a series of belief statements.... The real essence of Christianity was *experiencing* the truth, and that lay beyond belief." Much later than that 1902 meeting in West Virginia, the following slogan would come to be accepted widely as a brief way of identifying many congregations of this movement: "Where Christian experience makes you a member."[8] Such a phrase does not intend to de-emphasize the theological content of faith. The purpose is to highlight the necessity of being involved personally in radical, life-changing obedience to the call of God, the source, focus, substance, and end of all true doctrine.

When the Christian faith is reduced to a matter of intellectual awareness and mechanical assent at the rational level, real understanding is compromised. To apprehend Christian faith adequately, one first must approach and embrace it with all of oneself. Then, by an enabling divine grace, one continues in the understanding process through embodying the faith in the realities of this present world. The knowing process is far more than memorized creeds. It is life and mission, believing and questing, all in constant interaction.

So the theological focus of this movement has tended to be on direct change in one's life rather than on any isolated, routinely repeated, and often arid confessional formulation of Christian faith. In fact, the usual process by which Christian communities have written and confessed formal creeds has been criticized and avoided by the movement. In part this is because the severely divided Christian community has tended to use such theological formulations in institutionally protective ways that shield many believers from real life change and significant social impact.[9] Such formulations often

---

6. John W. V. Smith (Anderson, Ind.: Gospel Trumpet Co., 1956).

7. See the article "Lovers of Truth" by Merle Strege in *Vital Christianity* (August 24, 1986), 22-23.

8. "A united church for a divided world" is another common self-designation of this movement, used for years on the movement's national radio broadcast in the United States and Canada, the Christian Brotherhood Hour.

9. "Fundamentalism" is the common term for a rigid and protective theological stance. Martin Marty says that the base theological feature of modern fundamentalisms is "oppositionalism." Their agenda is "set by what they feel or calculate demands their resistance, by what they most contend against" (in Hans Küng, Jürgen Moltmann, eds., *Fundamentalism As An Ecumenical Challenge*, London: SCM Press, 1992, 3). Today that target is "modernism" in its many forms. An irony is that the rationalism of modernism (the Enlightenment influence) is used extensively by Christian fundamentalists in their vigorous defense of the truth as they see it.

become tools to justify and maintain the dividedness of some Christians from others whose creeds or practices differ even slightly.

Church of God people seek to be clearly convictional without being narrowly and prematurely creedal. They are conservative, to be sure, but they seek to avoid being "denominationalists" in their view of the church or "fundamentalists" in their theological method. There is an appreciation for process and a disposition to be committed to the whole of truth that lies beyond the apprehension of any one tradition within the Christian community. Thus, "catholic" is an important addition to any "free church" designation of this movement.[10]

Pioneer leaders of the Church of God movement recognized that truth, beyond needing to be *experienced*, tends to be *progressive*. New light had begun to shine on the gathered darkness of church life, and surely there yet would be "more light." All such light had been and always would be thoroughly biblical in its substance, but human understanding of it inevitably is partial and always should be growing. Although there is only one biblical revelation on which the faith is founded, that revelation grows on us and we in it. In this sense, it is progressive (not that it evolves, changes, and is added to over time).

The essential relationship of Christian experience, the process of knowing truth, and the related stance of openness to "new light" should not be misunderstood. These commitments are not intended to encourage movement leaders to be rash and individualistic, stepping outside the mainstream of Christian faith by exhibiting theological novelty in their thinking, believing, or acting. No one has sought or claimed any new divine revelation that surpasses what is available to all Christians or is not wholly consistent with traditional, "orthodox" thought. No "prophet" has received revelation from God that in any way has added to the substance of the biblical revelation. The task is to reform in light of enduring biblical truth, not to extend and change that truth. This movement "is not committed to ecclesiastical standards or doctrines repugnant to human reason. We do not believe in extremism or fanaticism of any kind. We have no sympathy for strange or freak doctrines that are maintained only with subtle arguments or with forced and unnatural interpretations of Scripture."[11] There is no rash novelty, only commitment to taking seriously what is authentic, enduring, and essential to Christian life and mission.

---

10. These phrases, while fairly descriptive of the movement's aspirations, were rarely used by the movement of itself. At first there was little focus on church history other than as the arena of apostasy. Thus, the "free-church" tradition, as such, was little known prior to the work of Charles E. Brown in the 1940s and 1950s. Since Roman Catholicism was viewed as a prime example of falsely institutionalizing the church by human hands, the word "catholic" understandably has been avoided as a primary movement self-description.

11. Frederick G. Smith, *Brief Sketch of the Origin, Growth, and Distinctive Doctrines of the Church of God Reformation Movement* (Anderson, Ind.: Gospel Trumpet Co., 1927).

How does the authentic, enduring, and essential become known? Jesus is reported in John's gospel to have called God's Spirit "the Spirit of truth" (Jn. 14:17; 15:26; 16:13). The Spirit of God is linked closely by the New Testament with the truth of what was being accomplished in the life of Jesus. Jesus is inseparable from the Spirit who communicates truth, especially the truth that is in Jesus himself. Those who worship the Father are instructed to do so "in spirit and truth" (Jn. 4:23-24)—and Jesus is "the truth" (Jn. 14:6), the truth conveyed to us by the Spirit.

The real challenge, Church of God leaders have insisted for generations, is to walk constantly in the light as God gives light, not ever canonizing the spot on which one stands or institutionalizing the perception one may hold at any given time. Faith always is a pilgrimage, a journey guided by the Spirit toward more and more light. Believers are to be following the light. These hymn lyrics express it well:

We limit not the truth of God, to our poor reach of mind,
By notions of our day and sect, crude, partial, and confined.
No, let a new and better hope, within our hearts be stirred:
The Lord hath yet more light and truth, to break forth from the Word.[12]

---

2. Journey of Daniel S. Warner (1842-1895), The Movement's Primary Pioneer[13]

In its earliest decades the Holiness Movement in America sought to be a reforming force within existing church structures. Eventually, many movement adherents, often reluctantly, became separatists, judging themselves forced out of the established churches because of their commitment to holiness. Rather than "reformationist," the separatists were more "restorationist" based on "primitivist" ideals often associated with their holiness emphasis.

Daniel S. Warner

Daniel S. Warner helped inspire this separatist process, although his motivation was anything but the

---

12. Verse one and refrain of "We Limit Not the Truth of God," words by George Rawson (1807-1889), based on parting words of Pastor John Robinson to the Pilgrim Fathers, 1620.

13. This brief essay essentially reproduces the material on Daniel Warner written by Barry L. Callen that appears in Melvin Dieter, ed., *The 19th-Century Holiness Movement* (Kansas City: Beacon Hill Press of Kansas City, 1998), 395-401. Dr. Callen was a "Volume Advisor" for this publication. For a full presentation of the life and ministry of Daniel S. Warner, see Callen, *It's God's Church!*

further dividing of the church by setting up another human organization, even one justified by a concern for holiness. He longed for the church's unity and came to see holiness as the biblical and experiential basis on which authentic Christian unity was possible

Warner came from a difficult home background in Ohio, was converted to Christ in 1865, and soon was actively engaged in pastoral ministry and church planting in Ohio and then Nebraska. The church body with which he had become affiliated, the Winebrennerian Churches of God, was not tolerant of holiness revivalism at the time—nor was Warner initially. In 1877, however, Warner came into close and positive contact with holiness people. By then he was hungry for a deeper spiritual life and continued to be burdened about the hurtful divisiveness he saw everywhere among Christian people. Then came his fruitful holiness contacts. At first they featured the spiritual experiences of his own wife and her parents. When he and his family visited the Ohio farm of his in-laws in April, 1877, Warner immediately sensed that something was different. His wife's family always had been good Christian people, but now he noticed that they had recently "made a more full consecration to God and realized an increased experience of holy joy." He observed in his journal that now "God's presence still more pervades the happy household of sanctified children of God."

The keys to true holiness were thought by Warner to be thorough human consecration, a pervasive divine presence, and resulting joy, known by individual believers and in the body of Christ, the church. He was curious, open, and spiritually hungry but had to be convinced because of much hypocrisy he had seen among declared holiness people. Later in 1880, while addressing the Western Holiness Convention in Illinois, he recalled:

> When I went to the first holiness meeting I ever attended, what do you think I expected? I thought they would work themselves up into a high state of feeling, and get their seekers so wrought up also, that they would finally get to the point of a physical sanctification. But I really found them, each with a Bible in his hand. They were so much one that I could not tell who was the leader of the meeting. And they all searched the word.

On April 8, 1877, Warner's wife Sarah went forward to the altar and claimed her own "sanctification." Daniel was pleased, supportive, and yet still quite cautious. He thought of himself as already committed to Christ and obedient to the Spirit. He certainly had sought to be disciplined in his faith and faithful with his gifts. Was there really more to be experienced? The holiness workers said there was a "second work of grace." Members of his own family now professed such a work, and their lives witnessed to its meaningfulness. They told him that he also needed to be sanctified. On April

16, 1877, he noted in his journal: "Since I rose this morning my constant prayer has been to God to lead me in all things. I pray God to take me like an old sack and shake me until entirely empty, and then fill me with the fullness of God."

The search continued. On July 5 Warner was leading a holiness meeting in Mansfield, Ohio. After a time of Bible reading and congregational testimonies, he issued the usual invitation, then himself stepped down to the altar to seek sanctification. His spiritual life was not yet satisfying. Now, very publicly, he was seeking more of God's transforming grace for himself. That very evening another service was in progress in the same place. When the time came, he did as in the morning, kneeling at his own meeting's altar. He reported later in his journal that "all was dark" and he felt "ashamed to bow at the altar and seek sanctification of 'soul, body, and spirit' after I had invited sinners to, and labored with them, at the same altar." Pride can be a real problem, especially for a respected public leader. The next morning he read 1 Peter 5:10, "But the God of all grace, who hath called us unto his eternal glory in Christ Jesus, after that ye have suffered a while, make you perfect, stablish, strengthen, settle you." He so hoped that God somehow would perfect, settle, and establish *him*. Then he read Ephesians 3:14, 16-19. There it was! He had only to accept the Spirit's work by faith.

His journal entry of July 7 is pivotal. From this day on his life and ministry would be different. What his soul yearned for now had been found! His testimony of this day reads in part:

> Today we fasted all day. Met in the Bethel at 9 A.M. and held meeting until after 4 P.M. without intermission. Evening, met at a quarter to eight. Mighty power filled the house. The altar was filled from one side to the other. Several were seeking sanctification. Glory to God, this night he [God] began to give me some of the evidences (besides my hitherto naked faith) that I had got out of the wilderness into Canaan. Jesus, my blessed Savior, just cut me off one bunch of the sweet grapes of this "land." Oh, glory to God, once more I was a little child! I felt the blood of Jesus flowing through my entire soul, body, and spirit. Heaven on earth! Hallelujah, it is done!

From July 7, 1877, to his last day of life in 1895, Daniel Warner was a committed holiness evangelist and writer. By July 28, two weeks after the sacred cleansing and empowering, he already had written two articles on holiness for the *Church Advocate* [periodical of the Winebrennerian Churches of God] and was anxious to cooperate with the National Holiness Association. Shortly he would begin work on his first major book, *Bible Proofs of the Second Work of Grace* (1880). The beginning paragraphs of chapter one are presented here. They share Warner's central conviction and concern for the well-being of the church and the key role that holiness must play in that well-being.

> After the kindness and love of God our Savior appeared unto me, removing the veil of ignorance and deep prejudice from my heart, enabling me to see and appropriate Christ as my sanctification, all the longing of my heart seemed to center in a desire that all God's dear children should enter this "valley of blessing so sweet."
>
> I wondered that we should have tarried so long in the "first tabernacle" when but a thin veil, and that rent by the death of Christ, separated between us and the "holiest of all" where the glory of God forever dwells, even that glory which Christ has given to the church "that they may be one" (John 17:22).
>
> I soon perceived that it was for want of someone to *give the trumpet a certain sound,*" or set forth perfect holiness as the privilege of all Christians, attainable *now,* by a *definite act of faith.* In order to experience either justification or entire sanctification, these blessings must be presented to the eye of faith as a definite object of pursuit. Hence, under the pall of formalism, where the change of heart is but vaguely and indefinitely taught, it is rarely experienced.
>
> Hence, also, the great mass of the church, who have actually come out of spiritual Egypt, are yet with the murmuring host in the wilderness battling with their inbred evil nature, because, under the generalizing preaching of the present day, no further application of the blood of Christ is pointed out to meet the deeply felt want of perfect heart purity. And the great day of reckoning will disclose the solemn fact that thousands have turned back to the double bondage of Egypt, and are now eternally lost, who, with definite teaching in the way of holiness, would have been washed in the Redeemer's blood, had their "fruit unto holiness, and the end everlasting life."
>
> The church is God's appointed means of saving the world. But perfect holiness is her normal condition. And holiness is only attained by a definite grasp of faith, and it cannot be thus appropriated until presented to the mind in a definite form.
>
> Having, therefore, a clear conviction that upon the preaching and testimony of entire sanctification, as a distinct experience subsequent to justification, more than upon all else besides depends the salvation of immortal souls, the safety of converts, the purity and consequent power, peace, and prosperity of the church, and the glory of God. And perceiving that this "second grace" is the ultimate end of Christ's death, and the great burden of the apostolic

ministry, I was constrained to dedicate forever unto the Lord all the energies of my being for the promotion of this great salvation. (7-9)

The focus of Warner's ministry had shifted, and this shift soon would bring change in his thinking and church relationships. His was a poet who wrote numerous texts that became the lyrics of new gospel songs. Soon these songs would inspire thousands of holiness people and would become part of the hymnology of a new holiness movement to be known as the Church of God (Anderson). One of several of these songs still appearing in the 1989 hymnal of the Church of God reads:

Fill me with Thy Spirit, Lord, Fully save my longing soul;
Thru the precious cleansing blood, Purify and make me whole.

Fill me with Thy holy light, I would have a single eye;
Make me perfect in Thy sight, 'Tis Thy will to sanctify.

Fill me with Thy perfect love, Naught of self would I retain;
Losing all, Thy love to prove, Lord, I count a happy gain.

Fill me with Thy mighty pow'r, Father, Son and Spirit, come;
In my soul the unction pour, Make me ever all Thine own.

Fill me with Thy presence now, Lord, Thyself in me reveal;
At Thy feet I humbly bow, To receive the holy seal.

Refrain
Come, O Spirit, seal me Thine; Come, Thy fullness now bestow;
Let Thy glory in me shine, Let Thy fire within me glow.

About a month after his experience of holiness, Warner sat under the teaching of Daniel Steele, a prominent holiness advocate, and began filling his journal and personal library with books and references to a range of classic holiness works. Warner now fed on such literature. Then he heard a Brother Rice, a Methodist minister, preach a sermon on sanctification, only to learn that this preacher had just had his ministerial license taken away by the Northwest Ohio Conference of that denomination. The reason was that Rice was preaching holiness (presumably he was thought to be a divisive voice in the tradition of the Wesleys). Such a painful experience soon would come to Warner himself in the form of being put on church trial by the West Ohio Eldership of the Churches of God (Winebrenerian).

The charges brought against Warner were these: (1) transcending the restrictions of the Eldership; (2) violating rules of cooperation; and

(3) participating in dividing the church. The concern was that Warner had been drawn into a parachurch euphoria of emotionally charged and unauthorized holiness meetings that were drawing people and resources away from a reasoned faith and the established churches. Warner, of course, viewed the concern and his resulting dismissal quite differently. He insisted that he had been disfellowshipped "for preaching full salvation, for following the Holy Spirit, and for helping to save over 150 souls [in Findlay, Ohio]."

Now Warner was affiliated only with the Holiness Alliance in Ohio. He began to reflect on the implications of holiness teaching for the unity of all Christians. Clearly he viewed his own ministry as uniting and not dividing. Reads his journal (Jan. 30, 1878) regarding the charge of dividing the church:

> I showed that the only results of the holiness meeting were fifty-three sinners converted and 118 believers sanctified, and that all the division and confusion was caused by the carnal and wicked opposition on the part of the rest of the church, just like the envious Jews stirred up the people at Thessalonica and Berea (Acts 17) and interrupted the apostles in their peaceable work of leading souls to Jesus.... The apostles, of course, had to bear the blame, and. . .bonds and prisons awaited them; and I, too, was ready to suffer affliction with the people of God for the sake of Christ.

For the rest of his life Daniel Warner would never pastor again, but always be an itinerant evangelist, writer, and editor. He would be an unapologetic and relentless advocate for the holiness of Christians, a liberating holiness that, in his view, should enable a divinely-inspired unity among Christians. He would place special stress on such matters as the unity of believers in Christ, the reality of a victorious Christian life cleansed and empowered by the presence of the Holy Spirit, and the kingdom of God as a present spiritual reality, with Christ as its King.

Warner recorded in his personal journal in March, 1878, that he now had this "new commission" for his own ministry:

> On the 31st of last January the Lord showed me that holiness could never prosper upon sectarian soil encumbered by human creeds and party names, and he gave me a new commission to join holiness and all truth together and build up the apostolic church of the living God. Praise his name! I will obey him.

This building up included a passion for enhancing the unity of God's people through a common sharing of the holiness experience. Warner became an early "come-outer" with his insistence that holiness had radical implications for Christian unity outside Spirit-impeding and "man-made" ecclesiastical structures. Holiness, he wrote and preached widely, is the instrument both of the individual's need for heart purity and of the church's final reformation—final in that it can and will purge the last element of the sin of the church, sectarianism. He even challenged the appropriateness of organizing a denomination because that usually comes from divisive motivations and leads to sectarian ends.

This radical vision of the perceived proper results of holiness revivalism was an embarrassment to the mainstream Holiness Movement, which Warner separated from in 1881 when the Indiana Holiness Association, which he had served as a vice-president, refused his request that it modify its membership requirements in order to allow persons like himself to continue participating without needing to present denominational credentials. Consequently, he announced in the *Gospel Trumpet*, which he then edited: "We wish to cooperate with all Christians, as such, in saving souls—but forever withdraw from all organisms that uphold and endorse sects and denominations in the body of Christ." Warner became the primary pioneer of the Church of God movement (Anderson) which was to become one of the larger of all the holiness bodies, the one with "light on the church" that leads to a holiness-unity vision and speaks a prophetic voice to wayward denominational, ecumenical, and even holiness structures.

Editor's Note: For more on the life and legacy of Daniel S. Warner, see Barry L. Callen, *It's God's Church! The Life and Legacy of Daniel S. Warner* (Anderson, Ind.: Warner Press, 1995) and Callen's *Contours of a Cause: The Theological Vision of the Church of God Movement (Anderson)* (Anderson University School of Theology, 1995).

3. Winebrennerian Context of Daniel S. Warner's Beliefs

by Barry L. Callen

If preaching was to be Daniel Warner's life calling, presumably some church affiliation was necessary.[14] So, during the summer of 1867, while preparing for his marriage in September, Warner sought wisdom on the question of the best available church connection. With care he examined the

14. Andrew Byers recalled this time in Warner's life and interpreted it this way: "To join a sectarian denomination is never by divine prompting, but is urged from human source. A young convert possessing the spirit of Christ is naturally at home in the Lord and with Christians anywhere.... Accordingly, our young brother was only 'acting natural' when he manifested no particular anxiety to 'join the church'" (*Birth of a Reformation*, 1921, 51).

practices and beliefs of the churches in his Ohio community and sought to compare them with his own growing understanding of biblical teaching. The final choice was a small body known as the General Eldership of the Churches of God in North America. This denomination had been organized in 1825-30 in Harrisburg, Pennsylvania, by John Winebrenner, a former German Reformed minister whose revivalism had separated him from his parent body.[15]

Warner was licensed to preach by the West Ohio Eldership at its eleventh annual meeting convened at Findlay, Ohio, in October, 1867. His first pastoral assignment was the congregation in Mount Blanchard just south of Findlay. In his journal nine years later (Oct. 1, 1876) Warner was overcome with emotion as he recalled this Eldership meeting in Findlay. "I had not expected a license; but how I trembled with fear and dread when I learned that a license and a field of labor were given me!. . . Having begun an invalid, supposed by many to be a consumptive, my strength has gradually increased through God's blessings and mercies."

The stances of the Churches of God (Winebrennarian) attracted Warner because they appeared so biblical to him. In fact, Warner's "self-imposed course of private biblical and theological studies. . .and his very mental furniture bear the Winebrennerian stamp."[16] What was this theological stamp? It focuses on a five-point theological transformation experienced by John Winebrenner during the 1820s, a transformation inspired by revivalism and his interaction with leaders of groups such as the United Brethren in Christ. The points reflect roots in German Pietism and other "radical" elements of the Protestant Reformation that had been transplanted to America and had become part of America's revivalism. By 1830 these points had led Winebrenner to a rupture in his relationship with the German Reformed Church. Now in the 1860s the same points were shaping the early vision of Warner:

> 1. The Bible is the Word of God, the only authoritative rule of faith and practice. This "only" left no place for church tradition, including human inventions like creeds, catechisms, rituals, etc.

> 2. Spiritual regeneration, being born again, always is necessary for a person to become a real Christian and church member. Thus the Christian faith is rooted in the Bible and in such spiritual experience.

---

15. See Forney (*History of the Churches of God*, 1914), Richard Kern (*John Winebrenner: Nineteenth Century Reformer*, 1974), and Harvey Gossard ("John Winebrenner: Founder, Reformer, and Businessman," *Pennsylvania Religious Leaders*, 1986).

16. L. Leon Long, "To What Extent Was Warner a Winebrennerian?" *Church Advocate* (Feb. 1976), 6.

3. Humankind possesses free moral agency and the ability, with the Spirit's assistance, to repent, believe, and be saved. Thus denied were the Reformed doctrines of predestination, providence, and perseverance.

4. Baptism and the Lord's Supper were gradually seen as symbolic "ordinances" rather than grace-conveying "sacraments." Baptism necessarily is to be preceded by belief and regeneration and is best administered by immersion (eliminating the appropriateness of infant baptism).

5. Regarding the church, the only requirement for membership in a local congregation is having been born again, and the true biblical name for a local congregation or for the Body of Christ as a whole is "Church of God."[17]

John Winebrenner had no intention of founding a new denomination, bodies he stigmatized as "sects." He saw no church organization as legitimate if it limited the freedom of local congregations, which should accept no human creed, name, or ordinance. It's *God's* church, he insisted, not a contrived *human* arrangement in God's name. In this way Winebrenner saw a basis for the unity of all Christians and churches. This general anti-denominational view, when joined with the Wesleyan teaching of holiness, was to become the view and vision of Warner in his later years. He also would not intend to found a new denomination and would insist that *it's God's church!*

In his booklet *The Church of God*, Warner restated several Winebrennarian themes and recast them in light of his Wesleyan experience of entire sanctification. He had concluded that the cleansing love of God is the "bond of perfectness" which can restore the unity of the church (21). As Merle Strege concludes: the Church of God (Anderson) was born "the child of a marriage of two different theological traditions. To an essentially Wesleyan soteriology Warner had joined a restorationist ecclesiology that closely resembled that of the believers' churches" (*Tell Me Another Tale*, 1993, 10).

Editor's Note: For a full discussion of the Believers' Church tradition and its relation to the Church of God movement, see Charles E. Brown, *When Souls Awaken: An Interpretation of Radical Christianity*, 1954 and Barry L. Callen, *Radical Christianity: The Believers' Church Tradition in Christianity's History and Future,* 1999).

---

17. Harvey Gossard, "Winebrenner," 89-90.

4. The Carson City Resolutions (1881)

Editor's Note: The first two congregations to "step completely out of Babylon" and take as their sole basis the New Testament church were located in Beaver Dam, Indiana, and Carson City, Michigan. The "saints" in Carson City, as an expression of their position and intentions, developed and affirmed the following in 1881.

Whereas, we recognize ourselves in the perilous times of the last days, the time in which Michael is standing up for the deliverance of God's true saints (Dan. 12:1), the troublesome times in which the true house of God is being built again, therefore,

Resolved, that we will endeavor by all the grace of God to live holy, righteous, and godly in Christ Jesus, "looking for, and hastening unto the coming of the Lord Jesus Christ," who we believe is nigh, even at the door.

Resolved, that we adhere to no body or organization but the church of God, bought by the blood of Christ, organized by the Holy Spirit, and governed by the Bible. And if the Lord will, we will hold an annual assembly of all saints who in the providence of God shall be permitted to come together for the worship of God, the instruction and edification of one another, and the transaction of such business as the Holy Spirit may lead us to see and direct in its performance.

Resolved, that we ignore and abandon the practice of preacher's license as without precept or example in the Word of God, and that we wish to be "known by our fruits" instead of by papers.

Resolved, that we do not recognize or fellowship any who come unto us assuming the character of a minister whose life is not godly in Christ Jesus and whose doctrine is not the Word of God.

Resolved also, that we recognize and fellowship, as members with us in the one body of Christ, all truly regenerated and sincere saints who worship God in all the light they possess, and that we urge all the dear children of God to forsake the snares and yokes of human parties and stand alone in the "one fold" of Christ upon the Bible, and in the unity of the Spirit.

Editor's Note: A part of this early vision of Church of God people was commitment to a free and unstructured fellowship with almost a total absence of ecclesiastical machinery (which was seen as signs of fallen humanity and the apostate church). There was fear that introducing virtually any kind of organization would subvert the true church by reducing it to a human institution not controlled by the Holy Spirit. The pioneers of this movement sought to avoid human organization in the church and carried on a polemic against the "sects" and their "man-made" structures. For a rather different view by a major and more contemporary Church of God leader, Samuel G. Hines, see Entry 173.

Frederick G. Smith

5. The Last Reformation in Prophecy

by Frederick G. Smith, *The Last Reformation*
(Anderson, Ind.: Gospel Trumpet Co., 1919), excerpts
from 223-256.

Editor's Note: This selection is a good example of an early self-understanding of the Church of God movement, seeing its life and mission in the midst of a "final reformation" of the church by God, as understood graphically through interpreting the Book of Revelation. This line of interpretation was launched by Daniel Warner later in his life, was greatly popularized by F. G. Smith, and later was carried forward capably by Lillie S. McCutcheon (*The Symbols Speak*, 1964, rev. ed., 1999).

The scene changes (Revelation 14:1-5), and again we have the picture of God's chosen people set in bright relief against the dark background of Protestantism and the still darker shades of papal apostasy....

What a contrast with the beast powers described in the preceding chapter of the Revelation! This redeemed company is on Mount Zion, not hidden in the darkness of the wilderness. They are with the Lamb, not wandering after the beast. Instead of being oppressed and overcome by opposers, they are singing the joyful song of redemption and harping with their harps; and instead of having the "mark of the beast," they have their *"Father's name written in their foreheads."* The manner in which this joyful, redeemed company is distinguished from the host of beast-worshipers brought to light under the preceding symbols, proclaims unmistakably the fact that we have here a description of the true people of God who have obtained victory over the apostasy. In other words, a distinct reformation is predicted....

Here we are brought face to face with some of the most solemn truths contained in the Book of God. The very powers of apostate Christianity just described under the symbols of two beasts are now represented by the angel as Babylon; for, be it observed, the divine message is against those who worship the beast and his image. The image was made by the second beast. Therefore, Babylon includes both Romanism and Protestantism—the whole realm of formal churchianity; and beast-worship is here condemned in one of the most terrible denunciations found in all the Word of God. All the evils inherent in the false, unscriptural systems of so-called Christianity are here summed up under the one word Babylon....

The prophecies already cited make clear a mighty religious movement before the end of time, a movement designed to triumph over the apostasy. Since the apostasy was twofold in its nature, comprehending a corruption of evangelical faith and the development of ecclesiasticism, it is evident that the Last Reformation must both restore primitive truth and eliminate ecclesiasticism, thus bringing back to the world the original conception of the church as embracing the whole divine family under the direct moral and spiritual dominion of Christ. It is also evident from the prophecies that this is to be accomplished by literally forsaking the systems of man-rule just as ancient Israel was restored after the captivity by God's people, leaving Babylon and coming home to Zion. Zion represents the church in its primitive, unified condition under the government and law of Christ alone. Babylon represents a foreign rule and another law....

The sect system, wherein ecclesiasticism reigns and where the full truth in all its purity can not be taught and practiced, does not represent the true church, but Babylon. The system is foreign. It contains, however, many who are not Babylonians, but children of the divine family—Israelites indeed. The awful judgments of God pronounced against Babylon are directed against the false system itself and the real beast-worshipers it contains, not against the true people of God, who love their Lord and are willing to walk in the light of His Word as fast as they are able to understand it....

The movement to ignore sect lines and bring the true people of God into unity is not based upon a mere interpretation of prophecy, however. The necessity of such a work is being felt by the true people of God everywhere, even those who make no particular claims to knowledge of prophetic interpretation. Knowledge that the ecclesiastical systems of the present day do not represent the real church outlined in the New Testament is all that is absolutely necessary in order to stir the heart for reformatory action. Departure from the truth of God carries with it responsibility on the part of all those who become awakened to that departure—responsibility to return to the Bible standard. A final reformation there must and would be even if it had never been predicted by the prophets of old; for Christ, the great ever-living head of the church, would at the proper time pour out upon His servants the spirit of judgment against all unscriptural systems and forms of worship and demand the restoration of the pure church of the morning time of our era....

The final reformation is on. "Final," I say, because it leaves nothing to be restored as regards either doctrine, practice, or spirit. It stands committed to the restoration of the whole truth and the harmonious unity of all true Christians in one Christ-ruled, Spirit-filled body. In short, it stands committed to the restoration of apostolic Christianity in its entirety—its doctrines, its ordinances, its personal regenerating and sanctifying experiences, its spiritual life, its holiness, its power, its purity, its gifts of the Spirit, its unity of believers, and its fruits. This reformation will continue until it becomes a great mountain and fills the whole earth, until "the kingdom and dominion, and the greatness of the kingdom under the whole heaven, shall be given to the people of the saints of the Most High."

This reformation is the movement of God. It is not a humanly organized movement depending for its success on the ability of men to persuade people to leave other churches and join them. God himself is breaking down the barriers that divide, and in response to His call the redeemed are forsaking human sects and creeds, and their hearts are flowing together. The center of this movement is not a particular geographical location, nor is its nucleus a particular set of fallible men: the center and nucleus of this world-wide movement is OUR LORD JESUS CHRIST, and its operative force is the SPIRIT OF THE LIVING GOD, which draws the faithful together in bonds of holy love and fellowship. Multitudes already recognize no other bonds of union than that moral and spiritual affinity which is the common heritage of all the disciples of Jesus that know the blessed experience of the heavenly birth. Multitudes more are beginning to see the light of this glorious truth, and in due time Christ, the Light, will illuminate the hearts of all the saved ones. All hail the day that lies just ahead!

> Back to the one foundation, from sects and creeds made free,
> Come saints of every nation to blessed unity.
> Once more the ancient glory shines as in days of old,
> And tells the wondrous story—one God, one faith, one fold.

Editor's Note: In addition to his 1919 book *The Last Reformation*, F. G. Smith also authored *The Revelation Explained* (1908) and *What the Bible Teaches* (1914). These books were extraordinarily influential in the Church of God movement, especially in the first half of the twentieth century. The 1914 volume was condensed by Kenneth E. Jones (1955; rev. ed. 1999).

6. What the Pioneers Preached

by John W. V. Smith

Editor's Note: Historian John W. V. Smith has detailed "the basic theological presuppositions of these first proclaimers of what they called 'this present truth'" (*The Quest for Holiness and Unity*, 1980, 81-100). These follow, along with song references since much of the early theology of the Church of God movement was carried in music (see the doctoral dissertation by Robert Adams titled "The Hymnody of the Church of God [1885-1980]," Southwestern Baptist Theological Seminary, 1980). What did the pioneers preach?

• They affirmed the Protestant precept that the Bible is the sole foundation of the Christian faith. [Note: D. Otis Teasley's 1907 song, "Back to the Blessed Old Bible."]

• They affirmed the basic conviction that religion, for the Christian, is essentially experiential. [Note: Joseph C. Fisher's 1884 song, "I'm Redeemed, Praise the Lord!" and Barney E. Warren's 1907 song, "A Child of God."]

• They affirmed that God was calling them to proclaim and to model the visible earthly expression of God's one holy catholic church. That church could not be equated with any existing denomination. They had "light on the church." It was to be holy, unified, not controlled by any creed, structure, or tradition. [Note: Charles W. Naylor's 1922 song, "O Church of God."]

• They affirmed that they were participants in the fulfillment of a segment of divine destiny for all humanity. They understood their role as being the heralds of God's ultimate will for the church. The second coming of Christ was near and God had called into being a "final-reformation" movement. Increasingly this movement came to be understood by many of its leaders in the "church-historical" interpretative framework of Daniel/Revelation. The first article in the *Gospel Trumpet* to develop from prophecy a chronological timetable for the final renewal of the church did not appear until 1887. [Note: William G. Schell's song "The Biblical Trace of the Church" (appeared in *Select Hymns*, 1911), Daniel S. Warner's 1897 song, "The Evening Light" (published after his death in 1895), and Charles W. Naylor's songs, "The Reformation Glory" (1922) and "The Church's Jubilee" (1923).]

Historian John W. V. Smith concludes with the following:

> In summary it must be noted that the Church of God reform movement did not find the basis for its self-consciousness in any one of the basic concepts herein delineated, but found it in a combination of all four of them. Each depends on all others, and all give support to each. None of them have any meaning, for instance, without the principle that the sole foundation of the Christian faith is in the Scriptures. The personal experiential interpretation of the Christian life is necessary to understanding the nature of the Church and the unity of believers. The sense of destiny involves the Christian person individually and also corporately in the Church. The interlocking themes which tie them all together are holiness, unity, and mission. Of such was the Church of God as it emerged from a conglomerate variety of sincere people to become a united movement aware of its purposes in the accomplishment of God's divine will for all his people on the earth. (1980, p. 100)

Editor's Note: Two of the more influential theological books in the early generations of the movement were F. G. Smith's *What the Bible Teaches* (1914) and Russell R. Byrum's *Christian Theology* (1925). Their more contemporary counterparts are Barry L. Callen's *God As Loving Grace* (1996) and Gilbert W. Stafford's *Theology for Disciples* (1996). John W. V. Smith's *I Will Build My Church: Biblical Insights on Distinguishing Doctrines of the Church of God* (1985), not intended as a systematic theology, highlights eight doctrines designated as "distinguishing," not "distinctive." Smith clarifies that none of these doctrines is unique to the Church of God movement. All are said to be thoroughly Christian and all are based on Scripture. However, "this particular combination of teachings. . .each interpreted in the manner indicated, makes the Church of God approach distinctive and significant" (4). Also see the 1973 doctoral dissertation by Gilbert W. Stafford (Boston University School of Theology) titled "Experiential Salvation and Christian Unity in the Thought of Seven Theologians in the Church of God (Anderson, Ind.)."

7. Consultation on Doctrine (1970-1974)

by William E. Reed, excerpted from the booklet
Consultation on Doctrine
(Anderson, Ind.: Executive Council, 1974).

Editor's Note: After about eight years of the life of the Church of God movement, it was judged necessary by movement leaders to reassess the movement's teaching tradition. A major attempt at such reassessment occurred in the years 1970-1974.

Four years ago, in June, 1970, the General Assembly of the Church of God took favorable action on the following resolution:

The General Assembly sessions this year have helped us to not only see and handle our duties, but also see and know our strong differences of opinion. Many of the expressed differences concern agency programs and decisions that were vigorously debated against.

Whereas some of the expressed differences reflected a possible problem of attitudes as well as opinions; and

Whereas many of the differences reflect theological and doctrinal problems that need to be openly and honestly faced by this Assembly; and

Whereas some of these problems grow out of evidently changing patterns of our preaching, teaching, and publications across several decades.

Therefore be it resolved that we urge a serious restudy of the theological and doctrinal message of our movement, and that the Executive Council and the graduate School of Theology examine the feasibility of calling a Consultation of Doctrine to allow mutual discussion among us as leaders in faith and practice.

The intent is not to prepare a creed or definitive statement of our position, but rather to hear and examine anew the doctrinal concerns that are important to our life and work as a movement.

One year later, in June 1971, the Executive Council reported to the General Assembly that, in its opinion, the type of Consultation on Doctrine requested in the 1970 resolution was feasible and should be conducted. The Council offered the suggestion that the study focus sharply on the doctrine, "The Church, Its Nature, Mission, Polity and Unity." It was further suggested that the Division of General Service be requested to prepare and distribute the necessary guidance information for conducting the Consultation and that the Consultation be conducted primarily in state and regional assemblies throughout the Church of God.

The Division of General Service, in order to implement and carry out the assignment, appointed a thirty-member Design Committee to research and evaluate resource materials and to advise regarding the best way in which to conduct the Consultation. Since no funds were appropriated by the General Assembly to underwrite the expense of bringing the Design Committee together, the research and evaluation was conducted by mail, with the members of the Design Committee residing in Anderson constituting a coordinating committee.

The Design Committee constructed and adopted the following statement of purpose for the Consultation:

> To explore biblically and historically the Church's nature, mission, polity, and unity in order to find a common ground for the commitment of old and the nurturing of newer members of our churches. In order to accomplish this, we will:

1. Examine our biblical and theological rootage.
2. Identify doctrinal distinctives and their meaning and application today.
3. Appraise our affinities with other religious groups and the nature of the unity we seek.
4. Evaluate the doctrine of the Holy Spirit as it relates to the Church as the people of God.
5. Express programmatically the challenges to the Church for evangelism and mission.

In keeping with this purpose and with a view toward encouraging the broadest possible participation in the Consultation, the Design Committee selected four ministers to prepare short resource papers for use in presenting the four subtopics of the assignment as follows:

"The Nature of the Church"—Keith Huttenlocker
"The Mission of the Church"—R. Eugene Sterner
"The Polity of the Church"—Arlo F. Newell
"The Unity of the Church"—James Earl Massey

An opportunity was extended to each regional, area, state, district and provincial assembly to participate in the Consultation. The resource papers were made available to the participating assemblies in printed form. Guest leadership was also provided on an out-of-pocket expense basis. Over the past two years, 30 assemblies, including approximately 2,200 ministers, have participated in the Consultation. Several members of the Design Committee have been used as guest leaders. The Consultations on Doctrine have served a useful purpose in the following areas:

1. *An increased appreciation for the heritage which is ours in the Church of God.* As we have examined the theological and historical root system which has produced the movement, we have recognized the humanness of the pioneers of the past, while, at the same time, recognizing the rightness of direction which they gave to the movement. A reexamination of their posture regarding the nature of the church and the role of the Church of God as a reforming movement has given additional evidence that the church is of God and that God is still working in his church to call sinners to repentance, Christians to unity, and the world to judgment.

2. *An increased awareness of the relationship between sound doctrine and authentic experience.* In an age when so much false doctrine is being propagated and so much experience is being predicated on shallow emotionalism, the contribution of the Consultation at this point should not be minimized. Sound doctrine builds strong Christians. If, in the Church of God, we can continue to propagate sound doctrine, spiritual stability, and social relevance, the future of the Church is assured. On the other hand, if sound doctrine is neglected, the end product will be that of immature Christians and a lack of relevance for the Church in society. There is a recognized balance between doctrine and experience. As the word *doctrine* is used here, it is synonymous with the words *truth* and *gospel*. As this truth is declared, believed and practiced, it will build strong Christians, and, by building strong Christians, the Church will become strong.

3. *Some areas of polarization have been identified.* There is general commitment throughout the movement to the concept of oneness and unity among the people of God. There is not full agreement as to how unity can best be attained. Some are inclined to assess the role of the Church of God movement differently than others. This is not a new polarity. Rather, it is a continuation of a polarity which has characterized the movement from its beginning. There is a fine line

of distinction to be made here. On the one hand, there are those who might want to claim more for the movement and its particular prophetic and reformational role than what can be supported by a right interpretation of Scripture. On the other hand, there are those who might be claiming less for the movement and its purpose under God. It is encouraging to observe that, while there are differences on peripheral approaches to unity, there is a splendid consensus that unity is the gift of God and not a human achievement.

4. *The Consultations have also provided a vehicle which has encouraged openness in discussion.* In many instances, this has proved to be the best contribution of the Consultations. It has provided an opportunity for persons with differing points of view to sit together and discuss these differences without fear of judgment or ostracization. This has tended to break down the inclinations and tendencies to categorize each other as "liberals" or "conservatives." There has been an honest questing for a better understanding of the other person's point of view.

5. *An awareness that recognition in the Church should be predicated on participation in the Church's broader ministries.* At this point, the Consultations have served a significant purpose in encouraging the support of the Church in its local work, its state program, its national work, and in its world outreach. In several of the Consultations, black and white ministers have come together as brethren to talk for the first time about the nature, mission, polity, and unity in the Church. This has encouraged a significant step forward in the unifying of the Church at state and local levels. The contribution here may be more significant than what we presently realize.

8. Teaching Priorities

by Benjamin F. Reid, as originally written for and published in Barry L. Callen's *A Time To Remember: Projections* (Anderson, Ind.: Warner Press, 1978), 89-91. Dr. Reid (1937-1999) was a beloved pastor, preacher, leader of the National Association of the Church of God (see Entry 187), and trustee of Anderson University. He was awarded the University's honorary Doctor of Divinity degree in 1982.

Benjamin F. Reid

80

After one hundred years, where does the Church of God go from here? What ought to be our priorities? What goals and objectives ought we set? Where does God want us to go? Where is the Holy Spirit leading us? I suggest a few priorities for our future.

We Must Evangelize

The Church of God must become a divinely motivated force for soul winning in this present world. We must recapture soul-burden. We must renew our commitment to the great commission of Jesus to "go into all the world and preach the gospel to everyone." The tremendous motivations that propelled the "flying ministry" in the early days of this movement must be recaptured here and now. Millions in our cities, ghettos, rural areas, and small towns need to be won to Jesus Christ. Television, radio, newspapers, magazines, mass evangelism, door-to-door visitation, campus ministries, shopping center chapels, hospital and institutional ministries, telephone witness, dial-a-prayer, outdoor services, cooperative parishes—every means available must be used to get the gospel of Christ to a lost world. "By all means, we must win some!"

We Must Let the Wind Blow!

The Church of God has always had a sound theology of the Holy Spirit. With the current wave of Pentecostal fervor and charismatic phenomena swirling all around us, the Church of God must not become bashful and backward in its proclamation and appropriation of the biblical experiences of Pentecost. We must reject negative "knee-jerk" reactions to modern Pentecostals. Rather, we must seek to understand their search for a truly Spirit-filled experience. We must help them to understand that experiential emotions must be firmly rooted in biblical truth and that the Holy Spirit is given for the sanctifying of believers, the imparting of victory over sin, and the inspiring and empowering of the believer toward the task of being witnesses for Jesus. The impartation of gifts by the Holy Spirit must be acknowledged and accepted and the Church must be taught how all spiritual gifts are to be used for the edifying of the body of Christ. We must "let the wind of the Spirit blow" throughout the Church, unafraid of it, unconfused by it, and unsatisfied without it. Only then can we know the truth of the biblical imperative, "It is not by might nor by power, but by my Spirit, saith the Lord."

We Must Preach the Word!

The Church of God must proclaim its allegiance to, its faith in, and its determination to preach the Word of God. We must produce Bible scholars and first-rate theologians. Our publishing house must print books, heavy in scriptural content and profound in biblical insight. Our seminaries and colleges must produce preachers "mighty in the Scriptures" who can preach effective expository sermons.

Our intense desire for relevancy and up-to-dateness must not be allowed to dilute our faith in the Word of God and our building upon its firm and historic foundations. "Back to the Blessed Old Bible" must be more than a nostalgic reminiscence of our Bible-thumping, proof-texting pioneers. It must be the undergirding strength of our preaching, teaching, writing, and searching. Without getting bogged down in semantic battles about *plenary inspiration* and *infallible* versus *inerrant,* the Church of God must proclaim that the Bible is our only rule of faith and practice and is the only trustworthy revelation of God and his Christ and of God's will for us through the Holy Spirit.

We Must Break Down the Walls!

Yes, after one hundred years we are still grappling with the problem, prospect, and potential of Christian unity. How exciting is the prospect that perhaps in our second century, should Jesus tarry, we shall learn more effectively how to put into practice our proclamation that there is "one way and one Spirit, one hope and one God!" In our future, racism must continue to die among us so that we will no longer be embarrassed as we preach that we are a "united church for a divided world." Our arrogance must continue to die, so that truly we will "reach our hands in fellowship to every blood washed one" without our thinking that "coming home to Zion" means coming to our Anderson-centered organization.

We must see that union in Christ, fellowship in Spirit, and unity in one spiritual body do not mean amalgamation into one organization. We must be a spiritual movement that ignores, overlooks, and works around denominational structures and rejoices in, relates to, and recognizes always our fellowship in the Spirit with every member of the body of Christ, whatever their racial or cultural heritage and whatever their theological or denominational history.

The Church of God faces its second century with a full agenda marked "unfinished business." Our vitality is assured as long as our vision remains clear. Our internal unity is assured as long as our diversity is not destroyed. Our theological fidelity is assured as long as our faithfulness to the Word of God is constant. Our future growth is assured as long as we believe and accept the Great Commission as our way of life. Our future impact upon the entire religious world is assured as long as we remain open to the "wind of the Spirit!"

Editor's Note: See also Benjamin F. Reid, *Glory to the Spirit* (Anderson, Ind.: Warner Press, 1990; memorial edition 1999).

9. We Believe

Excerpts of a "Statement of Conviction on the Occasion of the
Centennial of the Church of God Reformation Movement,"
by Anderson School of Theology, 1979

The Church of God movement has maintained certain theological perspectives. . .which we judge to be worthy of serious consideration by all Christians. Accordingly, we declare our continuing commitment to this particular movement within the church because along with it:

WE BELIEVE. . .

That the gospel of Christ has the power to transform all persons who are willing to repent, believe in its promises, and obey its commands.

a. Persons are justified before God on the basis of the free and universal offering of divine grace which is made effective by faith, expressed publicly through baptism, and nourished by the Holy Spirit and the Word of God. "Therefore, since we are justified by faith, we have peace with God through our Lord Jesus Christ" (Rom. 5:1).

b. Persons are sanctified by the cleansing and empowering work of the Holy Spirit who establishes the lives of believers in perfect love and enables those lives to be lifted above the domination of sin. "For this reason I bow my knees before the Father. . .that. . .he may grant you to be strengthened with might through his Spirit in the inner man and. . . that you may be filled with all the fullness of God" (Eph. 3:14-19).

c. Jesus taught his disciples to lead disciplined and sacrificial lives of prayer, witness, and service. He washed the feet of his disciples as an action symbol of the servant life appropriate for all. He taught his disciples to act with courage and compassion in the face of evil and disease. He demonstrated the healing dimension of God's will for the body, mind, and spirit. "By this all men will know that you are my disciples, if you have love for one another" (John 13:35). "And he [Jesus] sent them out to preach the kingdom of God and to heal" (Luke 9:2).

d. Persons justified before God, sanctified by God, and serving in God's name willingly submit to the lordship of Christ in all areas of life. They are thus present citizens of the Kingdom of God and they anticipate the glorious consummation of that Kingdom at the return of Christ. "Unless one is born of water and the Spirit, he cannot enter the kingdom of God" (John 3:5). "For the kingdom of God is not food and drink, but righteousness and peace and joy in the Holy Spirit" (Rom. 14:17).

We are convinced that the Christian life is both intensely personal and compellingly social. It begins in God's grace, leads to God's service, and is fulfilled in God's eternity.

WE BELIEVE. . .

In a cluster of biblical teachings which form a vision of the church. Specifically:

a. God's church is the community of redeemed persons. It is not to be understood primarily as any or all of the humanly designed and historically conditioned organizations of Christians. It is a divinely ordered fellowship of all persons in harmonious relationship with God. A local congregation, then, is best understood as a local manifestation of the church universal (Eph. 2:14-21; 1 Cor. 1:2).

b. God's church is a community of divine-human partnership with Christ as Head. The church is all of God's redeemed children. It is the people of God made members one of another under the headship of Christ (Eph. 2:19-22). It is that unique body chosen for purposeful partnership in accomplishing the will of God on earth. Persons who are admitted to membership in the church by the grace of God (Acts 2:47) and equipped for service by the gifting of God (1 Cor. 12:4-7) are the Spirit-led persons who guide the life and work of the church, just as that Christian council at Jerusalem made strategic decisions in light of what "seemed good to the Holy Spirit and to us" (Acts 15:28).

c. God's church is a holy community. Its holiness does not center in its possession of sacraments as means of saving grace or in its being historically in line with a hierarchically conceived "apostolic succession." It is the "Body of Christ." Through the atoning work of Christ and the sanctifying work of the Holy Spirit, the church, through the individual lives of its members, is privileged to participate in and demonstrate that holiness (1 Cor. 1:2, 3:17; Eph. 5:25-27).

d. God's church is intended to be a unified community. The dividedness among Christian people today is not just unfortunate; it is

84

inappropriate and wholly unacceptable. Unity is clearly God's will for the church. Participation in the Lord's Supper dramatizes the intended unity of Christians as they celebrate their one Lord, one salvation, and one mission. But that unity, symbolized in worship, must find visible expression in the life and witness of the church. The goal is less a contrived peace treaty among deeply divided church organizations and more a radical reconsideration of what is an appropriate network of relationships among brothers and sisters in Christ (Luke 22:14-19; John 17:20-21; Romans 12:4-5; Gal. 3:28; Eph. 4:4).

We have committed ourselves to the implications of this vision of God's church. A unified life and witness among brothers and sisters in Christ is not optional. It is a natural outcome of the experience of grace and membership in the body of Christ. It is a crucial factor in the effectiveness of the church on mission!

WE BELIEVE. . .

That God calls his people to mission. All Christians are mandated to bear witness to God's saving activity in Jesus Christ (Acts 1:8; Luke 24:48) and to "make disciples of all nations" (Matt. 28:19). In this regard it is important to note that:

a. There is an unalterable gospel which transcends all denominational boundaries and controversies. Its essence is found in St. Paul's great statement: "God was in Christ" (2 Cor. 5:19), and in its corollary: "Jesus is Lord" (1 Cor. 12:3). In these statements we have a sufficient basis and reason for the Christian mission to all the world. The Holy Spirit bears witness to Jesus as Christ and Lord, and those who are filled with the Spirit will do the same.

b. Accomplishment of the Christian mission requires that Christians rise above private prejudices and party spirits to their sacred privilege and urgent obligation as members of the church. The grace of God in Christ should find embodiment in the life of the church and expression through the evangelical witness and sacrificial service of the church. Only in this way will the world come to know that the reconciling love of God is real and greatly to be desired.

c. Proper theological perspective is essential. We preach Christ! And in light of Christ we know that holiness of life and the "bond of perfectness" in the church are foundational for the all-important mission of the church. The church is on mission as the. . .

85

Elect from every nation, Yet one o'er all the earth,
Her charter of salvation—One Lord, one faith, one birth.
One holy name she blesses, Partakes one holy food;
And to one hope she presses, With every grace endued.

We are committed to God's church on mission. Christ is central. Love, holiness, and unity are crucial. A needy world is waiting!

WE BELIEVE. . .

In the principle of openness to all affirmations of the Christian faith which are expressions of the biblical revelation (John 16:13). This is a necessary stance for Christians who would venture on mission to the world with a desire to foster honest and growing relationships with fellow Christians from many cultural and creedal backgrounds.

The intended unity among Christians is not based on the achievement of full agreement on all theological questions. Rather, it is based on a common membership in the church through the grace of God and is anchored by a common commitment to the centrality of Christ and the authority of the Word of God.

As individuals, we seek to remain humble and open to the daily instruction and leadership of the Holy Spirit. As a movement, the Church of God seeks always to allow itself to be reformed so that, by avoiding any development of the stagnation of rigid creed or inflexible structure, it can remain a pliable instrument in the hands of God.

We are privileged to have received the basic truth of Christ in the biblical revelation, but we realize that our understanding and application of that truth are always subject to the continuing ministry of the Holy Spirit in our midst. The nature of the church requires that our theological understandings and church-related organizations be used to build bridges of hope to the world and not walls of division among Christians.

Editor's Note: In 1934, in the midst of considerable controversy concerning whether or not the Anderson campus was still loyal to the teaching tradition of the Church of God movement, campus officials published a statement of their belief. See Entry 33.

10. Functioning Above Sectarianism

Excerpted from an article by Leslie W. Ratzlaff in
Vital Christianity, June, 1985, 22.

Sectarian chains bind God's people, mar their work, and keep the church from reflecting God's full glory. To forever throw off sectarian cords takes eternal vigilance. The following points suggest transcending and rising above all sectarian cords:

1. The Church of God transcends any human beginning! God gave it birth on the Day of Pentecost as attested to in Acts 2. The year 1881 may be a year when bold action based on discoveries about the church of God was taken [beginning of the Church of God movement]. It, however, was not the beginning but the affirmation of a reality long in existence.

2. The Church of God belongs simply to the triune God! To be other than the church of God "from whom every family in heaven and on earth is named" (Eph. 3:15) is sectarian and to be called other than that presents a confusing witness.

3. The Church of God transcends any human geographical center! God's headquarters are not in Jerusalem (John 4:20-24) and certainly not in Anderson, Indiana. Yet each local congregation is planted in a specific geographical area and should be so identified.

4. The Church of God transcends any reformation movement! Paul took a firm stand against the tendency to a sectarian spirit (1 Cor. 1:10-13; 3:1-9). God uses human agents, but only God is to be exalted and glorified. The church of God is greater than any reformation movement. Neither does it exist to serve the reformation movement. Rather the movement exists to serve the church.

5. The Church of God with its biblical base honors and incorporates into its lifestyle all truth. It is greater than any or all of them; therefore, to call it baptist, pentecostal, presbyterian, or any of a host of other names restricts the church, its witness, and its commitment to Christian unity.

6. The Church of God transcends any human alliance! Alliance separates from fellow Christians. Cooperation, yes; formal alliances, no. The church of God is married to Christ alone and responds ultimately only to the Divine drumbeat.

In summary, let it be understood that the Church of God reformation movement, along with other reforming movements, is an important servant of Christendom. Its task is to help the church awaken and constantly measure up to God's standard. It plays a John-the-Baptist role in helping the church come into God's own. The reformation movement serves to provide agencies that help the church fulfill her Kingdom-building assignment.

The local Church of God congregation is under the sovereignty of God and is a divine-human organism answerable to God alone. Its relationship to the Church of God reformation movement is voluntary.

11. Receive the Holy Spirit

by Arlo F. Newell in his *Receive the Holy Spirit* (1978).

Editor's Note: Holiness and unity have been twin themes at the very heart of the vision of the Church of God movement. The first book ever written by a Church of God person was Daniel Warner's *Bible Proofs*. A more contemporary work on the subject is Kenneth E. Jones, *Commitment To Holiness* (1985). In 1978 Arlo Newell wrote on the subject in ways characteristic of much of the movement's teaching tradition. Excerpts of this work follow.

While the fruit of the Spirit is a part of every sanctified believer's life, reproducing in us the nature of Christlikeness, the gifts of the Spirit are not demonstrated in every life, nor are they fully understood.... The gifts entrusted to us are determined by the type of ministry to which God has called us....

If called to speak, the Holy Spirit enables us to communicate. If our calling is to serve in the most difficult of circumstances, God's Holy Spirit equips us to minister. If the Master has called us to bring healing to the sick, he will not fail to provide the power for the miraculous. Therefore, some divide the gifts into these three general areas: *Speaking* gifts; *Serving* gifts; *Signifying* gifts. Others prefer to use terms relating to the type of ministry carried out, such as the ministry of *helping*, the ministry of *directing others*, the ministry of the Word, and the ministry of the *spectacular*. Each pattern merely becomes a formula to help the student recognize the divine enduement for service and the responsibility to be stewards of these gifts....

The task of the Church as outlined in Matthew 28:19-20 would appear to be beyond our human capabilities. Yet God has assured us that "all things are possible to him that believeth" (Mark 9:23). Believing faith opens to us the resources of God for fulfilling his Great Commission. Through the Spirit we have been given new life in Christ. Then, as the life-giving Spirit rules within us, we are placed in the Body as it pleases him (1 Cor. 12:18). For that reason there are varieties of gifts (1 Cor. 12:6), with at least eighteen bestowments being mentioned in the Pauline texts. I believe that these are not exhaustive, but are only indicative of the power available through the Spirit to provide adequate ministry for any need that may arise within the body of Christ, the Church....

Having acknowledged the bestowal of such a gift [communication], what are the principles governing the use of gifts in the Church?

First, *the Giver is more important than the gift.* One should never seek for power, signs or evidence, but seek the Spirit who bestows gifts "as he wills."

Secondly, *gifts are always governed by the fruit of the Spirit, basic of which is love.* In all of Paul's writings about the *charismata* the qualifying factor is an attitude of divine love.

Finally, *the gifts are always given for the building up of the body of Christ.* No gift is for selfish exaltation. Serious questions should be asked if one claims a gift of the Spirit and is haughty or proud. At such times one would be wise to exercise the instruction of 1 John 4:1: "Beloved believe not every spirit, but try the spirits, whether they are of God: because many false prophets are gone out into the world."

God has a Pentecostal experience for you! Don't become alarmed—I am not referring to one with all of the audiovisual effects of wind, fire, and tongues. But I do mean that there is a purifying, ventilating, and exhilarating experience that will be known to you when the Holy Spirit becomes the obsession of your life. Samuel G. Hines, beloved pastor and evangelist, has said: "When the Holy Spirit becomes your obsession, then you become his possession." It is at that time that Pentecost comes to you personally. That is God's promise.

John's account of the post-resurrection appearance of Christ (John 21:19-29) does two things: First, it is the witness to the victory over death. To anxious hearts shut in by fear behind closed doors, Jesus speaks words of Peace (vv. 19, 21, 26). Secondly, it testifies that Jesus breathed on them, saying, "Receive the Holy Spirit" (v. 22)....

The disciples for whom Jesus was praying and upon whom he breathed these words *were already born of the Spirit.* They had believed on him (John 17:8), but he wanted them to experience the fullness of the Spirit. Too much time has been spent in theological debate regarding two works of grace. To say that it is impossible for one to be saved and sanctified at the same time is to limit God in what He is able to do. God is able to do all things, and he is not limited by our interpretation of his revealed acts in Scripture. However, to ignore the obvious intent of this passage in John 20:22, given to obedient followers and believers in Christ, would be equally in error. One must recognize that there is a deeper experience in the Holy Spirit beyond the initial experience of conversion. As Myron Augsburger has so helpfully stated, " The concern is not a question of time, but a question of reality."

89

Is your experience in Christ adequate for all that he has called you to do? Or do you need more of his likeness in your life? Paul, speaking to the Ephesians, asked simply, "Have you received the Holy Spirit since you first believed?" (Acts 19:2).... If you have not received God's promise for your life, I pray that you will discover the fullness of the Spirit-filled life and face the future with the assurance of ultimate victory in Christ. Even so, come Lord Jesus. Amen!

12. Consensus Statement of Faith

by the Task Force on Doctrinal Dialogue, 1996

Editor's Note: After several years of intense and insightful discussions among leaders of the Church of God and the Christian Churches/Churches of Christ, agreement was reached by participants on the following statement of faith. Not intended as a "creed" for either church body, it nonetheless held great meaning for those involved in its development. For a complete story of this multi-year dialogue and its purposes and outcomes, see Barry Callen and James North, *Coming Together In Christ,* 1997. This statement of faith and the names of the eighteen church leaders who signed it are included as Appendix I. The statement reads as follows.

Preamble

We, as two church movements, have much with which to enrich each other. We have begun to learn from each other and must continue to benefit by building meaningful relationships. Although we hold in common the lordship of Jesus Christ, we do not need to arrive at full consensus on doctrinal issues in order to be open to each other, influenced by each other, genuinely valuing and loving each other, and learning to minister with each other.

Affirmations

1. We have learned that the roles played by the Enlightenment and American Holiness/Revivalism have shaped the theological perspectives of our respective heritages. This awareness now influences our attitude and helps us to transcend certain limitations coming from our histories.

2. We appreciate the value of the historic Christian creeds, but we are unwilling to make any of these creeds a test of Christian fellowship.

3. We celebrate our common conviction that Christ is the authority for life and belief. Christ is revealed through the Bible, as interpreted by the work of the Spirit in the context of the community of faith.

4. We desire to recover for our time the essence of New Testament Christianity.

5. We recognize the church as the universal Body of Christ. Each local congregation is called to be a manifestation of this one body. We recognize the importance both of freedom in the Spirit and mutual responsibility among Christ's disciples.

6. We are agreed that baptism is commanded by the Lord Jesus to be practiced by all of His followers. This baptism is to be by the immersion in water of penitent believers. Baptism is symbolic of the atoning death, burial, and resurrection of Christ. By its nature as well as by biblical teaching, baptism is involved with forgiveness of sin. We take pains, however, to repudiate any doctrine of baptismal regeneration, holding that forgiveness is wholly a matter of God's grace.

7. We rejoice in the Lord's Supper as an affirmation of the new covenant of God's love poured out through Christ, the crucified, risen, reigning, and returning Lord.

8. We encourage our brothers and sisters in the Christian Churches/Churches of Christ and in the Church of God to give careful attention to these affirmations and to continue discussion of other issues concerning which there is a range of opinion among us. These include footwashing as an ordinance; women in ministry; the most desirable frequency of participating in the Lord's Supper; and the meanings and processes of the "sanctification" of Christian believers.

Editor's Note: In light of the first affirmation above about the wisdom that comes from historical perspective, note Barry L. Callen's *Radical Christianity: The Believers Church Tradition in Christianity's History and Future* (Evangel Publishing House, 1999). He identifies and locates historically a family of reforming Christians, the Believers Church tradition, and places the Church of God movement within this tradition. He says that "the quest is to find and live out a strong doctrine of both God's Spirit and God's church. Authentic Christian life requires a vital and growing relationship between the believer and God; it also requires a responsible relationship between the believer and other believers [thus, holiness and unity as core and coordinate concerns]. The Church of God, and this tradition generally, lives with a delicate dilemma. On the one hand, there is a strong reaction to the dominance and often deadness of establishment Christianity. On the other hand, there is a strong desire to be effective and accountable in being and doing what God intends for the church in the world. The twin and sometimes conflicting values are freedom in the Spirit and accountability within the church of the Spirit.

91

13. Two "Reformation Principles"

Defining principles of the Church of God reformation movement, as
affirmed by the General Assembly of the Church of God
(United States and Canada)

Editor's Note: Two "reformation principles" have been affirmed by
the General Assembly of the Church of God (United States and
Canada). They are the authority of the Bible in the church's life and
the lordship of Jesus Christ for all of life. For the content of these
principles and the contexts of their affirmations by the General
Assembly, see Entries 75 and 76. Also see in Entries 169 and 170
for the results of two "Dialogues on Internal Unity" that were convened in 1981 and involved these principles and related matters.

The ministerial *Credentials Manual* maintained by the Congregational
Ministries division of Church of God Ministries offers a good example of the
movement seeking to be convictional and faithful to a particular reformation
tradition without being "denominational" (see the 1997 edition). Note this
text from pages 9-10 which refers to the two "reformation principles" of
biblical revelation and belief in Jesus Christ:

> Occasionally in this *Credentials Manual* there is reference to
> beliefs, standards, or practices "widely embraced" or "gen-
> erally taught" in the Church of God (Anderson, Ind.). The
> intent of such references is to insure that ministers and con-
> gregations affiliated with the Church of God movement are
> appreciative and supportive of the distinctive heritage and
> commitments of this particular movement among God's peo-
> ple. They are not intended to be "denominational" in any
> exclusive or divisive sense. It is important in this regard to
> note that the distinctiveness of the Church of God movement
> features a commitment to the unity of all God's people.
> Faithfulness to the biblical revelation is judged central, with
> no accompanying assumption that all truth is known best or
> fully *by any church body*, especially when a church body
> chooses to isolate itself from honest dialogue with the rest of
> the believers in Jesus Christ.

The *Credentials Manual* adds this on page 45:

> Although the Church of God movement honors theological
> freedom within the bounds of biblically-based belief, those

to whom ordination is granted are expected to hold persuasions that are in general agreement with the teaching tradition of the Church of God movement. Each ordaining body should supply the ordination candidate with a list of recommended Church of God doctrinal books and expect their being read. Recommended are at least these:

1. Russell Byrum, *Christian Theology* (1925, 1982).
2. Barry Callen, *It's God's Church!* (1995).
3. Barry Callen, *Contours of a Cause* (1995).
4. Barry Callen, *God As Loving Grace* (1996).
5. Kenneth Jones, *Theology of Holiness and Love* (1995).
6. John Smith, *I Will Build My Church* (1985).
7. Gilbert Stafford, *Theology for Disciples* (1996).

TESTIMONIES

Editor's Note: Valued and especially influential in the history of the Church of God movement have been inspired and divinely gifted leaders who have shared their testimonies for the information and inspiration of others. What follows is a sampling of such testimonies, most from the first generations of the movement and some originating outside North America (India, Germany, and Australia). Other international witnesses may be found in Entries 199, 200, and 203. In all cases these witnesses include both the expressed joy of coming to Christ and some explanation of the circumstances of coming particularly to the Church of God movement.

In more recent years, numerous leaders have come to the Church of God in their home countries. One example is Obrad Nikolic of Serbia. In 1994 he opened the first congregation of the Church of God in Serbia after a long search for a compatible church association. In a handbook of denominations he discovered material about the Church of God and was immediately drawn to it for reasons not very different from what drew many others to the movement a century earlier. He said: "You have no creed but the Bible. You are a movement for the restoration of the unity and holiness of the church. Your worship services tend to be informal, accentuating expository preaching and robust singing. Baptism is by immersion; you also practice footwashing and observe the Lord's supper. And the Church of God maintains a strong interest in evangelism."

The following testimonies witness to the nature and role of the Church of God movement as it was understood and experienced by a range of persons of earlier generations.

14. That Victorious Spirit

Excerpted from an article by Andrew L. Byers in the *Gospel Trumpet*,
December 13, 1952, 11. Written in 1949.

Sometime in the early eighties of the last century, my parents learned of and subscribed for the *Gospel Trumpet*. They had already been taking several holiness papers and had accepted the doctrine. My father, who preached in both English and German in a small denomination known as River Brethren, began to preach holiness, and this brought my parents much persecution from the ministers of that body. When the *Gospel Trumpet* came into their hands, they received what was to them new light with regard to the one Church, unity through Christ etc. I remember those times very distinctly but could not then appreciate what my father and mother were going through because I myself had not yet become a Christian.

Our home was in northwestern Illinois near the Mississippi River, a few miles south of the city of Clinton, Iowa. Early in April, 1888, when I was eighteen, D. S. Warner and his evangelistic helpers came to our home. I had just finished teaching a winter term of school in Benton County, Iowa, and had engaged myself for the spring term. This gave me two weeks of vacation, which of course I decided to spend at home. What a coincidence for me that those two weeks should cover the time that those heavenly messengers were to stay with us while holding meetings in the vicinity! They had been on an evangelistic tour which took them as far west as Denver, Colorado, and were now returning.

My father and I went to engage a schoolhouse for the meetings. On our return we saw two men standing at our yard gate talking. One was Brother Warner. Could it be that such a wonderful man, an editor of a paper and one of whom I had heard so much, was really visiting us?

During the winter in Iowa I had attended a revival held by a River Brethren evangelist and had taken a stand for Christ by rising to my feet in response to a call. But I was given no instruction in faith whatever, and it seemed that for me the Christian way was to be rather tough going.

At the gate my father made himself acquainted and then introduced me to Brother Warner, informing him of my recent conversion. As that dear man reached to shake my hand he said humbly and appreciatively, "Well, that's good news," and there beamed from those soft blue eyes a Christian love and tenderness I can never forget. That he should so rejoice in spirit at the knowledge of my conversion seemed to give me a spiritual uplift and to place my estimate of salvation on a much higher level.

The week which followed was the brightest period and to me the most full of destiny in all my life's history. Our home was a paradise. There was something about the happy and victorious spirit of that little group which exalted Christianity in my conception and made it a thing much to be desired as a lasting possession. Brother Warner instructed me in my consecration for sanctification. As I became ready to venture on God's promise, he seemed to discern my faith and broke the way before me by claiming the promise with me. That was the beginning of the reformation for me!

15. Out of Sectarian Confusion

Excerpted from Mary Cole, *Trials and Triumphs of Faith*
(Anderson, Ind.: Gospel Trumpet Company, 1914), 120-126.

I was still a Methodist. The Methodists did not license women to preach; but when the preachers found out that God was using me in the salvation of souls and that I was not especially interested in building up any certain denomination, I had an abundance of calls.

God had already begun talking to my brother Jeremiah about the sin of division, and he was beginning to see the evils of sectarianism. The winter after I was healed, he had attended the Jacksonville, Illinois, holiness convention, and had met with Brother D. S. Warner, who at that time was editor of a holiness paper, *The Herald of Gospel Freedom*, then published at Rome City, Indiana. Brother Warner was already beginning to discern the unity of God's people, but he had not yet received enough light on the subject to sever his connection with the Winebrennerian denomination, of which he was a member.

During my brother's absence in evangelistic work I received several copies of the *Trumpet*. As soon as I read in the *Trumpet* about the sin of division and saw that the new paper opposed the licensing of preachers, my sectarian spirit was stirred. I thought that holiness would make the churches, as I called them, better. I was afraid that if people got hold of such literature as the *Trumpet* it would disgust them with holiness forever. I burned the *Trumpets* I had already received, and then sat down and wrote Brother Warner never to send me another copy. As I was traditionized, and had opposed the truth in ignorance, the Lord did not hold my opposition as a willful sin.

After my brother had got light on the one body, he was so enthused with the truth that he wanted to explain it to every one he met. While out walking one day the next summer after he discerned the one body, he fell into conversation with a man about the Scriptures. After talking a little while the man said, "I have a paper that reads just as you talk." Going to the house, he brought out the *Gospel Trumpet* and gave it to my brother, who went down the road reading as he went. He never stopped reading until he had finished the paper. At the earliest opportunity my brother wrote a letter to Brother

Warner, asking him if he had enough light on the one body to set it clearly before the people. He also asked him if any were accepting this divine truth. To the first question Brother Warner replied, "Yes," and to the second, "Yes, hundreds are discerning the one body." As soon as my brother learned that Brother Warner and many others had the same truth that God had made so clear and beautiful to him, he rejoiced greatly. He could not rest until he went where Brother Warner was; but, as I had neglected to walk in the light, I was left alone, and that, too, in more ways than one.

Some time before I discerned the body of Christ, I had some impressive dreams. In one I thought I was in a large building belonging to some denomination. A conference of that denomination was being held just outside the door, and the ministers wanted me to come and take part. I looked toward the door through which I must pass, and I saw two large worms with their heads together, lying directly across the threshold. In order to enter the room, I would have to step over the worms and would be in great danger of receiving a deadly bite. I said to myself, "I will not run the risk for any man's notions or ways," and, turning on my heel, I went out of another door.

I soon saw my dream fulfilled. The denomination that I had been holding a meeting for insisted that I should join their conference, saying that they would give me a license so that I could hold meetings in their territory. I knew that, according to their discipline, they could not license a woman to preach, and I said to the minister, "You don't dare to give me a license." "Well," said he, "I will tell you what you can do, Sister Cole, we can go to a place not far from here where you have had a good meeting, lay this matter before the people, and have them vote to give you a permit, so that you can hold meetings in any part of our district." I did not feel at all led to take such steps, and, as I had done in my dream, I turned in the other direction. I suppose God was using this method to get me ready for the truth.

The summer before I got out of sectarianism, an M. E. South minister invited me to come to their new chapel to attend the quarterly conference and to help hold a series of meetings. As the M. E. South denomination did not license women preachers, women were not allowed at the quarterly conference. They had arranged, however, that several other women and I should sit in a room adjoining the conference, so that we could hear the proceedings. This was on Saturday. On Sunday morning they held their quarterly love-feast, partook of the Lord's Supper, and listened to a sermon by the presiding elder.

In the afternoon and the evening, I preached. While the service was in progress, the ministers were holding a private meeting to decide whether or not I should proceed with the meeting I had come to hold. In this part of the country was a wealthy man, a sinner, who contributed very liberally to the support of the work. This man objected to women's preaching and opposed the continuance of the meeting.

It was decided that the meeting should not continue, but the pastor of the congregation did not tell me. The pastor and his wife were both present at the service on Monday night, and both seemed well pleased. On Tuesday evening the interest began to increase, and one or two raised their hands for prayer. Just at the close of the service a note was handed me requesting me to close the meeting, as they had decided not to continue at the present time, but to wait until later in the season.

I could not keep from crying. I had called the Methodist Church my mother; and now to think that my mother was treating me in this way made me feel very bad. I went home with a young couple who had been saved a short time before in a meeting held near this place. They felt very bad over what had happened, and we all cried together. The young people tried to encourage me as best they could.

I still continued to get calls from the sectarian preachers to go and help hold meetings. I responded to these, and held two or three meetings in different places. Late that fall I held a meeting at Rolla, Missouri. The preacher could hardly get an audience when he preached, so he sent for me, thinking that a woman preacher would be quite an attraction and would draw crowds. The crowds came. Although there were a number of ministers present, including the presiding elder, I occupied the pulpit, I think, during half of that meeting. Conviction came upon the people, and a number came to the altar; but not many of those who came seemed to get an experience.

On the last night of the meeting quite a number of bright, intelligent young people, some of them college students, came to the altar and some of them were getting saved. As the minister went to talk with the seekers one by one, God put it into my heart to listen to what they were saying. Not once did these preachers say, "Seek the Lord until you find him;" "There is reality in salvation;" "Never stop until you know you are saved." Their instructions were: "Join the church;" "Get baptized," etc. God opened my eyes right there to the awful work that these so-called ministers were doing. I said, "If they are going to help deceive souls that way and send them to destruction, I will never help them again." That was the last meeting in which I ever helped to build up Babylon.

16. Excitement in the Ozarks

Excerpted from John A. Morrison, *As the River Flows* (Anderson, Ind.: Anderson College Press, 1962), 100-107.

Daniel Warner planned an evangelistic tour to begin in June of 1887 and to last until late April of the following year. It was to take him as far west as Denver. The evangelistic party consisted of five persons: Warner himself, who at the time was forty-five years of age; Mrs. Sarah Smith, an elderly widow from Jerry City, Ohio; Miss Frances Miller from Battle Creek, Michigan; Miss Nannie Kigar of Payne, Ohio, who was in the early twenties; and Barney Warren of West Liberty, Ohio, a lad eighteen years of age.

Warner did the preaching and the four others composed a quartet to do the singing. Warner composed the words of the songs, and they were set to music by young Warren. Occasionally, Warner would join in the singing with his high tenor voice. The words of the songs were highly evangelistic. Also, they breathed a spirit of profound devotion. The singing of this group was electric in its effect upon the listeners. It so happened that the voices blended in an unusual harmony, and the little group sang with such utter and joyous abandon to the cause they represented that their singing had an emotional appeal almost unbelievable. Wherever they went, people thronged to hear them.

They were not particular as to where they sang. They sang in railroad depots as they waited for trains; they sang in wagons as they trudged along rough country roads; they sang in hotel lobbies and in the streets of towns and cities. They visited our Ozark county in 1887. In 1937, fifty years later, the old-timers were still talking about that singing. And now, seventy-five years after they were here, one still hears faint echoes of their singing from the children and grandchildren of the old-timers who actually heard the Warner party sing so long ago.

It was a hot sultry day in July, 1887 when the little party of three women and two men piled their luggage in front of the ticket window in the big Union Depot in St. Louis. They asked for five tickets to St. James, a tiny town on the Frisco Railroad, ninety-eight miles to the southwest of St. Louis, down toward the wild Indian Territory. To pay for the tickets the little group searched all their pockets. When the bill was taken care of they had left a total combined balance of one nickel.

Grandpa Morrison had sent a check for $100 to them at Keokuk, Iowa, where they had taken a steamboat down the Mississippi to St. Louis. All day long Grandpa had met every train coming into St. James from the east. Each train that came brought only disappointment. In relating the affair Grandpa said, "Early the next morning, I was at the depot waiting for the morning train. As I waited I heard singing across the way at the Snyder Hotel. 'What is that,' I said. A man standing near said, 'Your people came in last night on the midnight train.' I never heard such singing!"

Not by telephone, nor by telegraph, nor by television, nor by radio, but by word of mouth the news had gone over the hill country, into the hollows and across the valleys to house and hut and hovel—news about the meeting in the arbor of dry leaves, down on the ridge in the old Towell field. News about the preaching and the singing and the shouting. Sermons two and three hours long! Singing, such singing! Music, some said, with power to charm even the wild creatures in the thick woods round about.

So the people came crowding in. Some came to pray. Others came to curse. Grizzled old mountain men sat in the shade of the trees and whittled and squirted tobacco juice and declared, "We ain't never saw nothin' like it." Some were profane. Some were touched deep in their inner beings by what they saw and heard. Tears trickled through whiskers like brooks through brier thickets. Young and boisterous swains galloped in from the hills, their fiery horses kicking up clouds of dust; occasionally a pistol was waved over-heard and fired into the air.

So this Tuesday came to a close there on the dusty ridge. The July sun had disappeared with a mellow golden glow over the rim of the post-oak hills. In the evening service Warner had stood in the rough pulpit, with the flickering glow of the coal-oil torch on the pages of his big Bible, and sweaty and grimy from the heat and dust, had preached with terrific power. The songs had been sung. The invitation to accept Christ had been given. In the dark shadows of the big arbor the people had bowed their heads for a prayer of dismissal. All the lights in the arbor were put out, and this strange temple of worship was in black darkness, except as the moon coming up shot its beams of silver light through the leafy branches of the trees. The sounds of the rumbling of the wagons and the clattering of horses' hoofs had died away as the people homeward had plodded their weary way. The lanterns in the tents around the arbor had been blown out, and the tents were lighted only by the pale, gray light of the moon as it filtered through the canvas. The deep, brooding silence of the holy night had settled down over the bivouac of these pioneer pilgrims. No sound could be heard, save the voices of count-less katydids and jar flies as they chanted their love songs over the air waves of the night.

Editor's Note: Impacted by this evangelistic heritage in the Ozarks, John Morrison later would become principal (1923-1925) and then president of Anderson College (University) from 1925-1958.

17. Soon Won to the Truth

Excerpted from Albert F. Gray, *Time and Tides
on the Western Shore* (published privately, 1966), 12-13.

It was in November 1895 that G. W. Bailey and J. C. Peterman, minis-ters of the Church of God, came to Grand Forks, North Dakota. A group of people interested in holiness were holding cottage meetings. This group included Methodist, Baptists, Salvationists, Free Methodists, and a few oth-ers. This group held a meeting at our home which was attended by Brother Bailey. After several had bragged about their churches, Brother Bailey gave them a strong speech against division based on 1 Corinthians 1 and 3. I sat on the stairs and listened. Mother and Uncle Will Baldwin were soon won to the truth. A congregation of the Church of God in Grand Folks was begun at that time. Soon mother would go about the house singing:

> Oh, glory to Jesus, we hail the bright day
> And high on our banners salvation display,
> The mists of confusion are passing away.

Some of those present at that meeting resented the message and rejected the truth, including their leader, Joe Nixon, a Free Methodist minister. I liked Nixon, so was somewhat prejudiced against the new preachers. For a little while I was Baptist, Salvationist, and saint, but eventually was won to the truth.

Editor's Note: Albert Gray became a long-term and highly respected leader in the Church of God. His service included the presidency of Warner Pacific College, 1937-1957, and his functioning as chair of the governing board of Anderson University, 1931-1948, and chair of the General Assembly, 1934-1936, 1939-1954.

18. Light at Meeker Schoolhouse

Concerning Nora Siens Hunter (1873-1951), as excerpted from John W. V. Smith, *Heralds of a Brighter Day* (Anderson, Ind.: Gospel Trumpet Company, 1955), chapter 6.

Nora Siens Hunter

In the early days she was known as Nora Siens. She became involved in the "flying ministry" of this religious reform movement [Church of God] by way of a very complicated and, in a sense, tragic set of circumstances. She was born August 16, 1873, in a one-room "box" house near Chanute, Kansas. The first eight years of her life were comparatively uneventful, except that the home was saddened by the death of an infant sister during this period. Her parents, Robert C. and Anna Meeker Siens, were not well-to-do people, and her father often had to work away from home to supplement the meager farm income. The Siens were devout and religious people, though, and were very diligent in teaching their children to pray and read the Bible. The whole family went to church whenever there was an opportunity.

100

In the year that Nora was nine, however, multiple tragedy struck the Siens household. The first blow was the death of the mother. This left Robert Siens with four children to care for, one of them a six-weeks-old girl named Neenah. Within a very short time, though, there were only three, for Neenah became ill and died quite suddenly. Hardly had the shock of these losses been fully realized when four-year-old George was fatally injured in a fall from a wagon tongue. This left only Nora and her brother Ed Byron, who was two years younger than she.

For a time the father tried to maintain a home for himself and the two children, but he had to spend so much time away from home at work that it soon became apparent that other arrangements would have to be made. Because he was a Union Army Civil War veteran he was able to find a home for Nora and Ed in a soldiers' orphanage, so they were sent to Normal City, Illinois, to begin a new kind of life. The father married again and did not think it advisable to bring the children into his new home, so they were left pretty much to themselves. During this period Nora suffered a great deal from loneliness, but had no complaint about the treatment she received in the orphanage.

When Nora was fourteen some of her relatives in Kansas offered to let her come to live with them, and she took advantage of the opportunity. This brought her back into the familiar territory of southeastern Kansas. The relatives lived near the town of Galesburg. Here she entered into the activities of the community. Among her activities was regular attendance at a Sunday school held in the Meeker Schoolhouse not far from where she lived. After a couple of years she was teaching a class of children. She apparently took this job only because helpers were so badly needed, for she felt most inadequate, both from the standpoint of knowing how to do it and of being spiritually prepared for the responsibility. She tried her best, though, to improve her method and to make herself more of a student of the Bible. Despite these efforts she did not succeed in shaking off the feeling that her own spiritual condition was not what it ought to be. Beset by doubts and uncertainties, she was generally dissatisfied with the state of her own soul. She longed for real inner peace, but it seemed always to be just beyond her grasp.

In the spring of 1892 a new preacher began holding services in the Meeker Schoolhouse. He was Dr. S. G. Bryant, a former physician from Galesburg. His message struck a responsive note in Nora's soul. He described just the kind of spiritual experience which she longed to have. When he invited those who felt a need in their lives to come forward to pray about it, Nora decided to go. There at a public altar she found the peace for which she had longed. She testified exultantly to her new experience: "My whole heart swells with praise and thanksgiving, because I realize and know that I have complete victory over the world, the flesh, and the devil."

101

This Dr. Bryant who had been able to help Nora find the answer to her need was to influence her in other ways. He had some religious connections which were a bit different from the usual run of denominations with which she was acquainted, and he had some ideas about church membership and Christian unity which sounded new and strange. He condemned the divisions in the Christian church as being sinful and told about a magazine called the *Gospel Trumpet* which advocated the abandonment of all sectarian groups so that Christians everywhere could be united in one church.

As Dr. Bryant preached these doctrines he told of his own spiritual quest. He had been a successful practicing physician and owner of a drugstore in the city of Galesburg when a traveling preacher by the name of George R. Achor brought a tent into town and began holding services. Very few people responded to his preaching. After several days had passed Bryant found out that Achor also had been a physician, so he sent him some provisions. Mrs. Bryant, out of curiosity, attended the meeting one night and was converted, but she never got her husband to attend. Eventually, through the help of other ministers whom she invited to come, particularly Mary Cole and Lodema Kaser, Mrs. Bryant had been able to lead her husband into a solid Christian experience. He said that almost immediately he began preaching. He turned a dance hall which he owned into a meeting place and began holding services. He also felt the need to reach people in the surrounding communities. That was why he had come to the Meeker Schoolhouse.

This story thrilled Nora Siens. She felt that God wanted her also to be a worker in his kingdom. But she was young, only eighteen, and the opportunities were limited. It soon became apparent, though, that she would have difficulties multiplied if relatives were not sympathetic with her new approach to religion. She talked to Dr. Bryant about the matter, and he invited Nora to make her home with them. She gladly accepted, little realizing all that would be involved. Hardly had she moved to her new home with the Bryants when they decided to extend their evangelistic efforts beyond their own community. They began traveling from town to town in revival campaigns, and Nora went with them. For almost a year she accompanied them and gave assistance in the meetings which they held, mostly doing personal work and helping with the music. She then joined the William N. Smith evangelistic party and traveled for several more months.

The summer of 1893 found Nora in Grand Junction, Michigan, the home of the *Gospel Trumpet,* about which Dr. Bryant had spoken. She found a number of young people there who were helping in various aspects of the work. More help was needed at this particular time in the Children's Home, so she decided to stay awhile. It was probably while she was here that she preached her first full-fledged sermon. She was exceedingly nervous, as well a nineteen-year-old girl might be. It did not help matters as far as she was concerned to have D. S. Warner in the audience. She apparently impressed him as being quite capable, though, for that fall he asked her to travel in evangelistic work with him and his new wife, the former Frances Miller. She accepted this invitation also.

Editor's Note: In the 1930s Nora Hunter envisioned a new mission organization and then became the first president of the National Women's Home and Foreign Missionary Society of the Church of God, now Women of the Church of God. For additional detail about Nora Hunter, see Hazel Neal and Axchie Bolitho, revised by Marie Meyer, *Madam President: The Story of Nora Hunter.* For more detail on Women of the Church of God, see Entry 185.

19. Stepping into the Light

Concerning Frederick G. Smith, as excerpted from John W. V. Smith,
Heralds of a Brighter Day (Anderson, Ind.: Gospel Trumpet Company,
1955), chapter 5.

Frederick George Smith was born November 12, 1880, on a farm near Lacota, Michigan. His parents, Joseph F. and Mary A. Smith, had been for years sincere and satisfied members of the Methodist church. In January of 1883, however, two traveling evangelists came to their community and upset their state of spiritual satisfaction. Samuel L. Speck and Sebastian Michels preached that it was necessary for everyone to have a personal experience of regeneration and a second experience of entire sanctification and to withdraw from the sinful divisions which had destroyed the unity of Christ's church.

Being Methodist, the Smiths could easily go along with the first two of these points, but the third was somewhat disturbing. Before the meeting was over, though, they had accepted the challenge. Both of them "stepped out" into the "light" and took their stand for the "truth." From this time to the end of their lives they were enthusiastic supporters of the Church of God reformation movement.

Joseph and Mary Smith did not themselves become ministers in the strict sense of that term, but their farm home became one of the most active evangelistic centers in that part of the country. It was here that many revival services and prayer meetings were held. After the Gospel Trumpet office moved to Grand Junction, only a short distance away, the Smith home became a meeting place for the workers, and many were the occasions when songs of worship and praise could be heard coming from this two-story farmhouse. Whenever any traveling ministers came through southern Michigan it was usually in the Smith house that they were given lodging and food. There was seldom a day from the time of their conversion until the

Trumpet office moved to Moundsville, West Virginia, in 1898 that some activity connected with the movement was not in progress in their home.

It was in such an atmosphere as this that young Fred Smith spent the early years of his life. He never knew anything except all this church-related hustle during the time that he remained at home. It has been said that he was rocked in his cradle by A. B. Palmer, that he played as a boy with N. H. Byrum, and that he attentively listened by the hour to the long sermons and very adult conversations which took place when such men as Speck, Michels, Palmer, D. S. Warner, J. N. Howard, A. J. Kilpatrick, and many others visited in the Smith home.

Even as a boy Fred amazed his elders by the ease with which he could enter into discussions on doctrinal topics and by his extraordinary ability to memorize Scripture passages. He was not content just to know certain familiar Bible stories; he would select some of the heavier passages and commit them to memory.

Fred had many recollections of these boyhood days, but one incident stood out as a never-to-be-forgotten event. It took place almost before he was old enough to be aware of his surroundings in a way that could be remembered. His parents took him to the 1883 camp meeting at Bangor, Michigan, the first such meeting which the Smiths attended. One day a woman by the name of Emma Miller (later Mrs. A. B. Palmer), who had been blind and an invalid for nearly three years, was instantly and completely healed in answer to prayer. The rejoicing of the saints was of such magnitude that young Fred was frightened to the point that it was almost impossible for his older sisters to allay his fears and get him to stop crying. As this story was retold time and again in subsequent years, it made a lasting and growing impression on his mind. He never had to be convinced that God was at work among his people.

In the fall of 1890 when Fred was "nine, going on ten," he went one Sunday with his parents to a "protracted meeting" being held about six miles from his home. The evangelist was D. S. Warner. In the morning service he spoke of the children's meetings which had been conducted during the week and announced that another such meeting would be held that afternoon at one o'clock. The Smiths had planned to stay all day, so Fred decided to attend. He sat on the front row.

There was nothing particularly unusual about the meeting, but at its conclusion Warner asked if there were any of the children who wanted to give their lives to God. After a few had responded by coming forward, he looked around over the group who still remained standing and spotted the young lad he had talked with many times when he had been in the Smith home. He saw that the youngster had a troubled look on his face, so he spoke directly to him and asked point-blank, "Fred, would you like to get saved, also?" Fred looked up and blinked his eyes and swallowed hard. He managed to get out a feeble, "Yes," and went forward and bowed at the altar. Soon Warner was at his side, praying. His prayer was a simple one. "O Lord," he said, "take the stony heart out of this boy and give him a new heart and a new spirit." Just as he said that, something happened to Fred. He later said, "I thought my heart had actually gone out of me! Praise God! I wonder even yet how so much joy and glory could be poured into one little soul."

20. To the Chief Singer

by Barry L. Callen, drawing on works by F. G. Smith and Axchie Bolitho, concerning Barney E. Warren

Barney E. Warren

Barney E. Warren was born in 1867 to a musical family that moved from a farm near Buffalo, New York, to Van Buren, Michigan, when he was five years old. He was converted in a log-house revival near Bangor, Michigan, in 1884 and two years later joined D. S. Warner and his traveling evangelistic company as the bass singer. Gaining the freedom for this travel, however, was not easy, as F. G. Smith recalls in his "Introduction" to Axchie A. Bolitho's book *To the Chief Singer*, a 1942 biography of Barney Warren. Here is Smith's recollection.

It was back in the 1880s, when I [F. G. Smith] was but a small child and Brother Warren was still in his teens, that my acquaintance with him began.... The Warren family lived at the time only a few miles from my childhood home near Grand Junction, Michigan. My father and mother, Joseph F. and Mary A. Smith, heard and accepted the truth in January, 1883, and in the years immediately following their home became "home" for the pioneer ministers [of the Church of God movement], including Brother D. S. Warner.... It was here that I first met "Barney."

Brother Warren's mother was a precious, devoted saint of God; but his father, though possessing some admirable qualities, was at the time unsaved and was at first a great opposer of the truth. "Barney," the young boy, slipped away from his own home and came to my home, and borrowed extra clothing from my oldest brother, Hermy, in order to be baptized.

Brother Warren felt very definitely his call to the ministry. It was 1886 and Brother D. S. Warner, who was forming his first evangelistic company, was eager for Barney to go along as one of that company; but Tom Warren, the father of the boy, objected very strongly. The matter came to a head one day in my own home. I was a small boy, standing by and looking on, but the events were so striking that they made a lasting impression upon my mind. As I recall the circumstances, Brother Warner stood pleading for the boy, but Tom was obstinate. Suddenly Brother Warner seemed to be changed almost into another man. His eyes flashed as if with a sort of piercing fire; he stepped up close to the rebellious father, but did not touch him, and cried out: "Tom Warren, you are fighting against God, and you cannot get away with it." That strong man, a former wrestler, trembled and sank to the floor, while Brother Warner stood over him and said: "God has smitten you, and you cannot get up until you let Barney go." After a while he yielded, and said: "Barney is the Lord's." Then Brother Warner said: "Now you can get up"— and he did....

Later the father turned, became a friend of the cause.... One night. . .a band of ruffians entered the meeting house on our farm for the purpose of breaking up the service that was in progress. We children—and some of the older people as well—were alarmed. Suddenly Tom Warren, the strong man, sprang to his feet, seized the disturbers one by one and tossed them out the door, like pieces of cord wood. Then the meeting went on....

Eventually some 7,000 gospel songs would be attributed to the composing gift of Barney Warren. He set much of Daniel Warner's poetry to music. In 1900 he wrote words and music for a song that captures the sense of urgency of the young movement of the Church of God. Called "Every Hour For Jesus," the first stanza reads:

> Every hour for Jesus, shall our motto be,
> There is plenty of work we may do;
> We may all keep busy till the Lord we see,
> Till he comes for his faithful few.

Axchie Bolitho tells this story of the writing of this particular song:

In the early days of the movement there were few settled congregations and fewer pastors. Every minister felt himself a messenger with a "flying roll;" i.e., either an evangelist or an evangelistic singer. But pioneering is difficult and not everyone who felt the call of God upon him could enter new places and get for himself a hearing. So it came about that there were many "messengers" who had no place to deliver themselves of their "burdens." This state of affairs became a burden upon Mr. Warren's mind and he prepared a sermon on the subject and delivered it at the Moundsville, West Virginia, camp meeting.

The message had to do with the brevity of time and the necessity of each one doing all within his power before time should be no more.... There are multitudes all around who need instruction, encouragement, and conviction. What can we say to our Master if we waste our time?... As the message progressed, a deep solemnity took hold of the congregation and deepened even beyond usual in the soul of the speaker. After the service the pressure on his spirit made him seek a quiet place for meditation. There the words and music of this song came together as if the whole were really but one effort. Returning to the camp, Mr. Warren sang the song, from the manuscript, to the evening congregation. It appeared first in *Salvation Echoes,* a [1900] songbook which was brought out shortly after the above-mentioned camp meeting (109-111).

Editor's Note: See the dissertation done in 1996 by Wilfred V. Meeds at Claremont Graduate School titled "The Hymnody of Barney Elliot Warren."

21. I Found My True Home

Excerpted from James Earl Massey,
Raymond S. Jackson: A Portrait (1967).

Raymond Samuel Jackson was born March 20, 1892, on a farm in Cass County, Michigan. He was the fourteenth child in a family of fifteen children. His father was Abraham Isaac Jacob Jackson, a former slave. His mother was named Eliza, the daughter of Harrison and Sarah Ash, a pioneer family that also lived in that settlement located in Cass County called "Chain Lake."

In 1871, about twenty-three years after the time when Harrison and Sarah Ash, Eliza's parents, helped to incorporate the Chain Lake Baptist Church, Abraham Isaac Jacob Jackson became pastor there. The membership of the church then was twenty-six members. There he ministered until 1874, when a Reverend D. Rollens became pastor. The list of members at that time numbered about one hundred.

Abraham Jackson's second term as pastor of the Chain Lake Baptist Church was quite short, only one year. He had begun to see the evil of denominationalism. He had also begun to understand the biblical standard of Christian holiness. His concern to teach and preach a doctrine and polity more in keeping with the New Testament finally made it necessary for him to break with the Baptist church. He afterward established an Evangelical Christian Church in Vandalia, Michigan. This was his considered effort to promote a visible realization of what he saw and understood as the New Testament view of the true church. God had given Abraham Isaac Jacob Jackson a concern for some truths of which his son Raymond would be an able exponent in later years.

As a new convert, Raymond S. Jackson sought to establish a church connection for himself. He first attended meetings at a neighborhood congregation of believers identified organizationally with a Church of God whose headquarters were in Tennessee. It was a group with piety and spirituality, open and friendly in spirit. He and his wife shared the life of the group. During the course of their association Jackson maintained a particular interest in the doctrinal concerns of the congregation. He studied the available literature bearing on the beliefs promulgated. He also took notice of the group customs. He was impressed by the name "Church of God." It was biblical. He later learned, however, of another group bearing the same name, with headquarters at Anderson, Indiana. He was eager to study them. He soon got an opportunity to do so.

Raymond S. Jackson first attended the Anderson Camp Meeting in 1918. That was a particularly good year for him to have attended. Having recently heard about the Church of God reformation movement, it was a matter of divine fortune that he chose to attend at a time when the spirit of camp meeting was evident in the large attendance and the quality of the services. That was a good year for attending because Jackson heard firsthand about the work of the Church of God: the work of the Missionary Board was defined in one of the ministers' meetings; the case for a training school for ministers and gospel workers was presented, discussed, and endorsed; reports were made on the work among foreign language and nationality groups in America; the new tabernacle had been completed, in which he sat with hundreds of others—some also "first-timers," no doubt, listening with interest and stirred spirit at the words of some of the great preachers in the church—unaware that he would himself one day be one of the church's great preachers, and also stand there in that same pulpit as spokesman for God!

During that visit Jackson met some of the leaders of the Negro churches in the Church of God. He visited the literature tent, and carried away what he wanted from among the materials being freely distributed to those who wanted them. In the midst of reading and listening—listening several times to E. A. Reardon and F. G. Smith during the camp meeting, as well as following the thoughtful messages of E. E. Byrum, J. Grant Anderson, D. O. Teasley, Charles E. Brown, and R. H. Owens, among others—Jackson had determined to what group he must be linked. He heard James B. Prescod, a Negro from Barbados, tell of the work in the West Indies and South America. He witnessed several healings, which took place as a result of prayer for the sick. He listened with care to the approaches to the doctrine of healing as it was being expounded in the meetings by such men as L. H. Morgan, J. W. Byers and wife, Nora Hunter, among others. 1918 was indeed a good year for being introduced to the Anderson Camp Meeting.

Jackson enjoyed especially the general services where all attended together. The sermon by F. G. Smith on "What Is 'This Reformation'?" appealed to him as he was thinking about a possible relation with this people and group. There was another preacher whom Jackson heard during that meeting, a preacher he would afterward never forget: J. D. Smoot, who preached one night in the tabernacle on "What Must One Do to Be Saved?" Jackson and Smoot in later years became friends, sharing the confidence and encouragement of each other through many years to come.

Jackson knew at that camp meeting that this Church of God was his true home. He decided within himself that he would be known as part of it, without any reservations. He declared his decision openly in one of the meetings at that 1918 camp meeting.

Editor's Note: In honor of his outstanding life and ministry, in 1970 Anderson University granted Raymond Jackson an honorary Doctor of Divinity degree.

22. I Met the "Evening Light Saints"

by Barry L. Callen, concerning William Joseph Seymour (1870-1922)

Born in 1870 as an African-American in an area of the bayou country of Louisiana that was well acquainted with Ku Klux Klan violence, William Joseph Seymour had to be self-educated. His parents were former slaves and his birth was during years of poverty and intense institutionalized racism. Reared a Baptist, he drank deeply of the tradition of the Christian spirituals and then in 1895 headed north for Indianapolis, Indiana, in hope of finding greater freedom. Soon he associated with the largely white Methodist Episcopal Church, a symbol of his growing determination to foster racial reconciliation through the power of Christ's Spirit.

Smallpox hit his body and the use of one eye was lost. This helped to inspire him to quest for healing and sanctification in his life. By 1900 Seymour found his way to Cincinnati, Ohio, was influenced by Martin Knapp, the Methodist founder of the International Apostolic Holiness Union, and met the local representatives of a young reform movement being called the "Evening Light Saints" (Church of God, Anderson). Among these people he found his sanctification, his call to preach, and a supportive group of believers who formally recognized his budding ministry. These "Saints" were focused on the proclamation of holiness, healing, and an unusual inclusiveness of African-Americans. Now as part of this group, Seymour traveled frequently, preaching the reconciling good news of Christ. He heartily agreed with this movement that sanctification has church-wide, social personal implications.

Soon Seymour found himself in Houston, Texas, where he had some relatives. The choice was made to settle there. He began to function as pastor of a local congregation of the "Evening Light," and soon learned about a well-known Bible teacher, Charles F. Parham. Parham, a strict segregation-ist, impressed Seymour with aspects of his teaching, including his emphasis on tongues-speaking, a source of conflict that ended his local pastorate and direct relationship with the Church of God movement. Seymour at this point apparently did not experience this tongues gift (Parham would not allow Blacks to join others at a common altar where such was sought). Then a new ministry opportunity presented itself. Seymour's godly life had attracted some visitors from Los Angeles who invited him to come to the more racial-ly open West and help them develop a holiness congregation. He decided to go and began an inspired preaching ministry that included holiness, healing, racial reconciliation, and glossolalia, which he then believed was a sign accompanying the baptism of the Holy Spirit. This latter emphasis brought his rejection by the mission he was helping to develop.

Rejection was accepted as a new challenge. So he began conducting independent cottage meetings where he and others began to speak in tongues for the first time. Large interracial crowds began arriving at the services, which had to be moved to larger quarters on Azusa Street. These meetings between 1906 and 1909 are generally regarded as having effectively launched American Pentecostalism. When Seymour invited Parham to come and help, he did; but Parham quickly became openly critical of the "darky camp meeting" and tended to wrench the revival away from Seymour into a much more segregated mode—one contrary to the larger vision of the church fostered earlier in Seymour by the Evening Light Saints of the Church of God.

Although the Azusa Street Revival was shepherded by an ordained min-ister of the Church of God, this reform movement that so significantly shaped Seymour has not readily owned this man and his significant ministry, primarily because of the "tongues" issue. The two large histories of the Church of God movement (by Charles E. Brown and John W. V. Smith) do not list his name in their indexes. Cheryl J. Sanders, a contemporary African-American leader of the Church of God, has offered her view of this. Clearly and rightly proud of the legacy of racial openness left by Seymour, she adds:

> A point-by-point comparison of the September 1906 edition of Seymour's periodical *Apostolic Faith* with *What the Bible Teaches*, a compilation of early writings by F. G. Smith, editor of the Church of God publication *Gospel Trumpet*, reveals striking similarities. The only clear point of disagreement is the tongues doctrine. Moreover, the two documents are virtually in complete accord with regard to the two distinguishing doc-trines of the Church of God, holiness and unity…. [Seymour's] commitment to Christian unity had a dual grounding, in the

antisectarianism of the Church of God reformation movement and in the Pentecostal blessing of tongues-speaking as a ritual reenactment of the outpouring of God's Spirit on all flesh (31-32).

Here was a man nurtured by the Church of God movement and blessed by God, but one left out of the published histories of this movement, probably because of a controversial doctrine that was a blessing to some and very troubling to many others.

Editor's Note: For more detail, see D. J. Nelson, "For Such a Time as This: The Story of Bishop William J. Seymour and the Azusa Street Revival," unpublished dissertation, University of Birmingham (U. K.), 1981. Also, see the Index of this present volume for references to "glossolalia."

23. I'll Help with the Tent

by Barry L. Callen, concerning Elmer and Elizabeth Sowers, parents of Lillie Sowers McCutcheon (1921-1999). Excerpted from Barry L. Callen, *She Came Preaching: The Life and Ministry of Lillie S. McCutcheon* (Anderson, Ind.: Warner Press, 1992), 36-38.

In 1923, when Lillie Sowers was only two years old, her parents [Elmer and Elizabeth Sowers] finally were to experience that spiritual rebirth that would have a profound effect on her own life and, through her many years later, on the lives of tens of thousands of others. The event that really set their spiritual rebirth in motion seemed only incidental at the time.

Elmer Sowers was a welder, inventor, and master mechanic. Creative, practical, and brilliant in his own way, he was a hard-working and good-natured man. He happened to be six feet, eight inches tall, unusual for his day, and he had done some amateur boxing, once having been the sparring partner of Jess Willard. One day in 1923 that height and strength would lead to a revolutionary change in his life and in that of his wife. At the time, the whole incident seemed innocent and natural enough, just one of those things on the way home from work. But time would show that the hand of God had been especially at work this day.

Elmer always walked to work, a considerable distance down a hillside in the community of North Apollo, Pennsylvania, to the factory along the river below. On that eventful day in 1923 he was nearing home after work and reached an area where often his children would see him coming and run to get some little treat that he always seemed to have in his pocket. But this

111

day he approached an unusual scene in an open field area within sight of his home on Robbins Avenue. Two men much shorter than himself were struggling with a large tent they were trying to erect. Being a congenial man who never knew a stranger, Elmer stopped and offered the considerable benefit of his height and strength. When the center pole was in place and secured, Johnny Williams and Herman Ast, ministers of the Church of God movement, invited Elmer and his family to the revival tent meeting about to begin.

Rev. Williams was a Welshman, a zealous evangelist with twenty-five years of experience. Ast was a young minister newly graduated from Anderson Bible Training School in Anderson, Indiana. Elmer and Elizabeth decided to attend the meeting, and Elizabeth attended almost every night for a month. While she did not quite "see the church" at first the way the evangelists were preaching it, both she and her husband experienced Christian salvation.

The fruits of this newfound faith were to be expressed somewhat differently by Elmer and Elizabeth. Elizabeth was the dominant one with respect to the family's religious life. She would become a solid rock. Even while the Sowers family occasionally came to host the group life of the growing Church of God fellowship in North Apollo, Elizabeth continued to struggle with the call to "see the church," the one church of God, the body of all Christ's children free of sectarian divisions. She was determined to discover the truth for herself. One week Brother George Earl Sample preached a sermon on this subject in the Sowers home and then Elizabeth, continuing her quest privately, finally found her answer in John 17:21-23. She was, as she later put it, "convinced, never to doubt again. Thank God!"

Being a determined woman of action, Elizabeth went straight to the local Lutheran pastor and told him to remove the Sowers names from the church roll. Elizabeth had been baptized in the Lutheran church as an infant, but now she joined her husband in being baptized by immersion by Rev. Ast, the Church of God pastor across the river in Vandergrift. Their son Glenn was only seven years old at the time, but he never would forget the physical marvel of five-foot tall Rev. Ast successfully immersing his dad, who towered over the minister by nearly two feet in height! About a year later young Glenn himself was part of a three-week revival in the Vandergrift church with M. A. Monday and an exciting singer, Arthur Lynn, known as "America's Golden Tenor." Glenn bowed one evening at the altar and found his own salvation.

Editor's Note: A daughter of Elmer and Elizabeth Sowers, Lillie Sowers McCutcheon, was converted at age seven and baptized in the local public swimming pool at age twelve. She became a leading pastor and influential national leader in the Church of God from the 1940s until her death in March, 1999. Her brother Austin also became a leading minister, serving for many years as associate pastor of the Newton Falls, Ohio, congregation, while his sister Lillie was the senior pastor. Two lengthy obituaries were presented at the funeral of Lillie McCutcheon (March 8, 1999, Columbus, Ohio), one by Barry L. Callen and the other by Arlo F. Newell. These both appear in the Fall 1999 issue of *Reformation Witness*.

24. Holiness and Unity Joined

by James Edgar Royster, concerning John A. D. Khan. Excerpt from the Royster master's thesis, "A History of the Church of God in South India: 1897-1960" (Hartford Seminary Foundation, 1967), 73-78.

John A. D. Khan
India

The central personality in the early history of the Church of God in South India—and all of India for that matter—was John Alla-ud-Din Khan, a converted Muslim from East Bengal. Khan was born November 22, 1877, and was raised in a Muslim family. His earliest awareness of Christianity came when his uncle told him about hearing an evangelist deny the efficacy of a mere formal performance of religious duties. A few years later, as a school boy, Khan met an English missionary and bought several Christian books, including an English copy of the New Testament.

Prior to the chain of events that culminated in his conversion and baptism, Khan began rigorously to observe the pillars of Islam—praying five times a day, fasting during Ramadan, etc. This period of zeal and devotion to Mohammed came during his later primary and high school days. Young Khan had met an Arab priest who so soundly impressed him that he became a disciple following a "ceremonial repentance."

As a high school student at Mymensing, about fifty miles from Khan's home and the county seat of an East Bengal district, Khan began on August 6, 1893, to attend Bible classes conducted by Miss Ehrenburg, a converted Jew, of the Australian Baptist Mission. His interest was sufficient that he requested Miss Ehrenburg to offer daily rather than weekly classes. This she did, and in three months Khan had studied the Gospels and Acts. His conversion occurred on December 3, 1893. Of this experience he wrote, "I could scarcely find expression to give vent to the outbursts of joy within my soul."

Khan's first denominational association in Calcutta was with the Salvation Army. It was under their guidance that he was led to the experience of holiness he so desperately desired. Affirming the reality of this experience, Khan said, "The Lord sanctified my heart by a second and definite work of grace, subsequent to regeneration." He also came to know the Plymouth Brethren but did not affiliate with them because they did not advocate sanctification in the sense that he understood it.

Khan's perplexity at not finding in Calcutta a church teaching both holiness and unity, as he interpreted the Bible to set them forth, caused him to undertake a fresh investigation of the New Testament. After a six-month study he reached the following conclusions:

1. God has but one Church.
2. God's Church is named by God.
3. Christ is the head of the Church.
4. The Holy Ghost is the administrator of the Church.
5. He organizes the Church and appoints his ministers.
6. There must be unity in the Church in all matters of doctrine and practice pertaining unto life and godliness.
7. There are no sinners in the Church of God.
8. A hireling ministry and program worship are foreign to the Church of God.
9. The love of God is the only tie that binds believers together.
10. The Word of God is the only guide in all matters, doctrinal and spiritual.

Concerning the results of this period of intense Bible study, Khan wrote, "When I came to these conclusions from the Word of God, I found myself in an isolated place; I could not join any of the denominations then."

Khan shared his views with some fellow college students and one of them especially, Mozir Moses, was sympathetically impressed. During this period Khan made his first contact with the Church of God. The account can be described best in his own words.

> About this time I saw an advertisement in a paper, to the effect that a man in Texas was offering to send samples of holiness papers published in America, on receipt of a silver dime. I was very anxious to know what was going on in America, about this doctrine of holiness, and so sent my name with remittance to the party. Soon after I began to receive all sorts of papers from America, some of which I liked more than the others. Among these samples there came a copy of the *Gospel Trumpet* catalogue of books. Being fond of study, I was eager to find out what books they were;,and when I read the names and contents of those books, such as "Divine Healing of Soul and Body," "Salvation; Present, Perfect, Now or Never," "Church of

God," "What Church Should I Join?" etc., I was very eager
to get these books. I sent for them at once, and I need not tell
you that I was more than satisfied. I found in these books just
the things that the Lord was teaching me all those days.

On July 7, 1896 Khan wrote from Calcutta to the Gospel Trumpet
Company, then publishing from Michigan, and requested a subscription to
the *Gospel Trumpet.*

Editor's Note: A. D. Khan (1877-1922) had a great vision for evangelizing India and shared it with the readers of the *Gospel Trumpet*
in the June 23, 1898, issue. Khan came to the United States in 1903,
visited numerous congregations and meetings over a period of
months, and helped greatly in awakening the world consciousness
of the young Church of God movement.

25. Impressed by a Saintly Life

The Story of Richard D. Meyer, excerpted from the
1926 *Church of God Yearbook*, 12-13.

Richard D. Meyer was born in Seckenhausen, Hanover, Germany,
July 23, 1873 and passed peacefully away September 2, 1925 at Anderson,
Indiana. Brother Meyer was reared in Germany, a Lutheran. He came to
America in 1889, and returned to Germany on a visit in 1895, but did not
remain very long. Three years later he made a second tour to his fatherland,
visiting friends and relatives. Between those two tours he was converted.
From the beginning of his Christian experience he was a whole-souled, conscientious soldier of the cross. In fact, so conscientious was he that life was
a constant battle with accusation and discouragement because he sometimes
failed to reach his highest ideals.

While returning from his second trip to Germany, in the year 1903,
Brother Meyer came in contact on the steamer with our late beloved
missionary, Brother John A. D. Khan, of India. So impressed was brother
Meyer with the sainted, godly life of this converted Mohammedan, and so
convinced was he that the reformation principles preached by brother Khan
were heaven-sent, that he decided to embrace them. That same year he came
to the Gospel Trumpet Office and enrolled as a worker in the German type-
room, as the German work was then a part of the Gospel Trumpet Company.

He was an indefatigable worker, who looked beyond the cold type to the
burning, vital message made by its impression and scattered through the
mails all over the globe. "While he mused the fire burned" within his own

breast. It moved his pen, and for many years prior to the time of his late and severe affliction, his glowing, fervent exhortations appeared in the pages of both the *Posaune* (the German *Gospel Trumpet*) and the English *Gospel Trumpet*.

The Great World War [World War I] brought to him an intense burden for the suffering people of his fatherland. After the smoke of the battle had cleared away he determined to visit them, preach the Christ whom he loved to them, and start a publishing work which would continue the promulgation of the message of this reformation that he loved so well. He visited the war-stricken populace of Poland, held meetings among the cantons of Switzerland, but especially did he work in the Valley of the Ruhr, where he succeeded in establishing a European *Posaune* at Essen.

26. My Heart Set Aflame

by Harold Chilver

I was born at Armadale, in the state of Victoria [Australia] in 1905 and was one of three sons and two daughters reared in an atmosphere of a warm Christian home where Jesus was revered and his mandates obeyed as they were revealed in the Scriptures. Here we were taught the rudiments of Christian living and the first essential, that of allowing God prior place in our lives. Our family lived on a farm in an isolated district in Gippsland. Church services were few and Sunday school only infrequently conducted.

At the age of seventeen years I became a Christian through a new birth experience of deep significance and lasting impression. It is sufficient to say that from this time onward, God implanted in my heart a continuing desire to lead and teach in the work of the Church. I therefore, not surprisingly perhaps, gave myself constantly to study and writing. To be a wholehearted child of God was the prevailing urge in my life now, and I continually sought for more light on what the Bible taught.

My father had for a long time been disillusioned with denominationalism, although we were influenced by Baptist theology. Dad thought it wasteful and an unnecessary duplication to be so divided, and many were the discussions I heard on this subject. Later he saw further light on the Church, mainly concerning its spiritual nature, but had not, as far as I know, seen that an inward spiritual relationship should, and indeed, must reveal itself in an outward, visible, and tangible expression of unity. Dad was always vitally interested in these matters. How often we sat around the family table and listened to or took part in discussions on subjects such as this, especially if the local minister was with us, which happened when he had to spend the night in the area.

Into this fertile condition came a journal that was to enlighten my understanding and set aflame my heart with the blessed truths it emphasized. It happened this way. In those early years discussions and controversies were prevalent, particularly concerning religious and ethical questions. At this time of which I write, one subject stirring the district where I lived, discussion of which I entered into freely, was that of social dancing. Was it right for Christian folk to indulge in this pastime? Would it harm one's Christian witness? To help in those disputations, I decided to obtain a booklet advertised in a church paper we were subscribing to. The name of the booklet was, "The Lure of the Dance." The Reverend E. P. May had added an appendage of some length to conform more closely to Australian conditions. I addressed my request to the Gospel Trumpet Company, Sydney, New South Wales, and when I received the booklet it was wrapped in a portion of a magazine entitled the *Australian Gospel Trumpet.*

The booklet contained some vital information and instruction, but strangely I seemed to be held with a gripping interest by the articles in the pages of the incomplete journal. My heart thrilled to the deep spiritual truths which were written therein, and I determined to know more of the source of such vital material. Here was taught clearly the Bible concept of the oneness of God's people and how they, in this blessed inward spiritual relationship, should show forth the outward unity in the glorious nature of the Church of God.

And then there was the teaching on holiness—the cleansing of men's hearts and the strength to live free from the power of sin and its consequent guilt through the indwelling Christ by sanctification and full commitment to God's control of our lives. In short, a crucified life, directed by the Holy Spirit of God. How it lifted me to heights of spiritual joy! I dedicated myself even further to Christian work as far as I was then able. I asked for the paper to be posted to me for the small sum of seven shillings per year.

I also began to purchase books as they were listed in the *Gospel Trumpet.* Among them were *The Christian Church: Its Rise and Progress* by H. M. Riggle and *What the Bible Teaches* by F. G. Smith. Then there was a wonderful book by C. W. Naylor, *Winning a Crown*, a book for young Christians just like me. This book I loaned around and it traveled hundreds of miles from home, but I always got it back!

During this period (about 1920) I had regular correspondence with the Reverend E. P. May who had come from Anderson, Indiana, with limited funds to begin the publication of an *Australian Gospel Trumpet.* Brother May came to our home and spent some days with us. During his stay I and some others were baptized by him.

117

Part Two:
CLARIFYING THE LIGHT
CHARACTERISTICS, CRISES, AND RE-EVALUATIONS OF THE TRADITION

Editor's Note: Reformation of the church is always an urgent and ongoing process. Materials in this section seek to establish some guidelines for the reformation process, recall key occasions when the Church of God movement was itself faced with crises of challenge and change, and allow a few voices to try stating for the movement its enduring "marks of greatness" that remain across all the variations of time and place.

27. On Ministers Seeing "Eye To Eye"

Three articles by Daniel S. Warner, *Gospel Trumpet*, December, 1893, compiled and edited by Barry L. Callen

Editor's Note: Church historian John W. V. Smith reports that the teachings of the Church of God pioneers often spoke of their vision of the church being divinely organized (1980, 93). In part, this meant the elimination of all offices, titles (except Brother and Sister), committees, boards, and procedures which required formal elections or appointments—traditional signs of a humanly organized church. An exception to the use of such traditional signs was the ordaining of "elders" or ministers.

How uniform must be the thinking of these special leaders? Daniel S. Warner, primary pioneer of the Church of God movement, addressed the general issue of ministers "seeing eye to eye" in three articles in the *Gospel Trumpet* (December 14, 21, and 28, 1893). Excerpts of all three articles follow. Church historian Merle D. Strege concludes the following in relation to this series of articles by Warner:

118

Despite clear differences of interpretation, Warner did not use the authority of the editor's chair to enforce doctrinal uniformity. Instead, he appealed to the Word and Spirit of God and implicitly trusted in the ongoing conversation between minister and minister and between minister and editorial office. Together the participants in this conversation engaged in the practice of biblical interpretation, believing that the Word and Spirit of God would enter into their honest and sincere efforts, guiding them into "all truth" (in an unpublished 1995 essay titled "The Peculiar Impress of the Mind: Biblical Inspiration and Interpretation in the Early Church of God (Anderson)," 14-15).

Strege recalls these Eye-To-Eye articles of Warner in his 1993 book *Tell Me Another Tale*, pages 84-86. He concludes by stressing that what is most crucial is how we handle conflict in the church's life.

27a. "Do the Ministers of God See Eye to Eye?"

Daniel S. Warner, *Gospel Trumpet*, December 14, 1893

"Thy watchmen shall lift up the voice; with the voice together shall they sing; for they shall see eye to eye, when the Lord shall bring again Zion" (Isa.52:8).

The expression, "see eye to eye," evidently signifies that they are of "one heart and one way" (Jer. 32:39). In "one body, one spirit and one faith" (Eph. 4). "Perfectly joined together in the same mind and in the same judgment" (1 Cor. 1:10). "Stand fast in one Spirit, with one mind, striving together for the faith of the gospel" (Phil. 1:27). "Like-minded one toward another, according to Christ Jesus" (Rom. 15:5). They all agree in faith and doctrine, being in the one "faith of the gospel" (Phil. 1:27). They are of the same mind, and that is not what they have compiled in a creed and subscribed to, but that mind, faith, doctrine and practice is "according to Christ Jesus." This harmony of sentiment and teaching is attained and only can be attained by having our former education and our own wisdom destroyed and purged out; and be led of the Spirit of God into all truth, according to the promise of Christ (Jn. 16:13).

All being thus "taught of God," and receiving the Word from his mouth, interpreted by his Spirit, there must be harmony; for "God is not the author of confusion." And, upon the other hand, where there appears the slightest discrepancy or conflict in the teaching, it is because some person has not been brought perfectly under the light of the Word by the Holy Spirit; or has been carrying something along he had received and taught before wholly sanctified. But on the authority of God's word we affirm that it is the privilege and solemn duty of all God's messengers to understand and teach the word of God in perfect harmony. This does not, however, imply that they all have the same gifts or abilities, nor yet that they have all attained unto the same degree of knowledge in sacred truth; but "whereunto we have attained we walk by the same rule," and what we have not learned of the Lord we do not presume to teach. Hence there is harmony in all that is taught, so long as each teacher is confined within that measure of truth received by the Holy Spirit.

In this article it becomes our duty to notice a very few points in which there has not been perfect agreement manifest among the watchmen who have returned to Zion.... [Warner proceeds to discuss "hell redemption" and purgatory.]

By the help of the Lord we will follow this article with others that are needed for the complete unification of all who walk in the evening light, and we sincerely ask the prayers of all the dear saints that only the wisdom that comes from above may guide our thoughts and pen, and the love of God mould our words. Amen.

27b. "The Ministers of God Must See Eye to Eye"

Daniel S. Warner, *Gospel Trumpet*, December 21, 1893

Another point in which we think there has not been uniformity in the teaching of all God's ministers is in reference to what Christ meant when he said, "It is easier for a camel to go through the eye of a needle, than for a rich man to enter into the kingdom of God."

The teaching throughout Babylon has been this, "There was a gate through the wall of Jerusalem that was called the Needle's Eye." It was of such straightened dimensions that a camel could, with great difficulty squeeze through it; but that only by unloading and crouching down upon its knees. And to this supposed door, it is supposed that Jesus had reference. And we learn that some dear brethren in the evening light have carried along with them that education received in sectism, and so teach. Now we firmly believe that the theory is simply based upon the two suppositions we have named above. If any brother or sister can truthfully say that the Holy Spirit gave you that interpretation of the matter, we would love to hear from you.

But let us examine the Word and find out the mind of the Spirit that spoke through the Son of God....

And now beloved, if we are going to fulfill the prophecy of a holy ministry returned from Babylon confusion, to see eye to eye, and teach the same things, be sure that you take up and teach nothing that only has the traditions of sectism to sustain it. Only teach what you know by the sure Word and Spirit of God, and there will be harmony.

27c. "The Ministers of God See Eye to Eye"

Daniel S. Warner, *Gospel Trumpet*, December 28, 1893

We continue our investigation of points upon which all God's dear ministers have not all come to a full understanding, by taking up the word "Hades" which involves the subject of the intermediate state. Let it be remembered that this is also a point that does not materially affect uniformity in any principle of practical righteousness, not in the present truth, it being wholly a matter relating to the future. Nevertheless, it being a scriptural word, it is our privilege to understand its meaning, and so come to a uniformity of knowledge respecting it, and by consequence, harmony of teaching.... [Warner explores extensively biblical uses and meanings of words related to "hell."]

My dear brethren, if we wish to see eye to eye, and teach uniformly, we must look into things more narrowly than to hold and teach a thing simply because we "always thought it meant so." For that which we always thought is generally what we were educated into back in Babylon....

Editor's Note: See Entries 169 and 170 for more recent examples (1981) of the Church of God engaging in serious internal dialogue about important matters that were being debated at the time.

28. Organizing for World Mission: Formation of the Missionary Board, 1909-1910

by Barry L. Callen

The first organized ministry of the Church of God movement was the publishing work, the Gospel Trumpet Company (see its history written by Harold Phillips, *Miracle of Survival*). The second arose from the experienced need for some form of organization to coordinate the missionary outreach of the Church of God. This need became evident by 1909 after twenty years of voluntary and independent missionary endeavors, some of which had led to overlapping work, differing mission philosophies, poor communication, improper preparation for cross-cultural ministry, and financial inefficiency. Missionaries went out on faith, raising their own support. Obvious inequities had developed.

Many ministers began asking if there were not a better way. Note this quotation from the June 12, 1909, entry in the diary of George P. Tasker, regarding the historic decision made by the body of ministers at the annual Anderson Camp Meeting of 1909:

> On June 12, 1909, after an address on "Government in the Church," H. M. Riggle, after presenting our plans for a missionary paper, to be called the *Missionary Herald*, recommended that "certain brethren should be recognized amongst us, by common consent, as having and exercising in behalf of the Church, the responsibility and care of the foreign missionary work. They should be capable of advising, instructing, encouraging and restraining." The names here presented, and that were acknowledged by the immediate rising to their feet of the entire assembly of ministers, were D. O. Teasley, J. W. Byers, E. E. Byrum, E. A. Reardon, G. P. Tasker, H. A. Brooks, and D. F. Oden. Brother Riggle then said, "it is intended that the entire ministry should cooperate with these brethren," to which all said, "Amen."

For a movement critical of the downsides of formalized organization in the life of the church, this was a significant step—one not agreed to by all and requiring biblical justification.

H. M. Riggle supported the legitimacy of some organization in the life of the church in a sermon at the 1912 Anderson Camp Meeting. He said, "Government and system need to be recognized in the church. Such recognition will not show that we are a sect; on the contrary, these things being God's order, our recognition of them will be one of the surest signs that we are the Church of God." The new Missionary Board, he implied, was clearly one such sign. In *Our Ministerial Letter* (Nov. 1912), J. W. Phelps wrote "Our Mission Work" and included this:

> It will be seen that sectarianism results, not from attempts on the part of God's children to plan to do the work of the church in an orderly, systematic manner, but from attempts to bind upon men as doctrines things not required by the letter or spirit of the Word, or to release men from obligations which the letter or the spirit of the Word requires (8).

The first formal meeting of the Missionary Board of the Church of God convened in Anderson, Indiana on June 8, 1910. The officers elected were D. O. Teasley, chair; E. E. Byrum, vice-chair; and G. P. Tasker, secretary-treasurer. The board assumed responsibility from the Gospel Trumpet Company for all funds that had been raised for mission work. The new board stated its purposes as: "(1) to act as an advisory board in the matter of missionaries going to foreign fields; (2) to have charge of all collections and disbursements of missionary funds; and (3) to take a general interest in the dissemination of missionary information." In the first meeting of the Board, twenty-seven missionaries were recognized: British Isles, four; China, two; Japan, four; British West Indies, two; Germany, four; and India, eleven. The first missionary appointments by the board were accomplished in this meeting. They were N. S. Duncan and his wife for assignment in Barbados. By 1914 the board was legally incorporated in the State of Indiana, with eleven members and the ability to hold property, carry on legal business, and register for similar functions in other countries.

For additional detail on the board's formation and its extensive work in the following decades, see Lester Crose, *Passport for a Reformation,* Warner Press, 1981.

29. William G. Schell: A Journey Into and Out of Darkness

by Barry L. Callen

Editor's Note: The case of William G. Schell is a prime example of an ad hoc and grace-filled process of discipline and restoration that operated in the early years of the Church of God movement.

William G. Schell was born June 30, 1869 in Darke County, Ohio. He was converted in a Methodist revival at the age of fourteen and united with that denomination until August, 1886, when he attended a holiness meeting. It was conducted by A. J. Kilpatrick and J. N. Howard. Reports Schell

> When I entered the congregation Bro. Kilpatrick was in the pulpit. There seemed to be such a holy awe about those men and such a sweet influence of God's Spirit flowed out from the words they were uttering to my heart as I had never experienced before. In a few minutes I was made to see clearly that they had an experience of salvation beyond anything I had ever attained unto, and my heart within me seemed to melt like wax.[1]

The next Sunday Schell returned and heard these preachers speak on the "pure church" and was so thoroughly convinced that he resolved to no

1. Henry Wickersham, *A History of the Church* (Moundsville, W. Va.: Gospel Trumpet Publishing Company, 1900), 361. Wickersham reproduced an autobiographical piece by Schell written March 21, 1900.

longer "have my name recorded on any book, except that one which would contain the names of all the blessed in that great day." He decided that there would be one less Methodist because "I felt that for me a membership in the church of the living God only was needed."[2]

Persecuted at first by many former friends in the vicinity of his home in West Liberty, Ohio, Schell soon was preaching locally and then in other states. Having thus begun his ministry in 1886, it was not until June, 1888, that he had opportunity to attend his first general camp meeting of the Church of God. It convened in Bangor, Michigan and featured exciting reports from Daniel S. Warner and his company who had just returned from an evangelistic tour in the western states. This inspiration helped motivate Schell as he proceeded to hold meetings in Ohio, Indiana, and Pennsylvania—sometimes assisted by Brother Warner, B. E. Warren, and others. He gained such respect in the Church of God that he was called on to preach the funeral sermon in Grand Junction, Michigan, when Warner died in December, 1895. Observes C. E. Brown,

> He was a man of an unusually fertile and brilliant mind, a mag-
> netic and eloquent preacher, and a voluminous and interesting
> writer.... Many thought that he would be chosen to take the
> place of D. S. Warner after the latter's death. Although another
> man took this position [Enoch E. Byrum], William G. Schell's
> influence continued unabated.[3]

For instance, in 1893 the Gospel Trumpet Publishing Company, then in Grand Junction, Michigan, had published Schell's *The Biblical Trace of the Church*, the first major work to develop a prophetic identity for the Church of God movement—his line of thought appeared also in the form of a song by the same title.[4] Schell's book *The Better Testament* was released in 1899 when the publishing work and Schell's family had relocated to Moundsville, West Virginia. Here the company was first incorporated and Schell was one of the leaders. It was in this new location that trouble boiled to the surface.

Schell had moved to Grand Junction in the spring of 1896. From there he had continued his active ministry, traveling, for instance, with E. E. Byrum through the southern states in the winter of 1896-97 and that fall preaching in Washington, Oregon, California, and Arizona. Then came the trouble. In 1898, according to historian Henry Wickersham,

A delusive spirit became manifest in several of the ministers,

---

2. Ibid., 364.
3. Charles E. Brown, *When the Trumpet Sounded* (Anderson, Ind.: Warner Press, 1951), 124.
4. William Schell's song "The Biblical Trace of the church," in Select Hymns (Anderson, Ind.: Gospel Trumpet Company, 1911).

that was causing them to oppose the doctrine of sanctification.... The work suffered greatly under the influence of these men until they were renounced through the *Trumpet*, and the church took a decided stand against them at the general camp-meeting at Moundsville, in 1899."[5]

The pioneers of the Church of God movement understood sanctification to be a central doctrine and held essentially the same understanding of it as was taught commonly in the American Holiness Movement of the time. It was thought of as a definite and instantaneous second work of grace, subsequent to justification, that frees believers from their inherited Adamic nature, cleansing them from the love of sin and enabling them to live a life free from sin in this present world. Soon, however, the "second cleansing" aspect of this teaching came into question. Some ministers of the movement claimed that the believer is cleansed completely with the initial experience of justification. Count Nicholas von Zinzendorf (1700-1760), a leader of the Moravians, had taught that one is entirely sanctified at the moment of justification. Those who decided to espouse this "Zinzendorfism" in the Church of God eventually were labeled the "anti-cleansing heresy." By 1898 the *Gospel Trumpet* was dealing pointedly with this issue. W. G. Schell wrote a two-part series entitled "Zinzendorfism Refuted" (March 1899), viewing the one-work theory as heresy.

Soon, however, Schell himself became the target of heavy criticism. In the June 18, 1903 issue of the *Gospel Trumpet,* D. O. Teasley and H. M. Riggle jointly wrote an article titled "Departed From the Faith." They reported that "a number of those whom we had learned to love and esteem in the ministry have fallen prey to false spirits and doctrines." For the sake of the "safety of his [God's] precious cause," it had become their painful duty to inform the church of those who had "fallen away." Specifically named was William G. Schell who had "apostatized from the faith."

What were Schell's false and dangerous new teachings? Three are named by Teasley and Riggle. (1) He no longer "considers the present reformation to be of God." (2) He questions the truth that foot-washing is a New Testament ordinance. (3) He had come to favor triune immersion as the best form of baptism. Thus, the Church of God at Moundsville, West Virginia, where the publishing work and Schell then resided, had acted to "reject him as being unworthy of their fellowship and unfit for this ministry." Teasley and Riggle now asked the church generally to cooperate with this decision.

In 1908 Schell wrote to E. E. Byrum, editor of the *Gospel Trumpet,* expressing penitence and asking for forgiveness and prayer for his ailing

---

5. Wickersham, *A History of the Church*, 386.

body and searching soul. Published in the February 20, 1908 issue is a lengthy article of Schell's titled "Seven Years of Darkness." He speaks of himself as the prodigal son whose "soul went into darkness" in 1901. He writes candidly of his having been tempted by the devil who had caused him to make "a great mistake." He had joined with two minister friends who were sharply criticizing another minister. Hatred entered his soul and "the blessed experience of holiness had departed." But, after seven years of painful spiritual darkness he declared, "I have just been lifted by the mercies of God."

What an eventful seven years of darkness it had been! He had gone from Moundsville to Morgantown, West Virginia, entered the grocery store business, did things that were "worldly and devilish" (sold tobacco, went to theaters, etc.), lost everything that he had invested in the business, tried farming on borrowed money in North Dakota ("what I knew God did not want me to do!"), and suffered crop failures and more debt there and back in Morgantown and Moundsville. Then there was a failed mission he attempted in Minneapolis ("I found myself drifting into the truth to such an extent that the sectarians began to see that I was opposed to sectism and they abandoned me, went back on their pledges. . ."). The Schell family was in poverty and suffered a series of significant illnesses. Soon William Schell was desperately reaching out to God. He managed to find work in the beet-fields of Montana in 1906. Word began reaching him of people in the Church of God who still cared for him and were praying that he would be restored to his earlier ministry. Finally he was deeply convicted and wrote a letter of confession to E. E. Byrum. He sent it to the Trumpet Office now located in Anderson, Indiana and received a warm response of prayerful openness.

Hope had returned. As soon as possible, Schell journeyed to Anderson, "confessed my wrongs both to God and to the brethren, and God has most graciously saved my soul." "O brethren," he then wrote in his 1908 *Gospel Trumpet* article, "help me to praise God for his mercy to me!" He added this plea:

> To all the dear souls who have backslidden from the evening light, let me say to you in love, there is no victory for you but in Zion. You can not get saved under a lower standard of light than that you have received.

Forgiveness was sought from any who had been wronged by his sojourn into spiritual darkness and the process of paying his debts began. In 1910 William G. Schell became the first pastor of the Church of God congregation in Bellefontaine, Ohio. In 1922 he published a significant volume titled *Sanctification and Holiness: The False and the True* which carefully critiques "second cleansing" teaching.

126

30. The Case of Missionary George P. Tasker

by Barry L. Callen

In the 1920s some ministers of the Church of God began worrying that the movement was evolving within itself a sectarian spirit not unlike the one it had always been quick to condemn. One who became worried was George P. Tasker (1872-1958). He sat as a member of the first Missionary Board of the Church of God, serving as Secretary-Treasurer for its first two years of operation (1910-1911). Then in 1912 he and his wife accepted a call to missionary service in India. A close relationship developed with A. D. Khan, an inspiring Indian church leader. But soon the relationship between Tasker and the Missionary Board in the United States began to sour. Khan and Tasker preferred a Christ-centered fellowship to a church-centered one, a preference that brought opposition in years when the Church of God in the U. S. was becoming more centrally organized and, at least in the opinion of Tasker and some others, more "sectarian"—the very thing the movement had come into existence opposing.

On June 12, 1924, J. W. Phelps, then Secretary of the Missionary Board of the Church of God, wrote to missionary G. P. Tasker in Calcutta, India. He began by saying that it was his "painful and disagreeable duty" to convey a resolution passed by the board at its annual meeting, June 11, 1924.

> Whereas a mass of correspondence between our Secretary and Brother G. P. Tasker reveals the fact that Brother Tasker has grown out of sympathy with the work which this Board seeks to do in India; and

> Whereas very numerous complaints have come to us from influential brethren in this and foreign lands vigorously protesting against our supporting a man whom they believe to be working at cross purposes with the vast majority of the brethren in the home land: therefore be it

> Resolved that this board sever its relations with Brother G. P. Tasker and wife at once; and that both he and the Field Secretary of India be notified at once to this effect; and be it further

> Resolved that we instruct the Field Secretary of India to look after and provide for the temporary support of the Taskers until

127

such a time in the near future when the board can honorably be relieved of their support, such term not to extend beyond January 1, 1925. The Field Secretary of India will take the necessary steps as soon as possible to close up or otherwise arrange for the work in Calcutta formerly under Brother Tasker's care; and be it further

Resolved that this act shall not be construed as affecting in any way Brother and Sister Tasker's ministerial status, which is not within the jurisdiction of this Board; and be it further
Resolved that we would not by this action cast any reflection upon Brother Tasker's moral character. We have known him for many years as a gentleman of high moral character and still regard him as such. In like manner we esteem his wife to be a lady of the highest moral character. It is with feelings of deep sorrow that we terminate the relations of many years, but we do so driven by the convictions of our consciences that in our trustee capacity it is our duty to support missionaries on the foreign field who are able conscientiously to teach in harmony with and work for the accomplishment of the purposes sought by the people whose gifts we administer.

In response to this decisive board action, G. P. Tasker prepared and released from India in October, 1924, an extended pamphlet carrying the key correspondence between the Board and himself beginning in 1921, the above board action, Tasker's own explanations, and other related materials. Called "An Appeal to the Free and Autonomous Churches of Christ in the Fellowship of the Evening Light," this pamphlet of Tasker began with this:

The situation that has developed between Brother and Sister G. P. Tasker, missionaries to India, and the Anderson, Indiana, Missionary Board of the Church of God (U. S. A.), under which they have been working, has reached a point where an appeal to the churches appears to be necessary, that they, as the ultimate earthly court of appeal (Mt. 18:17), may have a chance to decide for themselves what seems to have been decided without them.

In a March 5, 1923, letter from J. W. Phelps to Tasker, the "gist of all the charges" against Tasker was said by Phelps to be,

. . .that your sermons, your missionary lectures, your private conversations, and your general attitude toward the church, have in them so much unbalanced liberalism that they widen out the boundaries of this reformation until, to use the words of

Brother [F. G.] Smith, "like a river in the desert without banks it spreads until it loses itself in the sand where it evaporates, and nothing is left but the barren desert of denominationalism.". . .The heart of the whole matter is that this organization of which we are a part is the church of God. This Board is the Missionary Board of the church of God. You are a missionary of the church of God. As preachers, Board, and missionaries we must, to be true to our calling and profession, faithfully represent the thought of the people with whom we claim fellowship and whom we profess to represent.

Tasker, in his pamphlet (p. 11) reacts strongly to Phelps' sentence, "This Board is the Missionary Board of the church of God." He says,

Observe the small "c". Whether he means it or not, Brother Phelps virtually says in that sentence that this Board is the Missionary Board of the whole Christian church! (1 Cor. 10:32). It would be more reasonable and true to say it is "a Missionary Board of the church of God," or "the Missionary Board of a church of God," but to say it is "the Missionary Board of the church of God" is too much altogether, since an infinite majority of the true Christian church know nothing of the doings of Anderson, Indiana.

Elsewhere in his responding pamphlet (pp. 42-43), Tasker concludes,

I am ready to work peaceably, fraternally, and heartily with you in this Mission to the heathen, subject to the policies and rulings of the Board, and in harmony with all my fellow missionaries, if they will not require me to believe and say about ourselves what I can not say. This is no question of *names* and *claims,* but of *being,* of *character,* of *spirituality* and *conformity* to the *mind of Christ,* the Church's living HEAD. It is a matter of spiritual FACT. Let us *show* that we are "the true church" and we won't have such a hard job making spiritual people believe it.

What were Church of God leaders in Anderson saying about "ourselves" that Tasker was not prepared to endorse? Phelps had said that a missionary was responsible to "faithfully represent the thought of the people with whom we claim fellowship and whom we profess to represent." He had specific reference to the reformation movement that authorized the work of this Missionary Board. But what in the movement's self-perception and teaching emphasis troubled Tasker, a troubling which the Board was no longer prepared to tolerate?

Tasker speaks of the key issue in his view as "ecclesiasticism" and "a betrayal of the Divine principle of this movement as it came to birth in the soul of D. S. Warner." Tasker wished to represent the church—the whole body of believers in Christ. To the degree that the Missionary Board was insisting that Tasker remain faithful to the thinking of the Anderson-related body, as though it were *the* church, he would protest and stand true to the "church of God of the New Testament, which is the only church we both [Tasker and the Board] have been professing to recognize" (p. 23). The center of the troubling issue, then, had to do with a differing interpretation of the method of attaining the "grand ideal" of the Warner-related movement. There was, judged Tasker, a common Tasker-Board affirmation of the following:

> . . .God's reform is a movement of the Spirit of God in this one body which is destined to bring its present earthly members into right and intelligent relationship to one another in Christ, so that the Church's spiritual and fundamental unity may have its proper outward expression everywhere throughout the world and that her great evangelistic Mission in the earth may be furthered (p. 24.)

Here was Tasker's perception of the methodological disagreement:

> You [Phelps and the Board] believe that this result is to be brought about by a geographical coming out to us, that we are nucleus, vanguard, refuge, rendezvous, center and so forth, all of which terms, my dear Brother Phelps, indicate an idea which I believe, if you will calmly apply them to an individual Christian and think out the psychological effect of that idea upon him, you will begin to see something of its dangerous character and can judge of its effect when applied to a people.... Why should we be rendezvous? Do you think for a moment that when "the last reformation" struck the Christian Church it struck it only at one point, Beaver Dam, Indiana? Or, to make it a little larger, the United States of America? I can assure you I don't. The reform movement we are in is of GOD, the God of the whole earth and the entire Church. It must move *in that Church,* not in just one little section of it, for God is in the whole (24-25, 27).

Tasker was direct indeed in his observations, particularly in light of the prominence of F. G. Smith in Anderson-based decisions and his teaching influence in North America. Wrote Tasker:

> I am therefore cordially against *sectarianism* wherever I see it. It is egocentric, Christ-obscuring, ignoble and *sinful*. And I tell you only the sober truth when I say that the people of the most sectarian mind and attitude that I have ever met in all my life have been and are just those people who have most fully imbibed our doctrine and spirit of geographical come-out-ism.... Appeals to "what the church believes" and to "the fathers," when these expressions are used in the narrow restricted sense in which you have used them in your [Phelps] letter, sound altogether too much like the language of the apostasy, when men began to defend their own ecclesiastical views instead of trying them constantly and ruthlessly by the Word and Spirit of the Lord. (31, 30)

While his formal missionary association with the Church of God movement in America was severed in 1924, George Tasker remained in missionary service in India until 1946, when he retired to Canada.[6] Three years after retirement, when he was seventy-four years old, Tasker was attending a Church of God congregation in British Columbia where an eighteen-year-old recent convert named Douglas Welch had become active. Welch was deeply impressed by the older man and the exciting world of missions which he represented and shared. Tasker passed on to the young man a rich legacy which Welch would extend for decades in Church of God mission work in East Africa and then instructionally at Anderson University School of Theology.

31. Reviewing the Goal of Christian Unity

by Russell R. Byrum, written in 1928.

Did God give to the Church of God reformation movement the whole truth on unity fifty years ago, or may the Spirit give us fuller light on the subject now? Do we have a creed other than the Bible—formal or informal, written or unwritten—which binds us to the views of the past, or which prevents our receiving clearer light?

6. For further information on George Tasker and the Missionary Board of the Church of God, see Lester Crose, *Passport for a Reformation* (Anderson, Ind.: Warner Press, 1981) and Merle Strege, *Tell Me the Tale* (Anderson, Ind.: Warner Press, 1991), chapter 1.

A number of our oldest, most prominent and loyal ministers say that they consider our old position inadequate. Too many ministers have left us in recent years because they say they can no longer hold to our theory of the church and unity. I do not pretend to justify them in their separation, but I wonder if we are not in some measure at fault in holding a too-narrow doctrinal position. Most of our ministers and churches have changed their attitude and practice in relation to Christians of other bodies, so that at present our doctrine is no longer in harmony with our practice. Our failure to adjust our doctrine to our changed attitude has caused some to think that they are more different from us than they are in reality.

Christians generally are calling for unity today. Many of the efforts for it may be misdirected, but the realization of it is coming to be a chief concern of the most outstanding leaders of the various denominations, as shown by world conferences on unity. I recently read a book giving chapters by eighteen leading religious leaders in which each sets forth his ideas on how to attain unity. I fear some of these men take the matter of real unity of all Christians more earnestly than some of our own good brethren. We must beware lest we lose our vision of real Christian unity and degenerate into mere Church of God sectarians.

What is Christian unity? Some think of it as being almost an absolute uniformity in doctrinal belief, in type of religious experience, and in conduct. The New Testament does not so represent Christian unity. We never come to perfection in knowledge of truth. We never claim to have perfect knowledge. We have unity of faith in degrees but never in absolute uniformity in belief. The Spirit usually teaches us truth through the natural process of the mind and only occasionally by mystical direct insight. The importance of the Spirit showing us truth has been considerably over stressed by us in the past. The abuses and errors resulting therefrom have now led us to be more cautious on this line.

Neither does Christian unity consist in uniformity in practices and methods. It does not mean sameness in forms of worship or ritual. One local church may kneel in worship, another sit, and a third stand. One may have considerable ritualistic worship and another will have almost pure spontaneity in its public services, yet all these may be in true Christian unity. Nor does unity consist in following the same methods in church work. One congregation may stress the revival method, while another employs the method of religious education as a means of leading men to Christ. But they need not therefore criticize each other because of their differences. Rather they should have unity in love with diversity in methods. Congregations may even subscribe to different church papers or send their money though different mission boards and yet have genuine Christian unity.

Early Protestant churches usually thought their creeds contained all the truth, and that unity could be attained by all Christians joining that particular sect. But they have found through contact with one another that their claim of doctrinal perfection was immodest and untenable. Not a few persons among us in the past have supposed that all true Christians would soon leave their denominations and come to us, acknowledge the *Trumpet* as the only true church paper, our missionary work as the only missionary work approved of God, and our ministers as the only true ministers of God. But our contact with sectarians has led us to see that many more are saved than was supposed; and as a consequence the hope of all Christians coming to us grows weaker. Probably few thinkers among us at present expect all true Christians to come to us, or to come into an operative unity with us. Some still try to hold that position or shrink from recognizing that they no longer hold that narrow theory, because it would be unorthodox and seems to them to be a surrender of the Bible doctrine of unity. Such brethren need to find a truer ground for unity.

A feeling of brotherhood is fast growing among Christians, and this will become more pronounced. Creeds as a test of fellowship are being repudiated and will doubtless be less in favor as time passes. Christians will recognize and accept the truth each other has held. Denominational lines will gradually fade out as they are beginning to do now and rivalries will consequently cease. All Christians will feel free to worship together and to help each other in Christian work. Cooperation in Christian work will be common and is now becoming so. True Christians will gradually come to the true basis for unity by God's working in their consciousness. They will eventually wake up to find themselves in loving fellowship with division walls gone.

We should hold up the ideal of Christian unity as we have always done in the past. We may well lead Christians to cease upholding creeds and sects, and to take a stand definitely for the biblical position. We may further promote unity by refraining from sectishness in our attitude and also from holding an unwritten creed. Let us be brotherly to others and not antagonize them. We should cooperate in charitable and other Christian work. We may be loyal to our work without being sectish.

Editor's Note: A good example of efforts to be loyal without being sectish is the book by John W. V. Smith, *I Will Build My Church: Biblical Insights on Distinguishing Doctrines of the Church of God*, (1985).

32. Problems of Christian Unity

Excerpts of a sermon by E. A. Reardon delivered at the annual meeting of
the General Ministerial Assembly, Anderson, Indiana, June, 1929.
Published previously in Barry Callen, *The First Century* (vol. 2, Warner
Press, 1979), 635-638.

E. A. Reardon

There is today a leaven working among the Christian people of the world with reference to the matter of Christian unity. As a body of Christians we [Church of God movement] have been advocating this for nearly fifty years, and now it is a source of no little satisfaction to see some of the fruits of the Spirit's working. Indeed, this is a very live subject and is engaging the sincere attention of the best minds in Christendom. The best thinkers and the best living people in denominational-ism are fast losing their sectarian attachment to creeds and are gravitating to a more brotherly attitude by which they are enjoying a sweeter fellowship and a more hearty cooperation in things spiritual. Efforts are being made constantly to promote union among certain religious groups whose beliefs are largely the same. This union, of course, is not God's ideal; but the drift of sentiment in this direction does show which way the spiritual wind is blowing. It seems to me that the time has arrived for us to examine seriously both our spirit and our attitude with reference to this matter....

It is a live question among some of our people as to whether we, as a movement, are the hub and center of Christendom. We wonder whether or not God's scattered sheep in the whole world are going to be gathered to us in this reformation. It is true that God is calling his scattered people out of confusion so they may abide alone in Christ and walk on the plane of his holiness and truth and gather together in congregational groups. Yet this does not necessarily mean that they are going to be gathered to us as the center of God's great movement on earth. I do not discount this gathering; but I am convinced that the gathering that God is most interested in is our gathering unto Christ, and there never will be one centralized and centrally-governed movement that will take in all the children of God on earth. There is no one place on earth from which God is directing all the affairs of his Kingdom and his salvation work. There is no one body of people on earth who can claim an exclusive right to Christ and to all his light and truth. If Christ were here in person, he would certainly put to confusion those bodies of his professed followers who make themselves his exclusive people. He would certainly jump over every fence and work wherever he could find believing hearts. If Christ were here on earth today, I cannot conceive of him as confining his operations exclusively to this movement, and I am quite sure that the representative minds and spiritual hearts of our people do not hold such a view.

Christ would certainly ignore our reformation exclusiveness and cultivate, first of all, that unity which is in himself. Christ-exclusiveness and reformation-exclusiveness are not identical. The expectation that all the sheep of the Lord in the world are eventually coming to us as a movement is not at all necessary to the success of God's plan. Anyhow, this movement is only one phase of the great reformation work that God is doing among his people in the world. It is true that this reformation is a concrete expression of the working of God's Spirit in the Christian world, and it has its place, but it is not all there is of God's reformation work. But someone may ask, "If God's sheep are called out of confusion, won't they naturally be gathered to us?" My answer is, "No." If we happen to be the people who preach the message to them, they will naturally come to us, but there will be many others gathered out of confusion, they will abide alone in Christ, they will have the same standard of truth, they will gather in congregational groups, and all this they can do under the leading of God's Spirit without knowing about us as a distinctive movement.

The Spirit of unity is wider than our movement and cannot be confined to us. The message of the Lord in these days must have a wider preaching than our present views will permit. There are many good Christians in the world who have much the same light as we have, but for certain reasons they may never identify themselves exclusively with this movement. In fact, as they see it, they would narrow their influence if they should. They see the truth and enjoy it, but they will never confine themselves to us. They are men who can reach the ears of the Christian world better than we can and they can get a hearing where it would be impossible for us to do so. And further, I feel like venturing this thought, that there are able men and women among us, who no doubt could be far more influential for Christ and the spread of reformation principles if they were not confined and hobbled by a critical and narrow spirit in some of our own people. They are too capable and useful to be confined forever to our limited field. Their influence is wider than this work....

While I do not advocate federation with other movements, yet I do suggest that we consider prayerfully why it is that we are so far away from others of God's people who have so large an amount of grace and truth, and why we have so little to do with them. Is it not a fact that, while some of them have what we would say is 75% of the truth, yet we are not able to cooperate with them to the extent of 5%? Have we the right attitude toward them when we reject them on the ground that they have not the light that we have on a few points? Perhaps we are not conscious of some of the barriers which we have built up against others of God's people.... Many [in our movement] seem to have imbibed the spirit of exclusiveness to the extent that they are seriously prejudiced against even that which is good in others, simply because it does not have our stamp upon it. They have shut themselves up in the reformation and bolted the door.

This attitude can be felt by other people of God, and it appears to them to be sectarian, and I confess it is. Some time ago I heard a trusted minister say that he was born and brought up in this movement and yet he found he had to get rid of a sectarian spirit. I heard of another minister, one of our own brethren, who went to a revival held by a preacher who was not among us. He preached a good straight gospel, and our good minister acknowledged that it was the truth, but said he wasn't going in the back door of Babylon to get it. Such unreasonable and unChristlike statements are made of the worst kind of sectarian cloth, and that kind of a spirit should be condemned among us. This work can be killed by sectarianism as well as by liberalism.

We must guard against that teaching and attitude that will make us narrower than the Word of God. If we advocate a universal brotherhood in Christ, we must cultivate a spirit of brotherly love toward all Christians. If we are in a world-wide movement, we must have a spirit that corresponds. Of all the people on earth, we should be the last to exemplify a sectarian attitude. In order to be right ourselves, it is by no means necessary to believe that everybody else is wrong.... We can never hope for cooperative unity among believers so long as we insist on a too strict submission to all our doctrinal views. Many of our own brethren in the ministry do not yet see all things alike and how can we expect others to do so?...

As I look out upon the horizon of this movement, it seems to me that I can see a tendency to sectarianize it. If this tendency is allowed to go to seed, it won't be long until we shall be numbered among the dead. I believe in a clean, separate, and distinct work for God, but I also believe that we should keep the sectarian stink out the distinction. It seems to me we need to be on the watch for this deceptive thing, for when it comes in it will be under the guise of loyalty to the reformation. There is such a thing as stressing the reformation to such an extent as to cause our people to be reformation centered, reformation sectarians....

I wish to reaffirm my loyalty to Christ, to His church, and to this movement. I do not question the movement or its message, but I do most earnestly plead for a better attitude on the part of our people toward others of God's people, an attitude that is less antagonistic, more conciliatory and, shall I say it, less sectarian. I hope I have made it clear that I am not advocating a compromise of truth nor an alteration of God's message, but a more Christ-like attitude and a spirit that corresponds with the position we profess to hold. Of course, there are serious dangers for God's work on every hand, but He is at the helm and will see it through. If we get a clearer vision of His great work and a larger portion of the Spirit's power, this work will grow and nothing can stop it. On the other hand, if we yield to any influence that will sectarianize it, we will soon fossilize and be in the Babylonian Museum ourselves.

33. The Case of Anderson College and President John A. Morrison

by Barry L. Callen

President John Morrison and Dean Russell Olt, Anderson College (University)

In the 1934 Anderson Camp Meeting and General Ministerial Assembly there came the final showdown. President John Morrison's ratification for a new term as president of Anderson College and Theological Seminary was under consideration by the ministers. Between 1929 and 1934 opponents of both the idea of a church-sponsored liberal arts college and the continuing reports of "liberal" teachings at the college in Anderson had joined into an organized attempt to force some changes. F. G. Smith, then pastoring in Akron, Ohio, was known to want the college controlled by "last reformation" teachings. He mistrusted Morrison in this regard and used his own considerable influence in the "field" to encourage opposition to Morrison's continued school leadership. Those opposing the school in its existing form and with its existing leadership were calling for an immediate end to the liberal arts curriculum and the placing of the school's administration "in the hands of men who are known to be wholly committed to this TRUTH, men who can and will pass it on, both in theological instruction and in burning reformational emphasis, to the body of students." A key document is the following resolution from Ohio that originated in December, 1933.

Adopted Unanimously by the Ordained Ministers of the Church of God Assembled at the Mid-Winter Session of the Ohio State Ministerial Association Toledo, Ohio, December 28, 1933

Whereas, there has for several years existed in many quarters grave questions concerning Anderson College & Theological Seminary; and

Whereas, many of our ministers no longer support this institution, because they are convinced that the College is not truly representative in doctrinal teaching and emphasis of the ideals firmly held by this reformation, and evidently these ministers will not give support so long as present conditions exist; and

Whereas, the Ministerial Body of the State of Ohio assembled at the State Camp-Meeting at Springfield in August, 1933, passed a resolution asking that the College phase of the institution be eliminated, and the work restored to a Bible Training School and Seminary only; THEREFORE BE IT HEREBY FURTHER RESOLVED:

1. That we insist that the Anderson School give its students the same doctrinal teaching and emphasis as has, and still does, characterize the great body of our ministers, including such truths as the present-day call of God to his people to come out of all sectarianism, Papal and Protestant, and modern Babylon.

2. That upon this condition only can the School hope to receive our moral and financial support.

3. That after the lapse of several years, during which time we have hoped for a change to be brought about within the School itself—such a change as will bring it into full harmony with the church and its teachings—we are now convinced that the only way this can be brought about is for the ministers in general to insist that the School be placed in the hands of, and be directed and managed by, men who are known to be wholly committed to this TRUTH; men who can and will pass it on, both in theological instruction and in burning reformational emphasis, to the body of students.

4. That as far as we are concerned we shall vote to ratify officials of this kind only.

5. That until the aforementioned changes are definitely and unequivocally made we can not urge our young people to attend the School, neither can we urge our congregations to support it.

AND BE IT FINALLY RESOLVED: That the Secretary of this Ministerial Assembly be instructed to mail copies of this Resolution to all ordained ministers of the Church of God in the United States as listed in the Year Book.

One response of the campus to this "Ohio uprising" appeared in the March–April, 1934, issue of its *Broadcaster* publication (p. 10). It was a statement of beliefs signed by eleven campus leaders, including President John Morrison and Dean Russell Olt. Presumably it was hoped that this statement (admittedly uncharacteristic of a non-creedal body) would be reassuring to the ministers; but it was not. The statement read as follows:

> 1. We believe in and teach the doctrine of Christian unity as set forth in the New Testament.

> 2. We believe and teach that there is but one Church, the Church of God, that it was built by Christ Himself, and that the only door of entrance is through Christ by means of the experience of the new birth.

> 3. We believe and teach that the divisions of Christians into sectarian bodies is wrong and unscriptural, and, therefore, in love and humility we urge saved people to repudiate the walls of sectarianism and to abide only in the one true, spiritual Church, which is the body of Christ.

> 4. We believe and teach that Christ and his truth, divinely and authoritatively revealed, is the only basis of true Christian unity and the only center to which all Christians can possibly be brought, and that we should fellowship all who believe on the Lord Jesus Christ and are saved by faith in him.

> 5. We believe and teach that this reform movement, which has as its grand ideal the unification of all true Christians, should not inculcate in its members a denominational consciousness or emphasize denominational legislative authority, and that it should guard against the spirit and practice of sectarianism.

> 6. We have urged and do urge our young people to go forth with enthusiasm and conviction to carry this great message to the ends of the earth.

When the showdown time arrived in June, 1934, President Morrison secured the majority vote required for ratification of his election to another term as campus president—but by only the narrow margin of 243-231! A long meeting followed between trustees, faculty, and church leaders in an attempt to reconcile as many differences as possible for the sake of church unity. There was candid exchange, a reaffirmation by all of commitment to reformation perspectives on doctrine, and agreement by college officials to add a course in the school on distinctive doctrines of the Church of God.

> *Editor's Note*: For the fuller context of the above story, see Barry L. Callen, *Guide of Soul and Mind: The Story of Anderson University,* 1992, chapter 4. For a statement of belief issued by Anderson University School of Theology in 1979, see Entry 9.

34. There Were "Watchmen on the Wall"

The Movement's Internal Struggle in the 1940s,
featuring Criticism of the National Work
by Rev. L. Earl Slacum and Others.
Also see Entries 49 and 203.

by Barry L. Callen

Despite the prevailing expansive mood of a rapidly growing Church of God movement, by the mid-1940s there were internal rumblings and dissident voices that for a few years would become quite disruptive to the work of the national agencies and many local congregations. Summarizes church historian John W. V. Smith,

> In reviewing the large volume of criticism which was voiced and circulated, it becomes apparent that the primary target was the national leadership of the movement. Over a period of time there had developed a general feeling of uneasiness about the growing and bigger-spending agencies in Anderson. Questions were sometimes raised and unsatisfactory answers given. Many ministers and a few laypersons across the country harbored some suspicions about the "big boys" who were "running things" in the church's national work. (*The Quest for Holiness and Unity*, 1980, 326).

The mistrust included these kinds of concerns and accusations: national movement leadership was steering the movement away from its historic beliefs and practices; Anderson leaders were "letting down the standard" in regard to some personal, social, and business practices (consulting doctors instead of divine healing, engaging in "worldly amusements," publishing indecent materials for commercial customers through the Gospel Trumpet presses, etc.); there had developed a "power bloc" by which a few powerful Anderson leaders held multiple leadership positions, had cornered the decision-making processes, and had left no room for the "little guys" to be heard.

Rev. L. Earl Slacum, then pastoring and preaching on the radio in Muncie, Indiana, published an article titled "Is Apostasy Emerging?" in the September 16, 1944, issue of the *Gospel Trumpet* (pp. 7-8). Then on September 19, 1944, he delivered a sermon at the annual meeting of the Church of God ministers of Indiana. It was titled "Watchmen on the Wall." Reflecting all of the above concerns, and prompted in part by a proposal from the Board of Church Extension and Home Missions to have states call "state evangelists" to coordinate the evangelistic work in their states, Slacum said he was alarmed and proceeded to denounce the evolving of an "ecclesiastical octopus entwining around the activities of all phases of the work."

This launched several years in which Slacum was the key stimulator of severe agitation in the life of the movement. Unfortunately, beyond the substantive concerns involved, over time there also were as many personalities attacked as there were principles defended. A primary communication vehicle for the opposition was a paper edited by Slacum and called *Watchmen on the Walls*. He included his September sermon in the first issue, sent a copy to every minister listed in the *Yearbook* of the Church of God, and appealed for response "so that some action may be taken. . .to correct this thing." Slacum received enough support that the agitation continued for seven years.

The 1946 General Ministerial Assembly appointed a Committee on Research and Improvement to put an end to all unsupported charges and restore harmony within the church. The investigation included several meetings with Rev. Slacum and his supporters. Also, longtime leader F. G. Smith was elected president of the Gospel Trumpet Company and was asked to return to Anderson from his Ohio pastorate as "Director of Public Relations." He did and traveled the country spreading renewed confidence and stability. Although finding considerable success in his crucial efforts, he died of a heart attack on April 24, 1947. That June the General Ministerial Assembly heard from its committee that most of the personal charges had no apparent basis in fact and that there was no "habitual" relaxation of doctrinal and behaviorial standards. While no out-of-control ecclesiasticism had been found, it was recommended that the agency structures be studied further. Thus, the assembly created the Committee on Revision and Planning that worked over the next several years and passed a resolution reaffirming faith in the national agencies and condemning Slacum for his actions (see Entry 49). Slacum judged that a reprimand and another committee were unfair and inadequate assembly responses, almost a "whitewash" or cover-up of the real problems.

A number of ministers and congregations rallied around Rev. Slacum to constitute a "reformed" reformation or the "Watchman" movement that soon had affiliated with it a Bible School in Plymouth, Indiana and the World Missionary Society of the Church of God newly established in Ashland, Kentucky. In response to this perceived defiance of the General Ministerial Assembly's resolution, Slacum's name was removed from the 1948 *Yearbook* and the Indiana Ministerial Assembly declared him no longer in fellowship with the Church of God movement.

The numbers and organizational complexity of the Slacum movement soon increased until the irony of the situation was more than Slacum could tolerate. His own movement was taking on the same characteristics which he had been criticizing in the Anderson agencies! So in May, 1951, he wrote a letter announcing his displeasure that the new movement of his had developed more structure in five years than Anderson had in twenty-five years! He sought an end to the division and the Watchman movement soon ended. In 1953 he was reunited with the Indiana Assembly of the Church of God. The work of the Committee on Revision and Planning continued and some changes were introduced, stimulated in part by the concerns raised during these years of unfortunate turmoil.

35. The Pastors' Fellowship

by Barry L. Callen, excerpted from his biography of
Rev. Lillie S. McCutcheon, *She Came Preaching*
(Anderson, Ind.: Warner Press, 1992), 288-293.

Lillie S. McCutcheon

One major aspect of the ministry of Sister Lillie McCutcheon to the church nationally was her inspiring and then leading for many years what became known as Pastors' Fellowship. She functioned as the original inspiration and the guiding light of this rather informal and yet rather large and sometimes influential organization within the life of the Church of God movement in the United States. As chair of the Fellowship's national Steering Committee for many years, Sister Lillie was very visible in its operation and deeply appreciated almost as a spiritual mother. There were older ministers who rejoiced at hearing again at regional rallies of this organization the Christian truths that had motivated their ministries for decades. There were younger ministers who sat as admiring disciples both of Christ and of senior leaders, including Lillie McCutcheon who seemed an authentic prophetess in their midst. Together they were looking back in the early teaching tradition of the Church of God movement to rediscover the best way forward. They seemed willing to risk being caught in some cold ashes of the past in exchange for being exposed to the heat of a living flame they believed was more present in the earlier generations of the Church of God movement.

Frequently the judgment was made by critical observers that Pastors' Fellowship was a thrust into theological nostalgia, that too naively it just repeated century-old sermons and sentiments, that in gentle disguise it was for some mostly an effort at gaining control of national church life or, if that failed, creating some new life they did control. But whatever reading was present in any given conversation on this subject, the name of Lillie McCutcheon likely was involved. She was the primary force that had brought into being this annual series of regional gatherings of pastors and other church leaders. She was at its heart and for its first years was its most frequent and respected voice.

142

The occasion of beginning had been in 1972 when the General Assembly of the Church of God, in a very close vote and with Sister Lillie the leader of the opposition, resisted the intent of Anderson University to affiliate the church's seminary with a forming consortium of seminaries in Indianapolis, which included a small Catholic seminary. Officials of the University and about half of the Assembly tended to see resistance to this affiliation as reactionary, an unfortunate attempt to close doors of educational opportunity, ecumenical outreach, and good stewardship of available educational dollars. Sister Lillie and a large body of ministers, while in principle not opposed to education, ecumenicity, or good stewardship, had significant concerns about the general direction the Church of God seemed to be moving in this and other matters. A segment of the church's leaders claimed to feel powerless, not taken seriously. There was concern about a major compromise of theological integrity and even the potential of a major split in the church if the many who felt this way were not somehow brought meaningfully into the larger process of things.

Sister Lillie later put it this way: "I'm the one who started Pastors' Fellowship. Some said I was trying to split the church. I really was trying to hold the church together! I think the general result over the years has been a stabilization of church life. Pastors' Fellowship has tended to hold us together rather than drive us apart." Of course, all would not agree, but Rev. Charles Wood, Sister Lillie's associate minister during those years [Newton Falls, Ohio] who accompanied her to most of the early meetings, was sure of at least a few things. Lillie never did anything for personal gain. She never wanted to encourage a separatist move in the church's life, but a distinctive voice within the church and for the good of the whole church. At times people did press her to speak and act in certain ways because she was seen as one who could be forceful and influential. Yes, she knew she was vulnerable to being "used" on occasion, the risk a leader sometimes has to take. Her central concern, nonetheless, was for the future of the Church of God movement. So many young ministers had little or no anchorage in the "founding truths" of the movement. Without exposure to these truths, she had concluded, they surely would at best only stumble their way into rooted and inspired ministry. Means had to be found to fill this dangerous vacuum.

Paul A. Tanner, retired Executive Secretary of the Executive Council of the Church of God, wrote to Sister Lillie on December 21, 1988, on the occasion of her retirement and said to her: "Few people are aware of the steadying influence you have been in keeping the pendulum from swinging too far either to the left or to the right. It has not always been easy, but you have been faithful." That was indeed an insightful analysis. She loved pastors and she loved the church, all pastors and the whole church. She also had strong convictions and, in the process of maintaining balance, in fact as a key way of maintaining balance, she wanted these convictions to receive a fair and open hearing. She was sure that the best way into the future for everyone involved an appreciative affirmation of key beliefs central to the past heritage of the Church of God. Developments in church life never should ignore or debunk prematurely earlier visions and convictions.

One of these heritage convictions was a strong aversion to denominationalizing God's church, including any sectarianizing of the Church of God movement itself. This conviction encouraged some leaders to believe that a championing of "our distinctive doctrines" was itself an ingrown, narrowing approach, setting the Church of God back many years. But the same conviction encouraged others, often associated with the Pastors' Fellowship, to assert almost the opposite, namely that no one should be captured by the current "headquarters" thinking, policies and programs. All should be free to believe and function as the Spirit directs—and the Spirit was directing them to preach again with boldness a range of classic themes and viewpoints commonly heard in earlier generations of the movement's life.

Rev. Robert Lawrence shared his own view:

> Few people have the courage, concern and conviction to take on 'the establishment' and boldly declare God's truth. Lillie S. McCutcheon is one of those prophetic few. She has reminded us that the Bible is still God's inerrant Word from heaven, that lost people must be born again, that God still wills our sanctification, and that the Bible still calls the saints to come out of the Babylon of denominations to be the Church of God.... She has been the person God has chosen to use to stem encroaching liberalism and lift up truth.

Sister Lillie once offered "A Prayer for Reformation" that made very clear some of the deepest concerns of her heart. She wrote these words in *Reformation Witness*, October, 1988:

> The gospel day is far spent. Awaken the church, we pray, to the sound of the trumpet for the final conquest.... Our souls cry, O Lord, revive the fervor of the Reformation, unite the army of Christians.... You are our Commander at this our Armageddon. Help us make the Reformation alive and continue the proclamation of truth until the God of Elijah brings judgment fire to destroy all evil.

The burden of that prayer probably is understood best in the context of something she wrote in 1981. The saints, she said, need equipped "for battle against deceptive winds of doctrine. Erroneous teachings divide God's children. . .rendering the church impotent." But she went on to caution her readers with this: "One of the most treacherous winds of doctrine in the church today is the *crosswind of individualism.* Heat waves of uncontrolled emotions strike like lightning, setting fires of mistrust and misunderstanding. To talk glibly of a 'split' in the movement may be an evidence of ulterior motives." So, in the March 8, 1981 issue of *Vital Christianity,* she concluded, "Some who speak in such a manner are already carried away with a desire for their own independent kingdom and seek for some spiritual failure in the movement to justify their action of withdrawal" (3). Her goal was to highlight truth, not to lead a revolt.

No one felt herself more loyal to the Church of God movement as a whole than Sister Lillie. She was committed to its institutions and corporate ministries. This was seen in the Newton Falls congregation's liberal giving to the national budget of the Church of God over the years and the superb service given to the church's Board of Pensions by both her husband Glenn McCutcheon and then her son Robert McCutcheon. But she also felt free to minister and support ministry wherever and however God might direct. She risked, on the one hand, an ad hoc church polity which permitted the launching of the volunteeristic Pastors' Fellowship movement and her visible support of the para-church ministry Project Partner With Christ. On the other hand, she was so aware that the Church of God needed more cohesion, increasingly organized and energized effort to reach out and make a difference in the future....

This combination of loyalty to and yet freedom from the "official institutions" of the Church of God is an example of the highest vision and the deepest dilemma of this movement. Sister Lillie embodied very clearly both the vision and the dilemma. She was completely loyal, but never passively in line. Doing things efficiently and together was only sensible in her view; building any self-serving and restrictive church establishment, however, was to be resisted at whatever personal price in the name of the best of the teaching heritage of the Church of God and for the sake of successful Christian mission. This was a delicate, sometimes awkward, often misunderstood middle way. She saw it as the only way. She saw it as very "Church of God" to be cooperative and accountable, and yet remain free to serve the whole church as God might direct.

Editor's Note: The mission statement of the Pastors' Fellowship speaks of a burden "for faithful and on-going preaching, re-preaching, declaration and dissemination of those doctrines and teachings that brought this Reformation Movement of the Church of God into existence. It is our purpose and mission to continue, by every means available, to carry this same vision to our generation and those who follow" (as printed in *Reformation Witness*, Spring 1999). The periodical *Reformation Witness*, currently edited by A. Wayne Burch, and Reformation Publishers operated by publisher Steven V. Williams, have emerged as two of the means for carrying out the mission of Pastors' Fellowship.

36. Reforming the School of Theology
(1972-1976)

Editor's Note: In the first years of the 1970s, Anderson University School of Theology, the seminary of the Church of God, was in transition and became the subject of considerable controversy in the General Assembly. To review this, under the caption "Christian Higher Education" see the several seminary-related actions of the General Assembly between 1972 and 1976.

Founding leaders of Anderson School of Theology.
Standing, L. to R.: T. Franklin Miller, Burt E. Coody, John W. V. Smith,
Adam W. Miller, Robert A. Nicholson.
Kneeling, L. to R.: Robert H. Reardon, Gene W. Newberry, Harold L. Phillips.

37. Before the Sun Sets

by Charles E. Brown.
Appeared as the article "Objectives of the Reformation"
in the *Gospel Trumpet*, May 4, 1940.

When we observe that the spiritual element in Christendom has been laboring for reform for eight hundred years, it gives us a sense of pain to see around us a Christianity which seems to have lost nearly all this great historic religious urge. Even in our own group [Church of God movement] there are those who object to the term "reformation," although that was a precious word to the heroic men and women who preceded us in this work some sixty years ago. We seem to live in an age where the caravans of Christianity are glad to rest, each in its little oasis of methods, budgets, building programs, regular services—counting its gains in percentages, glad enough to break even, anxious to keep the good will of the public, fearful of violating any of the fine points of etiquette, and forgetting entirely the high calls of sacrificial service and deathless devotion which have hummed in the ears of all the great saints of the past.

We are told that it is only a hopeless task to journey toward and seek to realize the Apostolic Church and its form, experience, and doctrine. To this we reply that first, even if we could not immediately realize our objective, it is in a search like this that all of the church's dynamic possibilities are made real. For centuries the great saints of evangelical Christianity have accomplished their miracles of service to humanity, simply because they were in search of the Apostolic Church. Even if they did not realize their goal, think of the good they did in attempting to do so.

At first thought, it seems that we might rest easier if we gave up our great task which seems to many an impossible one. To this, the answer is that if we gave up this task we should find many little tasks which would simply break our hearts. In fact, I think many of us would have our hearts broken as soon as we gave up this great undertaking. We should not find rest; instead we would find despair.

Again, I would like to say that the objectives that this reformation has set before itself are of two kinds. First, it has always believed that any local congregation could come to realize the three goals of the Apostolic Church within its own membership. That is to say, it could be a church with the apostolic experience, the New Testament doctrine, and the spiritual democracy of the primitive church. At the present day we believe that this ideal has been realized to a greater or lesser extent in hundreds of congregations, and is in process of continuous realization.

Second, this reformation has taught that this work must continue until the whole of genuine Christendom shall realize these three ideals of the Apostolic Church. Now that is a challenge to our faith, a challenge greater than some of us seem able to answer. Nevertheless, if we take earnestly and seriously the prayer of our Lord that we all may be one, we believe this ideal to be not only within the range of possibility, but it is an accomplishment toward which the Lord Jesus Christ has himself set his hand, and which he will see realized ultimately, whether we continue to co-operate in his purposes or fail him through our unbelief. With the reformers of the 1880s, we confidently take our stand in the unshaken conviction that the prayer of Christ for the organic unity of his people shall be fulfilled before the sun of history shall set.

Editor's Note: For further development of Dr. Brown's view of the apostolic ideal, see his book *The Apostolic Church,* 1947.

38. Abandon Our Theories of Prophecy

by Barry L. Callen, concerning the life and critical reflections of
Charles W. Naylor

Charles Wesley Naylor (1874-1950) is thought by some to have been a giant among Church of God persons, although at his death after many years of physical disability he was buried in Anderson, Indiana, largely isolated from the community of faith he loved. Born in Ohio and first becoming a Methodist, he was soon influenced by the Church of God preachers Barney Warren and Samuel Speck and joined the reformation movement in 1893. Ordained in 1899, he was an energetic traveler and prolific reporter, poet, columnist, and author. He had genuine enthusiasm for "the cause" of the Church of God movement.

Trouble came early and severely. In 1908 Naylor was seriously injured while helping with heavy timbers under a tent at a meeting in Sidney, Florida. The next year a further injury while riding in a truck compounded the first, with devastating results. Naylor would be confined to a bed for the rest of his life in Anderson, Indiana. Nonetheless, his mind was alive, his interests broad, and his spirits inspired by his sturdy Christian faith. Over the years he wrote about 150 gospel songs and hundreds of articles for Church of God publications. The songs included the basic "marching songs" of the Church of God movement: "The Church Has One Foundation"; "O Church of God"; "The Reformation Glory"; and "The Church's Jubilee." A total of twenty-five of his songs appear in the 1989 hymnal of the Church of God, *Worship the Lord.* A bestseller was his book *The Secret of the Singing Heart,* 1930.

Otto F. Linn

In the early 1940s Naylor took careful note of the recently published work of Otto F. Linn which provided an alternate interpretation of the Book of Revelation from the "standard" approach of F. G. Smith. He decided to review the whole matter and take a critical look at some of the major biblical interpretations espoused by D. S. Warner and others in the early days of the movement. He was candid in calling into question much of the prophetic perspective used by Warner to locate and validate the Church of God movement.

Reformation conservatives were highly displeased with this new analysis of Naylor and the officers of the Gospel Trumpet Company wanted no part in publishing Naylor's booklet. So it was published privately (n.d., 1942?) under the title "The Teachings of D. S. Warner and His Associates" and was circulated with the help of a "Committee On Distribution" (appreciative friends of Naylor).

Naylor notes in this publication that Brother Warner assumed the imminence of the second advent of Christ and the end of the world. On this primary assumption, according to Naylor, rested all of Warner's prophetic teaching and that related to the reformation itself. *Now* was the "day of his preparation." The year 1880 was accounted by Warner a "prophetic year" and marked the beginning of the work of preparation for the advent of Christ. Recalls Naylor: "Since only Brother Warner and the few associated with him 'saw the light,' upon them was laid the responsibility of proclaiming it and bringing about 'the reformation' of the church, which must needs come at once." Since, however, Naylor had now concluded that "our movement has no chronological setting in the Scriptures," he proceeded to reevaluate generally the whole prophetic scheme that, at least until the 1940s, had become so much a part of the self-identity and preaching of the Church of God movement. Following are excerpts from Naylor's booklet "The Teachings of D. S. Warner and His Associates."

I know that the more truth is investigated the brighter it shines, therefore I have had no hesitation in seeking to know to the limit of my capacity the facts, and all the facts, that I might discover. I have earnestly and prayerfully sought the truth without respect to what anyone else thought, believed, or taught. Truth will stand by itself; it needs no support. It vindicates itself, so I have sought it eagerly and without restraint....

I knew D. S. Warner and loved him with reverential affection.... I knew nearly all of the ministers who were associated with him.... I agree with all those principles we have taught that are clearly taught in the New Testament.... [Warner's] teaching on a pure and spiritual church, incarnating anew the Christ and speaking to the world as the voice of God, was a potent message which should remain central in all our teaching.... It is chiefly the field of prophetic interpretation and application that seems to demand rethinking....

"Threshing Babylon" never was God's plan. It did a great deal of harm. It created a great deal of prejudice, most of which was unnecessary. It has greatly hindered our work. What we said about the denominations and their preachers was often slanderous. We might as well face this. I am glad that most of us have stopped that sort of preaching.... Brother Warner had an extreme view of unity. He advocated a type of unity that never existed, and never can exist in this world. He was sincere and thoroughly believed what he taught, but we have seen the necessity of modifying his teachings to make them conform more nearly to the possibility....

149

We are not the only body of people who claim that the church ceased to exist during the Apostasy and had to be reconstituted. Some of the Baptist bodies teach this same thing; likewise, the Mormons, the Seventh Day Adventists, the Church of Christ, the Russellites, a number of holiness sects and other bodies, all teach that to them was given the task of reconstituting the lost church. They have built up bodies which they claim are the church. Nothing outside their bodies is the church. Our claim is on a par with theirs. I think we shall do well to see what effects their making such claims has had upon them in making them feel superior to others, proud of their movement, intolerant. When their attention is called to others who make the same claim that they make, they say, "Oh, but they are wrong; we are right. God has called us to re-establish his church, not them." Let us be warned by their example....

I am not a pessimist nor a kill-joy, but I know that indulging in rosy daydreams that are impossible of realization is futile. I am a realist and like to look the facts of any situation squarely in the face and adjust myself to those facts rather than ignore them.... Brother Warner expected all Christians to be brought into this movement in a single generation—this I know from his own lips.... His expectations are not only far from being realized, but they have not even begun to be realized.... One can be a member of a denomination and yet be wholly unsectarian. On the other hand, one can be undenomninational or antidenominational and still be thoroughly sectarian. The task of reuniting Christians is a most difficult task, and it will take a long time; but it must be done by all means by which it can be accomplished.

I love our movement. I have given my life to it. I love its people. They are my dearest friends. I expect to end my days on earth in this movement and to contribute all I possibly can to its advancement. But I long to see it freed from the things that have impeded its progress and have caused it to be misunderstood. I am sure that better, richer, more glorious days lie ahead of us for we are making genuine progress and getting rid of many of the things that have stood in our way.

If we would stop preaching our theories of prophecy which few will ever believe, and with power preach salvation, righteous living, true unity, a spiritual church—and exemplify these things—we would prosper and be blessed as at no past time, and our message would not be misunderstood as it has been so far. The way of victory is the way of simple, plain, gospel truth, loved, preached, and lived in the Bible way. If instead of being doctrine-centered or movement-centered we would become more and more Christ-centered, we would find many of our problems automatically solved and the glow of holy fervor would melt all hearts together.

Editor's Note: See the 1983 thesis done at Anderson University School of Theology by Robert E. Koeth and titled "A History of Anti-Catholicism in the Church of God Reformation Movement."

39. How Right Were Our Pioneers?

by Albert F. Gray.
Excerpted from the *Gospel Trumpet*, January 7, 1950.

It is not enough for us to say that we stand for the grand old truths preached by D. S. Warner. It is well to take stock to determine just how much meaning we can honestly give to that statement. There may be among us those who "garnish the sepulchers of the prophets" who would stone them if they were alive. We do not seek to be Warnerites; we should feel bound to disagree with Brother Warner to whatever extent he may be found out of harmony with the truth. If there be disagreements which are fundamental, effecting the central theme of his message, then we should repudiate both him and his message. The question with us is this: Was this movement in its fundamental aspects, as established by our early brethren, the work of God, or was it the result of a misdirected zeal?

Many people mistakenly believe that these early brethren held that this movement as such is the Church of God. On the contrary, they maintained stoutly that the Church of God *includes all the saved,* both those among us and those not associated with us. They referred to the movement as a reformation—the "last reformation." They felt that in this movement is found the ideal demonstration of the church in unity, which ideal would eventually envelop the entire body of Christ. Any confusion over the Church of God as the universal body of the saved and the Church of God as referring to a group of people as distinct from other Christians is of later origin.

It was the sincere belief of these brethren that God had especially raised up a group of ministers to effect a great reformation in the church. In all humility they accepted this responsibility. They had no intention of starting a new organization or of securing for themselves positions of leadership or power. Some of the brethren fully expected the return of Christ during their lifetime. They believed that, in preparation for that event, all of God's people would be gathered out of sectism so that the bride might be ready to meet the bridegroom. We know that Christ did not come as they expected he would, and judging by our preaching on the subject (or lack of it), the return of Christ does not seem as immanent to us as it did to them.

We know, too, that sinners are still being saved outside of this movement and that there are probably more Christians in the denominations now than when we first began calling them out. It is evident that God's people will not be freed from sectism as rapidly as these brethren expected, and perhaps not altogether by the process by which they expected it to be done. In view of their great sense of divine mission, and their great faith in the message, it should not be hard for us to overlook their extravagant expectations.

The appeal to prophesy in support of a position is a common practice today and was indulged in quite extensively by our early brethren. We have come to recognize that the practice of spiritualizing employed by them is not good exegesis, and we have felt compelled to discard some of their interpretations. However, the fact that these interpretations were of questionable value does not invalidate the position they were intended to support. Whether this movement is of divine origin does not depend on the interpretation of a prophecy, but rather on the truthfulness of its message and the results that it achieves.

The extreme anti-organization attitude of our early brethren resulted from their failure to differentiate between organizations that are divisive, breaking fellowship and destroying Christian liberty, and those that make possible the voluntary cooperation of Christians in the things that we can do best together. They did not always distinguish between the more common-place things which we may plan ourselves and the more spiritual things in which divine guidance is necessary. Believing as they did in a life completely controlled by the Spirit, they saw little need of human plans. So long as the work was small and in the hands of strong spiritual leaders whose guidance was sought and gladly accepted, there was little need for organization.

With the growth of the work there arose problems of cooperation which required planning and organization. We have come to feel that to plan together to carry on our work is not a mark of division but quite the opposite. We should not fail to recognize, however, that these early brethren saw real danger in human organization and man rule, for such danger *did* exist and *still* exists. Whenever human authority invades the sacred relations between men and their God or between Christians in the realm of spiritual fellowship, or stifles the conscience of the believer, or makes demands not agreeable with the Word of God, it has exceeded its right and become a mark of apostasy.

While our early brethren held to the position (and, to a large extent, to the practice) of extending fellowship to all who possess the spirit of Christ, they felt that all such persons would readily see and accept the truth concerning the church and the unity God's people. In their zeal for the truth they were sometimes too insistent and forced the issue before people were prepared to make a decision; and thus, alas, some were driven from the truth who might have been won with more brotherly treatment. At times these brethren became unwittingly responsible for division in their effort to cure it—a fault from which not all of us have yet found freedom.

In their effort to bring about unity, these early brethren demanded a uniformity of doctrine and practice which went beyond that required by the Bible. They felt that they must see "eye to eye" in almost everything and hence left little room for difference of opinion [see the "eye-to-eye" articles by Daniel Warner in Entry 27]. The standards held sometimes encroached on Christian freedom. To them unity was more important than individual liberty.

In criticizing the excesses that existed among our early brethren we are doing *just what they would do if they were still alive.* It was always their expressed intention to walk in clearer light as it comes. Changes did occur in the first few years of the movement affecting unimportant doctrines. These brethren soon repudiated some of their own prophetic interpretations when they saw they were not sound. Doubtless they expected progress for they sang, "Purer light is coming fast." We do well to hold the same attitude.

40. Marks of Movement Greatness

From *The Early Morning Light* by Robert H. Reardon, (Anderson, Ind.: Warner Press, 1979), 88-94.

During the 1941 Anderson Camp Meeting dinner to honor the three oldest then-living pioneers of the early work of the Gospel Trumpet Company (E. E. Byrum, N. H. Byrum, and B. E. Warren).
L. to R.: C. E. Byers, J. A. Morrison, H. M. Riggle, N. H. Byrum, B. E. Warren,
A. T. Rowe (standing), E. A. Reardon, C. E. Brown, Raymond Jackson, and F. G. Smith.

Now looking back over this past half-century, what are the marks of greatness which emerge in our movement? Do we have any great stars left in the sky? Yes! I shall touch briefly on a few.

1. *The Centrality of Christ.* Daniel Warner and our other pioneers had a high Christology. Christ was savior, Christ was healer, Christ was Lord and guide, Christ was teacher, Christ

was head of the Church. We may smile at many of the strange ways in which this came to be expressed, but one can never honestly search the record and come up with any other conclusion than that our forefathers had a deep, relentless, searching hunger after Christ and a profound commitment to be like him in spirit and conduct. This expressed itself in earnest prayer, constant study of the life of Christ, and the most humbling expressions of dedication I have ever known.

2. *People of the Covenant.* Central also in early Church of God teaching was the biblical concept that God has acted in history to bring into being a people, called by his name, through whom he was going to attempt in a special way to do his redemptive work. This ancient article of faith, born in the time of Abraham and fulfilled in the commissioning of the early church, is as valid today as it has ever been. It is this ancient root system that anchors our movement into the vast, universal, catholic church. It is here, rather than in any prophetic scheme, that we discover today who and what we are and what our mission is to be.

3. *Freedom from Sectarian Bondage.* There was the strong ring of truth in our early preaching that called for the redeemed to renounce every vestige of sectishness and step out into a life of freedom to join heart and hand with every child of God on the face of the earth. Seen against the shameful denominational quarreling and bickering of the 1880s and the high creedal and organizational walls of the times, this was an exciting and exhilarating stand to take. Naylor, our foremost doctrinal songwriter, wrote:

> The Church that was built when Pentecost came,
> The Church that is kept in one faith and one Name,
> Shall shine on resplendent, forever the same;
> I'll never go back, I'll never go back.

This membership in the great family of God through the new birth, standing in Christ alone, reaching hands in fellowship to every blood-washed one, is still a powerful, scriptural, and compelling idea. We have existed now for nearly a hundred years without church joining and its false securities. The idea is sound and needs to be shared.

154

4. *Spontaneity.* Although there was a great deal of freewheeling in the early days in our common worship, still there was a refreshing spontaneity and excitement. Church was where the action was: testimonies to salvation, witnesses to miraculous healing, ringing songs of victory, powerful and stirring preaching, lives being saved and transformed. When it went to excess—as J. A. Morrison used to say, "whopping it up"—it was a disgrace. At their best, however, these services were a powerful relief from the crusty, dead, formal rituals that were standard fare in most denominations. It would be great to recapture it at its best.

5. *Central Place of the Word.* The pioneers were first, last, and always students of the Bible. It was the written *Word* that gave authority; the *Word* that was the vehicle of the light; the *Word* that spoke to the kind of lives we were to lead; the *Word* which provided guidance, direction, and food for the soul. Fortunately, the movement never got caught up in the great fundamentalist controversies that rocked the religious world early in the century. Nonetheless, a part of our greatness in the past has been derived from a diligent study of the Word. No renewal of the life of our movement will come any other way.

6. *A Deep and Relentless Hunger for the Presence and Power of the Holy Spirit.* I have spoken earlier of some of our excesses in handling the biblical doctrine of sanctification. This beautiful gift to believers sets their life apart for the Lord, strengthens and empowers them for service, assures them of the undergirding presence of the Holy Spirit, and purifies their inner being. It is one of the great treasures of the Church of Jesus Christ. Rightly and sanely understood, it bears witness to one of the timeless hungers of humanity—the yearning after holiness.

7. *Richness of Inspired Hymns and Spiritual Songs.* One of the great legacies of our movement is our treasury of songs. The entire theology of the Church of God could be reconstructed from such songbooks as *Reformation Glory* (1923). A whole cadre of songwriters made their appearance in the first twenty-five years. Warner, Byers, Teasley, Warren, and Naylor flooded the publishing company with exciting music. One of the most attractive features of our early work was the singing. Accompanying most evangelists was a troupe of singers who

155

sang enthusiastically in railroad stations, street corners, homes, schoolhouses, and nearly anywhere. It was ringing, boisterous music, and it attracted and inspired people everywhere. Dozens of songbooks came off our presses....

8. *A Clear, Authentic Vision of the Church.* This vision of the people of God which fired Warner and his associates asked for a "called out" community of the firstborn, the entire congregation of the redeemed, with Christ as the head, the door, the energizer, the organizer, the Lord who sets the members in the Body, distributing gifts and callings through his wisdom. Through the years this biblical view of the church has held solid as the Rock of Gibraltar and its truth has not been shaken. It is the only basis upon which true unity between Christians can come. We need not fear that such a foundation will erode with the passage of time.

9. *A Global Vision.* From the earliest days our leaders saw theirs as a global mission, one destined in H. M. Riggle's familiar phrase to "encircle the globe." Something dynamic and exciting had broken into their time, and their vision was to get the message out to the whole world. It was to this task that the presses at the Gospel Trumpet Company were dedicated as they turned out tons of Christian literature that found its way into country after country around the world. This vision of great adventures and victories for God challenged the pioneers to new and creative methods of evangelism and outreach. It was carried forward with loyalty and devotion. It captured the imagination. It engendered boundless enthusiasm which swept aside the little currents of extremism, and brought the saints to their feet at camp meeting as they sang, "There's a mighty reformation sweeping o'er the land" and "I'm on the winning side."

Editor's Note: Also see Robert Reardon's 1943 thesis for Oberlin Graduate School of Theology and titled "The Doctrine of the Church and the Christian Life in the Church of God Reformation Movement."

THE GENERAL ASSEMBLY
UNITED STATES AND CANADA, 1917–2000

Editor's Note: The primary focus of the life of the Church of God movement is intentionally placed at the level of the local congregation. Increasingly, however, congregations join with other congregations to pursue cooperative ministries. In recent decades such cooperation has been prominent at the level of state or area assemblies. Some of these assemblies have developed to the point that they need to employ a state minister or area administrator.

Now there is an *Association of Area Administrators*, a fellowship of those persons who have been designated by their respective state or area assemblies to serve those assemblies in executive administrative leadership. Responsibilities typically include ministerial credentialling, camp meetings, evangelism and church planting, and other cooperative ministries beyond the local congregation and other than those pursued at the national and international levels. These administrators meet together at least annually. Following is a list of the current North American assemblies which employ such administrators and thus through them participate in this Association.

Assemblies	Administrators
Alabama	Anthony Weiger
Arizona	James Cox
California—Northern (includes Hawaii, Northern Nevada)	Cynthia James
California—Southern	David Winn
Canada—Eastern	Arthur Krueger
Canada—Western	John Campbell
Chesapeake/Delaware/Potomac	Wayne Harting
Florida	John Boedeker
Georgia	Paul Rider
Illinois	David Hall
Iowa	Clyde Castleton
Indiana	Richard Shockey, Dewayne Repass

Assemblies	Administrators
Kansas	William Ramser
Kentucky	Charles Shrewsbury
Louisiana	Raymond Cheeks
Michigan	Gerald Nevitt, Kenneth Wiedrick
Mississippi	Lloyd Bowen
Missouri	Jim Duncan
North Carolina	Maxine McCall
Ohio	Vernon Maddox
Oregon	Samuel Dunbar, Bill Martin
Pennsylvania—West	Vernon Allison
Pennsylvania—East (Boyertown)	Harold Kaefer
Tennessee	Arley Cravens
Texas	Marvin Sanders
Virginia	Donald Neace
Washington	Jerry Phillips

From the first generation of Church of God leaders, there has been a world vision calls Christians together in ministry. Soon there were regular gatherings of ministers to discuss and even plan for the work of the church. Early into the twentieth century this pattern evolved into what now is the General Assembly of the Church of God (United States and Canada).

I. THE GENERAL ASSEMBLY: INTRODUCTION

The General Assembly of the Church of God (United States and Canada) is not a standard denominational body that exercises governance and establishes doctrine and policy for the movement as a whole, and especially not for its state, regional, and provincial assemblies and its local congregations. Nonetheless, it is the most representative body of the Church of God movement in North America and as such has been very important in the movement's life since 1917. The materials in this part of the book introduce the reader to the central aspects of the Assembly's life and work across the twentieth century. It has acted and spoken often and on a wide range of issues. While it cannot be said that the General Assembly speaks officially for the Church of God movement, the Assembly certainly has been a major voice speaking to the movement and sometimes from the movement to the wider church and society.

Position and action statements made by this Assembly are widely regarded within the Church of God movement, especially in North America. For example, note the following from the ministerial of the *Credentials Manual,* prepared and administered by the Congregational Ministries division of Church of God Ministries:

> This *Credentials Manual* does not attempt to list or reproduce the many historic actions of the General Assembly of the Church of God that may bear on the standards by which ministers in the Church of God are recognized, advised, and disciplined. It does, however, acknowledge the existence and potential relevance of such Assembly actions in given circumstances (7-8).

The content of all such actions follows.

41. Parallel to a Local Church Business Meeting

by Russell R. Byrum, as in the 1922 *Yearbook* of the
Church of God (Anderson, Indiana), 6.

The General Ministerial Assembly of the Church of God[1] is the ministers of the church at the International Camp Meeting assembled in business session. The General Ministerial Assembly is for the purpose of giving general direction to the business and to the various business agencies of the church in general. It sustains practically the same relation to the general church that a business session of a local congregation sustains to the local church. As the local church assembled in business session discusses and determines its business policies in a general way, and appoints financial officers, trustees, or other business agencies for the accomplishment of its work, so the General Ministerial Assembly discusses and determines in a general way what general business interests the church shall conduct and appoints certain men to be responsible for the carrying out of certain business policies. For example, it elects the twenty-four members of the Gospel Trumpet Company, the members of the Church Extension Board, and the registrar of the Clergy Bureau.

---

1. In 1965 the word "ministerial" was removed from the Assembly's name, as increasing numbers of laypersons were being included in the Assembly's membership. See Entries 53, 56, 59, and 64.

It is also parallel with the local church business meeting in that it has no power to determine standards of doctrine or practice, to confer ministerial authority upon any one, to appoint ministers to particular fields, or to do any other thing that is properly the work of the Holy Spirit in his church. Its officers consist of a chairman and a secretary and it is organized under constitution and bylaws according to common parliamentary practice. Only ordained ministers have the franchise.

42. A Modest Beginning Motivated by Need

by Marvin J. Hartman

Editor's Note: This historical reflection by Marvin J. Hartman is excerpted from his B. D. thesis submitted to the School of Religion of Butler University, Indianapolis, Indiana, 1958, and titled "The Origin and Development of the General Ministerial Assembly of the Church of God, 1917-1950." The report by Charles E. Brown is based on a Hartman interview with Brown, October, 1957.

Much of the information concerning the background of the General Ministerial Assembly has been lost in the history of the movement. Because there was no organization, much of the discussion that took place in the early ministers' meetings was never written down. Indeed, there seems to have been an aversion to writing deliberations down. One wonders if this was not done because it may have been an indication that there was not full and strong unity. It must have been frustrating for those who believed so strongly in the unity of the saints to have to admit that the saints did not always agree.

Although it was not until 1917 that the General Ministerial Assembly officially organized, there were, prior to that time, what were called "general assemblies." These seemed to have a pattern across the church of taking place whenever a group of ministers got together to discuss their work. As early as 1902, at Yellow Lake, Indiana, this happened. Charles E. Brown reports:

> The first Assembly that I remember attending took place at the Yellow Lake Camp Meeting in 1902. The ministers present at the camp meeting assembled in the men's dormitory and sat around on the beds and talked. The only touch of a formal organization in this meeting was the appointment by this informal gathering of one man to represent the group in talking to the railroads concerning the availability of clergy rates.

160

Dr. Brown suggests that 1917 is only the formalizing date of an already existing organization. As early as 1906, there was always held—in connection with the Anderson Camp Meeting—a general assembly. This, indeed, was like the other general assemblies that took place whenever ministers got together. The main interest in these general assemblies was preaching. Influential ministers would exhort and encourage the brethren along the lines of the true doctrine. Sometimes in these early assemblies a discussion would take place. The discussion generally would go far enough along to start drawing various differences of opinion. Frequently, at this point "one of the more influential brethren would stand and say, 'Now, brethren, this is the way we believe the question.'"

Evidence of the significant role played by the Gospel Trumpet Company is seen in the very first meeting of the temporary organization of the assembly which was held on June 14, 1917. At this meeting, the Gospel Trumpet Company submitted a slate of nominees for company membership. This was significant because prior to this time the company membership was chosen in a self-perpetuating manner. This change was a wise move. It gave the ministry a feeling of participation, and set a precedent, both legal and moral, for future organizations tied legally with the assembly to have their membership likewise elected by the assembly [in 1995 such elections would be changed to ratifications of prior board elections]. Although the voting was done by yes and no votes on a slate of twenty-four candidates, there was remarkable unity at this first thrust of responsibility.

The other modest business taken care of in that first General Ministerial Assembly meeting is shown in the following items listed from the minutes of that first meeting (June 14, 1917):

A motion was made that in the temporary organization only ordained ministers of the Church of God have the right to vote. Motion seconded. Motion carried.

Motion was made and seconded that all ordained ministers of the Church of God in the congregation be requested to rise and stand for purposes of identification. Motion carried.

A motion was made and seconded that a majority of votes of the Assembly shall be sufficient for election to any office for which the Assembly may hold election. Motion carried.

Motion that voting and elections be by ballot. Motion seconded. Motion carried.

Motion that members of the Gospel Trumpet Company who are ordained ministers have a right to vote in this Assembly. Motion seconded. Motion carried.

Motion moved and seconded that the chair appoint a committee of five to draft a constitution and a permanent set of bylaws to govern the Assembly. Motion carried. [The five were J. W. Phelps, A. B. Frost, H. A. Sherwood, O. E. Line, R. R. Byrum. These names were written in pen, in long-hand in the minutes, with these two words after their names: "were appointed."]

Temporary organization was effected by nominating R. L. Berry, A. T. Rowe, and E. A. Reardon as chairmen pro tem. E. A. Reardon was elected.

Since the Anderson Camp Meeting in these early days was ten days long, the committee to draft the constitution and bylaws had time to work on that task. Evidently for this reason there were no other meetings of the Assembly for a week. Then on June 21 the report of the committee on the constitution was read and approved.

The *Gospel Trumpet* gave considerable space to comment on the 1917 General Ministerial Assembly. It, no doubt, was concerned with reaffirming in the minds of the ministers who were there the wisdom of this step, and also in communicating to those who were not there exactly what happened. There would always be a danger that some of those who were against organization might misrepresent or misquote to those who were not there. Therefore, the brethren were prompted to give considerable space to this historic 1917 meeting. Indeed, while the meeting was going on, the *Trumpet* said in the June 28 issue (no doubt written a week prior to its publication), the following:

> All things of the meeting have been marked by a sweet spirit of unity that is most convincing to those who visit these camp grounds that God is truly in our midst.
>
> The business interests of the church are receiving more careful attention than ever before. The Lord has given the ministry a larger vision of our unparalleled opportunities for spreading the pure gospel to the end of the earth. A deep desire is manifested to see a great forward movement along lines of activity and gospel work—both in the homeland and in the foreign fields. Our vision is not localized, but worldwide in its scope and purpose. In order to insure a sound financial basis for these increased activities, better business methods are being considered for the future than we have been accustomed to in the past.
>
> It has also been felt for some time that there should be a more direct legal relationship existing between the publishing work and the general body of the ministry. Steps have been taken to place this great work in more immediate touch with the ministry, and thereby increase their responsibility for and their interest in this important phase of gospel work. New members have been added to the Gospel Trumpet Company, increasing the number to twenty-four. These

twenty-four names were ratified by a vote of the ministers in session at the present camp meeting.

The motivating drive and power which characterized all the development of the organizational machinery of the General Ministerial Assembly seemed to be one of "need." To do the work of God, the early leaders discovered they had to "render unto Caesar" in some areas. The government—local, state, and national—made certain requirements regarding corporations, holding real and personal property, and so forth. The railroad needed a sponsoring national agency to clear membership of clergy for discount in rail travel. The boards and agencies were forced to comply with certain restrictions, which in turn affected the assembly. In short, the General Ministerial Assembly found it could not do the work of the Lord unorganized in a highly organized society. Many times, as the organizational pattern was developing, the thread-worn (but nonetheless, answer of the hour) phrase, "We can organize the work of the church but not the church," was marshaled in defense of the developing organization at Anderson.

43. Constitutional Guidelines

Editor's Note: The following three Articles are from the
Constitution and Bylaws of the General Assembly, 1998 revision.
The remaining ten Articles are not reproduced here.

ARTICLE I: Name

The name of this body is the *General Assembly of the Church of God* (hereinafter referred to in this Constitution and Bylaws as *Assembly*), with general offices located in Anderson, Indiana.

ARTICLE II: Purpose of the Assembly

The purpose of this Assembly shall be to function as a temporary presbytery in the conduct of (1) the general business of the Church of God in the United States and [in certain regards] Canada and (2) its annual International Convention. In the ongoing fulfillment of this purpose it shall provide for and devise measures to create and maintain a legally incorporated coordinating body, Church of God Ministries, governed by a Ministries Council accountable to the General Assembly in ways specified below.

ARTICLE III: Voluntary Association

This Assembly shall be regarded as a voluntary association. It shall not exercise ecclesiastical jurisdiction or authority over the Church of God in general or over individual congregations in particular. It shall, however, retain the right of a voluntary association to define its own membership and to declare, on occasion, when individual ministers or congregations are not recognized by the Assembly as adhering to the general reformation principles to which the Assembly itself is committed. See Entries 72 and 73 below for identification of these principles.

44. Elected Chairs of the General Assembly, 1917-2000

Editor's Note: The following persons have been elected by the Assembly to function as its Chairs over the years. They represent some of the best known, loved, and trusted leaders of the movement.

Samuel G. Hines

E. A. Reardon	1917–1919
Robert L. Berry	1919–1923
J. Grant Anderson	1923–1925
Charles E. Brown	1925–1927
Joseph T. Wilson	1927–1929
Charles E. Brown	1929–1931
Joseph T. Wilson	1931–1932
E. E. Perry	1932–1934
Albert F. Gray	1934–1936
Joseph T. Wilson	1936–1939
Albert F. Gray	1939–1954
Harold W. Boyer	1954–1968
Arlo F. Newell	1968–1974
Leonard Snyder	1974–1975
Arlo F. Newell	1975–1977
Paul L. Hart	1977–1983
Samuel G. Hines	1983–1989
Oral Withrow	1989–1990
G. David Cox	1990–1996
Robert A. Culp	1996 to present

45. Observations of a Longtime Assembly Member

Excerpts of the comments requested by and made to the General Assembly by Robert H. Reardon, President Emeritus of Anderson University (made near the conclusion of the Assembly's 1992 sessions).

Robert H. Reardon
Anderson University

I have attended this Assembly for forty-one years. There have been some years when we were so fearful of each other that we were afraid to talk. I thank God for the way we now are able to speak our minds and not be afraid of one another. That says to me something about the maturity of this Assembly—and that means a great deal to me.

My father, E. A. Reardon, was the first Chair of this Assembly. Once he came and made a speech to the Assembly in which he talked about a sectish spirit that was developing among us. We were building some high walls around ourselves, which never were intended to be. He was very blunt and it made a lot of the pastors in the Assembly very angry. They gathered in little knots, out under the trees on the campgrounds. They discussed what he said and they implied a lot of things in their discussions that he never said. At any rate, when they took the next vote, my father was voted off the Missionary Board, where he had been a charter member. He lost his office as a member of the Board of Anderson College and Bible School.

When the voting results were posted, it was the usual practice that all the ministers went by to see who got elected and who lost—and this time my father lost. So when the Assembly met the next day, everybody wondered what Dr. Reardon was going to say. He walked in, got recognized from the Chair, stood up in that Assembly and said, "Well, I've been over and looked at the Assembly vote. I see you voted me off both of these boards." There was dead silence. "I just have one thing to say to you," he continued. "The Assembly gave, the Assembly has taken away, blessed be the name of the Assembly." The next year they voted him back on!

There is a second event in this Assembly's history that I want us to recall. It always moves me very deeply. Brother F. G. Smith was the Editor of the Gospel Trumpet Company from 1917 to 1930. This man put a theological spine in the Church of God movement with his book, *What The Bible Teaches*. He surely used the power of the pen and effectively used his influence during his editorship. But as time went on there had begun to be in the Assembly a growing uneasiness about the centralizing of that much power.

So in 1930 the twenty-four members of the publishing company did not agree to re-elect Brother Smith as Editor, the most powerful office in our movement at the time. They then asked themselves the question, "Who are we going to put forward?" Now Brother Riggle was the Billy Graham of the Church of God, a powerful evangelist. They asked him. Brother Riggle agreed to be their candidate. They sent his name across to the Assembly to be ratified. The Assembly said "no." So the twenty-four went back and asked Brother C. E. Brown. He said, "I will do it on the condition that Brother F. G. Smith walk across the street with me and openly support the election." Brother Smith rose in the Assembly and did the gentlemanly thing, the honorable thing, the thing which showed where his love and loyalty really were. He supported Brother Brown, who became a very successful editor.

That is what makes an Assembly an effective Christian body. It is an evidence of the way the Holy Spirit works. It is a wonderful example of what charismatic church government is all about. Let us always proceed together in such a way.

II. GENERAL ASSEMBLY: POSITION AND ACTION RESOLUTIONS

Editor's Note: Following are the substantive position and action resolutions adopted by the General Assembly (United States and Canada) since its beginning in 1917. Editor's notes offer guidance to the context of an Assembly action and/or linkages to similar actions in other years. The resolutions are organized under seven sections and are listed topically and chronologically under each section. The sections are:

> Organizational Guidelines
> Identification of "Reformation Principles"
> Distribution of Resources
> Christian Higher Education
> Major Social Issues
> Emphases, Studies, Celebrations
> Church-wide Consultations

ORGANIZATIONAL GUIDELINES

46. Only Ordained Ministers Can Vote (June 1917)

Editor's Note: The General Ministerial Assembly passed its first motion in its initial year of formal existence. Because of the long pattern which this action established, not to be altered for decades, it is significant to note this motion as recorded in the Assembly minutes of June 14, 1917. It was moved that only ordained ministers of the Church of God have the right to vote. Motion seconded. Motion carried.

See Entry 53 which documents the elimination in 1965 of the word "Ministerial" from the Assembly's name. Entries 56, 59, and 64 record Assembly actions in the 1970s, 1980s, and 1990s greatly increasing the participation of laypersons in the Assembly's membership.

47. Establishment of a National Ministries Structure (Executive Council, June 1932)

The Golden Jubilee celebration in 1931 marked a time of historic review and future projections for the reformation movement. One result was the 1930 General Ministerial Assembly authorization of the appointment of a commission on Assembly reorganization. The commission's report, which included a plan to make the Assembly a delegated body, was rejected by the 1931 Assembly, but another action of the 1930 Assembly did become reality. It called for the consideration of a "business body" to manage the general interests of the church. In 1932 the Assembly altered its bylaws to provide for the creation and incorporation of the Executive Council of the Church of God. The June 20, 1932, minutes read:

> The objects and purposes of the corporation are hereby declared to be to promote the religious and benevolent work of the Church of God, and for such purposes such corporation shall have power to receive, take and hold real and personal property, donations of money and property, legacies and bequests, and to sell, transfer and otherwise convey such property, on behalf of the Church of God, to sue and defend any and all actions in any court, and to have, hold and enjoy all the rights, privileges and powers of corporations at common law.

In 1947 the General Ministerial Assembly authorized a Commission on Revision and Planning to study ways for achieving better coordination of the general work of the church. As a result, the 1954 Assembly amended the Articles of Incorporation of the Executive Council and in 1956 took even further action by increasing both the membership and responsibilities of the Council. According to Article III, Section I of the constitution of the Assembly as revised in June 1980:

> The Executive Council shall serve as coordinating council for the Assembly. It shall coordinate the work of the general agen-

cies authorized by the Assembly in their interrelated and cooperative functions, in their promotional and fund-raising activities, and in the services they offer to the Church at large. It shall promote the general welfare and cooperative work of the Church of God.

In 1991 the General Assembly approved a new set of expectations for the Council. Its name was changed to "Leadership Council." The following persons have provided significant leadership for the work of the Council (years listed are those of the respective Yearbooks where these names appear).

Presidents, Board of Directors

Robert L. Berry	1934–1937
Elver F. Adcock	1937–1946
John A. Morrison	1946–1948
William E. Reed	1948–1955
Steele C. Smith	1955–1960
Marvin J. Hartman	1960–1965
Carl M. Poe	1965–1970
Marcus H. Morgan	1970–1981
R. Dale Whalen	1981–1984
Betty Lewis	1984–1990
David Lynch	1990–1995
Merv Bennett	1995–1999

Secretary-Treasurers

W. Burgess McCreary	1934–1936
Earl L. Martin	1936–1937
Adam W. Miller	1937–1938
W. Dale Oldham	1938–1944
I. K. Dawson	1944–1947
Lawrence E. Brooks	1947–1955

General Secretaries (Directors)

Clarence W. Hatch	1955–1960
Charles V. Weber	1960–1971
William E. Reed	1971–1980
Paul A. Tanner	1980–1988
Edward L. Foggs	1988–1999
Robert W. Pearson	1998 to present

Clarence W. Hatch
Charles V. Weber
William E. Reed
Paul A. Tanner
Edward L. Foggs
Robert W. Pearson
General Director, Church of God Ministries

48. Join the Federal Council of Churches? (June 1944)

During the 1940s a wave of criticism rolled through the Church of God. Some pastors felt that all of the organizational and program growth had become dysfunctional, that a few "big boys" were trying to "run things" from Anderson "headquarters," that the national leadership was steering the movement away from its historic commitments.

One focus of this concern was an action of the 1944 General Ministerial Assembly establishing a committee to explore a possible relationship with the Federal Council of Churches. Critics saw the very idea of such exploration as a negation of the movement's understanding of Christian unity. The committee reported in 1946 that "due to the pressure of other duties" it had not yet accomplished its task. A motion to continue the committee was lost (149 yes, 158 no). The chairman stated his opinion that the Assembly could not commit the Church of God to membership in the Federal Council even if it so desired. E. F. Adcock, chairman of the committee, clarified that committing the church to regular membership in the Council had not been the intention of the committee. The case was closed.

Editor's Note: See the 1985 action on "Inter-Church Cooperation" (Entry 63).

49. Faith in the Integrity of the National Work (June 1947)

Editor's Note: In a time of considerable tension and misunderstanding, with many ministers in the Church of God openly distrustful of the integrity of the Anderson-based agencies of the church, the General Ministerial Assembly decided it must speak. In June, 1947, it adopted the following resolution.

WHEREAS sixty-seven years ago D. S. Warner and his associates in the faith brought into being a new religious movement conceived by the Holy Spirit and predicated upon the ideal of a pure and undivided church; and

WHEREAS to the promulgation of this ideal these hardy pioneers gave their time, talent, money and very lives, and died in the faith that through their humble instrumentality God was working a great work in the world; and

WHEREAS even in their brief day these pioneers hammered out the beginnings of effective organizational instruments for the publishing of this divine message; and

WHEREAS this Assembly has implemented and added to these instrumentalities as need dictated through the years; and

WHEREAS all through its history this work has been attacked both from without and within, but to no permanent avail, because of the strong foundation upon which our work rests; and

WHEREAS now for two and a half years a new attack has been waged against the work, an attack not upon one front of the work alone, but upon every front—a total attack upon the total program and leadership of the work—bitter and persistent, covering every part of our corporate program: evangelism, publication, home and foreign missions, education, Sunday school and youth; including charges specific and general against persons and groups, covering the grossest evils, such as ministerial apostasy, malfeasance in office, misuse of funds, falsification, fraudulent behavior, wholesale doctrinal defection, and extreme worldliness; and

WHEREAS if in the main these charges were true, our Christian conscience would demand that strong measures be taken to remedy such a situation, but since charges in the main are not true, then the same Christian conscience demands that such charges, false and deliberately made, and persistently circulated, be condemned as grossly unchristian, and that those responsible for such unbecoming conduct make proper amends; and

WHEREAS one year ago this Assembly appointed an Investigating Committee of seven competent and trustworthy brethren with the instruction that they investigate the truthfulness of these charges; and

WHEREAS this committee, at the expense of great labor on their part and at a considerable expenditure of money, have so investigated these charges; Now, therefore, be it

RESOLVED: First, that we hereby reaffirm our faith in and loyalty and dedication to the doctrines, ideals, and objectives which gave birth to the movement; and at the same time we express our confidence in the boards and general agencies which serve the Church at home and abroad under the authority of this General Ministerial Assembly; and

Second, that we emphatically disapprove of the spirit and methods employed in the attacks made upon the general work of the Church as unchristian, unbrotherly, and unfair; which attacks have resulted in division and discord among the ministry and the laity as well; and

Third, that this General Ministerial Assembly go on record as being opposed to this program, and to any program by an individual or group that is calculated to cause division among us and break the worldwide unity that has characterized our movement from the beginning; and

Fourth, that we call upon all those responsible for the program which has caused such confusion and division within the Church forthwith to discontinue all such activities; and this Assembly does hereby entreat with all Christian brotherliness of spirit Brother Earl Slacum and those associated with him in the present agitation to acknowledge their error and to make due amends, so that Christian fellowship may be restored and the unity of the Church be preserved; and

Fifth, that we strongly urge our ministers when faced with problems related to our general work, to handle all such matters through the proper channels in a definitely Christian spirit; and

Sixth, that we recommend to the Indiana Ministerial Assembly and to all other state ministerial assemblies where such a program of division may be carried on, if the decision of this General Ministerial Assembly as herein expressed is disregarded, that such disciplinary action be taken as will safeguard and insure the unity of the Church; and

Seventh, that copies of this resolution be mailed to all ministers of the Church of God, and that this action be recorded as a part of the permanent minutes of this Assembly.

Editor's Note: For the larger historical and organizational-growth settings of this resolution, see Entries 34 and 203.

50. Anderson Camp Meeting to Be Continued and Housed (June 1960)

Anderson Camp Meeting, 1940s

Editor's Note: It was not possible to convene the 1960 Anderson camp meeting because of the collapse of the south end of the large tabernacle in which the meeting had been held annually for some forty years. A debate followed in the Assembly concerning the appropriate course of action. The final decision read:

WHEREAS this Assembly has spoken in clear and unmistakable terms favoring the continuance of the Camp Meeting and the Annual General Ministerial Assembly meeting at Anderson, Indiana, and

WHEREAS facilities for such meetings must be provided; be it therefore

RESOLVED, that the General Ministerial Assembly does hereby authorize and instruct the Executive Council of the Church of God, its legal entity, to proceed at once to provide the facilities for such Camp Meeting and General Ministerial Assembly by one of the following possibilities:

1. The repair of the present partially existing tabernacle at an engineer's estimated cost of $70,500 plus;
2. The erection of a colorable Stran-Steel building over the present tabernacle floor, meeting the state of Indiana building code;
3. Or, some other similar priced construction. Be it further

RESOLVED, that the Division of World Service and the Budget Committee of the Executive Council arrange the necessary financing plan for covering the approved construction costs in cooperation with the Executive Council; be it further

RESOLVED, that authorization for awarding the construction contract be made jointly by the Executive Committee of the Executive Council and the Board of Directors of the Gospel Trumpet Company; [and] be it further

RESOLVED, that this Assembly express its desire on these possibilities by ballot in this meeting today.

Editor's Note: In 1961 the site for the present Warner Auditorium, an entirely new facility, was dedicated. The decision for the future had been made.

51. Establishment of the Commission on Social Concerns (June 1964)

WHEREAS there is manifest interest in a Commission on Social Concerns in the Church of God, and

WHEREAS the Executive Council has received from different sources requests for the establishment of such a Commission on Social Concerns, and

WHEREAS there is manifest urgency for the careful and prayerful study of ways in which articulate calls may be given to the congregations for them to carefully consider Christian responsibility in the fields of temperance and general welfare, particularly with alcohol problems, gambling, tobacco, pornographic literature; in areas of peace and world order, particularly with military policy and legislation for conscription, disarmament and nuclear weapon control; and in the area of human relations, particularly in race relations, civil liberties, church-state relationships, housing, and civic responsibility, and

WHEREAS the Executive Council through its Executive Committee and the National Association of the Church of God (West Middlesex, Pennsylvania) through its appointed standing committee on race relations, have concurred in the call for the establishment of a Commission on Social Concerns, and

WHEREAS in other years this Assembly has appointed committees and commissions with responsibility in the areas of social Christian concerns, therefore, be it

RESOLVED, that the General Ministerial Assembly authorize the establishment of a permanent Commission on Christian Social Concerns responsible to the Assembly through the Executive Council, and be it further

RESOLVED, that this Commission on Christian Social Concerns shall be established with the purpose, the general areas of concern, the grant of power and lines of responsibility, the determination of membership, and other similar factors within the limitations described in the recommendation from the Executive Council to the General Ministerial Assembly which is attached to this resolution, and which is dated June 15, 1964.

Editor's Note: For thirty-four years this Commission was an active body, sensitizing the General Assembly and the Church of God generally to a wide range of social concerns, often initiating the texts of resolutions on which the Assembly acted. While the concerns remain for the church, the Commission itself was disbanded in 1998 as part of the restructuring of the national ministries.

52. Establishment of the Committee on Christian Unity (June 1965)

Editor's Note: Church historian John W. V. Smith welcomed the establishment of the Committee (later Commission) on Christian Unity and explained his view as follows in 1967.

After eighty-four years we finally, in 1965, got around to giving serious attention to our own responsibility in removing barriers by authorizing, through the General Assembly, a

Committee on Christian Unity.... Its very existence introduces a new dimension in our approach. No longer do we just preach unity and wait for the Holy Spirit to bring it about; we now accept the possibility that the Holy Spirit may be seeking to lead other Christians also along these same lines, and we are willing to join them in the quest. Inherent in the whole process, of course, is the frank admission that not all the "saints" have "come out" of the denominations. There are many still in "Babylon," we now realize, who are sensitive to the Spirit's voice and sincerely desire to make a reality of Christ's prayer that "they all may be one" (9).

WHEREAS for several years there has been manifest interest in a Committee on Christian Unity, and

WHEREAS resolutions have come from several state ministerial assemblies to the General Assembly or Executive Council calling for such a committee, and

WHEREAS the All-Board Congress and Planning Council expressed deep concern for and the need of such a committee, and

WHEREAS the General Assembly has instructed the Executive Council and its Division of General Service to study the need, structure, and responsibility of such a committee and bring a report to the General Assembly, and

WHEREAS representatives of the Church of God have already been in conversation with the representatives of certain other church groups who have sought to become acquainted with the Church of God, therefore, be it

RESOLVED, that a Committee on Christian Unity be authorized by the General Assembly and responsible to the Assembly through the Executive Council, making annual reports, with its concluding report in June 1969....

Editor's Note: The life of this Committee was extended to 1975 when the General Assembly recast this body as a permanent Commission on Christian Unity because (a) "the need and responsibility for unity and cooperative work among Christians is so strategic to Christian witness and world evangelism" and (b) "the Church of God continues to need a representative group to make contacts, hold conversations, and develop lines of cooperation with other church bodies of similar spirit and concern." While the concern for initiatives on behalf of Christian unity clearly remains, the Commission itself was disbanded in 1998 as part of the restructuring of the national ministries.

53. Name Change to "General Assembly" (June 1965)

Editor's Note: In 1958 the General Ministerial Assembly redefined its own membership to include "laymen who are elected or appointed members of the Executive Council, a subordinate board, committee, or commission of the Assembly." Although this was implemented immediately, the inconsistency of such action and the name of the Assembly was not addressed until 1965. The June, 1965, action read as follows.

INASMUCH as we now have some seventy-five laymen who are duly elected and authorized members of this Assembly, which in fact, makes this a General Assembly rather than a General Ministerial Assembly, therefore, be it

RESOLVED, that the term "General Assembly" be hereinafter used to designate the title of this Assembly and such changes be reflected in the Constitution and Bylaws and other official papers. Article I—Name—to read: "The name of this body is the General Assembly of the Church of God (hereinafter referred to in this Constitution and Bylaws as 'Assembly') with general offices located in Anderson, Indiana." and, be it further

RESOLVED, That Article I, Section 2, of the Bylaws be amended by striking out the words, "Any ordained minister of the Church of God in good and regular standing," and inserting the words, "Any member of this General Assembly," making this part of Section 2 read, "Any member of this General Assembly shall be considered eligible for election or appointment to these offices."

54. Establishment of the Office of Associate Executive Secretary (June 1974)

Editor's Note: This General Assembly action sought to address the need for a more visible and formalized tie of the Black constituency of the Church of God to the organization of national ministries.

The Executive Council recommends to the General Assembly that authorization be given for the employment of an Associate Secretary to serve with the Executive Secretary in the administration of the Council's work on behalf of the Assembly and the Church of God. The Executive Council further recommends:

1. That the office of an Associate Secretary be filled initially by a carefully selected black person who is to be nominated by the Board of Directors of the Executive

Council, but with election by the members of the Executive Council and ratification by the General Assembly in the same manner as is the office of the Executive Secretary.

2. That the term of office for the proposed Associate Secretary shall be for five years, beginning January 1, 1975, subject to the Assembly's approval of this recommendation.

3. That the General Assembly grant the Executive Council the privilege of submitting the name of a person to fill this office for ratification prior to the adjournment of its June 18-20, 1974, meeting.

4. That the General Assembly approve the budget for the operation of this office recommended by the Budget Committee and by the Executive Council.

5. That the General Assembly will amend its Bylaws, Article V, Ratification of Officers, by adding sub-paragraph (14) to read: (14) "Associate Secretary to the Executive Secretary of the Executive Council."

Editor's Note: With the above action was a lengthy description of this new position. The following are two central portions of that description.

The Associate Secretary is to join with the Executive Secretary in interpreting the policies and decisions of the General Assembly and the Executive Council to other agencies of the Church of God and to any person or groups needing such information. In turn, he is to interpret to the Executive Council and the General Assembly his readings of what is happening on the field and recommend procedures for the strengthening of understanding and cooperation.

The Associate Secretary is to serve in a liaison relationship between the Executive Council and the black membership of the Church of God. His special assignment will be that of trying to bring about closer ties and relationships within the Church. He shall be responsible to keep the Executive Council, its Board of Directors, and the Executive Secretary fully aware of the needs, feelings, and developments in the black church.

55. Cooperation in Missionary Work (June 1975)

Editor's Note: The 1974 General Assembly authorized the appointment of a twelve-member committee to:

1. Study the work and impact of the several "mission groups" at work in the Church of God;

2. Study their relationships with the duly constituted national agencies of the Church of God;

3. Study the implications of their promotional efforts on the total programming and fund raising for the agencies authorized by the General Assembly, state assemblies, and other national assemblies.

The report of this committee, presented to and adopted by the 1975 General Assembly, included the following five recommendations.

1. We recommend that the Executive Council of the Church of God study the feasibility of inviting each of the following organizations now serving the interests of the Church of God to appoint an observer to attend and participate in the annual meeting of the Council when budgeting is done for the general work of the church: Project Partner with Christ; Vacation Samaritans; Men of the Church of God. The purpose of this recommendation is twofold:

   (1) To provide opportunity for a para-mission organization to receive current information on programmatic and budgetary decisions reached by the Executive Council;
   (2) To provide opportunity for the Executive Council to receive current information on the operations and activities of para-mission groups and to give counsel on how coordination can best be achieved.

2. We recommend that the following groups set up a regular schedule of meetings to review planning and coordination of programmatic concerns: The Missionary Board of the Church of God; The Board of Church Extension and Home Missions; Project Partner with Christ; Vacation Samaritans; Women of the Church of God; Men of the Church of God. The Executive Secretary of the Executive Council will convene the initial meeting of this group.

3. We recommend that the para-mission organizations which solicit their financial support from the general body of the Church of God congregations and members in the United States report on a yearly basis their financial operations. In implementing this recommendation, it is requested that a copy of the annual Statement of Financial Condition be filed with the office of the Executive Secretary of the Executive Council for placement in the files of the General Assembly and its Executive Council.

4. We recommend that para-mission organizations, which receive their primary support from the Church of God as represented by the General Assembly and its Executive Council, always consider themselves to be morally and ethically related to the Church of God and follow the practice of selecting a majority of persons of Church of God membership to serve on their Boards of Directors and in their corporation memberships.

5. We recommend that each para-mission organization, which receives its primary support from Church of God congregations and members, include in its Articles of Association and Bylaws a provision whereby in case of dissolution the assets of the corporation will be retained for the benefit of the Church of God and not inure to the benefit of any private persons.

56. Increasing the Participation of Laypersons (June 1979)

WHEREAS this Assembly has authorized its Committee on Bylaws and Organization to study ways of increasing lay participation in the General Assembly of the Church of God, and

WHEREAS said committee has spent three years in such a study and has developed a suggested "model" for reconstituting the membership of the Assembly to include more laypersons, therefore, be it

RESOLVED, that the committee be instructed to prepare copies of this "model," along with a packet of explanatory materials, to be sent no later than October 1979 to each congregation listed in the current *Yearbook of the Church of God*, and be it further

RESOLVED, that each congregation be asked to discuss this model and to respond to the Bylaws Committee no later than April 1, 1980, on a form provided, and be it further

RESOLVED, that the committee bring to the 1980 Assembly specific recommendations for changing the Assembly's bylaws along the lines suggested by a consensus of responses from the congregations.

Editor's Note: The model referred to is that the membership of the General Assembly should be newly defined to include all members of all Church of God congregations who are present at designated meetings of the Assembly; from this group a selected number would be identified as voting members to provide a manageable and representative base for decision making; the voting members would include all ministers and laypersons who currently constitute the General Assembly and, in addition, at least one layperson designated by each local congregation. The Bylaws Committee did bring to the 1980 Assembly the results of a congregational survey for the purposes of information and further clarification. No action was requested. The committee brought to the 1981 Assembly a review of the history of the question and proposed that "this same model for increasing lay representation in the General Assembly remain before us for continued refinement and discussion and that it be brought before the 1982 General Assembly for a vote." See Entry 59. The Assembly's Task Force on Governance and Polity recommended to the 1991 Assembly a plan for a major increase in lay membership based on congregational delegates. The recommendation was approved (Entry 64) and became effective in 1993 and then was made a permanent arrangement by action of the 1996 Assembly.

57. Procedure for Grievances (June 1980)

Editor's Note: The 1980 General Assembly sessions included criticism directed at a national agency of the church, Anderson College. The criticism had been focused publicly by an "open letter" mailed by a minister to all Assembly members just prior to the convening of the Assembly. Apart from the substance of the criticism, the attention of the Assembly was directed toward affirming more appropriate ways for future grievances to be handled. Thus, the Assembly adopted the following resolution as procedural guidance for the future. It should be noted that in the 1985 Assembly, in the midst of criticism being directed at another national agency of the church, Warner Press, the Assembly's Business Committee reaffirmed this 1980 action, redistributed it to Assembly members, and urged that it be honored. In 1989 the Executive Council and General Assembly reaffirmed a modest revision and annual reissuing of this procedure. The original resolution read as follows.

The National Agencies of the Church of God are servants of the church and have been brought into being by action of the General Assembly. Each agency is incorporated and governed by a board of trustees duly elected by this Assembly, and answerable to this Assembly.

It is likely that some agency decisions will be unpopular. Members of this Assembly must know that they do have a voice and that their voice will be heard. Therefore, an accepted procedure for sharing differences, grievances, and suggestions is needed. The Business Committee recommends that the biblical basis found in Matthew 18:15-17 be the accepted norm and procedure. The following process shall then be our guide:

1. Agency

    a. A letter to the chief executive officer of the agency in question shall be written seeking an answer or solution. If a solution is not easily resolved by mail, an official meeting with the chief executive officer shall be established at the convenience of both parties.

    b. If such a meeting is unsatisfactory, it will then be appropriate to seek a meeting with the elected officers of the corporation, including the chief executive officer, to seek a solution.

    c. If no solution to the problem is found, attempt shall be made to have the larger governing group of the corporation consider the matter.

2. Executive Council

    a. If the above steps to solve the problem with the agency in question have been exhausted, consultation with the Board of Directors of the Executive Council may be sought to see if proper negotiation can be achieved. The Board of Directors may make the concern an agency item for the Executive Council.

3. General Assembly

    a. If the concern is not satisfactorily resolved, the grievance may be presented to the General Assembly, through its Business Committee.

    b. If the Business Committee does not agree to make the concern an agenda item, it may be brought to the floor of the Assembly. By a two-thirds vote of the members present it may then be dealt with directly by the Assembly.

Editor's Note: The 1989 revised form of this 1980 grievance procedure laid stress on resolving differences with agency administrators and governing boards at the agency level. The General Assembly was referred to as "the body of last resort" only.

58. Maintaining a Responsible Business Committee (June 1981)

Editor's Note: The established procedures for conducting the business of the General Assembly seemed to some members of the 1980 Assembly to be designed to obstruct their full participation. One minister stated with considerable frustration that, while Assembly members were urged to follow orderly procedures, some members often found it difficult to get through the proper channels. Therefore, a motion was adopted that called on the Bylaws Committee of the Assembly to take appropriate action in regard to this concern. The specific recommendation was that any item of business be permitted on the Assembly floor if a majority of voting members so desired (instead of the two-thirds vote traditionally required).

In conflict with this specific recommendation, however, was another action also taken by the 1980 General Assembly. Because of an "open letter" distributed nationally by an Assembly member just prior to the 1980 Assembly, and in the face of widespread questioning of the appropriateness of this means of bringing a concern to the attention of those in positions of responsibility, the Assembly approved a policy governing grievance procedures (see entry 19). The first step called for in this procedure was written contact with the chief executive officer of the agency related to the concern in question. The final step in this procedure, should all else fail to bring some resolution of the problem, was a bypassing of the action of the Business Committee of the Assembly by a two-thirds vote of Assembly members, thus allowing direct action on the floor of the Assembly. This grievance procedure also was forwarded to the Bylaws Committee for appropriate action.

The Bylaws Committee saw the conflict in these two actions of the 1980 General Assembly, one calling for movement from two-thirds to a majority and one specifically retaining the two-thirds vote necessary to bring an item of business to the floor when the Business Committee of the Assembly has not agreed to make that concern an agenda item. In light of this conflict, in view of the long-standing two-thirds bylaw of the Assembly, and with the knowledge that the two-thirds guideline is widely accepted as sound parliamentary procedure, the Bylaws Committee recommended to the 1981 Assembly that its standing bylaw not be changed. The Assembly accepted this recommendation.

59. Lay Representation in the
General Assembly (June 1982)

Editor's Note: In light of the action of the 1979 Assembly and the subsequent church-wide study, the following was presented to and approved by the 1982 General Assembly.

Background

The Bylaws Committee, through its extensive studies, has noted wide-spread support for some increase of lay representation to the Assembly. The committee has decided to bring a proposal for adoption to the Assembly this year. The committee acknowledges its responsibility to listen carefully to the church and that its proposals should reflect procedures that enhance the unity we desire. Therefore, this proposal differs from the one given to the Assembly previously. This proposal comes as a result of the committee's desire to achieve Assembly-wide consensus on this question.

Proposal

Therefore, the Bylaws Committee proposes that the Constitution of the General Assembly, Article IV, Membership, Section 4, which now reads:

One layperson may be selected by each state (district), or provincial assembly, to attend the General Assembly as an observer.

be changed to read:

One layperson selected by each recognized state or provincial assembly; a representative selected by each recognized state or provincial organization of Women of The Church of God; and a representative selected by each recognized state or provincial organization of the Church of God Men, International.

Explanation and Effect

"Recognized" is understood to mean:
(1) State or provincial assemblies which are recognized by the General Assembly of the Church of God through its Division of Church Service;
(2) State or provincial organizations of the Women of the Church of God which are recognized by the national organization of the Women of the Church of God;
(3) State or provincial organizations of the Church of God Men, International, which are recognized by the national organization of Church of God Men, International.

The effect of this change is to bring those persons now designated as observers in the Assembly into full membership in the Assembly. In addition this change brings into the life of the Assembly key proven leaders of two of the church's vital national organizations. Both organizations endorse heartily the possibility of their participation in the Assembly. The likelihood of faithful participation by these persons is good because of their demonstrated concern for the work of the church and the high percentage of their attendance already in the convention. The potential addition to the Assembly is approximately one-hundred and thirty-five persons.

Editor's Note: See Entry 56 for an earlier action in this regard, and Entry 64 for another action approving a significant further expansion of lay Assembly members beginning in 1993.

60. Ratification Procedures for New Executives (June 1984)

WHEREAS the General Assembly prescribes in its bylaws that certain agency executives shall be presented to it for ratification; and

WHEREAS it is appropriate that the General Assembly know the qualifications and central convictions of persons they are asked to ratify; and

WHEREAS the size and setting of the General Assembly do not make it feasible to engage in a lengthy cross-examination style of questioning; and

WHEREAS a board duly elected by the General Assembly has already reviewed the qualifications of, and elected, the person to be ratified; and

WHEREAS the Assembly requires pre-Assembly mailing of information about nominees; therefore be it

RESOLVED, that the corporate agency presenting the name for ratification state the qualifications, home church, and credentials of its nominee; and be it further

RESOLVED, that the candidate to be ratified share in writing his/her own experiential testimony and spiritual pilgrimage, including a personal statement of doctrinal convictions; and be it further

RESOLVED, that the Executive Council mailing to General Assembly members in May include both of these documents for their advance study and reflection; and be it further

RESOLVED, that should any agency fail to have such materials ready for advance mailing, such information shall be given to the General Assembly, in session, at least one day prior to the ratification vote; and be it finally

RESOLVED, that no person shall be ratified by the General Assembly on the same day that his/her name is presented to the Assembly for ratification.

Editor's Note: The 1996 Assembly acted to clarify the limited meaning of a ratification action of the Assembly (see Entry 67).

61. Warner Press: Concerns and Dramatic Changes (June 1983-1986, 1997-1998)

Editor's Note: During 1981-82 criticism was heard from several sources about various structures and practices of Warner Press. In response, the Publication Board of Warner Press named a Consultation Committee which brought to the 1983 General Assembly a progress report of the early stages of its work. The committee reported that it was studying the following.

1. The function and purpose of Warner Press in relation to the Church of God;
2. The propriety and sufficiency of the organizational structure of Warner Press regarding the relationship of the president and editor in chief;
3. The latitude and freedom of the editor in chief to pursue and fulfill this defined function;
4. The editorial policy and its manner of determination; and
5. The sufficiency of the present organizational structure for oversight or review of Warner Press (from the General Assembly through the lowest echelon).

The committee promised to report again to the 1984 General Assembly. In that Assembly the chair of the Publication Board spoke for the committee, which had already mailed its final report to Assembly members. With the support of the officers and Consultation Committee of Warner Press, there was introduced and adopted a resolution from the Winchester, Kentucky, and Pryor, Oklahoma, Pastors' Fellowships. This resolution noted reception of the report of the Consultation Committee, expressed concern that "spiritual considerations be given preeminence over the financial and operational policies of Warner Press," and called on the Publication Board to bring to the 1985 and 1986 General Assemblies a full report on the implementation of the changes outlined in the final report of the Consultation Committee.

Prior to the 1985 Assembly, in which the president of Warner Press was scheduled for ratification for a new term, renewed criticism was directed toward Warner Press. In its annual meeting in May, 1985, the Executive Council heard the grievances and appointed a Special Committee on Warner Press Grievances, comprising persons outside Warner Press, and charged it to report to the 1985 General Assembly prior to the ratification vote on the company's president.

In the 1985 Assembly the Publication Board of Warner Press brought its scheduled implementation report, which was followed by the report of the Special Grievances Committee. This latter report spoke specifically to the issues of bonuses, salaries, and the tenure of board members and called for the ratification of the president of Warner Press for an abbreviated two-year term. It was reported that the Publication Board had agreed to implement all of the recommendations made. Consequently, the president's special two-year term was voted.

The Special Grievances Committee made an additional and extensive report to the 1986 Assembly. It included a review of the committee's assignment and work, a summary of expressed concerns about the publishing work, and a series of recommendations grouped in four areas. They were: the mission and operational philosophy of Warner Press; the renewal and expansion of the publishing ministries; the utilization of income; and restructuring for effective leadership.

A decade later concerns turned into a financial emergency as great as the Church of God movement had ever faced. Without public warning, Warner Press suspended the publication of *Vital Christianity*, to the surprise and shock of many in the church, and retired the office of editor-in-chief. These were the publication and the role that had been at the center of the movement's beginning and early growth and had been its central communication vehicles throughout the twentieth century (*Vital Christianity* previously had been called the *Gospel Trumpet*).

By January, 1998, the company's situation seemed bleak. It had sold a large portion of the company without realizing proceeds nearly adequate to resolve its escalating financial problems. By the convening of the General Assembly in June, 1999, an all-church plan had been developed that included the participation of Anderson University, the Board of Church Extension and Home Missions, Women of the Church of God, and the then new Church of God Ministries organization of the national ministries. Key persons working toward a viable solution to a most complex and difficult problem included Edward Foggs and Merv Bennett of the Leadership Council, J. Perry Grubbs of the Board of Church Extension, and James L. Edwards of Anderson University.

This major financial problem would be solved only over a period of years, the large facilities of Warner Press would be remodeled into the new home of Church of God Ministries, and the much smaller Warner Press would be controlled by the national ministries body. The volume by Harold Phillips recording the history of Warner Press is titled *Miracle of Survival* (1979). The dramatic and nearly tragic events altering the company in the 1990s reflected another scramble for meaningful survival and the continuing presence of God's gracious miracles.

62. Limitation of Terms for Board Members
(June 1985)

Editor's Note: For some years it had been the conviction of some members of the General Assembly that the church would be better served if a limitation were placed on the number of consecutive years that any one person could serve on a governing board of a national agency. In the Assembly of 1985 the Bylaws Committee presented a recommended bylaws change which, as amended on the floor to be even more restrictive, was adopted as stated below.

No person shall be nominated for membership on any subordinate Board who has already served as a member of that Board for two consecutive five (5) year terms or ten consecutive years until after a lapse of two years.

In 1986 this limitation was broadened to three consecutive five-year terms for those governing the institutions of higher education. Then in 1990 the maximum of three terms (fifteen years) was applied to all persons affected by the original 1985 action.

63. Acceptable Inter-Church Cooperation
(June 1985)

Editor's Note: The following resolution was developed and adopted by the Committee on Long Range Planning (April 1985) and approved by the Executive Council of the Church of God (May 1985). It then was presented to members of the 1985 General Assembly for information and guidance.

WHEREAS the Church of God Reformation Movement has historically affirmed the unity of the Body of Christ as expressed in its many forms, yet one; and

WHEREAS the Church of God Reformation Movement for over eighty years has participated in mutually supportive relationships with other communions through its national and state agencies in missionary education, missions education, and ministerial continuing education; and

WHEREAS ministers and laypersons of the Church of God Reformation Movement have been involved in significant ways in local cooperative ministries such as community concerns, leadership training, and evangelism; and

WHEREAS the Commission on Christian Unity of the Church of God in its 1983 Statement of Concern and Guidance on Christian Unity urged the church "to work toward an intentional togetherness to exercise a willed movement toward each other"; and

WHEREAS the 1984 Consultation on Mission and Ministry established as one of its five priority areas of concern that of being the body of Christ, with one of its stated goals "to expand ministries through voluntary relationships with Christian groups outside the Church of God Reformation Movement and seek to live out the vision of unity through broader interdependent relationships that serve mutual needs for training, fellowship, and witness"; therefore, be it

RESOLVED, that the Committee on Long Range Planning supports the historical stance of the Church of God Reformation Movement to seek intentional inter-church relationships through which its own ministries are strengthened and enriched and which provide opportunity for the Church of God Reformation Movement to live out its message of Christian unity through enriching the entire Body of Christ; and be it further

RESOLVED, that all Church of God Reformation Movement national, state, and local structures be encouraged to participate in inter-church relationships as a means of expressing our belief in Christian unity and our desire to effect cooperative ministries.

Editor's Note: The 1987 General Assembly heard criticism of the National (U.S.A.) and World Councils of Churches and the suggestion that national agencies of the Church of God might be involved with them inappropriately. It adopted a resolution calling for the establishment of a special committee to study, document, and evaluate the current involvements of general agencies of the Church of God with the National Council of Churches (U.S.A.) and the World Council of Churches. This committee's report was presented and received with appreciation by the 1988 Assembly. It excluded discussion of the World Council since no involvement was found except an occasional "observer status." Portions of this report follow.

Summary Perspectives

The study committee is united in its strong conviction that the Church of God must find increasingly effective ways to express its commitment to Christian unity and to fulfill the mission of the church in the world. We are called to make a difference, but we cannot do it alone.

Diversity and interdependence are both facts of contemporary church life. There is considerable and increasing diversity of backgrounds, beliefs church traditions and priority agendas now seen in Church of God congregations and among Church of God leaders at all levels of church life. Church of God colleges increasingly are being populated by students from other than Church of God congregations. Many Church of God pastors participate actively with local and area inter-church bodies that provide fellowship and/or cooperative ministry opportunities. Often these bodies include a wide spectrum of church traditions, commitments, and agendas. Pastors have the freedom to participate as they judge appropriate and sometimes they do in very visible, formal, and influential ways. Interdependence among Christian communities appears necessary for the effective accomplishment of some ministry goals. It also appears to be a natural implementation of the burden for Christian unity carried by the Church of God reformation movement.

Church of God general agencies, with major ministry mandates and limited resources in a complex world, also have evidenced need for "outside" ministry relationships and resources. In a very few instances they have developed limited relationships with working units of the National Council of Churches in Christ as a partial means of fulfilling this need. In such instances the agencies have been especially sensitive to public allegations made against the Council and they have walked carefully the narrow path of restricted involvement designed only to enrich their own work and witness without formal membership or direct involvement in the larger life of the Council itself.

Admittedly there are risks in all sharing relationships; but the isolationist alternative would be a denominationalizing of the Church of God reformation movement, an alternative which inevitably would bring its own high price. Given the risks associated with all alternatives, then, the study committee seemed to face a choice between (a) calling for a blanket prohibition of all such participation with working units of the NCCC or similar inter-church bodies and (b) calling for no action, thus leaving the general agencies free to relate to whom and as they see fit. The committee judged neither of these choices acceptable. Rather, the committee saw wisdom in developing a set of Relationship Guidelines which the General Assembly would be asked to adopt for the guidance of general agencies accountable to the Assembly. These guidelines are viewed by the committee as reasonable expectations, ones open where ministry needs justify and limiting where limitation clearly appears necessary.

Proposed Relationship Guidelines
Any general agency, commission, division or committee, accountable to the General Assembly of the Church of God in the United States, which chooses to relate in any manner to any working unit associated with the National Council of Churches in Christ or other inter-church body should do so only within the assumptions, affirmations and limitations contained in the following guidelines:

1. Any inter-church relationship should be guided by the clear understanding that the Church of God, as represented by the Executive Council and the General Assembly, has not and should not become formal institutional members of the National Council of Churches in Christ. Such organizational identity is not the best way to express Christian unity!

2. Any inter-church body involved in a relationship should be committed publicly to the divinity and lordship of Jesus Christ. He is central to the meaning and the mission of the church!

3. Inter-church relationships should be seen as opportunities to serve and witness in light of the distinctive heritage of the Church of God reformation movement. We have something important to share as well as receive in any such relationship!

4. An inter-church relationship should not be maintained if that relationship gives support to beliefs or actions which clearly violate beliefs or actions generally held to be true and proper by the Church of God reformation movement. We in the Church of God must be accountable to each other and maintain the integrity of our doctrinal heritage!

5. Any Church of God participants in an inter-church relationship should not attempt to speak in the inter-church setting for the Church of God reformation movement as a whole. Participants always should make clear that they function by individual or agency choice and do not necessarily represent their brothers and sisters at large!

6. Church of God general agency staff or dollar resources invested in an inter-church relationship should be limited to the ministry function justifying that relationship. The Church of God does not control and sometimes does not condone all that large inter-church bodies say and do!

Postscript

The study committee wishes to affirm an important call issued to the Church of God by the Consultation on Mission and Ministry of the Church of God in 1984. It was a call "to expand ministries through voluntary relationships with church groups outside the Church of God reformation movement" so that we can "achieve our mission more effectively and expand our ministries." This present committee report and the relationship guidelines proposed above are intended to support, not impede this call. It is the committee's hope that such guidelines will enrich appropriate inter-church relationships and, at the same time, avoid inappropriate ones. It also is our hope that the Church of God will give continuing attention to the opportunities associated with working relationships among Christians for the sake of the church's mission in the world.

64. Expanded Lay Membership of the General Assembly (June 1991)

Editor's Note: The General Assembly's Task Force on Governance and Polity recommended to the 1991 Assembly a plan for expansion of lay membership of the Assembly. The recommendation was approved, to be effective with the 1993 Assembly, but to be reviewed by the 1996 Assembly in light of the plan's initial years of implementation. The plan was so reviewed and then made permanent by action of the 1996 Assembly. The plan established as members of the Assembly laypersons who are properly named, present in any meeting, and fit within the following limits:

a. One layperson from each congregation, AM attendance to 100;
b. Two laypersons from each congregation, AM attendance from 101-500;
c. Three laypersons from each congregation, AM attendance from 501-1,000;
d. Four laypersons from each congregation, AM attendance over 1,001.

65. Recommendations: Task Force on Governance and Polity (June 1992)

Editor's Note: In 1987 the General Assembly established a "Task Force on Governance and Polity" to "undertake a wide-ranging analysis of present governance and polity traditions, assumptions, structures, and relationships; to develop recommendations for enhancing the effectiveness of governance and polity—congregational, state and national—to the end that mission and ministry are strengthened." The Task Force brought to the 1992 Assembly a series of affirmations and nine recommendations. All recommendations *except #4* were approved. They were as follows.

1. Resolved, that the General Assembly encourage each congregation of the Church of God to have in place current mission, vision and covenant statements as its ministry moves into the 21st century.

2. Resolved, that the Division of Church Service convene representatives from the groups presently conducting in-service training and programs, to extend dialogue and joint planning, and report annually to the Executive Council.

3. Resolved, that the Executive Council be authorized to undertake a study of the possibility of holding one International Convention and General Assembly elsewhere; that the study when completed will be brought to the Council for action and to the General Assembly for decision no later than 1994.

(4. Resolved, that the General Assembly approve the establishment of the "Mission and Ministry Triennial" as described here and in Exhibit A.)

5. Resolved, that the General Assembly concur with the Executive Council in changing its name to "Leadership Council of the Church of God" and its chief executive officer's title to "General Secretary": that it authorize steps to amend its bylaws accordingly.

6. Resolved, that the General Assembly favor the direction proposed in the above recommendation regarding services to the ministry of the Church; that it support a study group with members from the Council and Division, to propose means by which these recommendations may be implemented.

7. Resolved, that the General Assembly commend and encourage the Commission on Christian Higher Education and the member institutions in their efforts described above to enhance interdependence and accountability.

8. Resolved, that the General Assembly accept the above recommendation of the Task Force regarding church-wide discussion, coordination by the Executive Council, and reporting to the General Assembly in 1994 [about possible restructuring at the national level].

9. Resolved, that the General Assembly approve the above recommendation that "fresh efforts, styles, and initiatives in program coordination and collaboration begin immediately": that it support the process described above.

Editor's Note: See Entries 71 and 203.

66. Conflict of Interest (May 1993)

Religious institutions are under scrutiny more than ever with respect to the ethics of how they conduct business. This scrutiny is coming from self-monitoring by the church, governmental bodies, and the general public. One of the most sensitive arenas of concern lies in the matter of conflict of interest.

The Leadership Council proposes that those general agencies answerable to the General Assembly and those para-church or other groups which draw their primary financial support from the constituency of the Church of God have in place a written conflict of interest policy which addresses at least the areas identified in this document.

A conflict of interest may be defined or described as follows:

1. When a person has a duty to promote one interest but chooses to promote a competing interest instead;

2. When an institutional insider (board member, officer, or staff person) chooses to promote an interest in competition with that institution's ministry;

3. When an institutional insider (board member, officer, or staff person) stands to profit personally by promoting his/her own interests or the interests of friends, relatives, or business associates.

Examples of potential conflicts of interest are:

1. When institutional insiders have an interest in a vendor to the institution;
2. When employees of one institution are loaned to other organizations;
3. When institutional fund raisers give financial advice to donors;
4. When an attorney represents two clients with conflicting interests;
5. When institutional employees accept gifts from vendors;
6. When institutional insiders are also insiders of a related organization.

Conflicts of interest are not always avoidable and may not necessarily be unethical. Certain actions, however, are essential to avoid questionable and unethical conduct.

1. Conflicts of interest must be disclosed to the institution as soon as any conflict is discovered.

2. After disclosure is made, the insider with a conflicting interest must not participate in judging the merits of that interest. This, at a minimum, would require one to abstain from voting and to refrain from otherwise promoting the outside interest. It could, under some circumstances and at the discretion of the body, call for one to absent him/herself during the period of the discussion and/or action on the matter of interest.

Many institutions, religious and secular, require their board members to complete an initial conflict-of-interest questionnaire when they become board members and to make periodic (often annual) declarations regarding personal conflict of interests. The Leadership Council has not attempted to formulate a uniform conflict of interest policy. It does, however, urge the General Assembly to adopt this statement as a reference document for guidance to general agencies and others in formulating their own conflict of interest policies. [Approved, Leadership Council, May 6, 1993.]

67. Governing Boards To Elect, the Assembly To Ratify (June 1995, 1996)

Editor's Note: During 1994-95 an Election Study Committee worked in relation to a series of General Assembly election/ratification issues of concern to some members of the Assembly. In response to its report to the 1995 Assembly, the Bylaws Committee of the Assembly brought proposed bylaws changes. They were approved. The main one was the change from the Assembly *electing* members of the agency governing boards (from a pair of names nominated by the boards) to the Assembly *ratifying* those members elected previously by the boards. Prompted by two circumstances where the implications of Assembly ratification actions were extended beyond the Assembly's (unstated) intentions, the 1996 Assembly approved the following formal clarification:

The General Assembly's ratification is a simple concurrence in the prior election of the board in question. Such ratification in no way assures the elected person claim to the full tenure or compensation of that office. The electing board retains the right and responsibility for performance evaluation, continuance in office, and appropriate compensation. The Assembly expects each electing board to have and follow fair and formally stated severance standards and procedures.

68. Toward United Credentialling Bodies (June 1996)

Whereas, the essential unity of God's people is one of the foundational Biblical convictions of the Church of God Movement; and,

Whereas, cultural, racial and social uniquenesses are present within the Movement contributing varied resources which should be seen as strengthening our united Kingdom efforts; and,

Whereas, a lack of unified practice and process in the credentialling of ministers and churches has developed and perpetuated in some areas fostering confusion, misunderstanding and a negative witness: and,

Whereas, several states or regions where overlapping credentialling entities exist have already provided model efforts toward creating unified credentialling bodies and,

Whereas, the recently assembled Credentials Congress affirmed that unified credentialling bodies are a worthy goal for the Church of God Movement.

Therefore Be It Resolved, that Church and Ministry Service does hereby call upon each state, region or province with two or more credentialling assemblies to:

1. Begin immediate dialogue for the purpose of bringing about reconciliation in credentialling practices that will heal divisions, celebrate uniqueness, and bring about a greater realization of cooperation in the Church of God Movement.

2. Establish dated goals for unifying the various assemblies at least in terms of credentialling functions by June 1999;

3. Commit to creating credentialling committees and/or boards that are reflective of the various, unique constituencies which they will serve;

4. Seek assistance, mediation or whatever other tools are needed to bring about the desired result of unified credentialling procedures for the Church of God.

69. Provision for Absentee Ballots (June 1996)

Editor's Note: Given the voluntary nature of the General Assembly, with its membership each year defined in part by physical presence, it long was a perception that, since the Assembly always convenes in Anderson, Indiana, those not living in the central region of the United States were not proportionally represented. Beginning in 1987, there was put in place a temporary provision for absentee balloting for certain elections in the General Assembly. A study later was conducted of the actual use and impact of such a privilege. Determining that this privilege was significant and its use not a negative in the Assembly's life, the 1996 Assembly made absentee balloting a permanent part of its electing process.

70. Provision for Special Mail Ballots (June 1997)

Editor's Note: As initial projections were being made for the necessary decisions to implement in a timely fashion a major restructuring of the national ministries, it was judged that provision needed to be made for the Assembly to be able to act between its regular annual sessions. Thus, a provision was approved by the 1997 Assembly for its ability to conduct a special mail ballot. It read:

> The nature and/or timing of an issue may require General Assembly action by a special mail ballot between regular sessions of the Assembly. Judgment concerning the need for a special mail ballot shall be made by the Assembly. When circumstances require, the judgment shall be made by the Executive Committee of the Assembly. A special ballot shall be sent to all persons who were certified to have been eligible voting members of the Assembly most recently convened prior to the mail ballot. Information about the issue in question will be provided. For the voting process, a minimum of at least five weeks for response will be provided from the date of the mailing of ballots. Only votes received by the stated deadline will be counted. All issues will be determined by majority vote, unless by Bylaws of the General Assembly specify otherwise.

71. Restructuring the National Ministries
(June 1996-1997)

Editor's Note: In his 1988 annual report to the General Assembly as General Secretary of the Leadership Council, Edward L. Foggs identified several areas that he judged would need major addressing by the Church of God during the decade of the 1990s. Included were:

1. Our need for a greater sense of partnership and interdependency.
2. Our need for more effective leadership accountability nationwide.
3. The function and structure of the church's ministries.
4. Long-range planning for effective engagement of the church's limited resources.

In his final report to the General Assembly as General Secretary (June 14, 1999), Foggs noted that the path of addressing such concerns had indeed "engaged the decade of the nineties." The process, he said, "has tested our wisdom, our creativity, our courage, our patience, our maturity, and our grace." In the end "we are the better for the journey we have traveled." Recalling the work of the Task Force on Governance and Polity (1987-1992) [see entry 64], the Leith Anderson consultation, and the Implementation Task Force and Transition Team, the result had been needed restructuring of the national ministries of the Church of God in the United States and Canada. "We stand prepared," he concluded, "to enter the twenty-first century with new vision, fresh perspective, and gifted leadership as Church of God Ministries, Inc., sets the pace for an ever-expanding reach in the church's mission and ministry." The theme for the 1999 International Convention in Anderson, Indiana, was "Great Expectations: A New Day Dawns!"

In 1996 the General Assembly heard an extended report and set of recommendations from consultant Leith Anderson. Following an affirmative action of the Leadership Council, it approved overwhelmingly "in principle" this proposal for a significant restructuring of the national ministries (vote of 954-104). Prior to this vote, the "concept" was identified as seven general points:

1. The intent is to enhance the ability of the national ministries of the church to function with maximum responsiveness to congregational needs.

2. The General Assembly is affirmed as the one clear voice for governance in the church.
3. The Leadership Council will become a single, central, implementing board.
4. The Leadership Council will have operating divisions uniting similar and compatible functions, probably under the titles Global Ministries and Church Ministries.
5. Certain agencies of the church will be known as endorsed agencies, identified as having a clearly defined relationship to the General Assembly and the Leadership Council.
6. Certain other agencies will be known as affiliated agencies and will have a strong fraternal relationship with the church based on covenants.
7. A visioning convocation will be convened periodically, perhaps every three (3) years, to function outside activities of governance, bringing together the leaders of the church from all sectors to develop, affirm, and recommend the central motivating visions for the whole church.

A refined organizational plan, in line with the above concept, was presented to the 1997 Assembly and approved for immediate implementation. Given the considerable legal, personnel, facility, and other implications of the new plan, full implementation was not complete until December, 1999. In 1998, the General Assembly approved a complete rewriting of its own *Constitution and Bylaws* to accommodate this major restructuring and its various relationships to the General Assembly. See Entry 43. This rewriting was prepared by the Assembly's Bylaws Committee, Barry L. Callen, chair, and P. Roger Brewer, vice-chair. It showed the new organizational plan of Church of God Ministries. Governed by a Ministries Council elected by the General Assembly and administered by a General Director, the cooperative ministries were now organized into three Ministry Teams or Divisions, each with a Director. They are: Congregational Ministries, Jeannette Flynn, Director; Outreach Ministries, Michael Curry, Director; and Resource and Linking Ministries, James R. Martin, Director.

Robert W. Pearson	Michael Curry	Jeannette Flynn	James R. Martin
General Director	Team Director	Team Director	Team Director
Church of God	Outreach Ministries	Congregational Ministries	Resource and
Ministries			Linking Ministries

For a broad perspective on these organizational changes in the larger context of the history of the Church of God, see Entry 203.

IDENTIFICATION OF "REFORMATION PRINCIPLES"

Editor's Note: The teaching tradition of the Church of God movement has not featured rationalistic theological formulas and restrictive creeds. To the contrary, such things have been viewed as a divisive plague on the Christian community. Instead, Robert Reardon has spoken of the movement's "marks" that have given it character and significance (see Entry 40). Barry Callen's 1995 book is titled *Contours of a Cause*, suggesting that the teaching tradition of the Church of God has been more of a "cause" than a creed, although the cause does have some definable "contours." The General Assembly of the Church of God (U. S. A. and Canada) has not laid out a creedal base for its own existence and membership, but it has reserved the right to monitor its membership, in part on the basis of adherence to "general reformation principles." Typical of the movement's non-creedalism and its non-ecclesiastical nature, the Assembly never has explicitly identified any such principles. However, two Assembly actions in the 1980s in effect have made two identifications. Following an insightful 1929 piece by Andrew Byers that helps to set the scene, the Assembly's two reformation principles follow.

---

72. Principles of the Reformation Movement (1929)

Excerpt of an address by Andrew L. Byers to
Church of God ministers, Eugene, Oregon, 1929.

The reformation principles, upon which our movement of the Church of God may be defined, may be expressed as follows:

1. Divine spiritual life received in regeneration and witnessed to by the Holy Spirit, and more than this, a true consecration to God, constantly maintained, which permits of no interposition of selfish ambition in the progress of the movement;

2. A disposition to obey the truth and the truth only and to let the Holy Spirit have his way and rule;

3. An attitude entirely receptive to, and which really welcomes, any further light and truth, one which assumes no infallibility and which is not satisfied with interpreting

Christianity and the Scriptures in the light of traditions and old ideas;

4. Acknowledgment of good wherever found; regarding no door into the church other than salvation, and no test of fellowship other than true Christianity possessed in the heart. The placing of no barrier that would exclude any who might be Christians. A regard for souls, whether believers or not, as far-reaching and inclusive as that of Christ's.

No person can truthfully say he is of this reformation who is not of its principles, even though he may take the Gospel Trumpet, worship in the Church of God, and testify that he is saved and sanctified. These principles characterize the true church in her unity and integrity. They are as narrow as the New Testament on the one hand and as broad as the New Testament on the other. It is by lacking in one or more of these essentials that a sect is a sect. We have assumed these principles; therefore, we have much at stake. It is easy to fail or come short by reason of such a high standard. All that a sect assumes is their creed, or system, or belief. We have assumed the whole and must not permit ourselves to be carrying out only a part.

A minister whose activities are along this line is truly a reformer. We must not think only of the pioneers in this movement as reformers; the reform spirit must continue, and characterize the whole movement. If it does, great results will follow, for we indeed have the greatest message ever preached since the apostles' days, and I sometimes think it is even greater than theirs. Billy Sunday said, not so long since in a sermon at Niagara Falls, when referring to the line of reformers, that the principles advocated by D. S. Warner (mentioning him by name) would one day sweep the world. The fact is, these principles are the bedrock of truth, and nothing can get under it to upset it. But the question is, Are we keeping to these principles? To the degree that we do we shall see the fruits of true evangelism.

73. General Assembly Reserves a Right

Editor's Note: For many years the General Assembly has reserved for itself the right to define its own membership, partly by the process of passing judgment on adherence to "general reformation principles" (see Entries 75 and 76). Two related matters are crucial.

One was a positive Assembly action in 1990. It regarded the status of persons whose names were appearing on Assembly ballots (nominated by various national bodies) but who were not attending or supporting local congregations of the Church of God. That action follows.

WHEREAS some members of this General Assembly of the Church of God are very much concerned about the appearing in the ballots of names of persons who are not attending or supporting local congregations of the Church of God; and

WHEREAS these persons are being placed into positions of vital importance to this reformation, i.e., college boards of trustees and agencies; and

WHEREAS many of us in this Assembly recognize the latent danger to the biblical and historical message of this reformation movement by such continuing practices; be it

RESOLVED, that all future "Who's Who" for General Assembly balloting include in parentheses the home congregation of said candidates, that we of this Assembly may be better informed and thus enabled to vote more intelligently.

Editor's Note: The other related matter involved a negative Assembly action. In 1991 the Assembly addressed an issue related to religious affiliation and Assembly elections or ratifications. In 1990 a motion had been introduced calling for the Assembly to "go on record as requesting that all agencies, committees or commissions not place on ballots to be presented to this Assembly for election or ratification the names of persons who do not attend or support local congregations of the Church of God." This motion was referred for study by the Commission on Christian Higher Education—of particular concern for the memberships of college boards of trustees. In the Assembly of 1991, then, the Commission recommended that the 1990 motion not be adopted. The Assembly concurred. The Commission's report included an extended rationale, summarized by these concluding paragraphs.

Careful review by the Commission on Christian Higher Education has revealed that adequate criteria are in place for membership on all our boards and that sensitivity to and compatibility with the message and tradition of the Church of God have been considered in nomination processes. The colleges in particular have missions which, in part, involve their positioning themselves for service in the larger arena of the Christian community and sometimes beyond to the general public. These missions call for creative and courageous flexibility and they need increased attention and understanding both by the church and the other constituencies being served.

An absolute restriction against any inclusion in collegiate governance structures of committed Christians with unusual understanding and influence who may not be actively affiliated with the Church of God would seriously hinder the accomplishment of institutional missions. Thus the Commission recommends that no additional restrictions be placed on the nomination processes of the several boards.

In summary, there is the Assembly expectation that persons, to be associated with the Assembly, will be "in fellowship and doctrinal unity," and it is preferred that typically they will be living out their lives of discipleship in relation to Church of God congregations. Doctrinal unity is to be defined by the direct teaching of the Bible (see Entry 75).

74. Executive Council Can Decide Adherence to Reformation Principles (June 1977)

WHEREAS Article II of the Constitution vests in this General Assembly of the Church of God the authority "to declare on occasion when individual ministers or congregations are not recognized by the Assembly as adhering to the general reformation principles to which the Assembly itself is committed"; and

WHEREAS this body only meets regularly one time annually; and

WHEREAS this General Assembly has heretofore caused to be created an Executive Council of the Church of God, Inc., with specific purposes, including the following:

Section 3b: "To coordinate the work of the general agencies of the Church of God in their inter-related and cooperative aspects as authorized by the General Assembly"; and

WHEREAS the General Assembly finds it necessary and expedient to delegate to the said Executive Council of the Church of God, Inc., between the annual meetings of the General Assembly, its authority to declare on occasion when individual ministers or congregations are not recognized as adhering to the general reformation principles and practices to which the Assembly itself is committed; and

WHEREAS this General Assembly finds the above-quoted language of Article III of its Constitution to include authority to find that a minister or congregation is no longer in fellowship and doctrinal unity with the Church of God; now, therefore, be it

RESOLVED, that its above-quoted authority under Article III of its Constitution be hereby delegated to the Executive Council of the Church of God, Inc., to exercise in its sole discretion between annual meetings of this General Assembly.

Editor's Note: Until the 1981 General Assembly none of these "general reformation principles" had been identified formally by the Assembly. In 1981, however, one such principle was identified. It was the principle of the central authority of the Bible in the life of the church. The statement of this principle follows as Entry 75.

75. Reformation Principle One: Biblical Authority in the Life of the Church (June 1981)

Editor's Note: During 1980-81 concern was expressed across the church that the authority of the Bible in the life of the church needed to be reaffirmed pointedly and publicly. Resolutions seeking to accomplish this purpose were passed in at least two area fellowships of ministers. These resolutions, however, contained "inerrancy" and "binding" language. Such language aroused widespread opposition, including arguments that inerrancy, as popularly understood, is a controversial theory of the Bible's inspiration not clearly taught by the Bible itself and not accepted by millions of evangelical Christians and scholars. Further, the call to "bind" was said to be contrary to the constitution of the General Assembly and alien to the heritage of the reformation movement of the Church of God.

A new resolution finally was drafted by a group of concerned ministers in an attempt to accomplish the central intent of the area fellowships without including the controversial concepts of "inerrancy" and "binding." This resolution eventually was presented to the General Assembly, but with the word "requirement" added in the final paragraph at the last minute by the Business Committee of the Assembly. The Assembly, however, acted to reinstate the word "expectation," thereby maintaining integrity with its understanding of its own Constitution and clearly affirming its opposition to the very idea of binding creedal statements being established in the church.

The following, then, is the resolution as finally approved. It is a clear statement of a "reformation principle" to which the Assembly is committed, namely, the genuine inspiration and central authority of the Bible in the life of the church.

PREFACE

For a century the reformation movement of the Church of God has pro-claimed a vision of the church which transcends the artificial and divisive barriers of rigid denominational structure and restrictive creedal statement. In this context, the General Assembly of the Church of God has limited itself as follows:

> This Assembly shall be regarded as a voluntary association. It shall not exercise ecclesiastical jurisdiction or authority over the Church in general nor over individual congregations in particular. But it shall, however, retain the right of a vol-untary association to define its own membership and to declare, on occasion, when individual ministers or congrega-tions are not recognized by the Assembly as adhering to the general reformation principles to which the Assembly itself is committed.

The continuing rightness of this self-limitation of the General Assembly is recognized and reaffirmed.

Without intending to exercise ecclesiastical authority, this General Assembly nonetheless desires to record its conviction and expectation in regard to the authority of the Bible in the life of today's church. The follow-ing, then, states a general reformation principle to which this Assembly is committed.

WHEREAS the intent of this resolution is to be understood in the light of the self-limitation of the General Assembly as stated in its Constitution (as quoted above) and is meant in no way to violate the reformation princi-ple that "the spirit of the movement is to acknowledge good wherever found and to regard no door into the church other than salvation and no test of fellowship other than true Christianity possessed within the heart" (A. L. Byers, *Birth of a Reformation*, Anderson, Indiana: Gospel Trumpet Company, 1921); and

WHEREAS from its beginning the reformation movement of the Church of God has been committed to the general theological stance that the Bible is our only creed and Christ alone is Lord, so that the Bible, supported by the interpretative ministry of the Holy Spirit, has had a central signifi-cance among us; and

WHEREAS a public restatement of this historic commitment to the authority of the Bible in the life of the Church appears timely in light of the secular humanism and doctrinal confusions of our day; therefore, be it

RESOLVED, that this Assembly declare its convictions that the Bible truly is the divinely inspired and infallible Word of God. The Bible is without error in all that it affirms, in accordance with its own purpose, namely that it is "profitable for teaching, for reproof, for correction, for training in righteousness, that the man of God may be adequate, equipped for every good work" (2 Tim. 3:16-17, NAS), and it therefore is fully trustworthy and authoritative as the infallible guide for understanding the Christian faith and living the Christian life; and be it further

RESOLVED, that this Assembly call the reformation movement of the Church of God to a new dedication to faithful biblical scholarship and proclamation, based both upon a commitment to its authority as described above and upon a fresh quest for studied insight and divine guidance in the crucial tasks of responsible biblical interpretation, teaching and preaching; and be it further

RESOLVED, that this Assembly state its expectation that all programs within this reformation movement of the Church of God reflect a genuine commitment to the Bible as the inspired and authoritative Word of God; and be it finally

RESOLVED, that this Assembly state its expectation that governing boards and elected officials, charged with oversight of the operational policies of agencies and the credentials of ministers related to this Assembly, will act responsibly and forthrightly in establishing the central significance of the authority of the Bible and in interpreting and implementing the teachings and directives of the Bible in their respective areas of the work of the Church.

Editor's Note: As one way of fulfilling this concern, in the 1991 Assembly a resolution was passed endorsing the "Discover Life In Daily Bible Reading" program and urging every congregation to enlist persons in reading through the Bible during 1992. For historical perspective, see Merle Strege's 1995 unpublished essay, "The Peculiar Impress of the Mind: Biblical Inspiration and Interpretation in the Early Church of God (Anderson)." Also see Kenneth E. Jones, *The Word of God.*

76. Reformation Principle Two: The Lordship of Jesus Christ (June 1985)

Editor's Note: See above the 1985 General Assembly action titled "Inter-Church Cooperation" (Entry 63). In part, it reads: "Any inter-church body involved in a relationship [with national ministry bodies of the Church of God] should be committed publicly to the divinity and lordship of Jesus Christ. He is central to the meaning and the mission of the church!" This, in effect, joins the authority of the Bible (Entry 75) as an assumed "general reformation principle."

DISTRIBUTION OF RESOURCES (WORLD SERVICE BUDGET)

Editor's Note: Since the 1920s with the introduction of the Associated Budgets, the Church of God movement has pooled resources in a common budget that has sought to carry forward cooperative ministries in North America and around the world. Following is a brief history of the raising and distribution of these resources.

77. Establishment of a Coordinated Budget Plan (June 1927)

Editor's Note: The 1927 General Ministerial Assembly received favorably the report of its Coordinated Budget Plan Committee. Robert L. Berry presented the plan, which previously had been agreed upon by the various national boards. It called for "boards or agencies having work that calls for general church support" to prepare annual budgets which would be examined by a "General Budget Committee." This committee would then "determine the sum to be set as the goal for each individual cause." It further called for "the program coordination of all promotional plans, whether of advertising or of special field representatives" and it designated guidelines for the distribution of designated and undesignated gifts. Finally, the Assembly, prepared to activate this plan immediately, authorized its chair, Charles E. Brown, to appoint five members to this General Budget Committee.

The concept of "Associated Budgets" was implemented in the years to follow. By 1941 the unified effort was known as "The World Service Commission." After reorganization of the Executive Council in 1955, the name was changed to the "Division of World Service."

78. Allocation of World Service Budgets

Editor's Note: The following are percentages of the annual World Service budgets as approved by the General Assembly for national solicitation and formula distribution to the several agencies and causes listed. The total budget figures used for determining these percentages include all basic, nonleveled, and restricted categories for each year in question, except for anticipated relay, budget promotion, and treasury/stewardship transactions and expenditures.

Allocation of World Service Budget by Percentage

Missions	1970-71	1980-81	1990-91	1995-96
Missionary Board	35.05	36.47	39.84	39.69
Mission Latin America	3.41	0.00	0.00	0.00
Church Extension/				
Home Missions	14.79	8.63	10.36	8.81
Hope Hill				
Children's Home	0.00	3.22	3.15	5.47
Mass Communications	4.10	3.78	4.26	4.07
Literature Evangelism	0.95	0.46	0.00	0.00
Disaster Fund	0.00	0.08	0.00	0.00
World Hunger	0.00	1.54	2.10	2.97
Million for Missions	0.00	3.45	0.00	0.00
TV Special	0.00	3.84	0.00	0.00
Church Planting	0.00	0.00	0.23	0.00
Vision 2 Grow	0.00	0.00	0.00	1.37
Contingency Reserve	0.00	0.00	0.00	0.18
SUB TOTAL	58.30	61.47	59.94	62.56
Education				
School of Theology	0.00	3.96	4.16	3.15
Seminary Tuition Fund	0.00	1.84	1.52	1.09
Anderson University	11.65	6.98	6.72	8.46
GBC/Mid-America				
Bible College	4.42	3.85	7.26	7.04
Warner Pacific College	7.56	7.21	6.03	6.71
Board of Christian				
Education	5.51	4.82	5.46	4.33
Black Ministerial				
Education	0.00	1.15	0.00	0.00
SUB TOTAL	29.14	29.81	31.15	30.78
Service				
Leadership Council/				
General Service	3.87	3.62	6.98	5.32
Special Committee/	0.00	0.00	0.06	0.00
Properties				
General Assembly	4.42	2.86	0.00	0.00
Board of Pensions	1.91	1.05	0.49	0.35
Division of				
Church Service	1.68	0.85	0.96	0.76
Ministers Aid	0.68	0.34	0.42	0.23
SUB TOTAL	12.56	8.72	8.91	6.66
TOTAL %	100.00	100.00	100.00	100.00

79. Giving Response of the Church

Editor's Note: The following total giving figures include all gifts that received credit from the Division of World Service, including any relay funds handled.

YEAR	MEMBERS	PER CAPITA	INCREASE (DECREASE)	TOTAL GIVING	INCREASE (DECREASE)
1970	147,752	16.36	8.4%	$ 2,416,513	9.1%
1971	150,198	17.20	5.1%	$ 2,582,497	6.9%
1972	152,787	17.04	-0.9%	$ 2,603,428	0.8%
1973	158,264	18.51	8.6%	$ 2,930,226	12.6%
1974	159,733	20.05	8.3%	$ 3,202,307	9.3%
1975	165,928	22.96	14.5%	$ 3,809,844	19.0%
1976	169,372	26.12	13.8%	$ 4,423,982	16.1%
1977	172,756	27.57	5.6%	$ 4,762,919	7.7%
1978	173,940	30.98	12.4%	$ 5,388,512	13.1%
1979	175,405	34.93	12.8%	$ 6,126,234	13.7%
1980	177,407	37.20	6.5%	$ 6,599,349	7.7%
1981	180,772	38.99	4.8%	$ 7,047,486	6.8%
1982	187,485	38.69	-0.8%	$ 7,254,160	2.9%
1983	191,508	38.82	0.3%	$ 7,433,992	2.5%
1984	195,105	38.14	-1.8%	$ 7,440,912	0.1%
1985	197,713	40.04	5.0%	$ 7,916,592	6.4%
1986	197,625	43.60	8.9%	$ 8,216,543	3.8%
1987	203,226	42.71	-2.0%	$ 8,679,527	5.6%
1988	203,552	42.30	-1.0%	$ 8,610,006	-0.8%
1989	200,062	45.64	7.9%	$ 9,131,141	6.1%
1990	202,215	44.75	-2.0%	$ 9,049,443	-0.9%
1991	206,445	45.47	1.6%	$ 9,387,502	3.7%
1992	213,872	45.35	-0.3%	$ 9,698,167	3.3%
1993	217,614	46.04	1.5%	$10,468,594	7.9%
1994	217,681	49.94	8.5%	$10,870,948	3.8%
1995	224,061	52.13	4.4%	$11,679,417	7.4%

CHRISTIAN HIGHER EDUCATION

Editor's Note: For a broad background and brief historical sketches of the several colleges and seminary in North America, and the Commission on Christian Higher Education, refer to Barry L. Callen, *Preparing for Service: A History of Higher Education in the Church of God* (Anderson, Ind.: Warner Press, 1988). In this history,

Callen notes the following about the early years of the Church of God and formal education:

> In the earliest years of the history of the Church of God movement it happened just about the way one would have expected. Given an experience oriented, anti-institutionally minded, generally rural body of Christian people, full of zeal and urgency for a gospel cause, living in the middle of revolutionary changes in American higher education that rarely were friendly to the faith, founding colleges was not a high priority. To the contrary, formal learning and evangelistic believing tended to be seen more as competitors than as companions. Education was identified as a typical part of the sectarian scene that God was calling to an end.... Being formally trained was announced as merely the process of a person being boxed in a human institution and tied by human thinking. It was understood to be a key element of the diseased backbone of the denominational system.
>
> Of increasing prominence during the early years of the movement was the growth and industrialization of cities. To these complex and problem-ridden settings came pioneer ministers of the Church of God who were burdened for the lost and the destitute. "Missionary homes" began to appear as teams of gospel workers conducted revival services, distributed literature, and helped the needy. Probably the first such home was started in 1895 in Chicago by Gorham Tufts. It operated as a rescue mission, an evangelistic center, and later, under the leadership of E. A. Reardon, a place for a wide range of worship, service, and educational activities. Young people were attracted to this and similar urban homes. They had energy for service to others and they had needs of their own for growth and training.
>
> It was typical in these settings that informal counseling and study sessions became regular classes for enthusiastic young gospel workers. Several of the homes developed the name "Bible School" or "missionary training school," including the Kansas City Bible School and Spokane Bible School. Some general softening of the harsh attitudes toward formal education had become evident. In a real sense the missionary homes were bridge institutions between what was slipping into the movement's past and what was about to come. They served for about a generation as the only existing "higher education system" of the Church of God (12-13, 18-19).

[Then came Anderson Bible Training School in 1917 (now Anderson University), an outgrowth of the movement's publishing ministry, the Gospel Trumpet Company, by then located in Anderson, Indiana.]

In the Church of God movement, early resistance to Christian education grew out of its supposed tacit denial of the need for a new birth or conversion. It was also suspect simply because most of the mainline denominations practiced and promoted it, because a long-range educational program was not compatible with the expected early return of Jesus, and because its organizational structure was thought to inhibit the free working of the Holy Spirit—it might become a substitute for revivals. Nevertheless, through the persistent efforts of a few far-sighted leaders, the values of the educative process were recognized and over many years there emerged a robust and widely accepted movement in Christian education. In the June 1, 1889, issue of the Gospel Trumpet, E. E. Byrum gave a strong defense of the Sunday School and included instructions on how to set up and conduct them. A Sunday School was organized on the Grand Junction, Michigan, camp grounds in 1892, but Christian education as an integral ministry of the congregation was not enthusiastically accepted for another twenty years.

By January, 1891, the Gospel Trumpet Company had begun publication of *The Shining Light,* a paper mostly for children, but promoted also for adult use. This was the beginning of printed curriculum materials for the Church of God. The first Sunday School quarterlies were published by the Gospel Trumpet Company in 1910, based on the International Uniform Lesson Series. In 1911, D. O. Teasley's book *How to Conduct a Sunday School* was published and widely used by the more than 300 Sunday Schools then functioning in the movement. By 1923 there were about 500 Sunday Schools. That year the national Board of Religious Education and Sunday Schools was organized. A primary program emphasis was leadership training, in cooperation with the International Council of Religious Education. A boost to the cause came in 1930 when Miss Pearl Johnson was employed by the Board to travel as a field worker to promote Christian education. She was succeeded in

1934 by Esther Boyer (Bauer). Strong proponents of excellence in Christian education were Bessie Byrum and Walter S. Haldeman, early teachers in what now is Anderson University.

A dramatic forward move came in 1939 with the Board's employment of Irene (Smith) Caldwell. She was named national Secretary of the Board of Christian Education (full-time beginning in 1941) and worked closely with A. T. Rowe, General Manager of the Gospel Trumpet Company, whose unbounded energy, fearless

Irene (Smith) Caldwell

courage, and innovative leadership helped move Christian education beyond its narrow horizons. Irene (Smith) Caldwell would go on to have a significant teaching career at Warner Pacific College, Anderson School of Theology, and Warner Southern College. The work of the national Board was carried on by T. Franklin Miller beginning in 1945. Miller, like Smith before him, combined evangelistic passion with commitment to educational excellence. They contended that a bird needs two wings to fly, evangelism and education. There was rapid growth at the local, state, and national levels. The publishing house produced training texts and better curriculum materials.

In 1965, when T. Franklin Miller left to become President of Warner Press, he was succeeded by Donald A. Courtney and later by Sherrill Hayes. New, expanded, and innovative programs indicated that the cause of Christian education in the Church of God, although struggling for half a century for full acceptance, had become a stable component of the ministries of evangelism, discipling, and nurture in most congregations of the Church of God. In recent years a key component of the resourcing of Christian education in many Church of God congregations has been the fully graded BRIDGES Curriculum for the church school.

T. Franklin Miller

Following is a brief overview of the institutions of higher education now related to the Church of God in the United States and Canada, along with their chief executive officers.

Institutions of Higher Education	Chief Executive Officers	Years In Office
Anderson University (Anderson, Indiana)	Joseph T. Wilson	1917–1923
	John A. Morrison	1923–1958
	Robert H. Reardon	1958–1983
	Robert A. Nicholson	1983–1990
	James L. Edwards	1990 to present
Anderson University School of Theology (Deans)	Earl L. Martin	1950–1953
	Adam W. Miller	1953–1962
	Gene W. Newberry	1962–1974
	Barry L. Callen	1974–1983
	Jerry C. Grubbs	1983–1988
	Barry L. Callen	1988–1989
	James Earl Massey	1989–1995
	David L. Sebastian	1995 to present

Bay Ridge Christian College (Kendleton, Texas)	J. Horace Germany	1959–1982
	Charles G. Denniston	1982–1987
	Robert C. Williams	1987–1991
	Wilfred Jordan	1991–1993
	Percy Lewis	1993–1995
	Seth Beverly	1995–1996
	Verda E. Beach	1996 to present
Gardner College (Camrose, Alberta, CA)	Harry C. Gardner	1933–1953
	Gordon Schieck (Acting)	1953–1955
	Thomas M. Hall	1955–1957
	Harry C. Gardner	1957–1961
	J. Milton Chugg	1961–1964
	Albert F. Irving	1964–1966
	Hugh C. Wolkow (Acting)	1966–1967
	Gordon Schieck	1967–1974
	David W. Davis	1974–1975
	Gordon Schieck	1975–1977
	Robert Hazen	1977–1989
	M. Bruce Kelly	1989–1997
	John Alan Howard	1997 to present
Mid-America Bible College (Oklahoma City, OK)	Max R. Gaulke	1953–1973
	John W. Conley	1973–1989
	Forrest Robinson	1989–1999
	John Fozard	1999 to present
Warner Pacific College (Portland, OR)	Albert F. Gray	1937–1957
	Milo L. Chapman	1957–1962
	Louis F. Gough	1962–1966
	E. Joe Gilliam	1966–1979
	Milo L. Chapman	1979–1981
	Marshall K. Christensen	1981–1996
	Jay A. Barber, Jr.	1996 to present
Warner Southern College (Lake Wales, FL)	Leslie W. Ratzlaff	1968–1969
	Leroy M. Fulton	1969–1990
	Gregory V. Hall	1990 to present

Deans of Anderson School of Theology, L. to R.:
David L. Sebastian, James Earl Massey, Jerry C. Grubbs,
Barry L. Callen, Gene W. Newberry.
Not pictured: Earl L. Martin, Adam W. Miller

The actions of the General Assembly related to higher education follow.

80. Proper Restrictions for a Church College (June 1918)

Editor's Note: The establishment of Anderson Bible Training School in 1917 was seen by some in the church at the time as a questionable or even dangerous event. In the 1918 General Ministerial Assembly the following report from an appointed committee was read and accepted.

Your committee appointed for the purpose of considering restrictions for the Anderson Bible Training School submits the following report:

1. We believe that such a school can be conducted to the glory of God and the welfare of the ministry and church if kept within certain bounds.
2. We believe that no effort should be made to create a sentiment to the effect that young ministers must attend this school in order to secure recognition.
3. It is our opinion that in many cases the education of ministers can best be obtained in those sections of the country where their ministerial work is to be done so that the practical can be more definitely combined with the theoretical. In other words, we do not believe that the Anderson Bible School should supersede or replace other training schools of the church.

212

4. Students should be left free to choose their own course of study from among such branches as the school provides.

5. No recommendation or diploma should be given any student. Satisfactory gradings in school constitutes no proof that an individual is called of God to preach the gospel. Hence every student must be left on his own responsibility so that he will not possess in this respect any authority proceeding from this school which will give him an advantage over those ministers who have not attended school. In the Church of God every minister must stand on his own merits and earn his place of responsibility whether educated or uneducated.

6. We believe that the training of ministers in this school should include more than their intellectual development along educational lines. The most prominent feature must be their personal development in spirituality, faith, and the gifts of the Spirit of God.

81. Anderson Bible Training School Separated from the Gospel Trumpet Company (June 1925)

Gospel Trumpet Home, Anderson, Indiana.
The "Old Main" of Anderson College (University)
beginning in 1925.

WHEREAS the Anderson Bible Training School has heretofore been a part of the Gospel Trumpet Company's sphere of responsibility, but has outgrown the meager organization provided for it in the company's Bylaws; and

WHEREAS it represents one of the general phases of the work of the church and requires that it be constituted a legal entity; and

WHEREAS it desires to be separated from the Gospel Trumpet Company and organized in accordance with the same general principles upon which the other general boards of the church are organized; and

WHEREAS the Gospel Trumpet Company has thoroughly considered and approved the separation, as well as the school's proposed Articles of Association as now modified; therefore, be it

213

RESOLVED, that this Assembly approves the proposal to have the school separated from said company, and organized in the manner desired.

82. Pacific Bible College Becomes a National Agency (1956)

Editor's Note: The June, 1956, Assembly voted the necessary changes in its own bylaws to establish Pacific Bible College as a subordinate board of the Assembly. In 1959 the Assembly concurred with the action of the college's board of trustees changing the school's name to Warner Pacific College. In 1970 the Assembly took major action in assisting the college in a time of the school's financial crisis. For a brief history of Warner Pacific College, see Callen, *Preparing for Service,* chapter 9.

83. Establishment of the Commission on Christian Higher Education (June 1958)

WHEREAS the study Commission on Higher Education, authorized by this General Ministerial Assembly in June, 1952, after five years of study and research is convinced of the need of a permanent Commission on Higher Education, a conviction shared by those connected with our educational institutions as well as by ministers and laymen; be it therefore

RESOLVED, that this General Ministerial Assembly hereby authorizes the creation of a permanent Commission on Higher Education as outlined in the By-Laws herewith submitted, whose general purpose shall be to promote the cause of Christian higher education within the Church of God Movement, said Commission to function within the framework of the Executive Council, and be it further

RESOLVED, that immediately upon adoption of this resolution and its accompanying By-Laws, the educational institutions named in these By-Laws, the Board of Christian Education, and the Executive Council be hereby instructed to appoint those persons who shall constitute the Commission.

Editor's Note: For a brief history of the Commission on Christian Higher Education, see Callen, *Preparing for Service,* chapter 12. The Commission was disbanded in 1998 as part of the restructuring of the national ministries of the Church of God.

84. Policy on Starting New Colleges (June, 1964)

In this time of growth in higher education in America many church colleges are finding it increasingly difficult to remain in operation or to uncover the resources necessary for an adequate program. Within the Church of God it appears evident that: (1) at present there are enough colleges to serve the Church of God student population able and willing to attend those colleges; (2) adequate support is not being provided for existing colleges, most of which are struggling financially for their very lives; and (3) new colleges in the Church continually enter the talking/planning stage, are presumably designed to meet the needs of a particular geographic area, but generally are without adequate student and financial support necessary for existence and growth.

The Commission on Christian Higher Education of the Church of God believes it is imperative that great caution be exercised in the establishment of new Church of God colleges, acknowledging that considerable hurt may derive to the Church and its young people through a college not built on an adequate foundation. Specifically:

> We urge that a new college be contemplated only within the framework of careful consultation with the Commission on Christian Higher Education, recognizing that through this means we are most likely to achieve the coordination so necessary to the total advancement of higher education in the Church;
>
> We urge that in the establishment of any new college, careful plans be developed for financial support and underwriting, recognizing that the costs of maintaining an adequate program at the college level are enormous;
>
> We insist that, if a prospective college would ever expect or hope to seek the support and assistance of the total Church, it should seek that support and assistance in the crucial stages of planning and establishment.

The Commission on Christian Higher Education continues to make itself available to the Church and its educational institutions as a resource, a stimulus, and a guide in these days of unusual problems and opportunities in the Church and in higher education.

85. Gulf-Coast Bible College Becomes a National Agency (June, 1968)

WHEREAS Gulf-Coast Bible College, Houston, Texas, has served the Church of God since September, 1953, as an institution of higher education, and during these years has trained an increasing number of young people for Christian service; and

WHEREAS the Texas State Assembly of the Church of God, to which Gulf-Coast Bible College is responsible organizationally, adopted a resolution in 1963, with the knowledge and concurrence of the trustees of Gulf-Coast Bible College that requested the Executive Council of the Church of God that the college be permitted to share in the budget for higher education through World Service; and

WHEREAS at that time, in the judgment of the Executive Council, Gulf-Coast Bible College had not attained the status of a general agency of the Church of God and therefore the request was referred to the Commission on Christian Higher Education for study in depth and to recommend guidelines to the college in obtaining additional strength and to make recommendations to the Executive Council for further consideration of the request from the Texas State Assembly; and

WHEREAS during the past five years Gulf-Coast Bible College has cooperated closely with the Commission on Christian Higher Education in making a self-study and in the implementation of recommended guidelines whereby the college might obtain accreditation by the American Association of Bible Colleges (Gulf-Coast Bible College now holds an associate membership in the American Association of Bible Colleges and is working toward possible full accreditation in 1968); and

WHEREAS the Board of Trustees of Gulf-Coast Bible College and the members of the Texas State Assembly of the Church of God, in keeping with their indicated desire for the college to have the status of a general agency of the Church of God, have approved provisional changes in the charter, articles of association, and bylaws of the college in order to comply with the requirements of the bylaws of the General Assembly of the Church of God as pertains to a general agency and, by so doing, have indicated their willingness to abide by the regulations, privileges, and limitations of a general agency, and as a member within the family of agencies, organized by and responsible to the General Assembly of the Church of God; and

WHEREAS the Executive Council of the Church of God, in session February 21, 1968, voted (23-3) to recommend to the General Assembly of the Church of God that recognition be given to Gulf-Coast Bible College as a general agency of the Church of God; therefore be it

RESOLVED, that the members of the General Assembly of the Church of God, in session on June 18, 1968, recognize Gulf-Coast Bible College as a general agency of the Church of God, with understanding that such recognition will entitle Gulf-Coast Bible College to have representation in the membership of the Executive Council, and participation in the World Service Budget; and be it further

RESOLVED, that the Executive Council be authorized by the General Assembly to work with the Texas State Assembly and the Board of Trustees of Gulf-Coast Bible College in the implementation of this action.

Editor's Note: For a brief history of Gulf-Coast Bible College, later named Mid-America Bible College (1985), see Callen, *Preparing for Service: A History of Higher Education in the Church of God* (Anderson, Ind.: Warner Press, 1988), chapter 7.

86. Action Concerning the "Foundation for Religious Studies" (June, 1972)

Editor's Note: During 1971-1972, in the face of low enrollments, rising costs, and an apparent need for revitalizing the curriculum, the seminary's administration and board of trustees set in motion a series of changes in the School of Theology. Included was the establishment of the Center for Pastoral Studies and an affiliation with the Foundation for Religious Studies (an evolving ecumenical consortium of theological schools in Indianapolis, Indiana). The following resolution was offered (but did not pass).

WHEREAS we, members of the Board of Trustees of Anderson College, are assured that the effective education of pastors, evangelists, missionaries, and other Christian teachers and workers is one of the most urgent needs of the Church; and

WHEREAS this Board of Trustees, in its search to determine what set of relationships and circumstances will provide the best training and preparation for the ministry in the Church of God, initiated a major study of theological education during the past year through the appointment of a special committee composed of the chairman of the General Assembly, the executive secretary of the Executive Council, College and School of Theology administrators, and members appointed from the Board of Trustees; and

WHEREAS the committee, through its year-long study took testimony from pastors, faculty members, School of Theology alumni, and present students; and

WHEREAS the recommendations of the committee included the development of new and expanded programs in the School of Theology, including a Center for Pastoral Studies and certain cooperative relationships with the Foundation for Religious Studies and Asbury Theological Seminary; and

WHEREAS the expanded programming makes available new resources for theological education in the Church of God and lays greater emphasis on preaching, evangelism, and field work experiences; and

WHEREAS this board feels that the expanded program will result in well-prepared ministers who are able to preach the Word effectively, teach, counsel, evangelize, and build up the Church; and

WHEREAS certain questions have been raised relating to the scope and involvements of the expanded School of Theology program, be it, therefore,

RESOLVED, that the General Assembly of the Church of God, meeting in annual session in Anderson, Indiana, on the 20th day of June, 1972, call for the establishment of a special committee, composed of three (3) pastors appointed by the chairman of the General Assembly, two (2) members of the Anderson College Board of Trustees, and two (2) members appointed by the Commission on Christian Higher Education of the Church of God, to make a study of the School of Theology's expanded program during its third year, to assess the effectiveness of the program for the preparation of ministers for the Church of God, and to present a report to the Board of Trustees and the General Assembly.

Editor's Note: The above resolution was *defeated*. It was replaced by the following resolution, which was adopted by a 499-422 ballot vote (slim margin reflecting the controversy involved).

In view of the defeat of the resolution establishing a special committee to study theological education, we the following ministers whose names appear below, hereby move that the association with the Foundation for Religious Studies be dissolved within the next three months or at the end of the first semester of the academic year.

Editor's Note: For a brief history of the School of Theology, see Callen, *Preparing for Service,* chapter 3.

87. Recommendations of the Study Committee on the Seminary (June, 1973)

Editor's Note: The 1972 General Assembly, following considerable discussion and a negative action on the School of Theology's new relationship with the Foundation for Religious Studies (see Entry 86), authorized a one-year seminary study committee. It was commissioned to bring to the 1973 Assembly a report containing "recommendations for the continuation of a Church of God seminary, responsible to the General Assembly." A major report was so brought. It included a series of observations and suggestions and twelve specific recommendations. The total report was received and approved by the Assembly. The following is a brief summary of the recommendations, with page references to the fuller statement of each within the report itself.

1. Commission on Christian Higher Education consider broadening the program of the Center for Pastoral Studies (page 7).

2. World Service Budget show askings of both graduate School of Theology and Anderson College undergraduate program (page 8).

3. Move toward increased World Service support to the School of Theology (page 8).

4. Move toward per-student base in Anderson College support (page 8).

5. Budget Committee bring a viable plan to achieve these goals, for Assembly review in June, 1974 (page 8).

6. Promote for seminary student scholarship funds (page 8).

7. Executive Council establish Special Trust Fund (page 9).

8. Commission on Christian Higher Education give high priority to seminary needs and problems (page 9).

9. Provide for additional meetings of the Commission on Christian Higher Education (page 9).

10. Establish a "blue ribbon" committee to give particular and continuing attention to the School of Theology (page 9).

11. Assembly ratification of the seminary dean (page 9).

12. In June, 1977, General Assembly again test the thesis of a free-standing seminary—separate from Anderson College (page 10).

88. Seminary Budget in World Service Budget (June 1974)

Editor's Note: The Assembly chair recognized F. Eugene Fauntleroy, who called attention to a report titled "Budget Committee Recommendations" regarding a recommended increase of $40,000 in the basic budget allocation to Anderson College for its School of Theology in the 1974-75 World Service Budget and that the Division of World Service concur with the Budget Committee in recommending to the 1974 General Assembly that this plan of additional support to Anderson College be extended over the following four years, or through the 1978-79 World Service year. A copy of these recommendations and the assumptions upon which the Budget Committee based them is attached to the original minutes. Fauntleroy moved the adoption of these recommendations, seconded by Dan Harman. Fauntleroy clarified that the five-year proposal would amount to $200,000 by 1978-79. Motion carried.

89. Seminary Tuition Aid Fund (June 1974)

Editor's Note: The Assembly chair recognized G. David Cox, chair of the Seminary Advisory Committee. Cox moved and the Assembly concurred in the adoption of this resolution from the Committee:

> The General Assembly instruct the Division of World Service to establish strategy for raising a goal of $50,000 for the year 1974-75 to be retained as a separate account established by the School of Theology, to be activated in the 1975-76 year, for the purpose of defraying tuitional costs now required from the students. These funds are to be expended for tuition costs for Church of God students in the School of Theology and, if available, also for extraordinary moving expenses and then also for student aid in exceptional situations. This dollar goal should be reviewed annually by the Budget Committee and made a part of the World Service Budget.

90. Relationship of the Seminary to Anderson College (June 1976)

WHEREAS the General Assembly of the Church of God, in its June 21, 1971 meeting, charged the Commission on Christian Higher Education to make a thorough and extensive study of theological education and ministerial training in the Church of God; and

WHEREAS the General Assembly, on June 19, 1972, approved the appointment of a Special Advisory Committee to advise with the board of trustees and administrative staff of Anderson College regarding the program of the School of Theology, with the stipulation that this committee was to function "until the completion of the study which the Assembly in its June 1972 session requested the Commission on Christian Higher Education to make, but not beyond June 1977"; and

WHEREAS the Commission on Christian Higher Education has now completed its study and submitted its report to the General Assembly; and

WHEREAS the Seminary Advisory Committee, in a communication under date of March 15, 1976, has communicated the following information to the Commission on Christian Higher Education, to wit:

> We, the Seminary Advisory Committee of the General Assembly, unanimously and strongly reaffirm and wish to

220

further encourage the concept set forth by the General Assembly's Special Study Committee in its major report to the Assembly in 1973 that there must be "a willingness and commitment in the Church of God to concentrate its graduate and ministerial education in the seminary."

In the light of our work over the past three years and in the light of the very encouraging developments in the School of Theology during that period, we, the Seminary Advisory Committee of the General Assembly, see no reason to consider further the question of a free-standing seminary, and we hereby encourage the Commission on Christian Higher Education to concur in this judgment and to so recommend to the General Assembly in its 1976 report.

WHEREAS the Commission on Christian Higher Education, in its meeting on May 1, 1976, did consider the recommendation from the Seminary Advisory Committee, and did wholeheartedly concur in it; therefore, be it

RESOLVED, that the General Assembly of the Church of God affirm this recommendation mutually agreed upon by the Seminary Advisory Committee and the Commission on Christian Higher Education; and grant its approval, for the present time, for the seminary, the graduate School of Theology, to remain in coordinate relationship to, and under the administrative guidance of, the Anderson College Board of Trustees and its administrative officers; and be it further

RESOLVED, that special commendation be given to the board of trustees and administrative officers of Anderson College for the attention they have given to the School of Theology over the past four years; to the Seminary Advisory Committee for the excellent work they have done in keeping the needs of the School of Theology before the General Assembly; and to the pastors and congregations that have shown concern in the seminary by becoming covenant churches in the seminary internship program and in helping to underwrite the tuition costs of eligible ministerial students; and be it further

RESOLVED, that the General Assembly, by its adoption of this resolution, consider the work of the Seminary Advisory Committee terminated and that the assignment of the Commission on Christian Higher Education in regard to theological education and ministerial training is now complete.

91. Recommendations for Ministerial Education (June 1976)

Editor's Note: The 1972 General Assembly was the scene of extended debate over matters related to the education of ministers (see Entry 86). One result of that debate was a charge to the Commission on Christian Higher Education "to make a thorough and extensive study of theological and ministerial training in the Church of God." The 1976 General Assembly received and approved the final result of this commission study which was presented in the form of a lengthy written report. Included was a set of affirmations and proposals. These are to be found on pages 536-541 of *The First Century*, volume 2, edited by Barry L. Callen (Anderson, Indiana: Warner Press, 1979).

92. Black Ministerial Education Fund (June 1977)

Editor's Note: As part of its 1976 study (see Entry 91), the Commission on Christian Higher Education reviewed the statement in the Bylaws of the General Assembly pertaining to general agencies and the document adopted by the Executive Council in 1965 titled "What Is a General Agency." In the light of the provisions in the Bylaws of the Assembly and the findings of its study, the Commission and consultants unanimously agreed not to recommend general agency status for Bay Ridge Christian College (a status the college had been seeking actively). It was agreed that an alternative to general agency status would be in the best interest of training black leaders to serve the Church of God at the present time. The following resolution was presented and approved to accomplish this purpose.

WHEREAS in June, 1975, the General Assembly of the Church of God referred a request from the Southern Association of the Church of God to the Commission on Christian Higher Education concerning potential general agency status for Bay Ridge Christian College; and

WHEREAS the General Assembly recommended to the Commission a thorough study of the best way to train leaders to serve the black church in the South, to include an in-depth study of Bay Ridge Christian College if needed, and with the assistance of a team of black consultants and with the full cooperation of the administration of Bay Ridge Christian College and representatives of the Southern Association of the Church of God; and

WHEREAS the Commission on Christian Higher Education and its eight black consultants have unanimously agreed as a result of these studies that the need is urgent, complex in nature, and national in scope, necessitating an approach other than the recommendation of general agency status for Bay Ridge Christian College; therefore, be it

RESOLVED, that the General Assembly of the Church of God establish within the annual budget of the Commission on Christian Higher Education, beginning with the 1977-78 budget, a Fund for Black Ministerial Education; and be it further

RESOLVED, that the administration of the fund be done in consultation with representative black leaders of the Church of God; and be it further

RESOLVED, that the commission in the administration of this fund give priority consideration to the following areas of need: (a) the urgent need for the development of the academic program of Bay Ridge Christian College, (b) the underwriting of scholarships for eligible black ministerial students to attend Church of God colleges, and (c) the development, in cooperation with the Center for Pastoral Studies, of an in-service training program designed primarily for black church leaders with limited formal training; and be it further

RESOLVED, that in the World Service Budget for 1977-78, the Fund for Black Ministerial Education be $55,000, with the understanding that gifts for this purpose would receive World Service credit; and be it further

RESOLVED, that the Boards of Trustees of Bay Ridge Christian College and Gulf-Coast Bible College be encouraged to explore the possibilities of joint programming and other mutual uses of the available human and material resources and that each of these institutions give annual progress reports in this regard to the Commission on Christian Higher Education; and be it finally

RESOLVED, that the Commission be instructed to make an intensive evaluation of the fund and the above programming during 1979-80 and that the commission make a report to the General Assembly.

Editor's Note: Based on the research and recommendation of the Commission on Christian Higher Education, the 1981 General Assembly acted to discontinue this fund. This action included the future granting of World Service credit for funds channeled through World Service for Bay Ridge Christian College and a continuing assignment for the commission to identify and address "the gaps or shortcomings" of the several national programs of black ministerial education.

93. Anderson College Board Speaks to the Church (June, 1981)

Editor's Note: On June 16, 1981, the Board of Trustees of Anderson College (University) made a major report to the General Assembly. This report spoke directly to concerns of the Assembly as these had been focused in the 1980 Assembly and then by a select committee that worked with high national visibility between the 1980 and 1981 Assemblies. The concerns centered on certain of the existing policies and personnel of the college, including questions of clarification regarding the nature of the school's mission, particularly as that mission related to the church and its stated convictions. Following lengthy discussion, the Assembly voted the following overwhelmingly.

> The General Assembly register its appreciation for the thorough manner in which the Board of Trustees of Anderson College addressed the recommendations of the Select Committee, and that the General Assembly accept the report and commit itself to work with the college in the realization of these objectives.

94. Church and Colleges: A Call for Clarification

Editor's Note: The 1981 General Assembly accepted with appreciation a major report from the Board of Trustees of Anderson College (see Entry 93). In a section of that report identified as "Critical Issues Ahead," there was a call for clarification of the relationship between the church and its colleges. It read:

> Historically, the relationship of the Church of God to its colleges has been largely informal and undefined. There has been the relationship created by the election of trustees, the ratification of chief executive officers, budgetary support, and general reporting. However, there is little clarity regarding the Church's expectations of its colleges and there has not been a widespread understanding of what constitutes a responsible relationship between a church body and its institutions of higher learning. We urge an exploration of this subject.

95. Gardner Bible College: 50th Anniversary (June 1983)

WHEREAS Gardner Bible College, this year of 1983-84, will be celebrating its 50th year of service to the Church of God; and

WHEREAS Gardner Bible College is the second oldest Church of God institution of higher education in North America [Anderson College the oldest]; and

WHEREAS the Gardner Board, its faculty and staff, and the General Assemblies of both Western Canada and Ontario have reviewed the original purpose of the school and have affirmed its viability for the present and future and have recommitted themselves to that purpose (original purpose stated below); and

WHEREAS Gardner Bible College is filling a significant role in the brotherhood of Church of God institutions of higher education, be it, therefore

RESOLVED, that this Assembly commend Gardner Bible College on this milestone in its life and ministry, and be it further

RESOLVED, that this Assembly call upon the church to enter into celebration with the Canadian church wherever and whenever possible in this year it has set aside as Gardner Bible College's Year of Jubilee.

Editor's Note: Following is the original purpose of this school as stated in THE ACT OF INCORPORATION by the Province of Alberta, March 31, 1947:

THE PURPOSE of Gardner Bible College is the providing of intellectual and spiritual training for prospective ministers, missionaries, and gospel workers and of promoting the true principles and teachings of the Bible as taught and exemplified by Jesus Christ.

For a brief history of Gardner Bible College, later renamed Gardner College, see Callen, *Preparing For Service,* chapter 6.

96. Move of Gulf-Coast Bible College to Oklahoma City (June 1984)

Editor's Note: President John Conley of Gulf-Coast Bible College reported to the 1984 General Assembly on the finalized plans of the college to move its operations to Oklahoma City, Oklahoma, in the summer of 1985. Concern was raised from the Assembly floor that the Assembly should approve such moving plans since such a move would require a change in the college's articles of incorporation (a change in corporate Articles requires Assembly approval). A motion emerged from the floor calling for the Assembly to approve the moving plan already underway. This motion carried unanimously. Soon the school's unexpected inability to sell its former property in Houston, Texas, brought about a major financial crisis that had to be addressed by the national church.

97. New Name for Gulf-Coast Bible College (June 1985)

Editor's Note: The 1985 General Assembly approved the third restated articles of incorporation of Gulf-Coast Bible College. This restatement assumed the school's relocation to Oklahoma City, Oklahoma, and its intent to do business in Oklahoma under the name "Mid-America Bible College." It continues to date in Oklahoma City and under the new name.

98. New Process for Electing Warner Pacific College Trustees (June 1985)

Editor's Note: For years there was concern that many members of the General Assembly were not acquainted with any of the candidates from whom the Assembly elected members to the Board of Trustees of Warner Pacific College. That Board and the West Coast Ministerial Assembly now recommended and the General Assembly approved the following.

1. That nominations for lay members be voted on at the West Coast Ministerial Assembly, with the name of the final candidate brought to the General Assembly for ratification.

2. That the college continue to take nominations for each ministerial position on the Board of Trustees to the West Coast Ministerial Assembly and place the names of two candidates on the ballot of the General Assembly.

Editor's Note: In 1996 (Entry 67) ratification became the typical Assembly procedure in relation to all governing boards related to the Assembly.

99. Reconstituting the Membership of the Commission on Christian Higher Education (June 1985)

Editor's Note: Following a 1984 meeting of the presidents, deans, and board chairs of the Church of God colleges in the United States and the annual meeting of the Commission on Christian Higher Education in January 1985, the following proposal was presented to the Executive Council and then to the General Assembly. It received approval from both bodies. A central assumption was that the proposed new composition of the Commission's membership would enhance the Commission's functioning by assuring that key decision makers in higher education would participate fully in the work of the Commission. This action increased the size of the Commission and eliminated the category of associate non-voting members. Effective July, 1985, the Commission's membership was established as:

Anderson College president, dean, and board chair	3
Warner Pacific College president, dean, and board chair	3
Mid-America Bible College president, dean, and board chair	3
Bay Ridge Christian College president, dean, and board chair	3
Warner Southern College president, dean, and board chair	3
Anderson School of Theology dean	1
Azusa Pacific University president	1
Executive Council representative (staff director)	1
Elected representatives (General Assembly)	6
Board of Christian Education executive secretary	1
Gardner Bible College president, dean, and board chair	3
Total	28

Editor's Note: As part of the major restructuring of the national ministries of the Church of God in the late 1990s, the Commission on Christian Higher Education was disbanded.

100. Fiftieth Anniversary of Warner Pacific College (June 1986)

WHEREAS Warner Pacific College will be celebrating in 1986-87 its fiftieth (50th) year of service to the people and mission of the Church of God, having been founded as Pacific Bible College in Spokane, Washington, in 1937; and

WHEREAS the college moved to Portland, Oregon, in 1940, changed its name to Warner Pacific College in 1959, and received full accreditation in 1961; and

WHEREAS the college has shared the time of many of its distinguished leaders with the general work of the Church, including Albert F. Gray who served as Chair of this Assembly for fifteen years and Milo L. Chapman who was a long-term member and officer of the Commission on Christian Higher Education; and

WHEREAS these fifty years of the college's existence and service have been characterized by sacrifice and dedication in the quest for excellence, informed by the central convictions of both the Christian faith and higher learning; therefore, be it

RESOLVED, that the General Assembly of the Church of God, in session June 17-18, 1986, join with the Commission on Christian Higher Education in recognizing, commending, and thanking Warner Pacific College on this fiftieth anniversary occasion; and be it further

RESOLVED, that this General Assembly of the Church of God call upon the church to enter into the various events of the anniversary celebration and, by so doing, dedicate herself anew to the importance of Christian higher education in these troubled times.

101. Limitation of Terms: An Exemption (June 1986)

Editor's Note: In June, 1985, the General Assembly placed a limitation of terms on any person serving on the governing board of a national agency. The following year the Commission on Christian Higher Education initiated a request that this limitation be less restrictive for the board memberships of the colleges. The Commission argued that "the functions and procedures of members of the college boards are distinctive...." The Assembly agreed, extending to a maximum of fifteen consecutive years the allowable tenure of service of any one person (although after a lapse of two years that person could be renominated). In 1990 this broadened limitation of terms was extended to all persons affected by the original 1985 action. (See Entry 62).

102. New Name for Anderson College (June 1987)

Editor's Note: In 1986-87 the administration and Board of Trustees of Anderson College studied the possible wisdom of adopting for the institution the name "university" (in part to reflect better the breadth of its academic programming, including the graduate School of Theology). After the campus Board had made the decision to change the name, the Assembly then acted as follows:

RESOLVED, that this General Assembly of the Church of God, in its annual meeting assembled at Anderson, Indiana, this 17th day of June, 1987, hereby approves the recommendation of the Board of Trustees of Anderson College, Inc., that Article I of the restated Articles of Incorporation of said Anderson College, Inc., be amended, and does hereby adopt the following proposed amended Article I:

"NAME. The name of this Corporation is Anderson University, Inc."

103. The Year of Christian Higher Education (June 1988)

WHEREAS the Church of God (Anderson, Indiana) has a long and rich heritage of Christian Higher Education; and

WHEREAS the church supports the following predominantly Church of God colleges and university (Anderson University, Anderson University School of Theology, Bay Ridge Christian College, Gardner Bible College, Mid-America Bible College, Warner Pacific College, and Warner Southern College); and

WHEREAS the Commission on Christian Higher Education is celebrating thirty years of service to the Church of God; and

WHEREAS well equipped lay and clergy leadership will enhance greatly the church's concern for revival; be it

RESOLVED, that this Assembly go on record as affirming the ministry of Christian Higher Education; and be it

RESOLVED, that July 1, 1988, to June 30, 1989, be declared jointly as a year of Christian Higher Education and revival; and be it further

RESOLVED, that local congregations, state and regional agencies, and national agencies find ways to promote Christian higher education, to sensitize the church to the values of Christian higher education, and to lift up the importance of attending a Church of God college/university.

104. Covenant Relationship: Anderson University and the Church of God (June 1992)

Editor's Note: Anderson University, the oldest and largest of the institutions of higher education related to the Church of God movement, decided to reaffirm and state more formally its "covenant" relationship with the Church of God. The resulting ten-page booklet, presented to the 1992 General Assembly, was received with appreciation. Following are excerpts from this document.

Since the [Anderson] school's founding in 1917, there have been times of tension and debate with the church. There have also been times of affirmation and celebration. Throughout the school's history, however, there has been an unwavering commitment from both the university and the church to be vital partners in the larger mission of the church. Specifically, the university covenants with the Church of God:

- to maintain in an excellent manner its undergraduate, graduate, and seminary programs of Christian higher education;
- to respect and treasure the authority of the Bible and the distinctive heritage of the Church of God;
- to provide preparation for Christian ministry both in the undergraduate schools and in the graduate School of Theology; to offer meaningful in-service training opportunities to current ministers;
- to work diligently to attract and provide assistance to Church of God students who enroll in its programs; to be open, attractive, and hospitable to other students to whom it can minister effectively;
- to reflect in its community life a commitment to diversity as found in the life and mission of the Church of God;
- to represent the Church of God well in the world of higher education;
- to exercise good stewardship of its human, physical, and financial resources;
- to be accountable, through its board of trustees, to the Church of God which founded it and helps sustain it;
- to work with other ministries of the Church of God—international, national, state, regional and local—in a supportive and interdependent manner.

Editor's Note: The responding Assembly action in response to the University's covenant presentation was:

BE IT RESOLVED that on the occasion beginning the celebration of the 75th anniversary of Anderson University, we the General Assembly, in session June 16-18, 1992, receive the covenant statement and confirm the relationship between the University and the Church of God, and pledge to continue the activity to discuss, modify, and expand the covenant document through dialogue between the representatives of Anderson University and the Church of God.

105. Agency Status: Warner Southern College (June 1997)

Whereas Warner Southern College has served the Church of God as an institution of Christian higher education since 1968; and

Whereas Warner Southern College submitted to the Leadership Council Board of Directors in October, 1990, a formal application requesting to be granted general agency status; and

Whereas a special committee appointed by the Leadership Council Board of Directors, including a representative of the Commission on Christian Higher Education, did an onsite visit and reviewed pertinent institutional and financial documents and reported its findings to the Board of Directors; and

Whereas the Board of Directors identified specific matters Warner Southern College needed to address; and

Whereas, over a period of time, Warner Southern College has satisfactorily addressed those matters; and

Whereas, the Leadership Council in its annual meeting in May, 1997, recommended that the 1997 General Assembly be asked to grant general agency status to Warner Southern College; and

Whereas, the Commission on Christian Higher Education concurs in this recommendation;

Therefore be it Resolved that this General Assembly grant general agency status to Warner Southern College in conformity with other agency institutions; and

Be it further Resolved that Warner Southern College receive World Service crediting for church gifts beginning with the 1997-98 World Service budget year.

MAJOR SOCIAL ISSUES

Editor's Note: In his 1999 book, *Perfectionist Politics*, Douglas M. Strong explains a phenomenon in American Christianity in the middle decades of the nineteenth century. Many holiness advocates mixed their "perfectionism" with political vision and action. They were seeking the establishment of God's government in church and state—a holy church and a sanctified society. The Church of God movement, however, emerged later in the nineteenth century and evidenced much less political preoccupation in relation to public institutions. In light of the urgency prompted by belief in the soon return of Christ, its vigorous commitment to the significance of sanctification focused primarily on the cleansing of individuals and the reformation of a wayward and divided church.

Across the twentieth century the Church of God, through its General Assembly, did find numerous occasions to express its convictions and concerns about a wide range of social issues. Rarely advocating any political strategy as such, at least the Assembly's perspectives were stated formally out of the context of its Christian convictions. These stated perspectives also evidence the context of and interaction with the world which the Church of God movement has known. Church of God sociologist Val Clear notes that the church inevitably reflects to some degree the secular setting in which it finds itself. To be *in* but not *of* the world "requires profound commitment and diligent effort" (Clear, "Social Concerns in the Reformation Movement" in *Vital Christianity*, June 22, 1980, 58). Clear highlights racism and war as two especially prominent social concerns that have plagued the society known by the Church of God in North America and thus have caused stress in and reactions from the Church of God through its General Assembly. Such formal reactions follow. The date indicated for each action is that of the General Assembly in which the action was taken.

106. Support for Prohibition (June 1928)

Editor's Note: The prohibition of the sale and use of alcoholic beverages was written into the United States Constitution as the Eighteenth Amendment, effective 1920. By 1928, however, Prohibition was being challenged vigorously by some prominent politicians. Attempts were being made to repeal this law. The 1928 General Ministerial Assembly spoke clearly.

WHEREAS we regard this propaganda as a challenge to the morality and public welfare, therefore be it

RESOLVED, that we urge a strict enforcement of the present prohibition laws, and be it further

RESOLVED, that we put ourselves upon record as favoring no candidate or political party that favors modification of the present prohibition law.

107. Objection to Peacetime Conscription of Youth (June 1928, 1932, 1947)

Editor's Note: The General Ministerial Assembly of 1928 spoke sharply against "war as a method of settling international disputes" and declared itself "in favor of every effort being put forward...to propagate the principles of peace." Again in 1932 the Assembly addressed this subject by stating bluntly that "war is unchristian, futile and suicidal.... We will never again sanction or participate in any war." By 1947, with the tragedy of World War II still fresh on all minds, the Assembly spoke once again.

WHEREAS this suffering and battered world even yet staggers under the shock of wars past, present, and future; and

WHEREAS the only bright rays of hope appear in the valiant efforts of relief of hunger and suffering abroad and in the aid given toward achieving material and spiritual reconstruction; and

WHEREAS we as a religious body have participated in such efforts and expect to continue to do so to the extent of our abilities; but

WHEREAS there is a vigorous campaign for conscripting the youth of our churches and nation for compulsory peacetime military training; and

WHEREAS the alleged benefits of such training are nullified by exposure to immoral influences coincident with the military life; and

WHEREAS the use of atomic warfare techniques would nullify the use of traditional armed forces; and

WHEREAS such preparation for war is no guarantee of peace, but, rather, creates an atmosphere which crystallizes the threat of war into the actuality; and

WHEREAS education for peacetime pursuits for uplifting mankind would be replaced by education for death and destruction; and

WHEREAS the need of our day is the erasure of malice, suspicion, and misunderstanding; and for the promotion of brotherhood, mutual trust, and the ministry of healing; and

WHEREAS the democratic processes of our government would be threatened by further growth of the military establishment; therefore, be it

RESOLVED, that the General Ministerial Assembly of the Church of God, assembled at Anderson, Indiana, June 18, 1947, commend the leaders of our nation for the splendid work of relief and rehabilitation which they have directed; but be it further

RESOLVED, that we register vigorous objection to any plan for peacetime conscription of youth for military training; and be it further

RESOLVED, that the secretary of this Assembly be instructed to send a copy of this resolution to the President of the United States, to the presiding officers of both houses of Congress, and to their respective military affairs committees, and to the Secretary of War.

Editor's Note: For a 1966 General Assembly action on military conscription, see Entry 117.

108. Supreme Court on Segregation (June 1954)

WHEREAS the United States Supreme Court has rendered a decision to end race segregation in the public schools, and

WHEREAS this decision brings to focus certain tensions in the areas of employment, housing, transportation, dining, and other public facilities, and

WHEREAS the principles of brotherhood and unity of God's children without regard to distinctive racial groups have been commonly taught in our movement, therefore, be it

RESOLVED, that this Assembly go on record as being in accord with the spirit and intent of the Supreme Court ruling, and be it further

RESOLVED, that this Assembly recommend to our people: (1) Restraint, patience, and humility in meeting this problem of segregation; (2) That they take an active part in study and efforts in their respective communities to find wise means of solving the problems of segregation; and be it further

RESOLVED, that there be a continuous demonstration of Christian brotherhood and unity on these campgrounds [Anderson, Ind.], and that there be fair and equitable treatment of all peoples regardless of race or economic status, and

WE FURTHER RECOMMEND that we enter into a covenant of prayer and personal rededication to the end that the will of God be accomplished in the relationships of all people.

109. Federal Tax Funds for Education (June 1961)

WHEREAS there has been wide discussion in the public press and in the current session of the Congress of the United States concerning the issue of granting federal funds to education, and

WHEREAS there are many facets of this issue which are of particular concern to the churches of America, therefore, be it

RESOLVED, that we, the General Ministerial Assembly of the Church of God, met in annual session in Anderson, Indiana, this 22nd day of June, 1961, do hereby express the following convictions regarding the use of federal tax funds for education:

1. We reaffirm our confidence in and our support of the public school system as an indispensable means of providing educational opportunity for all children; we recognize the great problems now being faced by the public schools and urge provision for increased resources for the operation and improvement of these public schools within a framework of proper safeguards.

2. We oppose any grants from federal, state, or local tax funds for the operation and support of non-public elementary and secondary schools.

3. We are concerned that the historic principle of separation of church and state be maintained and promoted and urge all branches of the government to avoid any infringement of the ideal of religious liberty which would inevitably arise when taxes paid under compulsion by all people are used to aid non-public schools.

Be it further Resolved, that a copy of this resolution be sent to the President of the United States, and that additional copies be made available to the public press and such other media of communication as may desire them.

110. Separation of Church and State (June 1962)

In view of the tremendous pressure now being brought to bear on our federal government for subsidies and handouts by the Roman Catholic Church for its parochial school system, it is now apparent that a definite stand needs to be taken by those of us who favor and believe fervently in the separation of church and state. We believe in the basic principle of the sacred nature of man's relationship to God. We do not believe that this can be legislated nor that it should become a part of political jurisdiction which is a direct possibility if we were to accept government aid for parochial systems.

Be it, therefore, Resolved, that a special committee be appointed by the Executive Council of the General Ministerial Assembly to study the field of church-state relationships as it relates to our colleges, agencies, and local church problems and to return to this Assembly with a report as to our stand regarding the above-mentioned relationships.

Editor's Note: A major report of this special committee, dated June 17, 1964, was made available to the Assembly and was included with its 1965 minutes. A portion of that report reads as follows:

1. We believe in the public school system as an indispensable means of providing educational opportunity for all children.

2. While supporting the right of religious groups to establish and maintain schools that meet prescribed educational standards at their own expense, and the right of parents to decide whether their children should attend public or non-public schools, we have serious questions concerning:

   a. Grants being made from federal, state, or local tax funds for parochial elementary and secondary schools;

   b. Payments being made from public funds for tuition or scholarships for children to attend private or church-related elementary or secondary schools, and grants being made to parents for that purpose;

   c. Tax credits, tax forgiveness, and exemption from school taxes for parents whose children attend non-public elementary or secondary schools.

3. There seems to be community value in supplying dental or medical and welfare services. . .to all children in any school...when assurance is given that such services are known to recipients as public services and expenditures are administered by public authorities who are responsible to the electorate.

4. In any provision of federal funds for tax-supported elementary and secondary public schools:

   a. There be no discrimination among children on the basis of race, religion, class, or national origin;
   b. There be adequate safeguards against federal control of educational policy.

111. Major Statement on Race (June 1964)

In order clearly to define our stand as members of the General Ministerial Assembly of the Church of God, and to encourage Christian action, we affirm that:

Unity, equality, and fellowship for all who are in Jesus Christ.

We base our stand toward basic human rights on the teaching of the Scriptures. God has "made of one blood all nations of men" (Acts 17:26). "For we are all the children of God by faith in Jesus Christ. . .for we are all one in Jesus Christ" (Gal. 3:26, 28). The first of these speaks as to origin, the second as to relationship. We believe that in the Church of God there should be no racial barriers because we are all brethren in Christ. We believe that man was made in the image of God, that every person is of intrinsic worth before God, and that every individual has a right to the fullest possible opportunities for the development of life abundant and eternal. We believe that these rights are given by God and that the church has a responsibility to defend them and work for their guarantee.

Firmly believing that the New Testament teaching sets forth a brotherhood without racial discrimination, we will work to achieve an experience of fairness and honest love toward all our brethren, free from discrimination based on race. This calls for patience, understanding, forgiveness, and unselfish service from every member regardless of race. The law of love should be the rule by which we live under all circumstances. The General Ministerial Assembly defines its membership in this manner:

> Ordained ministers of the Church of God in good and regular standing who are present at any authorized and duly called meeting of the Assembly. Unordained ministers who are pastors or full-time associate pastors of recognized congregations. Laymen who are elected or appointed members of the Executive Council, a subordinate board, committee, or commission of the Assembly.

All members of all races who qualify are urged to participate fully in the Assembly business and to exercise the common privileges granted to all members. Membership on national boards, committees, and the programs of the International Convention are open on the basis of qualifications. Brethren of all races are urged to seek and develop those qualities which will make their ministries beneficial to the whole church and to remember that the ministry of prayer to undergird those in general responsibilities makes one a partner and co-worker in carrying them out, even though he may not hold an office or be on the program. We urge ministers of state assemblies to:

1. Make special efforts to get ministers of all races to work toward a united expression of brotherhood and oneness;
2. Attempt to see that persons, regardless of race, are nominated for committees and offices in the state work according to qualifications;
3. Where there are segregated assemblies, begin the steps which will eventually bring all the brethren into one working fellowship.

We commend the hundreds of our congregations whose life and doors are open to people of all races and urge that they make this fact known by appropriate announcement. We urge that local congregations make special efforts to integrate those of other races who come into their midst. Because strangers may be timid and fearful, special care and concern should be exercised for them.

We urge each individual member to examine his life patterns in the light of the nature of the gospel and to fully welcome into congregational life fellow members and all persons without regard to race, color, or nationality.

We urge all our congregations which have not practiced an open door policy to honestly appraise their position in the light of New Testament teaching and the commitment of the Church of God to its teaching.

We recognize the difficult situation of our brethren where the social pattern is fixed and hostile to the brotherhood of all people. In love we extend confidence to them in their difficult situation. We trust that through prayer they can find ways of applying the principles of brotherhood and human rights even though the environment might be unfriendly.

We urge that we will always be guided by sound biblical principles rather than the highly emotional pitch so prevalent in our world. Ours is a call to prayer and study and deliberate Christian action. We are not called to conform to the demands of the world or society. We are called to follow the Lord and obey Him. This call is to every one of us, regardless of race or culture.

We, the members of the General Ministerial Assembly, pledge our prayers, concerns, and moral support to those pastors, congregations, and members who are faithful to their Lord.

Editor's Note: See Entry 121 for a 1968 attempt to implement the "open door" aspect of this present action.

112. Civil Rights Legislation (June 1964)

WHEREAS our nation is currently confronted with a grave social revolution, and

WHEREAS the nation's conscience has become increasingly aware and sensitive regarding racial discrimination and injustice to minority groups in our nation, and

WHEREAS the United States Constitution gives a clear status in law to a fundamental Christian and American principle, namely, the Constitutional guarantee of equal freedom and equal justice to all citizens, and

WHEREAS there is currently before the United States Senate, civil rights legislation designed to protect the Constitutional rights of all citizens of our nation, and

WHEREAS the Church of God Reformation Movement believes that the principle of segregation based on color, race, caste, or ethnic origin is a denial of the Christian faith and ethic, which stems from the basic premise taught by our Lord that all men are the children of God, be it, therefore,

RESOLVED, that the General Ministerial Assembly of the Church of God, in session at Anderson, Indiana, go on record as favoring the passage of that type of civil rights legislation which will guarantee justice and equality to all our citizens regardless of race, nationality, or religion.

113. Constitutional Guarantee of Voting Rights (June 1965)

WHEREAS the General Assembly of the Church of God in its 1964 meeting adopted a "Statement on Race Relations" which contains this statement: "The right to choose a place of residence, to enter school, to secure employment, to vote or attend church should in no way be limited by a person's race or culture," and

WHEREAS the 1965 General Assembly continues to bear witness to the stand it has taken in the area of race relations, be it, therefore,

RESOLVED, that the General Assembly of the Church of God, in session at Anderson, Indiana, supports legislation in support of Amendment XV of the Constitution of the United States which guarantees equal voting rights for all citizens in all fifty states of the Union without any discrimination based upon racial, religious, or economic differences as early as possible. Be it further

RESOLVED, that a copy of this resolution be mailed to the President of the United States and to the appropriate legislative committees.

114. General Agency Initiatives for Equal Rights (June 1965)

WHEREAS the time for making ringing declarations against racial discrimination has passed, having moved from saying to doing, be it, therefore,

RESOLVED, that the General Assembly of the Church of God in session at Anderson, Indiana, encourage and support the general agencies of the Church to take the steps and risks they deem wise and necessary to involve the church more deliberately in the struggle for equal rights.

115. Involvement in Racial Justice (June 1965)

WHEREAS the General Assembly in its 1964 June meeting affirmed that we should boldly stand on the principles of basic human rights because they are Christian; and that the right to choose a place of residence, to enter school, to secure employment, to vote, or attend church should in no way be limited by a person's race or culture, and

WHEREAS the essence of integrity is to demonstrate ideals and not merely talk about them, be it, therefore,

RESOLVED, that the General Assembly of the Church of God in session at Anderson, Indiana, urge its members to take direct action as a religious duty to do their part in their local communities to see that voting, jobs, housing, education, and public worship facilities are available to all citizens, and be it further

RESOLVED, that the Assembly urge each pastor to encourage greater personal involvement on the part of individual Christians in the struggle for racial justice.

116. Stand Against Tobacco (June 1965)

WHEREAS we in the Church of God movement have traditionally stood solidly against the use of tobacco in any form and have observed the general undesirability of the habit; and

WHEREAS we observe the vast amounts of money spent for tobacco, which expenditure could not be considered a constructive part of life or a contribution to human welfare; and

WHEREAS we have actively taught that the human body and mind is the temple of God, to be kept clean, pure, and fit for the Master's use; and

WHEREAS we consider it of great importance to protect our youth from the insidious advertising which seems to make the use of tobacco desirable by glamorizing the stars of the entertainment and athletic worlds; and

WHEREAS the report of the Surgeon General of the United States has injected a decisive, authoritative, and scientifically based analysis showing the harmful effects of tobacco, substantiating what we have long believed to be true; therefore, be it

RESOLVED, that in this General Assembly we reaffirm our convictions and teaching regarding the use of tobacco; be it further

RESOLVED, that this Assembly urge every minister to take a positive stand in discouraging the use of tobacco, to teach constructively, to help safeguard our youth, to help church leaders realize the importance of setting a good example, to lead the church in a redemptive attitude and effort toward those who are victims of the habit; and be it further

RESOLVED, that this General Assembly urge ministers and responsible church laymen to write their Congressmen, calling for stricter regulations on the advertising of tobacco in the mass media and on items for sale.

117. Military Conscription: The Right of Conscience (June 1966)

Editor's Note: See Entry 107 for reference to other Assembly actions (1928, 1932, and 1947) related to military conscription and participation. Also see: the 1958 thesis of L. Leon Long done at the Graduate School of the University of Illinois and titled "Pacifism and War Participation in the Church of God"; and the April 1991 article by Merle D. Strege appearing in the *Mennonite Quarterly Review* and titled "Demise (?) of a Peace Church: The Church of God (Anderson), Pacifism, and Civil Religion."

Like all true Americans, we as members of the General Assembly of the Church of God meeting in regular session in Anderson, Indiana, this sixteenth day of June, 1966, view with deep concern the escalating military involvement and the conscription of our youth for military service. We believe that war represents our moral failures. We abhor the causes that lead to war. We stand by the teaching and example of our Lord, who taught us and showed us the way of radical, sacrificial love.

We are thankful to God that we live in a land of basic freedoms whose law makes provision for alternative service by those "who, by reason of religious training and belief, are conscientiously opposed to participation in war in any form." We encourage our young men who conscientiously object to war to engage in such civilian work which contributes "to the maintenance of the national health, safety or interest."

We respect the right of each person to arrive at his own convictions. We believe in the principle of freedom of worship and freedom of conscience. We respect the rights of the individual conscience within our fellowship. We have never set up an authoritative creed. Instead, we accept the entire New Testament as our rule of faith and practice, and we seek to lead every member of our fellowship to full comprehension and full acceptance of the Spirit of Christ as the guide for all conduct. What we seek for ourselves we seek for every citizen of our land—the right of individual conscience which no governmental authority can abrogate or violate. We do not condemn or reject that person who differs with our position or participates in war. We shall seek to follow such persons with a ministry of help and guidance, but this is never to be construed as approval of war.

We fervently pray for the leaders of our nation and of other nations, many of whom we believe to be sincerely striving for peace. We pray that efforts by negotiation among countries, through the United Nations and every possible channel, may succeed in bringing peace to our troubled world. Let this statement of conviction be construed by any and all to mean that we fully support young men of the Church of God who sincerely and conscientiously are opposed to participation in military service. We encourage them to seek the constructive alternatives intended to bring health, healing, and understanding, and which serve the highest interests of our beloved country and of the whole world.

118. World Hunger (June 1966)

WHEREAS government and relief organizations have been making special studies of world hunger, giving special attention to India and other countries of the Eastern Hemisphere; and

WHEREAS churches and voluntary agencies have been expressing during recent months a mounting concern for the hungry of the world, the two-thirds of the world's population who suffer daily of recurrent hunger; and

WHEREAS the United States government and other world governments have made substantial contributions in recent years and months to supply emergency food commodities to prevent famine and to aid the governments of countries where hunger prevails to use technical skills to produce more and distribute more effectively all available supplies of food; and

WHEREAS for the first time in history the capabilities and techniques exist to prevent the warping of lives and the deaths caused by hunger; and

WHEREAS it should be recognized with regret that the food situation and its distribution around the world are not totally removed from world and local economics and world and local politics; and

WHEREAS united steps are being taken through world relief organizations to attack the long-range problem by caring for emergency feeding operations followed by a mounting aid program to enhance agricultural production, more adequate distribution of processed food, land reclamation, water provision, planned parenthood, and all related issues designed to get at the root causes of world hunger; and

WHEREAS all Christians, particularly those living in affluent societies, are faced with the moral and spiritual responsibility for compassionate action by acknowledging our common humanity and by giving food to the hungry in the name of Christ; be it, therefore,

RESOLVED, that this specter of world hunger be brought to the attention of the Church of God constituency through the medium of this resolution, as well as through current articles appearing in church and secular magazines and in the press; to awaken the conscience of each and every Christian to exert all his energies and to cooperate with efforts to help alleviate world hunger; and be it further

RESOLVED, that in view of the prevailing need in India today caused by the worst drought in seventy years with a resulting 80% to total crop failure in areas hard hit due to lack of monsoon rain, and in view of the possibility that large numbers now suffering from hunger may starve to death unless immediate assistance reaches India quickly; all who wish to respond to this great need and the prompting of their conscience do so by sending their contributions for world relief to the Missionary Board of the Church of God, all monies to be distributed immediately to direct need through Church of God missionaries involved in relief or through Church World Service, the most capable church-related organization to understand and meet the emergency needs found in India and other countries of the world.

119. Racial Justice a Spiritual Priority (June 1968)

WHEREAS our Assembly has received various resolutions across recent years concerned about race relations in the Church of God; and

WHEREAS the abundant supply of resolutions on the matter of race relations continues to call attention to our need to correct evident deficiencies and solve evident problems; and

WHEREAS the 1964 report from this Assembly's Commission on Race Relations stated our deficiencies and recommended appropriate steps for correcting our needs; and

WHEREAS it is the work of this Assembly to authorize, mobilize, and direct the interests common to our life and work as a church—and has effectively done so more recently by solving problems of finance (appropriations for college needs, building of Warner Auditorium); and

WHEREAS the church looks to the Assembly to advise and give direction on the particularly spiritual concerns of church life and work; therefore be it

RESOLVED, that this Assembly declare that its previous resolutions on the matter of race relations remain as issues of spiritual priority; and be it further

RESOLVED, that our national boards and agencies be directed to make deliberate moves to secure Negro leaders for executive and/or administrative roles wherever and whenever possible, this being a way to show a more truly inclusive pattern for ourselves on the national level; and be it further

RESOLVED, that this Assembly direct the Commission on Social Concerns to serve the Assembly by preparing such aids and guides for congregational use in resolving differences that keep some of our churches racially separate; and be it finally

RESOLVED, that this Assembly call upon the Church to repent for the deficiencies and failures as a people on the point of race relations, turning to God for renewal and grace during this International Convention.

120. Resolution on Race (June 1968)

Editor's Note: In 1957 the Executive Council of the Church of God and the General Ministerial Assembly named a study commission on race relations to serve for a period of five years. In 1961, this study commission reported to the Executive Council and recommended elements of a positive strategy for reaching desirable goals in better race relations. These proposed action steps were as follows.

1. Proceed with all deliberate speed to integrate ratification procedures in all states immediately.

2. Let ministers in all states arrange for fellowship meetings together and pave the way for integrated assemblies, beginning, also, to synchronize meetings, and procedures, adopt similar standards, and so on. Breakfast meetings or one-day prayer retreats might be employed.

3. National leaders should enter into serious discussions toward the integration of national agencies, it being understood that leadership opportunity, representation, and expression would be on the basis of qualification regardless of race.

4. That recognition and support be given to certain experiences and developments which our national boards are carrying out. That encouragement

be given to local churches that are able to move ahead with courage in this field, and that these churches on the frontier of exploration be supported with prayer and the concern of the church, and to the churches of the community, whatever the racial situation may be.

5. Let the Executive Council and the General Ministerial Assembly pass resolutions directed to our own churches, urging inter-racial fellowship within the local church and among local churches, asking our people to press forward toward integration on a truly Christian basis.

6. To take a positive stance, by resolution and through publications, on the matter of integration and the employing of our rich traditions and spiritual resources toward the demonstrations of Christian principles at this point of need.

7. That our ministers and churches be encouraged to cooperate in inter-church and community endeavors toward overcoming the racial cleavages.

> *Editor's Note*: This 1968 presentation to the Assembly went on to make the following historical observations and resolution—which was accepted. In 1964, the Executive Council offered and this Assembly adopted a further major statement on race, declaring that the urgency for action was growing in society and the need for the church to begin within its own fellowship to make corrections was imperative. Action was called for on the local, the state, and the national levels of our work.

Much progress has been made since these recommendations were adopted. On the local level, a large number of our congregations are now, to some degree, integrated with families of other races. The call for an open-door policy for all races was made, but has never been followed up.

On the state level, several assemblies have been merged and others are in the process of merging. On the national level, there has been a ninety-percent increase in the number of black representatives serving on national boards and agencies. The Missionary Committee of the National Association of the Church of God has been merged with the Missionary Board of this Assembly. The program of the International Convention has become much more representative of all races.

While these gains are encouraging, they have not kept up with the changes in society, the progress is much too slow and the urgency is increasing. There are eleven states which still have two racial ministerial assemblies. Therefore, be it

RESOLVED, that this Assembly urge all state organizations to bring about full involvement and fair representation of Negro persons according to ability in the offices and boards and committees of the state organizations; and be it further

RESOLVED, that where there are Negro and white assemblies still existing, steps be taken in accordance with the recommendations adopted in 1964 to "integrate all ratification procedures in all states immediately"; and be it also further

RESOLVED, that state assemblies report the degree of progress now existing toward integration of assemblies as adopted by this Assembly in 1964, and that the Executive Council, through its Division of Church Service, be instructed to bring to this Assembly in 1969 a summary of the progress that has been made.

121. Open-Door Policy (June 1968)

Editor's Note: Assembly chair Harold Boyer recognized Robert Reardon, president of Anderson College. Dr. Reardon referred to Charles Naylor's hymn, "The Church's Jubilee," and quoted the verse which includes the words "Reaching our hands in fellowship to every blood-washed one." He stated that the Assembly had in the past expressed an "open-door policy for all races" (see Entry 111), but that there was a need for more positive action. He presented the following resolution, which the Assembly then approved.

In view of the open-door resolution passed by this Assembly in 1964, be it

RESOLVED, that this Assembly call upon local congregations of the Church of God in the United States and Canada to ratify the following declaration and to make it known publicly through whatever means possible:

In accordance with the teaching of the Scriptures, this congregation of the Church of God welcomes fellow Christians without regard to race, color, or national origin, to participate fully and without any reservation in its fellowship and work. And be it further

RESOLVED, that the executive secretary of the Executive Council of the Church of God is instructed to place the above declaration before each local congregation of the Church of God, and to make public those congregations ratifying this declaration.

122. Refugees (June 1973)

RESOLVED, that the General Assembly of the Church of God urge local congregations to search out and discover refugees and devise ways and means of meeting their needs by participating with other like-minded groups in discharging a basic biblical imperative; and be it

RESOLVED, that this resolution and its accompanying document of information be disseminated to state boards of evangelism and to the pastors and official boards of local congregations in the areas where these refugee problems might appear, with an urgent request for serious implementation; and be it

RESOLVED, that the General Assembly of the Church of God urge individuals in congregations to keep currently informed regarding any major refugee situation in the world and how immediate relief and ultimate rehabilitation can be accomplished as the political situation will allow, and that the above information be secured through the Committee on Refugees of the United Nations, Church World Service of the Division of Overseas Ministries of the National Council of Churches, the Missionary Board of the Church of God, or the Executive Council of the Church of God, as well as through the media of the press and news magazines; and be it further

RESOLVED, that the above resolution with the document "Refugee Settlement: Persons Outside the United States" be sent to all pastors of the Church of God, with the earnest request that the church be encouraged to study it and other available information to the end that it might bring Christian principles governing such matters to the attention of proper governmental authorities, both state and federal, in such a manner that the government and people of the United States might better serve their proper role in the settlement of refugee situations wherever and whenever they might occur.

123. Role of Women (June 1974)

The Church of God in its beginning and through its early history included both men and women in its ministry. Little or no thought was given as to whether one who went forth to serve in the name of the Lord Jesus Christ was masculine or feminine. The emphasis was on spreading the gospel of truth as proclaimed by the reformation movement. Women served in many capacities, as evangelists, teachers, musicians, and pastors. They have served well along with men down through the years.

A recent survey by the Division of Church Service, through a questionnaire, revealed that, while women make up around 55 percent of the membership of the congregations of the Church of God, the percentage of women in leadership roles has steadily declined.

Therefore, in light of the statistics which document the diminishing use of women's abilities in the life and work of the church, comes the following resolution:

WHEREAS women are equipped by their Creator to serve in a variety of roles, including that of homemaker, employment in jobs and professions, volunteer work, and full- or part-time Christian service, and

WHEREAS women have demonstrated their ability and their commitment to the church, and

WHEREAS God calls women to use their gifts and skills to their fullest potential, therefore be it

RESOLVED that more women be given opportunity and consideration for positions of leadership in the total program of the Church of God, locally, statewide, and nationally.

Editor's Note: For detailed information on women in ministry in the Church of God, see Juanita Leonard, ed., *Called To Minister, Empowered to Serve: Women in Ministry.* Susie Cunningham Stanley, a prominent Church of God scholar, has been a leader in calling together a series of ecumenical conferences on the many issues related to women clergy, especially in the Wesleyan/Holiness tradition. Another prominent Church of God scholar, Sharon Clark Pearson, has written a careful reevaluation of New Testament teaching on women in Christian leadership, titled "Women in Ministry: A Biblical Vision," the *Wesleyan Theological Journal.*

124. World Hunger (June 1975)

WHEREAS Christian people in the wealthy nations, especially Christian people in the United States, should be influential in bringing resources to help alleviate the current world hunger crisis; and

WHEREAS there has been a concern expressed in Church of God periodicals and in mailings from national agencies that feeding starving people should be a top priority of the Church; therefore, be it

RESOLVED that the church actively seek to raise $100,000 for World Hunger and Disaster Relief during the year of 1975-76. This effort would include the $25,000 that the Women of the Church of God are seeking to raise, the $7,500 listed in the budgets of the Missionary Board and the $20,000 Disaster Fund, leaving $50,000 to be raised by World Service. All money sent to World Service for World Hunger Relief will receive World Service credit.

125. Violence on Television (June 1977)

WHEREAS in recent years we have witnessed on television an alarming increase in the use of profanity and violence and the portrayal of life-styles inconsistent with Christian values; and

WHEREAS the television networks and program sponsors have permitted profanity, violence, and the portrayal of life-styles inconsistent with Christian values to be included in an increasing number of telecasts; and

WHEREAS we believe this trend to be detrimental to the well-being of our families—especially our children and youth; therefore, be it

RESOLVED that the General Assembly of the Church of God, Anderson, Indiana, adopt the following write-in plan to combat the use of profanity and violence and the portrayal of life-styles inconsistent with Christian values on television:

> The plan: Each congregation be asked to appoint a social action chairman (or the pastor may initiate this plan). The chairman (or pastor) enlist the entire membership locally to write a brief letter to the three network presidents and program sponsors stating their opposition to the use of profanity and violence and the portrayal of life-styles inconsistent with Christian values on television. This could be done over a period of two or three months. The size of the local congregation would determine how many letters could be assigned for each week.
>
> For example: A church of 100 members would enlist 8 persons each week so that in approximately three months all members would take their turn in writing to the television networks and program sponsors; be it further

RESOLVED that, if this plan is adopted, the General Assembly, through the Commission on Social Concerns, convey this plan with appropriate publicity to all local congregations, urging that every congregation of the Church of God be enlisted in this action.

---

126. Stand Against Homosexuality (June 1979)

Since the world is invaded by sex perversion in the form of homosexuality, we, the Church of God Reformation Movement, do hereby express our conviction concerning the issue:

WHEREAS we in the Church of God, being an evangelical people, committed to biblical holiness, give high regard to scriptural injunctions against homosexuality, we are also a redemptive body and seek to express love, compassion, and a chaste relationship in Christ for everyone; be it

RESOLVED, that the General Assembly of the Church of God go on record as affirming our conviction that biblically we believe homosexuality is sin. We hereby stand firmly opposed to the licensing, ordination, or approving of persons in leadership actively involved in this life-style; be it further

RESOLVED, that we stand opposed to any instruction in our church-sponsored institutions or the use of curriculum material which accepts homosexuality as either normal, desirable, or Christian.

Editor's Note: See Entry 140 for the General Assembly's 1993 action on this same subject.

127. Stand Against Abortion on Demand (June 1981)

Editor's Note: After years of activity in the United States directed at passage of an equal rights amendment (ERA) to the national Constitution and related decisions of the Supreme Court, the General Assembly decided to speak on the major social concern of the legal availability of abortion to almost anyone for almost any reason. The Assembly action read as follows.

WHEREAS the United States Supreme Court has declared unconstitutional all state laws regulating abortion, and has opened the way for abortion on demand for any reason; and

WHEREAS the rights of the unborn child are being stripped away by reinterpretation of the Constitution by the Supreme Court; and

WHEREAS this opens the door to possible elimination of other unwanted or undesirable human beings, and

WHEREAS the Bible contains reference to God's personal acquaintance with children prior to birth, inferring the fetus has life, such as:

1. In Jeremiah 1:4, 5 ". . .the Word of the Lord came unto me saying, 'Before I formed you in the womb I knew you, and before you were born I consecrated you; I have appointed you a prophet to the nations'" (NASV);
2. And in Psalm 139:13, King David, inspired by God, wrote: "Thou didst form my inward parts; thou didst weave me in my mother's womb. I will give thanks to thee, for I am fearfully and wonderfully made" (NASV); and

WHEREAS abortion on demand, we believe, greatly diminishes the moral values, not only of the one seeking the abortion, but of this whole nation; and

WHEREAS the unborn child cannot plead in its own defense; be it, therefore,

RESOLVED, that the General Assembly of the Church of God go on record as opposing abortion on demand, recognizing that the unborn fetus is a living human being and thus should be protected by the laws and Constitution of the United States of America; and be it further

RESOLVED, that the General Assembly of the Church of God urges all congregations to express compassion and concern not only to protect life before birth but to work to assure that the lives that are preserved may receive the care, attention, and help that God wants for all persons; to provide family life and marriage education that will foster such a reverence for God-given life that both the causes and consequences of unwanted pregnancies may be diminished; and that this resolution be publicized.

128. Nuclear Arms Reduction (June 1982)

The incineration of our planet may be imminent! Why? Because of the threat posed by the nuclear arms race in which our country and the Soviet Union are principal participants. Planning the future of our global community is begging the question about a future for this nuclear age. The nuclear arms race itself could end with its destruction of the human race. We believe that the proliferation of nuclear weapons is a sin against the Creator and against His creation.

Because it may be the most urgent moral issue confronting our generation, we call Church of God people everywhere to fast and pray for world peace, and for global leaders as they make decisions which affect the destiny of the human family. We welcome the decision of the United Nations to hold a Second Special Session on Disarmament, and we invite concerned persons and groups to join in fervent prayer during those crucial days. We urge that families, pastors, Sunday school classes, youth, and other groups in local churches give serious study to the question of nuclear disarmament.

We commend the growing number of concerned persons in the Church of God who are expressing opposition to the nuclear arms race in letters to congressmen, senators, elected government leaders, and to local newspaper editors. The positive results of personal letters have been confirmed by both supporters and opponents of nuclear disarmament. We urge that these efforts in sending handwritten letters be continued and accelerated.

The nuclear arms race is not our fate but our choice. There is an alternative. No sinister external force or internal political system is imposing nuclear weapons upon us. Today we are playing brinkmanship with a nuclear shootout because of the accumulation of decisions made by our policy-makers elected and supported by voters and taxpayers. The decision about whether or not we go over the brink into a nuclear holocaust will be made by us, not by persons now in kindergarten, elementary or high school.

The alternative is the way of negotiation and agreement. Just as Mr. Nixon made creative efforts to normalize our relationship with China, and as Mr. Sadat won the admiration of the world when he carried the olive branch to Israel, we call upon Mr. Reagan and Mr. Brezhnev to say to each other and to the people of the world: "Enough of this; let us live in peace."

Our deliberate choice is to be faithful to Jesus Christ and to his gospel of reconciliation. His purpose for all people is life that is abundant and eternal. To place our trust in weapons of mass murder and destruction is irresponsible and idolatrous. We encourage Church of God people to accept our historical imperative to choose life and to find and support alternatives to the nuclear arms race.

Editor's Note: The above statement was "received" rather than formally adopted by the Assembly so that members of the Assembly could feel free to act upon such convictions as they saw fit.

129. Turning the U. S. Back to God (June 1983)

WHEREAS it appears that our nation is being confronted with the destruction of the principles upon which it was founded; and

WHEREAS the Declaration of Independence clearly cites "our reliance on the protection of Divine Providence"; and

WHEREAS in many ways the nation's conscience has become insensitive to our reliance on Divine Providence and to the destruction of the moral principles upon which this nation was founded; and

WHEREAS the President of the United States is currently urging the government authorities in this country to permit Bible reading and prayer in the schools and to cease the approval and financing of abortion; and

WHEREAS the Church of God Reformation Movement does not believe in the forbidding of the reading of God's Word or prayer to God in public schools and has gone on record as opposing "Abortion on Demand" (June 1981); be it, therefore,

RESOLVED that the General Assembly of the Reformation Movement of the Church of God, in session at Anderson, Indiana (June 1983), go on record, and so notify the President and the Congress of the United States, that this church body does strongly support the President of the United States, and all concerned members of Congress, in their efforts to turn this country back to God.

130. Pornography and Obscenity (June 1984)

WHEREAS the 8-billion-dollar pornography industry in America has grown to epidemic proportions and invaded every segment of society; and

WHEREAS the life-style propagated by the pornographic industry is contrary to the New Testament teachings; and

WHEREAS family, church, and community values are being seriously threatened by the pornography industry; and

WHEREAS the Supreme Court in 1973 reaffirmed the right of the community to protect its standards; and

WHEREAS the erosion of values has contributed to the increase in teen-age pregnancies, child prostitution, and sexual assaults upon women; therefore be it

RESOLVED, that this General Assembly support the Executive Council and the Commission on Social Concerns in their effort to inform our congregations about the seriousness of the problem; and be it further

RESOLVED, that this Assembly designate October 28—November 4 as Pornography Awareness Week, issuing a call to decency; and be it further

RESOLVED, that this Assembly request resource packets for our congregations so that they will be equipped to take positive action; and be it further

RESOLVED, that this Assembly urge our congregations to become involved in a plan of action in their own communities as well as using their voice as a positive influence in the media and law; and finally be it

RESOLVED, that this Assembly direct its executive officer to write the President of the United States:

    a. Asking him to make a public declaration that enforcement of the Federal obscenity laws is a matter of importance to him;

    b. Requesting him to order the Justice Department to enforce the obscenity laws which are now on the books;

    c. Pledging him our prayers and support in this effort.

131. Apartheid (June 1986)

Jesus demonstrated and taught that we are to love God with all our hearts, souls, minds and strength and to love our neighbor as ourselves. The Good News is that God has reached out to all people with the offer of Salvation and Reconciliation and that we, having become beneficiaries of His grace, become ministers of Reconciliation.

Apartheid, the policy of racial separation in South Africa, obviously violates both the witness and the spirit of God for all people of that nation. Oppression and violence are instruments aligned with Apartheid and are further manifestations of the philosophy of racial superiority. Both in thought and in action, this policy is diametrically opposed to the witness of Christ.

Brothers and sisters of the National Association Ministerial Assembly of the Church of God have eloquently expressed their condemnation of Apartheid. They hold out for us an example of concerned, constructive involvement.

With them, we, the General Assembly of the Church of God, oppose Apartheid in South Africa and all that it implies.

We call upon individuals within the Church to become properly informed so that they might speak, write, and act to express their personal disapproval of Apartheid.

Finally, we encourage the Church of God to pledge her support to efforts at reconciliation and peace-making in South Africa.

Editor's Note: A subsequent motion was passed calling for the above to be sent to the President of the United States and other appropriate government officials. Rev. Samuel G. Hines, chair of the General Assembly from 1983 to 1989, personally became internationally influential in this reconciliation effort in South Africa.

132. Domestic Violence (June 1986)

WHEREAS we recognize that domestic violence is a major problem in the United States today, affecting thousands of families in every economic, social, and ethnic group; and

WHEREAS we believe that awareness of the severity of the problem is the first step in combating this evil; and

WHEREAS we recognize that misinterpretation of Scripture has permitted some persons to justify domestic violence as being consistent with Christian doctrine; and

WHEREAS we also recognize that breaking the chain of violence is imperative to resolving the problem so that future generations do not perpetuate the evil; therefore, be it

RESOLVED that we call upon the Church of God Reformation Movement to break the silence barrier on domestic violence by recognizing and addressing the problem within our communities and within our own communion; and be it, also,

RESOLVED that we urge careful interpretation of Scripture, realizing that correct understanding of the Bible affirms the value and dignity of each individual; and be it also

RESOLVED that we regard violence to be inappropriate as a means of conflict resolution between adult family members; and be it also

RESOLVED that we recognize as unacceptable any behavior that goes beyond normal chastisement measures to use any form of violence in the family that grievously injures, maims, or causes psychological impairment (i.e., severe beatings, kicks, punches, or verbal abuse and depersonalization); and be it also

RESOLVED that we in the church assist persons in our communion to find alternative means of resolving conflict within the family, rejecting completely the practice of violence as defined above; and be it also

RESOLVED that we in the church work to find specific ways to provide protection and healing for the victims of domestic violence; and be it further

RESOLVED that we also commit ourselves to working for healing for the perpetrators of domestic violence.

133. Nuclear Weaponry (June 1986)

We are a biblical people ... "The earth is the Lord's and the fullness thereof" (Ps. 24:1). We are called to stewardship of the earth, and life. We therefore oppose the use of nuclear weaponry by any nation because it has the capacity to destroy God's creation.

Editor's Note: A subsequent motion was passed calling for the above to be sent to the President of the United States and other appropriate government officials. See Entry 128 on nuclear arms reduction.

134. Pornographic Materials (June 1986)

WHEREAS there has been a rising tide of pornographic materials made ever increasingly available in the family marketplace of America; and

WHEREAS our movement, through the effective leadership of our Executive Secretary, has taken a leadership role in joining with other concerned persons and groups to raise the standard of decency; and

WHEREAS as a Movement we have historically believed in and attempted to call our world to righteousness; and

WHEREAS we note with thanksgiving that through these united efforts in this battle, we have seen some victories, in that more than 15,000 stores have removed pornographic magazines in the last four months, including such chains as Seven-Eleven Stores, Eckerds Drug Stores, Stop and Go Markets, and Super-X Drug stores; and

WHEREAS we are aware that there is still much to be done in the battle to rid our society of this degrading influence; therefore, be it

RESOLVED, that we salute the past efforts of our pastors and leaders who have been involved in this fight against the pornographic tide; and be it further

RESOLVED, that we call upon the Church of God to redouble our efforts to lift up a standard of righteousness and to continue working in cooperation with other like-minded persons and groups until total victory is achieved.

Editor's Note: This 1986 action was preceded by the above action of 1984 (Entry 130) and then supplemented in 1990 by a vigorous action calling for specific steps against illegal pornography, "a dangerous and harmful evil in American society which must be eradicated."

135. Ministry with Older Adults (June 1988)

WHEREAS the current United States population of persons 65 and over is now approaching twelve percent (12%) of the total population, with future estimates projected to be approximately 20% by the year 2030 A. D.; and

WHEREAS the Bible affirms old age as a time when persons are able to reflect earnestly on their lives, share wise counsel with others, and develop the deep spiritual resources of their experiences; and

WHEREAS the Church of God (Anderson, Indiana) has an abundant number of older persons who are able to make significant contributions to their church, community and society; and

WHEREAS the local church is the center of life for a significant number of older persons who look to the church for spiritual nurture, inspiration, and direction; and

WHEREAS the National Board of Christian Education has launched the National Fellowship of Older Adults and has printed an Older Adult Ministry and Program Manual to assist local church leaders and state/regional organizations to plan and implement effective ministries and programs for older adults; and

WHEREAS Anderson University (School of Theology) has received a grant to train pastors, ministers and other key lay persons in developing their skills to minister more effectively with and to older adults; and

WHEREAS some local congregations, state/provincial/regional organizations, and national Church of God agencies have begun to initiate programs for the aged; and

WHEREAS we believe that older persons are an integral part in the life of the Church of God on whom we have been able to build strong and viable congregations; be it, therefore,

RESOLVED, that the General Assembly of the Church of God (Anderson, Indiana) proclaims 1989 as the "Year of Ministry to and with Older Adults"; and be it further

RESOLVED, that pastors, local congregations, state and regional/provincial organizations be encouraged to join with the National Fellowship of Older Adults, Commission on Social Concerns, and national agencies of the Church of God in promoting ministries and programs for and with older persons.

136. Responsible Sexual Behavior (June 1988)

WHEREAS forces in society encourage sexual intercourse before marriage; and studies indicate that in society in general, by age nineteen, 80 percent of today's males and 67 percent of today's females are sexually active; and in the United States alone more than 1,000,000 unmarried teen-agers become pregnant every year; and

WHEREAS there is an epidemic of sexually transmitted diseases; and premarital sexual intercourse can damage physical, mental, emotional, and spiritual health; and

WHEREAS the home has come under attack on many fronts and the family is struggling against forces greater than those faced by previous generations, and as a result parents are seeking additional knowledge and skills for teaching scriptural principles concerning sexuality, sexual activity, marriage, and proper self-image; and

WHEREAS parents and teen-agers desire better communication with one another but may lack the basic skills to accomplish this; and the church, as a basic support group for the family, is called to address and minister to these needs, be it, therefore,

RESOLVED, that the Church of God reaffirm its commitment to the sanctity of marriage and the reserving of sex for marriage; and be it further

RESOLVED, that the Church of God seek to train parents and other significant adults for effectively communicating biblical principles, especially those related to sexuality, sexual activity, marriage, and healthy self-image to young people, and that the Church of God seek to develop among parents, other significant adults, and teen-agers improved relational skills in an atmosphere of love and acceptance; and be it further

RESOLVED, that the above-stated goals be addressed at every level and through every avenue of the church's ministry; through national agencies, through provincial, state, and regional ministries, through such major gatherings as provincial, state and regional youth conventions and camp meetings, through the Inspirational and International Youth Conventions, and through the local church; and be it further

RESOLVED, that the church avail itself of various excellent resources such as the "WHY WAIT?" materials supplied by Josh McDowell Ministry which have been adopted for use by other evangelical church groups. These materials, having been reviewed by a select group comprised of representatives from the national agencies of the Church, youth ministers and other special interest groups, are considered sound in their content, effective in their usefulness, accurate in their Biblical application, and are recommended for use across the church.

137. Thanksgiving and Responsibility (June 1988)

WHEREAS the celebration of a Thanksgiving season has been a national tradition observed by the people of the United States from the days of the early settlers to the present time; and

WHEREAS many of the great leaders of the nation, including Presidents George Washington and Abraham Lincoln, recognized the importance of setting aside a time of Thanksgiving, and presidential proclamations have established the last Thursday of November as a day of Thanksgiving; and

WHEREAS in 1941, the United States Congress established Thanksgiving as a permanent national holiday; and

WHEREAS we as a nation have been blessed above all other nations; and

WHEREAS the United States Constitution has adapted to changing times and is the oldest written constitution in the world; and

WHEREAS the people of the United States should better understand the history of this great nation; and

WHEREAS it is appropriate to give thanks to God for the everyday freedoms guaranteed by the Constitution that the people of the United States so often take for granted; and

WHEREAS the people of the United States should take time to appreciate a land of plenty, a nation of vast human and natural resources, while not forgetting the plight of the needy; and

WHEREAS the National Thanksgiving Foundation, which has as its purposes: "To promote grassroots and private-sector involvement to help in the elimination of hunger and homelessness and to encourage nationwide expressions of thanksgiving for the blessings of life and liberty in America" is sponsoring simultaneous "National Thanksgiving Dinners" on November 17, 1988, to assist the hungry and homeless; and

WHEREAS the Church of God of Anderson, Indiana, supports the objectives of feeding the hungry and housing the homeless as well as being thankful for the blessings of life and liberty in America; therefore be it

RESOLVED, that the Church of God of Anderson, Indiana, encourages its members and other groups and organizations to work together on this national celebration by holding National Thanksgiving Dinners or other such activities on November 17, 1988, to give thanks for our blessings and to raise funds to help the less fortunate.

138. Urban Mission of the Church of God (June 1989)

WHEREAS the Census Bureau reports that the U.S.A. is steadily growing more urban and that presently 75 percent of the population now live in metropolitan areas, and that in 1963 it was 63 percent; and

WHEREAS the world is rapidly becoming urban, with projections ranging from one-half to 80 percent of the world's population living in urban places by the year 2000 (83 percent for the United States and Canada), depending on how people are counted and how cities are defined; and

WHEREAS the original charter establishing the Board of Church Extension and Home Missions of the Church of God, Inc. (1921) assigns the Board the responsibility, among others, of engaging in urban mission, mentioning specifically encouraging "home missionary work among. . .city slums" and seeking "to establish churches in large cities and strategic centers or other places where work has not yet opened"; and

WHEREAS at the turn of the twentieth century the Church of God was intentional in its urban outreach ministry, establishing Missionary Homes as centers of urban evangelism and compassionate ministries in some 42 cities over three decades; and

WHEREAS many Church of God congregations today have moved away from the core city, largely leaving the urban mission of the church to ethnic minority congregations that often face overwhelming needs with impoverished resources; therefore, be it

RESOLVED, that the General Assembly affirm metropolitan/urban areas of the nation, in all their pluralism and problems, to be proper and fitting places for the Church of God to be on mission...; and be it, also,

RESOLVED, that the General Assembly go on record as urging:

(1) pastors of local churches to aggressively pursue a course of consciousness raising regarding our Lord's urban mission mandate;

(2) national agencies to target urban mission and city churches in developing resources for ministry within their assignments;

(3) Church of God colleges and the School of Theology to develop core curriculum that will assist students in understanding the city biblically, theologically, and missionally; and be it, also,

RESOLVED, that the General Assembly go on record as urging metro area churches to move beyond occasional fellowship and unity meetings to develop active ministry networks (within existing organizational structures)...; and be it further

RESOLVED, that the Board of Church Extension and Home Missions recommends that the General Assembly enthusiastically accept and endorse this resolution on the Urban Mission of the Church of God as in keeping with the "National Strategy of Church Planting for the Church of God for the Next Two Decades," approved by the General Assembly in June, 1984.

139. Sexual, Emotional and Physical Abuse (June 1992)

WHEREAS abuse, whether sexual, emotional, or physical, is a growing problem in society; and

WHEREAS the effects of abuse create lifelong problems for the abused, attacking their very self-understanding and their relationship to God and the Church; and

WHEREAS we increasingly recognize that the church community includes both the abused and abusers in significant numbers; and

WHEREAS abuse is often a cycle where those who have been abused are more likely to become abusers; and

WHEREAS both persons who abuse and persons who suffer the abuse are in need of the redeeming power of the gospel and support from the Church; and

WHEREAS we acknowledge that healing from abuse comes only as a gift from God; therefore be it

RESOLVED that the General Assembly designate the month of October to focus on the need for healing of the abused and the abuser; and be it further

RESOLVED that the General Assembly urge churches to set aside one Sunday in October to pray for healing for both those who are abused and those who abuse; and be it further

RESOLVED that the General Assembly urge churches to initiate programs to bring justice, healing, and restoration for the abused and the abuser; and be it further

RESOLVED, that the General Assembly urge all persons to support programs and efforts to end abuse and aid in healing from abuse in their communities and throughout their nations.

140. Homosexuality (June 1993)

The General Assembly has, from time to time, deemed it appropriate to speak to the church regarding matters of spiritual, social, and ethical importance. In 1979 the Assembly passed a resolution titled "Statement Against Homosexuality" [see Entry 126]. Since then the subject has emerged with spirited discussion in the public arena. It seems timely, therefore, that the

Assembly once again address the subject with biblical conviction, compassion, and caring:

WHEREAS, there is a current national focus on homosexuality, frequently viewing it as an acceptable alternative lifestyle; and

WHEREAS, there is long-standing biblical evidence that a homosexual life-style is perverse and destructive to individuals and to society; and

WHEREAS, we in the Church of God are committed to biblical holiness and hold in high regard scriptural injunctions related to homosexuality and, therefore, cannot accept, endorse, or condone homosexual behavior; and

WHEREAS, we believe that the sexual relationship between man and woman within the bonds of marriage is viewed as something natural and beautiful—ordained of God; and

WHEREAS, we are a redemptive body and seek to express love, compassion, and concern for those who struggle with sexual identity or homosexual orientation to assist them in a chaste relationship in Christ; therefore be it

RESOLVED, that the General Assembly call on congregational and institutional leaders of the Church of God to demonstrate love and provide counsel and materials to assist families and persons confused or distressed by homosexual behavior and to bring redemption and wholeness to those persons; be it further

RESOLVED, that we respectfully urge all persons inclined toward homosexual behavior to seek the grace of God and such other aid and counsel as may be conducive to their relief; be it further

RESOLVED, however, that the General Assembly of the Church of God go on record affirming our conviction that, biblically, we believe homosexual behavior is sin; be it further

RESOLVED, that the General Assembly stands firmly opposed to the licensing, ordination, or approving for leadership those who are involved in this life-style; be it finally

RESOLVED, that the General Assembly supports instruction which brings understanding to issues related to homosexuality, but opposes instruction which endorses or promotes homosexual behavior as an acceptable alternate or Christian life-style.

141. Mental Illness (June 1993)

WHEREAS, approximately thirty million adult Americans suffer from one or more mental disorders, and of these as many as ten million are afflicted with chronic or prolonged mental illness; and

WHEREAS, approximately one percent of this country's population (about 2.5 million) have or will have the disease of schizophrenia, and about six percent have or will have a major affective disorder (major depression or manic depression); and as many as twelve million children suffer from some form of mental disorder, three million of whom have a serious mental illness; and

WHEREAS, persons with severe mental illness are estimated to account for as many as one-third or more of the nation's homeless, and occupy twenty-five percent of all hospital beds in the country; and

WHEREAS, the economic cost to society of mental illness is above $70 billion annually, of which $14.4 billion is for direct treatment and support costs; and

WHEREAS, because of ignorance, fear, and prejudice, mentally ill persons are not only stigmatized and discriminated against in housing, medical insurance, and employment opportunities, and are denied adequately funded treatment and support services, but are also often denied supportive fellowship in the church; and

WHEREAS, the families of mentally ill persons are frequently burdened by these illnesses and often serve as the primary caretakers of their loved ones, needing the support and love of friends and church, and yet often feel abandoned and shunned; and

WHEREAS, the church is called to engage in Christ's ministry of healing and advocacy on behalf of those who are ill in body, mind, and spirit and those who are discriminated against, lonely, unaccepted, and neglected; therefore be it

RESOLVED, that the General Assembly call upon the clergy and laity of the Church of God to avail themselves of knowledge of the plight of the mentally ill and their families and of the latest medical and scientific research into mental illness so as to dispel fear and prejudice; and be it further

RESOLVED, that the congregations of the Church of God be asked to evaluate their ministry among the mentally ill and seek a fuller, more imaginative, and compassionate ministry among this sizable segment of our society; and be it further

RESOLVED, that agencies of the General Assembly of the Church of God that are responsible for education and congregational nurture and ministry, including but not limited to the colleges, the university, the School of Theology, the Board of Christian Education, and Warner Press, be specifically encouraged to seek ways to assist the Church in fulfilling the intent of this resolution.

142. Ministry With the Disabled (June 1994)

WHEREAS, there is a national and worldwide focus on the needs of disabled persons; and

WHEREAS, in the United States alone, seventeen percent of the population suffers some disability (43 million persons); and

WHEREAS, there is long-standing biblical evidence of God's love and compassion being repeatedly extended to the disabled; and

WHEREAS, we in the Church of God are committed to biblical holiness and hold in high regard scriptural references and instruction in reference to the disabled; and

WHEREAS, we are a redemptive body and seek to express love, compassion, and concern for those who struggle daily with disability; therefore be it

RESOLVED, that the General Assembly call on the membership of the Church of God to demonstrate love, compassion, and counsel to assist disabled persons and their families in their struggle with disability; be it further

RESOLVED, that the Church of God seek to avoid any implication, by act of omission or commission, that the disabled person is a second-class citizen, and establish an increased level of sensitivity toward disabled persons' needs related to church gatherings; be it further

RESOLVED, that this Assembly request all Church of God congregations to work toward providing total accessibility for all facets of church worship and related activities, and endeavor to reach out to the disabled in their immediate communities, assuring spiritual accessibility as well; be it finally

RESOLVED, that the General Assembly call upon the leadership of our institutions of higher learning to examine the field of disability ministry and seek to activate appropriate academic curricula to equip present and future students with sensitivity and specialized training.

143. Freemasonry and Christianity (June 1994)

WHEREAS, the Church of God Reformation Movement has faithfully proclaimed that the Word of God declares Jesus Christ "the Way, the Truth, and the Life"; and

WHEREAS, the Word of God declares that no one comes to the Father but by the Son and that Jesus Christ is above every name whereby men must be saved; and

WHEREAS, Freemasonry is a Christ-less religion that omits the very name of Christ in its prayers and ritual and has a false view of God and the nature of God's salvation; and

WHEREAS, there is great danger that the Christian who becomes a Freemason will compromise Christian beliefs or allegiance to Christ (perhaps without realizing it); and

WHEREAS, there has been a lack of information and understanding of the true nature and bondage of Freemasonry and other similar secret lodges, societies, and organizations; and

WHEREAS, the secret nature of such lodges contravenes the Christian's open witness, and the secret nature of the oaths should be repugnant to the Christian; therefore, be it

RESOLVED, that the Church of God Reformation Movement reaffirm its historic position which proclaims that membership in secret societies and lodges which are oath bound is not compatible with the Christian loyalty to Christ.

144. Racial Reconciliation (June 1996, 1998)

Editor's Note: The 1996 General Assembly adopted the following:

Whereas, there appears to be an unusual wave of racial and religious hatred in this country [USA], presently finding its expression in the burning of church buildings belonging to black congregations; and

Whereas, this renewed form of racial hostility sets back previous gains in racial harmony; and

Whereas, our sincere desire is to work always towards a life lived in harmony and expressed good will to all; and

Whereas, our desire is that the Church of God and all the work accomplished through the Cross-Cultural Consultation [see Entry 175] towards racial reconciliation among us not be hindered by the violent acts occurring throughout our country;

Therefore, be it Resolved that this Spanish American Council of the Church of God in the United States, Canada, and Puerto Rico, the National Association of the Church of God, and the General Assembly of the Church of God go on record as expressing our concerns for a deepened solidarity with our African American brothers and sisters, and that such a resolution be publicized throughout its congregations.

Editor's Note: The 1998 General Assembly then adopted the following:

Whereas we believe that God has given us his design for the church in Gal. 3:28 (NRSV): "There is no longer Jew or Greek, there is no longer slave or free, there is no longer male or female; for all of you are one in Christ Jesus"; and

Whereas we recognize that, as in Eph. 2:14-15 (NRSV), "For he is our peace; in his flesh he has made both groups into one, and has broken down the dividing wall, that is the hostility between us. . .that he might create in himself one new humanity in place of the two, thus making peace, that by Himself he might make the two into one"; and

Whereas we recognize that we, the Church of God, have fallen short of practicing visibly the unity we proclaim by permitting racial division among us; therefore,

Be it Resolved that the Church of God Reformation Movement re-affirm its commitment to demonstrating visibly the racial and ethic unity we proclaim; and

Be it Resolved that we admit that racial reconciliation is needed among us; and

Be it Resolved that we call upon the church to confess the sins of racism and racial prejudice and to take responsibility for seeking and receiving forgiveness and finding healing; and

Be it Resolved that we urge individuals and congregations to create new ways of relating across racial and ethic lines by becoming ambassadors of reconciliation.

---

145. Establish A Task Force on Racial Reconciliation (June 1998)

Whereas the Committee on Long Range Planning, the Commission on Social Concerns, and the Commission on Christian Unity, meeting together in Anderson, Indiana, on November 20, 1997, recognize and affirm the Church of God Reformation Movement's historical commitment to racial harmony; and

Whereas the Hispanic Council, the American Indian Council, the National Association of the Church of God, and the Leadership Council of the Church of God recognize and affirm the Church of God Reformation Movement's historical commitment to racial harmony; and

Whereas these bodies also recognize and deplore the current reality of racial division resulting from our failure to live up to this commitment; and

Whereas these bodies further recognize the need for systematic, long-term effort to heal the racial divisions and realize the harmony we desire;

Be it Resolved that the Ministries Council be requested to establish a task force on racial reconciliation that will (1) lead the church to recognize and confess the actions in our history that broke the racial harmony and led to both structural and spiritual division and (2) develop strategies for dealing with our history and moving to reconciliation; and

Be it Resolved that this task force be charged with leading the church into the "Next Steps in Racial Reconciliation" suggested in the Dialogue on Racial Reconciliation, namely:

1. Taking Responsibility
2. Seeking Forgiveness
3. Repairing the Wrong
4. Healing the Soul
5. Creating a New Way of Relating

Be it Resolved that this task force report annually on its progress to the Ministries Council and the General Assembly; and

Be it Resolved that the task force on racial reconciliation remain in existence until such time as the Ministries Council decides that its assignment is completed.

146. United Nations: Decade of Peace and Nonviolence, 2001-2010 (June 1999)

WHEREAS twenty-three Nobel Peace Laureates, including Mother Teresa, signed an appeal asking the United Nations to designate the first decade of the new millennium as "A Decade for a Culture of Peace and Nonviolence for the Children of the World"; and

WHEREAS the UN General Assembly *unanimously* adopted the appeal which has *the potential of changing the direction of the world,* and calls for the principles of nonviolence to be taught in the educational institutions of all member nations, and at all levels of society; and

WHEREAS people on every continent, at the close of the most violent century in history, are perplexed and frustrated by the traditional policies of retaliation and violence, and are expressing an international willingness to find a better way for local and global conflict resolution; and

WHEREAS we believe that God is bringing our movement into a new day of more effective organization and outreach, and because of our deep concern that children and all people everywhere hear the Good News of Jesus and accept Him and His teachings; now, therefore

BE IT RESOLVED: that the General Assembly encourage Church of God people to cooperate with the worldwide efforts to make the years 2001–2010 a decade for building a culture of peace and nonviolence.

147. Addressing Violence in Our Society (June 1999)

Editor's Note: In the late 1990s there were several instances of mass shootings in the public schools in North America. The following was a response of the General Assembly to this and to violence on television and generally in society.

Whereas, the Church of God believes that the home and school should be a leavening agent for peaceful and harmonious living in society, and

Whereas, the Church of God believes that the home and school should be a safe place for adults as well as for children and teenagers, and

Whereas, the Supreme Court has ruled that prayer and other religious symbols and documents be removed from schools and other public buildings, and

Whereas, there is a move among caring Christian people across America to intercede for our schools—their administrators, faculty, staff, and students;

Be it therefore Resolved, that the General Assembly of the Church of God agree to do all that is within its power to fight against violence in society, home, and schools;

Be it Further Resolved, that the individual members of this General Assembly be proactive in praying for our school officials and students in our local communities; and

Be it Finally Resolved, that upon the passage of this resolution we will take it back to our home communities for implementation.

EMPHASES, STUDIES, CELEBRATIONS

148. Declaration of a Seminary Year (June 1960)

WHEREAS, this General Ministerial Assembly, upon the recommendations of the Budget Committee of the Executive Council and the Division of World Service, did last year (June, 1959), designate the Special Project for the year 1960-61 to be the raising of $100,000 toward the erection of the first unit of the School of Theology building; and

WHEREAS, during the year 1960–61, when the campaign to raise this $100,000 will be in progress, those in charge of raising the fund wish to designate the year as SEMINARY YEAR IN THE CHURCH OF GOD, in order to focus the attention of the entire church upon the importance of training our young people for the Church of God ministry; be it

RESOLVED, that the General Ministerial Assembly hereby adopts the following proclamation:

To Every Member of the Church of God, Greetings:

Be it known that the General Ministerial Assembly of the Church of God and its several agencies hereby proclaim the year 1960-1961 as Seminary Year, during which time a special fund of $100,000 shall be raised for the erection of the first unit of the School of Theology building in Anderson, Indiana, for the training of ministers for the Church of God. Every congregation is urged to study this need and make provision to contribute toward this important work of the Church.

---

149. Greetings to the Zurich World Conference (June 1967)

In this 49th General Assembly of the Church of God, convened for the purpose of conducting the business of the Church, and the 78th International Convention, we as ministers and laymen pause to acknowledge our brethren in all countries of the world. We especially send greetings to you who are attending the Fourth World Conference in Zurich, Switzerland.

We feel a bond of love for you which is stronger than the tensions, misunderstandings, and estrangements which are so common between nations and cultures. The work of God in Christ has made us brothers and fellow workers.

The Assembly by a standing vote expresses to you its deepest Christian love and warmest fellowship. We live in a troubled and explosive world. Poverty, hunger, disease, illiteracy, social inequality, and rebellion are a part of our times. We pledge our faithful stewardship and cooperation with our brethren throughout the world in endeavoring to bring the peace of Christ and his deliverance, never letting up on the elimination of these evils.

While you are gathered in Zurich, we pray that the Holy Spirit will be real to each of you and that he will bring a flowing together of hearts so that you will truly experience fellowship at the deepest levels.

Where possible, we ask that delegates take our greetings and Christian love to the church in their home countries.

It was moved, seconded (Charles Weber-Albert Donaldson), and carried by a standing vote that these greetings be conveyed to the Fourth World Conference of the Church of God, Zurich, Switzerland. [See Entry 204 for a brief history of the World Conferences.]

150. Declaring a Year of Evangelism (June 1970)

WHEREAS, the Church of God has been invited to participate in the projected 1973 nationwide evangelism thrust, along with other religious communions; and

WHEREAS, the Board of Church Extension and Home Missions has offered its services in initiating the 1973 evangelism emphasis for the Church of God; and

WHEREAS, the Division of General Service sees great value in a carefully planned emphasis on evangelism, which will bring together interested agencies of the Church in a coordinated effort; and

WHEREAS, the Division of General Service has given its enthusiastic endorsement to the projected program and encourages the Board of Church Extension and Home Missions to initiate the planning, involving all interested agencies of the Church of God, for our participation in the Year of Evangelism Emphasis; therefore, be it

RESOLVED, that the Executive Council designate 1973 as the Year of Evangelism Emphasis, and that it seek the concurrence of the General Assembly by resolution, seeking its approval and support by urging each minister and each local congregation of the Church of God to cooperate fully in this program; and

RESOLVED, that we, the members of the General Assembly, do hereby concur in the action taken previously by the Division of General Service and the Executive Council in regard to the 1973 Nationwide Evangelism Thrust; and be it further

RESOLVED, that we pledge our enthusiastic cooperation in this concerted effort to make the Christian witness more vital and relevant in American society.

151. Call for a Consultation on Doctrine (June 1970)

The General Assembly sessions this year have helped us not only to see and handle our duties, but also to see and know our strong differences of opinion. Many of the expressed differences concern agency programs and decisions that were vigorously debated.

WHEREAS, some of the expressed differences reflected a possible problem of attitudes as well as opinions; and

WHEREAS, many of the differences reflect theological and doctrinal problems that need to be openly and honestly faced by this Assembly; and

WHEREAS, some of these problems grow out of evidently changing patterns of our preaching, teaching, and publications across several decades; therefore, be it

RESOLVED, that we urge a serious restudy of the theological and doctrinal message of our Movement; and that the Executive Council and the School of Theology examine the feasibility of calling a "Consultation on Doctrine" to allow mutual discussion among us as leaders in faith and practice.

The intent of the Consultation will not be to prepare a creed or definitive statement of our position, but rather to hear and examine anew the doctrinal concerns that are important to our life and work as a movement.

Editor's Note: For a review of the process that followed passage of the above resolution and a summation by William E. Reed of the useful purposes eventually served, see Entry 7.

152. Plan for a Centennial Celebration (June 1972)

WHEREAS, the Church of God, with general agencies in Anderson, Indiana, and with congregations in forty or more countries of the world, will reach its centennial at the end of this decade; and

WHEREAS, the Church of God around the world will want to celebrate its centennial in a way that pays tribute to those who have preceded us in this work and, at the same time, present an appropriate challenge to those in generations to come; therefore be it

RESOLVED, that the General Assembly, on this 21st day of June, 1972, concur in the recommendation of its Executive Council in confirming the time period for the Centennial Celebration as beginning with June, 1980, and extending through October, 1981; and be it further

RESOLVED, that the Executive Council be instructed to proceed through its committee on planning for an observance of the centennial in a manner commensurate with our spiritual heritage and our unrealized hopes.

153. Call for an Emphasis on Church Growth (June 1976)

WHEREAS, there is a continuous need for the Church of God to urgently and aggressively address its attention and resources toward a more adequate fulfillment of the commission given by Jesus Christ to His church; and

WHEREAS, in the last few years, there has developed a wide range of tools, techniques, and methods for stimulating church growth; and

WHEREAS, we believe God by His Holy Spirit is prompting the Church of God to intensify its efforts in a major evangelistic effort to win new persons to meaningful discipleship; therefore be it

RESOLVED, that the General Assembly of the Church of God, meeting in June, 1976, go on record, and hereby do, as endorsing a major effort within the church to stimulate church growth; and be it further

RESOLVED, that:

1. Such a church growth effort be launched July 1, 1978, and continue through June, 1980, in the midst of our centennial celebration, and that the program for church growth be designed and administered by a strategy committee as named earlier in this report;

2. The passage of this resolution mandates and pledges wholehearted support on the part of all national agencies of the Church of God in the United States of America for full cooperation and participation in a united effort for church growth;

3. The costs of this effort, as determined by the Strategy Committee, shall be funded through the budget of the Division of General Service by a grant approved by the Budget Committee, and included in the 1977-78 World Service Budget;

4. Members of the General Assembly who vote for this Resolution also pledge their full support to utilize the ministry and tools produced by the Strategy Committee for their congregations and areas;

5. The Strategy Committee will bring to this Assembly in June, 1977, a progress report on its work to date, and in June, 1978, the committee will bring a report setting forth specific and detailed goals for congregations, state and area assemblies, and national agencies, and a follow-through plan for reaching the projected goals;

6. The Division of General Service will bring to the 1981 General Assembly a summarization report on the effectiveness and accomplishments of the church effort.

154. Prayer and Plans for the 1980 World Conference (June 1977)

WHEREAS, it is the judgment of this Executive Council and General Assembly that immeasurable good has occurred as the result of the several World Conferences of the Church of God that have been conducted over the past several years [see Entry 204 for a brief history of the Conferences]; and

WHEREAS, the different World Conferences have had a unifying effect upon the Church of God in many different nations and have served to clarify our thinking on many crucial issues to broaden our understanding and appreciation for persons in the Church of God in other parts of the world; and

WHEREAS, this Assembly has in many ways across many years given strong encouragement and support to the development of the several World Conferences; therefore, be it

RESOLVED, that this Assembly extend to the World Conference of the Church of God a warm, cordial invitation to have the 1980 World Conference of the Church of God in Anderson, Indiana, in conjunction with the Annual Convention of the Church of God in June of 1980; and be it further

RESOLVED, that we instruct the executive secretary of the Executive Council to carry our Christian greetings and assurance of prayer and support to delegates meeting in the Strategy and Planning Consultation to be held October 17-26, 1977, in Nairobi, Kenya, East Africa; and be it further

RESOLVED, that we express our corporate concern for the success of this consultation and our promise of prayer for the guidance of the Holy Spirit by a standing vote of affirmation.

155. Goal-Oriented Plan for the Future (June 1983)

Editor's Note: During 1983 final plans were being made for the major Consultation on Mission and Ministry scheduled for April, 1984, in Indianapolis. Many members of the Assembly were concerned that the Church of God did not seem to have a definite sense of direction as it prepared to move into the final years of the century. They also were hopeful that the substantial effort being invested in this coming consultation would result in more than a few generalizations that would not focus and energize the movement's ministries. A motion, therefore, emerged from the Assembly floor calling upon the coming consultation to work toward a specific goal-oriented plan for the coming years in the life of the Church of God. The Assembly adopted this motion. For results of this consultation, see Entry 171.

156. Church Planting (June 1984, 1988)

WHEREAS, God has richly blessed the Church of God reformation with substantial congregational growth through the first century of its existence; and

WHEREAS, the General Assembly has established the Board of Church Extension and Home Missions to develop and provide services; and

WHEREAS, there is an urgent need for a more intensified effort in planting new churches among the Hispanics, Asians, Africans, Arabs, and more than 80 million unchurched Americans; and

WHEREAS, states and districts have assemblies, officers, state coordinators and Boards of Church Extension and Kingdom Builders to help do church planting and congregational revitalization; and

WHEREAS, the state coordinators, the national Board of Church Extension and Home Missions and the national Board of Christian Education have cooperated in selecting a State/National Task Force to seek ways to increase the planting of new churches; therefore, be it

RESOLVED, that the General Assembly recognize and affirm:

a. That the Church is most obedient to her calling when reaching the lost and unchurched of our nation and world;

b. That planting and nurturing new churches is biblical and an effective way to evangelize the lost;

c. That the ministry and support of church planting, as being done by state and district Boards of Church Extension and Kingdom Builders, continue to be done;

d. That there is a need for each indigenous congregation to consider sponsoring a new church; and,

e. That some persons are called and gifted as leaders for starting new churches and that they be urged to cooperate with a state and district Board of Church Extension and Kingdom Builders. And be it further

RESOLVED, that we recommend that the General Assembly enthusiastically accept and endorse the national strategy of church planting for the Church of God in North America for the next two decades as one of the major recommendations, goals, and ministries for the Church of God.

Editor's Note: In the 1988 General Assembly it was reported that since the 1984 action, 106 new congregations of the Church of God had been launched. They were located in 36 different states or districts, representing a good beginning to a central and long-term task.

157. Declaration of a Year of the Hispanics (June 1984)

WHEREAS, there has been a great influx of Hispanics in the 1970s and 1980s, principally in the southwest portion of the United States and in all major metropolitan areas; and

WHEREAS, Hispanic people constitute one of the largest and most rapidly growing minority groups in the United States; and

WHEREAS, an urgent need exists to evangelize and minister in Christian love to these new immigrants of Hispanic origin; and

WHEREAS, the Church of God is in a special position of responsibility and opportunity to broaden and increase its growing ministry among Hispanics; and

WHEREAS, there is great need to become better acquainted with Hispanic culture and language and to celebrate this contribution to the Church of God; and

WHEREAS, the Board of Church Extension and Home Missions, meeting in its annual session the 26th day of April, 1984, recommended to the Executive Council that 1986 be recognized by the reformation movement as

a time for special attention focused upon the Hispanic community; and

WHEREAS, the Executive Council concurred in its meeting on May 10, 1984; therefore, be it

RESOLVED, that the General Assembly designate 1986 to be celebrated as the "Year of the Hispanics" and encourage general agencies and state organizations of the church to find ways to evangelize and minister within Hispanic communities.

Fidel Zamorano

158. Year of the Sunday School (June 1987)

Editor's Note: In grateful recognition of the two hundred years of significant ministry of the Sunday school movement, the Board of Christian Education and the Publication Board jointly sponsored the following, which was affirmed gladly by the 1987 General Assembly.

WHEREAS, the Sunday school is a vital outreach and nurturing arm of the Church of God; and

WHEREAS, the Sunday school provides regular opportunity for teachers and learners to study the Bible for discovering God's instruction for contemporary living; and

WHEREAS, the Sunday school provides a time and a setting for unified and systematic study of Church of God doctrine and heritage throughout the Movement; and

WHEREAS, the Sunday school represents a rich history of strong lay involvement, enlisting the largest group of volunteer workers in the church; and

WHEREAS, the Sunday school provides opportunities for the training and development of leadership in the church; and

WHEREAS, the Sunday school is a basic component to church planting and growth strategies; therefore, be it

RESOLVED, that all agencies and congregations of the Church of God give support to the Sunday school and its leaders by declaring September, 1987 through August, 1988 to be "The Year of the Sunday School"; be it further

RESOLVED, that each congregation set September 13 as the date for launching of the Sunday school year; and be it further

RESOLVED, that we support the Sunday school through the use of "Journey With the Word" curriculum for the Church of God; and be it further

RESOLVED, that we enlist our Sunday schools in the Decade for Sunday School Development; and be it further

RESOLVED, that we emphasize the Sunday school through church growth and planting strategies.

159. Year of Revival in the Church of God (June 1987)

WHEREAS, the forces of Satan and sin continue their destructive assaults against the cause of Christ; and

WHEREAS, the Scriptures teach that true spiritual revival in the Body of Christ will not only restore God's blessing, power and healing to the Church, but will also bring healing to the land that has become sick unto death; be it, therefore,

RESOLVED, that the Executive Council of the Church of God designate as soon as possible, hopefully 1988-89, a "Year of Revival"; and be it further

RESOLVED, that the International Convention Program Committee for that year consider focusing on the "Revival" theme; and be it further

RESOLVED, that this resolution be sent to every national agency and that these agencies be encouraged to pick up on this emphasis in their planning and publications; and be it finally

RESOLVED, that during this time particular emphasis be given to the ministry of intercessory prayer and fasting.

160. Day of Prayer and Fasting (June 1987)

WHEREAS, there are many kinds of pressures that all persons, clergy and laity face as they minister in the Kingdom of God; and

WHEREAS, there is much disorientation about the morality, testimony, and life-style of Christians currently being witnessed by the world; and

WHEREAS, there is such an obvious need to reach this continent and the world for Jesus Christ; and

WHEREAS, the leadership needs of the church are so very great (the New Testament Church provides our example, see Acts 13:2-3); and

WHEREAS, the ministry opportunities to affect the spiritual and moral destiny of many people are numerous; and

WHEREAS, the Bible tells us that "our struggle is not against flesh and blood, but against the rulers, against the authorities, against the powers of this dark world and against the spiritual forces of evil in the heavenly realms" (Eph. 6:12) and we need divine help to stand; therefore, be it

RESOLVED, that the first Wednesday of each month during the 1987-88 fiscal year be a Day of Prayer and Fasting; and

RESOLVED, that every congregation of the Church of God be encouraged to promote and observe this Day of Prayer and Fasting; and

RESOLVED, that this program be administered by the office of the Executive Secretary of the Executive Council of the General Assembly of the Church of God; and

RESOLVED, that this observance begin July 1, 1987.

161. Year of Christian Higher Education (June 1988)

Editor's Note: Refer to Entry 103 for the content of this resolution highlighting the ministry of higher education in the life of the church.

162. Year of Canadian—United States Partnership in Ministry (June 1988)

WHEREAS, the Church of God in Canada has always been an integral partner in fulfilling the mission of the Church of God Reformation Movement in North America; and

WHEREAS, the population of Canada is approaching 30 million people comprised of many socio-ethnic cultures; and

WHEREAS, the nation of Canada has ten provinces and two territories, with the Church of God having 53 congregations located in six provinces; and

WHEREAS, the Canadian Church of God has established and supported the Christian higher educational institution, Gardner Bible College, to prepare laity and pastors for ministry and service, and has contributed numerous missionaries who have served in overseas assignments with the Missionary Board of the Church of God; and

WHEREAS, an urgent need exists to evangelize and plant congregations of the Church of God in Canada; and

WHEREAS, there is a great need to become better acquainted with Canadian congregations, and to recognize their contribution to the Church of God; and

WHEREAS, it is desirable to strengthen cooperation, improve relationship, and foster interdependence between the Church in the United States and Canada; therefore, be it

RESOLVED, that the two Canadian Assemblies along with the Board of Church Extension and Home Missions, Anderson, Indiana, recommend that the year 1990 be recognized by the Church of God in North America as a time to better understand the need and opportunities to evangelize and plant churches in the nation of Canada; be it further

RESOLVED, that the General Assembly designate 1990 as the "Year of Canadian—United States Partnership in Ministry" and encourage general agencies, state and area assemblies, and congregations to build supporting relationships with Canadian churches.

163. The National Association's Diamond Jubilee (June 1991)

WHEREAS, the National Association of the Church of God with offices in West Middlesex, Pennsylvania, had its inception in August, 1917, when a group of saints, known as "The Brothers and Sisters of Love," held their first camp meeting in West Middlesex; and

WHEREAS, the National Association (hereafter identified by NA) since its beginnings 75 years ago has grown from a small farming community with rolling hills and wooded land to a camp ground site with modern cottages, retreat and recreational facilities and buildings with an assessed evaluation of more than two million dollars; and

WHEREAS, the primary motive in starting the NA was a desire of "The Brothers and Sisters of Love" for fellowship with those who believed in and practiced holiness; and

WHEREAS, the pioneers of the NA had no intent to start a schismatic movement apart from the international work of the Church of God in Anderson, Indiana, but rather to meet the needs among the Black saints for worship, fellowship, and service, and to enlist and develop its people without racist overtones and segregation control; and

WHEREAS, the NA is a vital and significant organization in the life of the Church of God and continues to make valuable contributions to the national and international life and ministries of the Church of God; and

277

WHEREAS, the impact and influence of the NA upon the Black community of the Church of God has been significant and immeasurable in terms of its scope and ministry, and constituency in the urban centers of our nation; and

WHEREAS, the NA has served as a catalyst for social change and cohesion to a significant number of the Black constituency of the Church of God and, at the same time, the NA has raised the social and political consciousness of the Church, resulting in some positive changes in race relations, employment, and attitudes; be it, therefore,

RESOLVED, that the 1991 General Assembly of the Church of God join the NA in celebrating its Diamond Jubilee by encouraging local congregations, state and regional assemblies, and national agencies to participate in the week-long celebration scheduled to take place during the Annual Campmeeting at West Middlesex, Pennsylvania, August 11-18, 1991; and be it

RESOLVED, that all local, state, and national Church of God publications be encouraged to promote the NA Diamond Jubilee Celebration in their newsletters, magazines and other appropriate publications; be it further

RESOLVED, that this Assembly declare August, 1991, to July, 1992, as the year of the NA throughout the Church of God; be it also

RESOLVED, that all pastors and congregations be encouraged to acquire and read the NA's Diamond Jubilee Historical Publication; be it finally

RESOLVED, that local congregations, regional and state assemblies, and the national agencies join in partnership with the NA to seek ways to evangelize the world, seek to solve racial problems, resolve church conflict, empower the poor and disadvantaged, and utilize our material and human resources for the up-building of the Kingdom of God.

Editor's Note: For more detail on the National Association of the Church of God, see Entry 187.

164. Vision-2-Grow! (June 1991, 1999)

Rationale:

Jesus Christ, our Savior and Lord, commanded: "Go therefore and make disciples of all nations, baptizing them in the name of the Father and of the Son and of the Holy Spirit, and teaching them to obey everything that I have commanded you" (Matt. 28:19-20 NRSV);

The Mission Statement of the Church of God affirms that we seek "to enable persons. . .to experience the redemptive love in its fullest meaning through the sanctifying power of the gospel and know Jesus Christ as Savior, Master and Lord";

In the nineties, looking forward to the next century, by faith and vision we believe:

- The Church of God has an opportunity to grow, to win more persons to Christ and help them find their place in the fellowship and ministry of a local church;
- Visionary, courageous, and trained pastoral and lay leadership can be enlisted and are essential to growth;
- The Spirit of God is convicting persons of sin and calling the church to be intensely involved in ministries of evangelism and to meet other human needs;
- The rapid change in the structures of society and in culture provides the church with a unique opportunity to proclaim and demonstrate the gospel.

Goals:

1. Church Growth—The Charge for the Future!
   In response to the Great Commission, and in recognition of God's desire to increase the Church, we seek to:
   A. Plant 60 new congregations each year.
   B. Increase U.S. A.M. worship attendance to 200,000 by 1995 and to 225,000 by 2001, with similar growth in Canadian churches.
   C. Renew biblical foundations, strengthen the family, and provide avenues for spiritual maturity.
   D. Strengthen congregational response to world need.
   E. Target 15 pastors of growing congregations to serve as partners in developing Vision 2 Grow! strategies.

2. Leadership
   In response to the need for effective and visionary lay and clergy leadership we seek to:
   A. Establish an intentional and focused effort for recruiting ministers.
   B. Strengthen present tracks of ministerial enlistment training.
   C. Create alternate models for in-service training and support.
   D. Challenge and enable pastors and lay persons to: (1) Provide visionary leadership; (2) Exercise their unique gifts; (3) Be faithful to the trust placed in them.

Editor's Note: The following review of the implementation of Vision-2-Grow! Comes from the report of Edward Foggs to the General Assembly, June 14, 1999.

279

During the nineties we celebrated the growth of the church. You will recall the challenge of "3,000 for Christ" in 1996 under the leadership of Rolland Daniels as Director of *Vision-2-Grow!* Then came the call and achievement of "10,000 for Christ." Other challenges followed. Our average Sunday morning worship attendance according to the 1988 *Yearbook* of the Church of God was 199,127. Our 1999 *Yearbook* reports an average Sunday morning worship attendance of 234,311—an increase of almost 18 percent. To God be the glory!

Our growth focus has been multi-faceted. We have looked to grow not only in numbers, but in spiritual maturity and extended outreach ministries. *Vision-2-Grow!* launched several major efforts to strengthen congregational life, pastoral leadership, pastoral families, and lay development. I want to acknowledge successor Directors Oral Withrow and Joseph Cookston. All of these Directors. . .have helped the church engage more effectively in fulfilling the Great Commission (Matt. 28:16-20) and the Great Commandments (Matt. 22:34-40). All of this has happened because of the enthusiastic participation of pastors, lay leaders, congregations, and ministries whose priorities were centered on these distinctive Biblical mandates.

Editor's Note: Also see Entry 203.

165. Celebration of an Ethnic Sunday (June 1992)

In October, 1492, Columbus' landing on San Salvador in the Bahamas was a historic event that triggered a tidal wave of global change that even today continues: the collision of the two worlds, the old and the new. This year our nation will commemorate 500 years since Columbus "discovered" the Americas. To celebrate while ignoring the pain of the natives who were already present when Columbus arrived is to be insensitive to our call as Christian peacemakers.

WHEREAS, we are a people called by God to be ambassadors of reconciliation for Christ; and

WHEREAS, millions of Americans, descendants of the Indians, Hispanic, Black, Asian, and other minorities feel the birthday of their country has been slighted by the so-called "500-year birthday celebration" of the Americas; and

WHEREAS, historians past and present have generally ignored the separate histories of minorities in the United States; and

WHEREAS, our Executive Secretary has challenged us as leaders to "be actively involved in our local communities in breaking down the barriers that destroy the lives of men and women and children who were created in God's image";

THEREFORE, the Spanish American Council of the Church of God in the U. S. A. invites the total Church to join us in a celebration of ETHNIC SUNDAY on October 4, 1992, whereby we can promote our unity in diversity by:

- Inviting minority pastors and leaders for pulpit exchanges, conferences, or seminars to enhance greater cross-cultural understanding;
- Planning workcamps into local communities or overseas to encourage people reaching out and working together;
- Promoting regional prayer services or prayer vigils in order to intercede for racial harmony in our cities towns and nation;
- Giving monies to our university, colleges, and other institutions of higher learning designated for minority scholarships.

Though Different in Race,
We Are One By His Grace.

CHURCHWIDE CONSULTATIONS

166. All-Board Congress and Planning Council (June 1963)

Editor's Note: The following is excerpted from the final report of the Findings Committee of the All-Board Congress and Planning Council, 1963.

On April 30–May 2, 1963, an All-Board Congress and Planning Council of the Church of God was convened in Anderson, Indiana, to facilitate and focus wide discussion on crucial issues then being faced by the movement as a whole. Some 260 persons participated in this intense and searching experience, including all national board members, selected national staff persons, all full-time state coordinators, and one representative from each state. In October 1963, the Findings Committee of the Congress summarized the results as follows.

We call for a clearer, more relevant expression of the existing theological foundations upon which this movement stands. We see the need for a rebirth of doctrinal emphasis, starting with the pulpit ministry and extending through all phases of the Church's life. Such a rebirth, we feel, should be undergirded in our educational work by clearly stated expressions of our faith published in readily available forms and appropriate for our people of all ages and at all stages of their Christian development.

We are discontented with where we have now arrived in the promulgation of our doctrinal position and see the need constantly to call up our teachings for reevaluation, particularly to see how they communicate living truth centered in a living Christ. In this way and through constant vigilance we would hope to avoid arriving at a dry and rigid creedalism which would undermine individuals whose faith is growing in an atmosphere of Christian fellowship and freedom under God. Serious theological discussion should be carried forward.

We recognize the need to maintain and build up a greater sense of unity among ourselves, achieving better and more harmonious working relationships. Our witness must begin with a more adequate demonstration of what we teach.

We recognize that we are not alone in our concern for unity. We have found, in working with our fellow Christians of other groups, kindred minds and spirits. We feel the need to increasingly express toward others the unity we teach, extending the loving fellowship and remembering that this is the basis of unity rather than intellectual uniformity.

While we feel the need to cooperate with other Christian groups, we are not looking toward mergers. We feel the need for more serious study on unity, perhaps by a duly appointed commission, which would find ways to enter into more serious dialogue with our Christian brethren. We must maintain the polarity of our position, expressing it more adequately and clearly while, at the same time, accepting our brethren as equals and as Christians.

To seek distinctiveness as a kind of denominational rationale is unjustifiable. At the same time, a genuine demonstration of Christian unity and of vital personal experience is an invaluable contribution in today's Christendom. If we are to make any distinctive contribution, we want to make sure it is of this kind. Perhaps any distinction should lie precisely in not setting up distinctives in the denominational sense.

We feel that our openness toward fellow Christians and to the truth, our conception of membership by salvation, the absence of creedalism, and our emphasis upon the dynamic nature of living relationships in Christ offer us some opportunity for Christian witness. It may be that our combination of teachings is significant, unity being possible only on the basis of truth and experience emphasized in this movement across the years.

As a church we need to know who we are, and why we are. It is possible to live on the memory of a few strong personalities who were able to rally a good force about them and make the mistake of taking their concepts of truth and attempting to confront today's situations with them. We may be united to one another and our rich heritage rather than united in Christ. We dare not become so preoccupied with ourselves that we feel that we must grow as a movement, forgetting that our mission may be to permeate society as others are doing, as leaven that will benefit the whole loaf.

We register much concern that in the midst of our day-to-day ministry, in the press of pushing a program here and a project there, we have not given enough thought and prayer to developing and keeping sight of great, overarching goals. We feel our need of these to steer our everyday operations, to coordinate our efforts and measure our progress, and to draw us on as we take a long view of all the work that lies before us. We look toward such goals as means of helping us gain an enlarging sense of mission. Only in the light of such clearly defined major goals can we wisely discern the specific objectives we need to set before us. The big goals should not just lie in the haze of the horizon, but should be clearly drawn and carefully communicated.

A great theology, clearly understood, and great overarching goals, clearly conceived, mean little in themselves unless they are carefully harnessed to help the Church and its people carry forward significant ministry. We call for an increasingly adequate structure to serve as a channel for implementing our mission. We see a need for a broad study of national, state, and local structure in order to strengthen the work of the Church at every level in a coordinated way. We feel that increased lay representation is called for at all levels.

We see the need for strong local fellowships of the people of God to be of fundamental importance to the witness and outreach of the movement. Our total evangelistic thrust, our general sense of mission, our missionary out-reach demand strong local congregations.

The fact that a large percentage of our churches are perennially small, weak, and apparently lacking in resources to produce growth, was seen by the Congress to be a paramount concern.

The need to strengthen leadership, both layman and pastor, was felt to be of central importance. A better understanding of the autonomy of the local church was considered of basic importance. How can this freedom be used wisely in matters of congregational discipline, interpersonal relationships, seeking counsel, and the acceptance of guidance in choosing pastoral leadership?

We recognize the disturbing fact that the pastoral image needs upgrading, both within the Church and in our culture, that frequently the "parson" is no longer the important leader in the community, that often neither the man nor his congregation are thought to be of real importance in the community. There is need to face openly the relationship of "educational attainment" and the image of the pastor. There is need to understand the forces in society which help to create anti-clergy attitudes.

We recognized the growing and valuable role of our seminary in both the enlistment and training of pastors. Closer communication between the seminary and the local church and state-level organizations was seen as desirable.

Some means of in-service training for pastors was recommended. Continued, strengthened, and improved services on the part of the Division of Church Service was encouraged. Stronger state-level organization and better means of examining candidates as well as establishing higher standards of registration and ordination are desirable.

There is a strong feeling among us that we must seek and find a deep spiritual renewal if we are to find adequate motivation for the task ahead. It is not always more knowledge, better techniques, better training, or more tools we need—most of our people know more now than they are willing to use. There is definite agreement that we must cease striving for status or respectability as a church and return to a love for people that constrains us to give ourselves in Christian service because we care about the spiritual, physical, and social needs of others. This also will lead the church to be passionately concerned about winning others to Christ.

Evangelism is seen to be at the very heart of the Church. However, it is obvious that we are not getting the message to enough people fast enough. While in the early years of our movement we grew very rapidly, we seem to be settling down to the way of least resistance.

Major concern has been expressed regarding our knowledge of the world and its needs. Sometimes the sickness of the world communicates itself to the Church more than the Church communicates its life-giving message to the world. It would seem that we are using the language and meanings of another day to communicate with a modern and fast-moving generation. We need to say the same old message in new and different terms or at least bring this generation of new Christians up to date on our language.

We confronted the pressing need to involve the total ministries of the church, the need for full recognition of the scriptural concept of these ministries, and that of heightening the interest of the whole church in the so-called "lay ministries" beyond the usual "church work." A clarification of the lay and pastoral ministries is needed. Various kinds of preparation and training are needed to prepare the church to receive and adequately demonstrate the gifts of the Spirit in the total ministries of the church.

We need a strong emphasis on redemptive fellowship in the church. Often our acceptance of other denominations and even members of our own congregations has been conditional, based on whether or not they agreed with "Church of God" thinking. Perhaps we have forgotten the great inclusiveness of "being in Christ." People are going to church where they can receive help, healing, comfort, as well as where they can hear the Truth preached. We need to be mindful of the needs of the total man.

It would seem that our ministry must be concerned with local, state, national, and even international problems of a social nature. Sometimes the ministry of the Church is not appreciated because we have seemingly closed our eyes to situations which exist, such as racial segregation. We have not been without our own problems as a movement. Perhaps we need to spend time and prayer eliminating our own problems before we talk too loudly.

167. Consultation of the Church of God (June 1970)

Editor's Note: The 1970 Consultation of the Church of God was constituted (much like the one in 1963, see Entry 166) with representation from the general agencies and from the state assemblies. It met with full awareness of the 1963 Congress, the findings of that earlier meeting having been widely distributed and discussed and the delegates having been given a review of those actions which had been taken to implement the findings.

An opening presentation of "the state of the church" suggested three focal points to keep in mind during the discussions:

1. The scriptural and theological base and imperative inhering in the mighty act of God through Jesus Christ, which gives the church its very life;
2. The social and practical reality of our time when people are hurting and lost and when Christians are called to incarnational involvement;
3. The relative and changing position of the Church of God movement within Christendom as it is expressed in fellowship and united witness.

The major work of this Consultation was to be done in six areas: (1) Social Concerns; (2) Unity; (3) Lay Ministry; (4) Evangelism; (5) Missions; and (6) Leadership. Coordinators had been appointed for each area and asked to prepare "projections" as a basis for study, analysis, and evaluation. Each area had three work groups with sharing times among the groups. Following are some of the issues addressed and points of the consensus reached.

1. Social Concerns

Issues: (1) What balance of social and individual emphasis? (2) How can we make the gospel relevant to all persons? (3) How can the church minister effectively in missions, evangelism, and unity, without seriously undertaking to bring reconciliation and equality within its own ranks?

Consensus: (1) Initiate creative programs relating to social concerns and encourage church agencies to do more; (2) Anticipate and plan rather than merely read; help black churchmen prepare for primary executive positions in the church; (3) Redefine and strengthen role in eliminating racism;

(4) Disseminate success experiences in elimination of barriers; (5) Actively support churches and pastors who are attempting to overcome racism; (6) Develop and circulate courses of study setting forth biblical imperatives in social concerns; (7) Become a catalyst, prompting churches and pastors to programs of action; (8) Executive Council should clarify the function of the Commission on Social Concerns, giving it economic support and administrative integrity; (9) Continue dialogue between white and black churchmen that goes beyond polite conversation.

2. Christian Unity

Issues: (1) Where is the Spirit leading us in intra- and interchurch unity in the 1970s? (2) What is the nature of the unity we seek? (3) What opportunities and obstacles to unity confront the movement? (4) How can the Church of God best contribute to the ecumenical movement?

Consensus: (1) Polarities recognized were: inclusive vs. exclusive fellowship; social concerns vs. evangelism; "come-outism" vs. cooperative involvement; cardinal beliefs vs. tradition; diversity vs. uniformity; delegated assembly vs. general assembly; (2) Recognition of racial divisiveness and the need to press for the removal of it; (3) Need to rethink sainthood and servanthood; (4) Find ways to utilize a larger variety of ministries; (5) Remain a nonjoiner but initiate more conversations with other groups; (6) Clarify responsibilities of the Committee on Christian Unity; (7) Officially endorse cooperative endeavors overseas; (8) Share insights on unity wherever doors are open.

3. Lay Ministry

Issues: (1) How can laymen best be supported in their own call and ministry in the everyday world? (2) What kind of training do laymen need to maximize their opportunities? (3) How can we broaden our base of planning and strategy to allow for their active participation at the planning, decision-making level?

Consensus: (1) Laymen do want to be significantly involved in the decision-making process; (2) Pastors should see their role more as opening up opportunities and giving guidance rather than trying to do everything themselves; (3) Institutes for laymen on college campuses for task-oriented study are needed; (4) Training institutes of longer duration for retired persons could prepare them for full or part-time leadership; (5) Study should be given to ordaining for lay ministries and the relation of that to baptism; (6) Lay ministry should be more than merely assisting in some "church work"; it should help identify authentic calls and support people in them.

4. Evangelism

Issues: (1) Are we an evangelistic people or have we gained mostly by those coming from other groups? (2) Are our methods of evangelism largely pulpit-centered and adequate for today and tomorrow? (3) What is evangelism, what are the essential ingredients? (4) Can we distinguish between personal evangelism and "gimmickry?" (5) Is our structure conducive and adequate for effective evangelization?

Consensus: (1) Admit that we have not been very evangelistic and need to seriously address this lack; (2) An evangelistic church is one characterized by warm fellowship, effective preaching, involvement with people and community, and a practical program of evangelistic outreach; (3) The time is overdue for evangelism as the primary thrust of the church; (4) Techniques of some interdenominational groups could well be utilized; (5) Special attention should be given to the inner city.

5. Missions

Issues: (1) With the rapidly changing scene in other countries as well as in our own, how can we better address the total task? (2) How can we achieve wider understanding and more informed cooperation in the church? (3) How can we best coordinate existing interest in the church and deploy it in a manner consistent with sound missionary policy? (4) What employment should be made of experienced (perhaps retired) people for specialized needs?

Consensus: (1) Schools are vital on the mission fields; perhaps some relocation is advisable; (2) Missions should be approached on an international basis, perhaps through some kind of international board; (3) Lay people, with orientation and training, should be used at strategic places; (4) There is need for skilled staff personnel in securing large gifts; (5) Missions conventions should be encouraged and guided by the Missions Board; (6) Active recruitment of youth for missionary work is needed; (7) Missionary work means sharing in the ghetto as well as overseas; (8) We suffer a credibility gap in missions unless we find solutions to division at home; (9) To avoid the "brain drain," we should foster advanced education of nationals in their own countries.

6. Leadership

Issues: (1) What is the authentic role of the pastor? (2) Do we need a more structured approach to pastoral "placement?" (3) What is the rightful role of women in leadership? (4) What relationship exists between lay leadership development and the preparation of pastors? (5) What will be required of the leader in the new urban society? (6) Should the General Assembly agree on criteria for leadership? (7) What relation is there between leadership of the Holy Spirit and a reasoned, even structured approach to leadership development and deployment?

287

Consensus: (1) Pastoral leadership is crucial if competent laymen are to be actively involved in God's work; (2) There is a shortage of pastoral leadership, not quantitative but qualitative; (3) Ministerial drop-out is a serious problem. We need an effective support system for pastors; (4) There should be some youth representation on the Executive Council; (5) Leadership by the Holy Spirit mixes with human understanding and rational processes; (6) The minister should be "married to the mission, not to the church"; (7) Members of credentials committees should be trained with a code developed for their work; (8) We must help the church to think in terms of ability, not color; (9) Youth should be encouraged to select freely those with whom they wish to associate, regardless of racial differences.

168. Yokefellow Statement (1974)

Editor's Note: Eighteen members of the Division of General Service and seven state coordinators gathered at Yokefellow House in Richmond, Indiana, May 9–10, 1974, to give prayerful consideration to the specific objectives to which they judged the attention and resources of the Church of God should be brought to bear in the immediate years leading up to the movement's centennial celebration in 1980-81. They called for and pledged ourselves to objectives in five areas.

1. Identity

We affirm the reformational role of the Church of God movement and, in keeping with this affirmation, call the church to repentance, cleansing, and reconciliation—both among ourselves and toward God—to the end that we may reestablish and renew our covenant relationship with God and each other, restore the biblical root system of our heritage, and thus nourish those things that draw us together as a people on mission for God in today's rootless and fragmented world.

In order to accomplish this, we covenant together that we will stress through every available channel the crucial importance of responsible study and exposition of the Holy Scriptures in all of our preaching and teaching, with particular emphasis upon the centrality of Jesus Christ in his body, the Church, and upon the fulfillment of his mission in the world.

2. Relationships

In keeping with the historical dedication of the Church of God movement to Christian unity, individual freedom, and brotherhood, we affirm the importance of the unity that exists among us. While recognizing individual creativity and initiative, we call for responsible commitment to the Church's total mission at every level of its life and work, from the local to the worldwide, as our supreme objective. In our united opinion, this objective calls for:

1. Complete obedience to Christ and his Word;
2. Recognition of the dignity and freedom of human personality;
3. Commitment to each other as members of the Body of Christ;
4. Loyalty to, and support of the church's institutions and programs which we have created together;
5. Openness to the continuing revelation of God's Spirit in our common life.

It is our belief that the New Testament sets forth the ideal that all Christians should be able to learn from one another. We maintain, moreover, the conviction that this movement represents a force of reformation leadership within Christendom with its emphasis on ecumenicity based on unity rather than on union. To this end, therefore, we encourage through every means possible the establishing and maintaining of work relationships with other like-minded groups on the national, state, and local levels.

3. Ministry

The major purposes of the Church of God movement, so far as its origin and continuing life are concerned, must be clarified sufficiently to strengthen our ministerial and lay leadership in their preaching and teaching roles, with particular emphasis in the following areas:

1. To be more creative to discover, train, deploy, and conserve leadership;
2. To initiate programs and processes that are biblically centered for understanding and addressing social ills and injustices;
3. To promote the Christian ministry as a viable, exciting vocation and insist upon quality training;
4. To challenge our finest young men and women to give themselves in ministry;
5. To develop support systems for clergy where ministers and/or members of their families can find adequate counsel during marital, financial, physical, emotional, or vocational stress.

In keeping with the purposes of the Church of God movement, we urge that doctrinal concepts be periodically reviewed for strengthening the church's convictions. We further urge that the motivating force for ministry be rediscovered in order that the Church of God may have purpose for continued being.

4. Integration

The Church by nature is one; therefore, the Church must continuously work its way through and beyond racial relationships to functional unity. It must be recognized and admitted, in doing this, that racist attitudes are incompatible with the Christian gospel of oneness, brotherhood, and love. As we work toward functional and visible unity, the following objectives should be kept clearly in mind:

1. Continue to emphasize the positive things which are being done to include persons of different racial and cultural origins and backgrounds in the decision-making processes at all levels of the Church's life and work;
2. Increase dialogue among persons of all races and cultures with a view toward helping local congregations of the Church of God become more effective and inclusive in their evangelistic and missionary outreach programs in the homeland and abroad;
3. Encourage and make possible the enrollment and training of youth from minority and ethnic groups included within the membership of the Church of God in our church-related colleges;
4. Further explore the structuring of state, regional, and national organizations of the Church of God in order to more truly express the oneness of the Church in the fulfillment of its mission in the world;
5. Recognize that attitudes relating to race must always be interpreted in light of the social environment and climate in which the Church carries forth its mission, but without any compromise with the principles of the Christian gospel.

5. Polity

We affirm and recognize that the local congregation is the primary unit of ministry and outreach for fulfilling the Church's mission in the world, the stabilizing of the home, and in alleviating the tensions that undermine society. In order to strengthen the local congregation, we urge:

1. Better leadership preparation at all levels;
2. Stronger emphasis on personal and group study of the Word of God as a complement to public proclamation;
3. Development of greater stewardship commitment by individuals and congregations.

We further plead for the development of more precise lines of responsibility, cooperation, and communication between the local, state and national organizations of the Church of God that will reflect our interdependent relationships. Some areas in which this could serve a useful purpose are:

1. Providing for a greater degree of participatory democracy in the life and government of the Church;
2 Cooperative planning, programming, goal-setting, and budgeting;
3. Congregational and ministerial certification and credentials;
4. Establishment of new congregations and agencies.

---

169. Dialogue I on Internal Unity (January 1981)

Editor's Note: The period 1980-1981 saw significant controversy in the life of the Church of God. To assist helpfully in bringing the most significant issues into focus and in bringing representatives of varying viewpoints into direct and prolonged discussion about these issues, the Board of Directors of the Executive Council convened a dialogue on internal unity. Present were thirty leaders invited because of their leadership roles in the national, state, and local ministries of the Church of God. The group decided upon its own agenda, choosing three major areas with the first, biblical inspiration and authority, receiving the most attention. The results of searching and intense discussion were mailed to all members of the General Assembly. They were as follows.

Issue 1: Biblical

How can the Church of God more adequately understand our position on the authority, inspiration, and nature of the Bible?

- Where are we agreed in our view of Scripture?
- Where are we not yet agreed?
- How much diversity can we have and still maintain unity?

Affirmations—We Are Agreed That:

1. The Bible is the inspired Word of God—the source of authority for Christians in faith, doctrine, and practice (2 Tim. 3:16, 17).
2. The Bible is fully trustworthy and without error in its revelation of the will of God concerning man in all things necessary to salvation and Christian living.
3. We must depend on the Holy Spirit's guidance in interpreting the Scriptures.

4. The individual and corporate study of the Bible is essential to effective discipleship and mission in the world today.
5. Our technical differences pertaining to Scripture in no way call into question our commitment to the authority of Scripture.
6. In our view of Scripture there are still areas where we hold divergent views. This does not jeopardize our fellowship or our Christian commitment.

Issue 2: Structural

What form of structure and/or polity can best serve the Church of God as it moves into its second century as a reformation movement in such areas as:

- The selection of leaders to serve national corporations, state organizations, and local congregations?
- The establishing of channels of communication through which more adequate information can be shared with the General Assembly by those who serve in leadership positions and who are accountable to the Assembly?
- The place of lay persons in the decision-making processes of the church—nationally, state and local?

Some Recommendations

1. That a study be made of General Assembly functions which include frequency, location of and duration of meetings; the nature and format of the agenda. (Consider dialogue need and rotation of location.)
2. That a review be made of the nature of accountability of boards and agencies, Executive Council and its subordinate units and related para-church groups, and to develop guidelines by which that accountability can be expressed to the General Assembly.
3. The study should involve widespread participation of the church at large.
4. Recommended to the Board of Directors that it encourage the Committee on Long Range Planning to initiate a continuing process which will allow all ministers of the church to share their views regarding the costs and priorities of the several agencies.
5. Use state and regional meetings as settings for communication seminars (to inform how national agencies function and means of access to them).

6. To develop a design for prayer support groups for individual agency personnel and their work.

7. A serious concern is expressed that our colleges are essentially unrelated and competitive. Some initiative should be taken to speak to this major problem.

Issue 3: Relational

What kind of unity do we seek in regard to social and moral issues as we are confronted by the mandates of Scripture regarding these? More specifically, are we seeking agreement of stance on the various contemporary social, moral and ethical issues?

(a) as a united voice of the church?
(b) as a common view of the world?
(c) as a common interpretation of Scripture?
(d) as a test of fellowship?
(e) as a measure of acceptability of leaders?

Some Recommendations

1. We recommended the development of scholarly statements on crucial social issues confronting the church. These can be printed resources, tapes or video-tapes which can be used in church study groups. These should present the various sides so that persons can "think" through what their own stance is. Positions of respected Church of God leaders should be clearly stated.

2. Develop a pattern of bringing together the best minds from the diverse points of view to dialogue in depth on selected issues. Resulting information and conclusions could be used in preparation of resources for #1.

3. Explore ways in which existing meetings may be used to dialogue on the crucial issues faced in ministry; i.e., General Assembly and ministers meetings.

4. Make a better effort to include the conservative voice in deliberations on social issues from which study resources and position papers may be produced.

170. Dialogue II on Internal Unity (December 1981)

Editor's Note: The General Assembly was kept well informed about the results of the second Dialogue, convened in December, 1981, by the Executive Council. Paul Tanner, Executive Secretary of the Council, reported to the Assembly that "issues of general interest did provide a free and open exchange of views, but there was no overriding issue as experienced in Dialogue I." The twenty-eight participants representing fourteen different states decided to discuss three subject areas. They came to the following points of consensus and recommendations.

ISSUE 1: Priesthood of Believers

Consensus:

1. The Scripture does support an orderly process in the work of the Church, but does not prescribe a specific polity.
2. We believe in the priesthood of believers, but this concept does not determine the specific numerical composition of the General Assembly.
3. We value increased involvement of Spirit-gifted lay persons in the General Assembly of the Church of God and its various structures.
4. The present proposed model for increasing lay participation in the General Assembly will not likely be accepted by the Church.

Recommendations:

1. That lay participation be selected from and by existing formal assemblies.
2. Unless the Bylaws Committee can come up with a proposal that gives greater evidence of acceptability, that they request a year's further study.

ISSUE 2: Leadership Development in Higher Education

Consensus:

1. We have a genuine appreciation for the richness and diversity among our institutions of higher education and express concerns only out of a sense of stewardship for these resources.
2. We sense a great deal of frustration among ourselves over the competition and independency of action on the part of our educational institutions and other problems relating to the need for overall coordination and supervision of our higher educational process.

Recommendation:

That the Board of Directors of the Executive Council appoint a committee to study ways similar communions structure their institutions of higher education and make recommendations for the corporate structuring of our approach to higher education.

ISSUE 3: Church of God Response to World Issues

Consensus:

The Church of God has a biblical mandate to be involved in world issues by caring and doing.

Recommendations:

1. Need to cultivate greater awareness of what is being done and should be done, by focusing on these in church publications and news media.
2. Upgrade image and work of Commission on Social Concerns by changing the name and assure that the membership is more inclusive (not only those of vested or concentrated interest) to increase its effectiveness.
3. Suggest that the 1983 International Convention Program Committee develop a theme emphasis to speak to a response to world issues, with speakers who can/will focus on the positive, evangelical Kingdom—now.
4. Suggest that the editor of *Vital Christianity* consider an issue with the theme of Church of God World Responsibility in the areas listed.

171. Consultation on Mission and Ministry (1984)

Editor's Note: An intensive study and evaluation of the structure and function of the Executive Council was commissioned during the mid-1970s. Among the issues that emerged in that study was one expressing the need for the Church of God to be involved in long-range planning in a more aggressive and coordinated way. Up until that time the only instance of coordinated effort at long-range planning at the national level was lodged with the Division of General Service.

Restructuring was decided on and included the termination of the Division of General Service and the formation of the Committee on Long Range Planning. Very early in its work this new committee established its own priorities. It quickly recognized that it could not, on its own, formulate goals for the work of the church. This recognition gave rise to the idea of a national consultation that would be broadly representative of the total church in all of its diversity. Initial approval for such a consultation was given by the Executive Council in May, 1982.

Selected Church of God leaders from across the United States and Canada (total of 135) convened in Indianapolis April 2-5, 1984, for provocative and stimulating dialogue. The event was identified as a major Consultation on Mission and Ministry. It was the most representative and ambitious attempt of its kind in Church of God history. What follows is a brief summary of the central concerns and goals projected by this Consultation for the Church of God movement to the end of the century.

AREA I
Concern: Truth—Here We Stand!

Purpose: *To affirm the biblical foundations for the mission and ministry of the church and highlight central biblical teachings.*

Goal: *To establish the Bible as the authority for the faith and life of the church.* We live in a time when traditional authority is questioned and an increasing number of persons, even in the church, are biblically illiterate. The Bible must be accepted as authoritative in the church and its contents must be taught and preached with clarity, discipline, and integrity.

Goal: *To witness to those biblical truths central to the particular mission of the Church of God movement.* The effectiveness of the ministry of the Church of God depends heavily on its own understanding of its distinctive mission as a particular fellowship and movement among God's people. The biblical truths central to this distinctive mission must be clarified, taught, and lived out.

Goal: *To understand the church as a covenant community called servanthood.* Thechurch today lives in an unstable and materialistic society. To be a faithful, influential and relevant witness in the world, the church must become a covenant community dedicated to the service of persons for the sake of Christ. This will require a biblical understanding of covenant and servanthood. It also will require sacrifice, even suffering.

296

AREA II
Concern: Into All the World

Purpose: *To broaden the church's understanding of world concerns and to motivate the church to fulfill its mission and ministry in the world.* It is possible for the church to live in the world, but remain aloof and "not a part of the world." The church is called to act within the world but not let the world squeeze it into its mold. Let the church be the church—the model of ministry, care, and concern guided by its understanding of the world in which it lives and works.

Goal: *To work toward global awareness and to recognize our responsibility to the whole world in Christian action and concern for world issues.*

Amos Moore
Nepal

Goal: *To sensitize the Church of God to the cultural distinctives of all persons in our world and to affirm their God-given dignity.*

Goal: *To become involved as the people of God who work for change at those points where the gospel speaks to the world in which we live.*

Isai and Sheny Calderon
Guatemala

AREA III
Concern: Mission—Good News!

Purpose: *To understand the mission of the church to present the gospel to every person through the power of the Holy Spirit at work in us.*

Goal: *To develop a statement of the mission of the Church of God Reformation Movement.* The Church of God has always been a people on mission, a people with a purpose. As we seek to clarify our own understanding of our unique message and mission, state it forthrightly and communicate it to others, we will be able to live it out more effectively. [See Entry 174 below for such a mission statement.]

Goal: *To equip persons to evangelize, nurture, and bring to maturity all persons who are lost from God and separated from one another.* As we become more sensitive to the many ways persons are separated from God and eachother, we will become increasingly motivated to lead them to Christ. In response to the Great Commission we will go out in the power of the Holy Spirit to make disciples. We will continue to teach and equip one another for this task.

Goal: *To challenge the Church of God to redemptive action in relation to the social issues of our time.* To serve Christ is to serve in the arena of human need. Our ministry of reconciliation must take us into the middle of the world's problems with redemptive action. We will respond to Christ's call to "preach good news to the poor. . .proclaim release to the captives and recovering of sight to the blind, to set at liberty those who are oppressed!" (Lk. 4:18).

AREA IV
Concern: A Living Church

Purpose: *To live out a ministry that fulfills the mission of the church as the people of God.*

Goal: *To prize the family as the basic unit in God's design for human relationships.* The family, vital to every person's fulfillment, is an endangered species. Fast-paced living is emptying homes, making them temporary storage places and little more. But the family is of God's design, and we are stewards of this resource. The Church must help families to live in wholeness.

Goal: *To strengthen the competence and effectiveness of ministerial leadership in the church.* The care and feeding of leaders is essential to the living church. Many, however, are crippled in effectiveness, wounded in the line of duty, unprepared, undisciplined for the challenges of a changing world. The church must offer the guidance and support to heal our healers.

Goal: *To understand the biblical foundations for accountability and inclusiveness in ministry.* Congregational freedom has not offered redemptive or useful ways to bring accountability to ministry. Conflicts often become diseases of destruction rather than building blocks for new strength. Women are being called, trained, ordained for ministry, but few are called to local pastorates.

Goal: *To inspire all believers to use their gifts in the ministry of the church.* Preparation and call of lay persons to a ministry of the common life is needed to release some of God's best, but least discovered resources for ministry. Lay muscles will mobilize the church.

Goal: *To mobilize the church to implement the national strategy for church planting as adopted by the General Assembly, June, 1984.* A surge of renewal for the movement will happen as we plant new churches. Seven hundred and seventy-three new congregations in ten years is a goal which can revitalize the movement, but only by a massive strategy of cooperation. The involvement of everyone is needed to achieve such a goal.

AREA V
Concern: Being the Body of Christ

Purpose: *To develop mutually interdependent relationships that enable the church to be effective in fulfilling its mission and ministry within the whole body of Christ.*

Goal: *To affirm the value and to strengthen the practice of interdependence within the Church of God.* Throughout our history we have experienced a growing understanding of the importance of interdependence to thesuccessful in achievement of our goals. For both practical and theological reasons we know that "we really do need each other."

Goal: *To determine and develop the best structures that best express interdependence and enable ministry and mission in the Church of God throughout the world.* There is always more than one way to get a job done. Throughout our history we have sought to be sensitive to the Holy Spirit and responsive to the needs in creating structures to do the work of the church. We will continue to create structures that reflect our need for interdependence.

Goal: *To establish specific time-related goals to be implemented through the church's interdependent structures.* We increasingly sense the need for setting specific goals for implementing our mission and ministry. For the goals to have meaning they must be the result of the widest possible involvement of the church at all levels. We sense a special call to give attention to growth and evangelism goals.

Goal: *To expand ministries through voluntary relationships with church groups outside the Church of God Reformation Movement.* Our quest for Christian unity brings us into relationships with all members of the Body of Christ. Through voluntary relationships we can often achieve our mission more effectively and expand our ministries.

Goal: *To lift up the responsibility of every congregation for ministry to the whole world, affirming our interdependence in recognition of the enormity of the task of global evangelization.* The task of global evangelization is enormous. The common mission we share calls us to live out our Christian unity and to experience interdependence as we seek to fulfill our common discipleship in the world.

172. Glossolalia and the Church's Life (June 1986)

Editor's Note: During the 1985 General Assembly a resolution was presented from the General Assembly of Ohio. It called for the establishment of a study committee "composed of qualified individuals from the academic and pastoral fields to study the work of the Holy Spirit as related to glossolalia in light of Scripture, our historical perspective, and present happenings in the Church of God movement." The resolution was referred to the Executive Council through which a study committee was named. In June, 1986, the committee submitted an extensive report. The Assembly received it with appreciation and commended "for careful study and guidance throughout the Church of God the biblical guidelines, observations, and recommendations contained in this report." In part they were as follows.

With particular reference to the gift of tongues, the following are understood to be biblical guidelines for its definition and exercise:

A. A gift of tongues is listed in the New Testament as one of the gifts which a given believer might receive as God chooses. Defining and governing the exercise of such a potential gift are important and difficult tasks in the context of the life of the contemporary church and in light of the limited biblical teaching on the subject.

B. A gift of tongues, however defined, is not given to all Spirit-filled believers (1 Cor. 12:28-30) and is not the evidence of the infilling of the Holy Spirit. Paul's discussion of evidence, as seen in 1 Corinthians 12-14, clearly states that a life of love is the essential evidence. Chapter 14 must be understood in the context of chapters 12 and 13, particularly 1 Cor. 12:1-3 and chapter 13.

C.   Which gift or how many gifts a person is given is not a factor in that person's salvation or sanctification. What is a factor is the reception of the Gift, that of the Holy Spirit (Acts 1:8 and Romans 8:9). A gift of tongues, therefore, should not be regarded as proof of spirituality on the part of the speaker. Any insistence to the contrary lies outside biblical teaching and leads easily to distortion in the meaning and intended use of spiritual gifts.

D.   A gift of tongues, according to the instances recorded in Acts, probably was the supernaturally-given ability to speak in human languages not previously learned by the speaker. If so defined, the purpose of this gift was (1) to provide a tool for the multilingual proclamation of the gospel and/or (2) to provide a sign of the universal nature of the Christian faith.

E.   A gift of tongues, according to the teaching in 1 Corinthians, is less clear in its nature. While it could have been a deterioration of the phenomenon of tongues at Pentecost or an extreme emotionalism related to local pagan practices, it may well have been a gift to some Christians of the ability to speak in the presence of God, which speaking required interpretation in public worship (1 Cor. 14:2). Whatever its nature, its manifestations in Corinth involved a range of problems which called for strict pastoral discipline. The problems centered in wrong personal attitudes, a misunderstanding of spiritual gifts, and unacceptable public practices. These problems were addressed by the Apostle Paul in part through the giving of the following guidelines.

1. Unintelligible speech in public worship is unacceptable (1 Cor. 14:9).

2. A gift of tongues should be seen as the least of the gifts because the person who so speaks without interpretation (unless in private) addresses God and does not directly edify the church through exercising the gift. A gift like prophecy, the ability to communicate clearly the word of God, is to be valued as a greater gift (1 Cor. 14:1-12, 19).

3. A gift of tongues should not violate the assumption that Christian worship services should be characterized by dignity, orderliness and self-control (1 Cor. 14:23, 32, 40).

4. A gift of tongues, if exercised in a public service, requires the presence and exercise of another gift, the gift of interpretation. Because the purpose of spiritual gifts is the upbuilding of the church, this latter gift is needed to bring

the former back into the realm of common understanding and edification. If a gift of tongues is exercised publicly, it is to be governed by the following (1 Cor. 14:26-32):

a. Only two or three persons may so speak in one service;
b. Never should more than one person speak at the same time;
c. Someone must always interpret the speaking or it is not appropriate to proceed;
d. There should be no confusion, only decency, order and edification.

The following are offered as biblical guidelines for local church life.

1. Local congregations of the Church of God are urged to give careful attention to acquainting persons with the traditional beliefs and practices of the Church of God regarding glossolalia (particularly the biblical guidelines stated above).

2. Congregations also are urged to teach the central importance of the work of the Holy Spirit in the lives of believers and in the process of genuine Christian worship.

3. Corporate authority over individualistic assertiveness in congregational life is vital. Submission to each other in the Spirit of Christ is a key to harmonious church life.

4. Persons who feel that it is important to promote private manifestations and/or public demonstrations of a gift of tongues in violation of Biblical guidelines should not expect leadership positions in Church of God congregations.

5. Any proposal for major change in a congregation's worship style or practices should be implemented with sensitivity to the whole congregation and not merely in response to the preference of a few, including the pastor. Congregations contemplating such a major change might well seek counsel first from respected Church of God leaders outside the congregation.

6. While not wishing to build walls between Christians, serious concern is expressed about the negative effects on local

congregations coming from well-financed Christian groups promoting charismatic concepts and practices opposed to the Biblical guidelines stated above.

Editor's Note: For comparison, see Entry 11 by Arlo Newell.

173. Task Force on Governance and Polity (1987-1992)

Editor's Note: The Task Force on Governance and Polity was established by the June, 1987, General Assembly and given the charge "to undertake a wide-ranging analysis of present governance and polity traditions, assumptions, structures, and relationships; to develop recommendations for enhancing the effectiveness of governance and polity—congregational, state and national—to the end that mission and ministry are strengthened." One of the presentations to the Task Force was a paper titled "Authority in the Church" by Samuel G. Hines (March 1991).

Dr. Hines had been the respected Chair of the General Assembly of the Church of God from 1983-1989 (see Entry 44) and had received honorary doctorates from Gulf-Coast Bible College (1976) and Anderson University (1985). In light of the Church of God movement's long exposure of the evils of institutions burdening the church with restrictive humanity, Hines spoke prophetically to the Task Force. In part, he said:

> Authority is necessary for the development of the church's faculties. It is God's plan for perfecting the church and driving her beyond her inclinations to her destiny.... The pathology of yesterday's institutions must not be allowed to cause the death of today's church.... Without authority, a community falls on its face and wallows in the mire of indecision and lack of direction.... The authority we give to those who serve us is still ours and that ownership is never surrendered. Holding leadership accountable and maintaining the right to withdraw the authority we give are only a couple of the ways to make sure that authority delegated does not mean autonomy lost.... Authority in the church is not intended to elevate individuals, groups, laws, systems, or traditions. Authority in the church is power to command assent and to promote what the church is by Divine decree.... The Holy Spirit is the CEO of the church and He surrounds Himself with gifted and empowered people. Administration is one of the gifts He distributes and people with

that gift should be as welcomed in exercising their gift as any other.... I am convinced that the Church of God is asking us [the Task Force] to deal directly with the issue of authority. They want us to give some guidance in facing the challenge of the tension between authority and autonomy. We have been given the initiative and the permission to be progressive.... Authority is not a threat to the church. It is God's gift to the church. We must be good stewards, using it at all levels to glorify God and to accommodate His purpose in the church and in the world.

The assignment of the Task Force stretched over five years, with substantive progress reports being made to the Assembly annually. The fourth report was given in June, 1991. It detailed "emerging priorities" and identified as a basic issue "the tension between authority and autonomy." While the final report would come in 1992, the 1991 report presented five recommendations, all of which were approved by the Assembly. These follow.

1. Expanded Lay Membership in the General Assembly.

    We recommend that all categories of present membership. . .be maintained.... We further recommend that the following persons who are properly named and present in any meeting shall be members of the Assembly, effective with the General Assembly of 1993:

    - one layperson from each congregation, AM attendance to 100;
    - two laypersons from each congregation, AM attendance to 500;
    - three laypersons from each congregation, AM attendance to 1,000;
    - four laypersons from each congregation, AM attendance over 1,001.

    We further recommend that this action receive a full evaluation and after three years of operation, with the Executive Council directed to design and conduct the evaluation, recommend action related to continuation, and bring that recommendation to the 1996 General Assembly for ratification. [In the 1996 Assembly a recommendation was made and approved that the 1991 action of expanded lay membership be made a permanent provision of the Constitution and Bylaws of the General Assembly.]

2. Establishment of a Mission and Ministry Triennial.

> We accept the general recommendation. . .regarding establishing a Mission and Ministry Triennial. . .and request the Task Force to develop further details and projections in its 1992 report. [This Triennial was further recommended in 1992 and *rejected* by the Assembly, although a similar plan for periodic Visioning Conferences was approved in 1997.]

3. Expectations of the Executive Council.

   1. Act as the central corporate body for envisioning churchwide direction, formulating goals, and initiating follow-up to established directions and goals.
   2. Be the central coordinative body for national ministries of the Church.
   3. Provide a viable and strengthened linkage between national and state ministries.
   4. Call national agencies to accountability with respect to those directions and goals which the General Assembly or Executive Council has approved or established.
   5. Oversee the performance and management of the legal, administrative and financial responsibilities of the Council in its relationships with the national agencies, national and international conventions, and other segments of the work of the Church of God.

4. Executive Council: Membership, Name, Meetings.

> *Editor's Note*: Tentative thinking on changes in the Council's membership, name, and meeting time were presented. The Assembly concurred in general and asked for definitive recommendations by 1992.

5. Renewal Among National Corporations. We recommend that the following take place in 1991–92:

> • That the Task Force continue to nurture constructive dialogue among representatives (staff and boards) of these national corporations; and
>
> • That the Executive Secretary of the Executive Council, within the spirit of the earlier recommendations concerning that office, initiate fresh cooperative consultations among the national corporations, built around the service clusters listed above; that new programming be cleared through these consultations.

Editor's Note: The final report in 1992 contained nine additional recommendations, all approved except the proposed *Triennial*. One was altering the name of the Executive Council to "Leadership Council." Another was authorizing a study of possible restructuring of the national work of the church. Later in the decade such major restructuring was accomplished, including approval of a "triennial" concept (visioning conferences). See Entries 71 and 203.

Editor's Note: This Task Force published in 1991 a significant resource titled "Organizing for Ministry in the Local Congregation." Included is the following, highlighting a perspective and concern central to the whole work of the Task Force:

> We in the Church of God Reformation Movement believe in governance by the Holy Spirit…. But through the years we have learned—as did the newly commissioned church in the Book of Acts—that until definite goals are established, tasks defined, deadlines set, and decisions made about who will be responsible for doing specific tasks, little is accomplished…. Historically, the Church of God Reformation Movement has depended more on relationship (the influence of persons) than structure (authority positions) to fulfill its mission. Time, however, confirms the fact that when care is not given to how parts relate to each other (structure), the execution of responsibility of an office is likely to be crippled by unclear expectations, competing interests, poor communication, and lack of cooperation. Such conditions usually result in the overall mission objectives of an organization becoming under supported and under funded.

174. Mission of the Church of God (June 1988)

The mission of the Church of God is to be a caring community of God's covenant people under the Lordship of Jesus Christ and the leadership of the Holy Spirit:

- To proclaim the love of God, through Jesus Christ, to all persons;
- To enable persons throughout all the world to experience redemptive love in its fullest meaning through the sanctifying power of the Gospel and know Jesus Christ as Savior, Master, and Lord;
- To call persons to holiness and discipleship;

• To equip persons to be servants of Christ in the world;
• To live as citizens of the Kingdom of God here and now, work for justice, mercy and peace, and abide in the Christian hope;
• To build up the whole body of Christ in unity.

Editor's Note: This statement was developed by the Committee on Long Range Planning, endorsed by the Executive Council and General Assembly, and "commended to the Church as a resource and working document in the pursuit of its multi-faceted ministries."

175. Cross-Cultural Consultation (November 1993)

Editor's Note: Under the sponsorship of the Leadership Council of the Church of God, a Cross-Cultural Consultation was conducted in Anderson, Indiana, on November 9-11, 1993, at the North Anderson Church of God. Its primary purpose was to afford a broadly-based group from a variety of cultural and ethnic backgrounds as a forum to discuss hurts and healing, to consider commitment to each other, and to the common mission, to celebrate our unique distinctives, and to review ways to strengthen one another in ministry. The Consultation included the goals of communication, intentional commitment, building appreciation, rejoicing in victories won, planning together, and considering models of inter-cultural ministry underway.

The more than 100 persons in attendance included Black, Hispanic, Indian American, Middle Eastern, Asian, and White representatives. Also represented were all national agencies, the Board of Directors of the Leadership Council, Commissions on Christian Unity and Social Concerns, the national Long Range Planning Committee, the Divisions of World Service and Church Service, Area Administrators from states and areas, Women of the Church of God, the National Association, the Hispanic Concilio, the Native American Mission, and presenters of cross-cultural ministry models.

The Consultation gave primary attention to patterns of credentialing of ministers, expressions of racism and empowerment, concerns for interrelated worship and structure, desire to fully understand schisms in the Body, efforts to bring healing to hurts, and other such matters of faith in action. Early attention was given to knowing about and appreciating the stories of life and ministry each brought to the Consultation.

Concluding attention was given to possible action steps by which the total church might be strengthened to reach across cultural and ethnic lines to demonstrate for society the oneness of Christians on mission and to model how diversity and distinctiveness can be valued and utilized in a united witness. It was hoped that such consultations would be repeated at state and regional levels to bring a continuing sensitivity to this need.

176. Leaders' Visioning Retreat (January 1995)

Editor's Note: In light of the Assembly's decision in 1992 not to approve a Mission and Ministry Triennium, this ad hoc retreat of about 120 church leaders sought to fulfill such a purpose, at least on a one-time basis. It concerned at McCormick Creek State Park in Spencer, Indiana, January 16-18, 1995. The purposes were:

1. To fashion a statement of the unique purpose and mission of the Church of God as envisioned by participants in attendance;
2. To review Vision 2 Grow, past and present, and to project future direction;
3. To seek spiritual renewal and encouragement through worship, study, and fellowship.

From the process emerged a "Vision/Action Statement," which read:

> The Church of God Exists To:
> • Worship the Lord;
> • Reach the Lost;
> • Disciple Believers;
> • Equip for Ministry;
> • Celebrate the Unity of the Body of Christ;
> • Live out the Love of Christ.

Three obstacles to fulfilling this vision were identified as: (1) Structure at the national level; (2) Leadership empowerment; (3) Lack of finance. Plans were designed to begin addressing these.

177. Visioning Conference (1998)

by Barry L. Callen

A key component of the restructuring of the national ministries of the Church of God in the 1990s (see Entry 71) was the projection of periodic Visioning Conferences. The first was convened in Colorado Springs, Colorado, September 29-October 1, 1998. About 250 persons participated, the majority of whom were chosen by regional, state, and provincial assemblies across North America as visionaries of the church. The task was to discover God's will for the Church of God in the years immediately ahead. Chair of the Visioning Conference Program Committee was Joe Cookston.

This key occasion provided opportunity for the new General Director of Church of God Ministries, Robert W. Pearson, to state his vision for the cooperative work of the Church of God movement as it approached the beginning of the twenty-first century. A guest presenter was Dr. Leonard Sweet, a historian and futurist who helped the Conference body understand better the "postmodern" challenges facing the church in the early twenty-first century. The issue of "reconciliation" emerged as one central focus. A large number of vision statements finally were generated, with the following emerging as the most prominent categories of concern:

1. **Leadership Development**. Need to broader the existing leadership base. Included were concerns for distance learning, clergy care, mentoring, and assistance for students in Church of God higher education.

2. **Outreach**. Need for addressing the issues of technology, community, global partnerships, education, and communication in relation to missions, evangelism, and church planting.

3. **Unity and Reconciliation**. Need to narrow the gap between the church's unity teaching and its unity practicing, including racial division and ecumenical outreach.

In regard to all three of these categories, inspired and prepared leadership was seen as key.

The intent of this first and of future Visioning Conferences is that such focusing of concerns and vision would provide guidance in prioritizing programming and the distribution of the church's energy and resources, especially in the arena of the newly constituted Church of God Ministries, Inc.

Editor's Note: Also see Entry 203. The second triennial visioning conference is scheduled for September 5–7, 2001, and again will convene in Colorado Springs, Colorado.

Part Four:
HONORING THE LIGHT
ECUMENICAL AND CROSS-CULTURAL
VISION, INITIATIVES,
PARTNERSHIPS

Editor's Note: The materials that appear in Part One of this present book speak of the vision of Christian unity seen in the earliest generations of the Church of God movement and conveyed both by direct teaching and personal testimony. Materials that appear in this Part Four focus more on actions taken than on positions held. The Church of God has believed that it has been given "light" on the unity issue. Following are various ways that this movement has sought to clearly articulate and actively honor this light.

One way of honoring the light, of course, has been the Church of God movement's attempts at the education of its own successive generations. See, for example, the 1954 Anderson School of Theology thesis by Donald A. Courtney, "A Study of the Development of the Sunday School in the Church of God," the 1954 Butler University School of Religion thesis by Kenneth F. Hall, "A History of Curricular Materials in the Church of God," and the 1962 Anderson School of Theology thesis by Sherrill D. Hayes, "Concerns for Christian Education in the Church of God as Expressed by the program of the National Board of Christian Education."

178. A New Approach To Christian Unity

Excerpted from *A New Approach to Christian Unity* by Charles E. Brown (Anderson, Ind.: Warner Press, 1931), 149ff. This is a classic statement of the unity vision typical of the Church of God movement.

Step One

The first formal step necessary to get back to the freedom and unity of the apostolic church is to drop all official creeds insofar as they are official and authoritative definitions of denominational belief. The argument is made that it is foolish and absurd to expect to get away from creeds. Every group of people has its unwritten creed; and even every thinking individual has a personal creed. How vain then to think of escaping creeds by laying aside the great historic creeds of the church.

This argument overlooks a serious point. It is admitted that each thoughtful person has a creed. I admit that I have my own creed, in its way, and on some points as definite as the historic creeds of the churches. But my personal creed is not a division maker. No other Christian in the world is compelled to sign it in order to have fellowship with me. It is inclusive, not exclusive.

Again, my creed is capable of change. I can sit down with a devout Christian and after a few words of prayer we can discuss the Christian faith; and I may arise from that conference with my creed slightly amended. It is doubtless then a better creed; but I did not have to violate a solemn oath to change it a bit; neither did I become a heretic. But many persons are tied up so tightly to official creeds that if they change their own personal creed they have violated a solemn oath. This puts them in a difficult position; for if a man has taken an oath not to believe the truth when he hears it, he will take good care not to hear it; but if he should hear it, sometimes he is compelled to believe it in spite of his oath. Thus it may be seen that there is a world of difference between an official creed, the standard of faith of a denominational corporation, and the private, personal creed of the individual Christian.

The apostolic church unquestionably had an unwritten creed. It was the living and growing faith of the church. But this creed never caused division until it narrowed and hardened in the course of centuries into the official, written creed of a human corporation. Therefore, the first step to Christian unity is to disengage oneself from the historic creeds completely, reverencing them as much as he wishes, believing them as much as he can, but receiving them as mere relics of Christian theological history, and not as standing walls of isolation.

Personally I am an old-fashioned Christian; and I very much suspect that I actually believe the historic creeds much more strongly than the majority of the ministers of the respective denominations; but I would consider it sinful to arm myself with one against my brethren. The will of Christ, the fellowship of all Christians, and the unity of the church are far more precious to me than any human creed ever written.

Step Two

The second formal step to restore the unity of ancient Christianity is the total abolition of all formal organic denominational divisions among Christian people; not to merge the denominations, but to abolish them is our duty.

This will doubtless sound like anarchy to those dear old souls who have never thought through the inescapable evils of denominationalism. It will shock those who love the historic organizations of men better than the blessed unity of the body of Christ. It will seem revolutionary to the "stand-patters" who spend their time looking back to the good old days of the past. But to all such we would say there is a true place for conservatism in the kingdom of God. Let us look back to the good old days when the church had visible organic unity. Let us remember that the denominations are only a comparatively recent development in the two-thousand year history of the church. All signs point to their eventual abolition and the gathering of God's people once again into the blessed peace and unity of the ancient church.

I shall be asked how the practical business of the church could ever be carried on in such a system. To begin with, it is perfectly all right to organize the agencies of the church according to the very best examples of systematic and orderly management of business. We have divine authority for this.

When the Greek-speaking Jews complained because their widows were neglected in the daily ministration, the apostles committed the matter to the church and the church chose several believers to handle the problem (Acts 6). Notice that the church, and not the apostles, chose them. Also, the Gentile churches appointed a committee to bear their gifts to the poor saints at Jerusalem (1 Cor. 16:3; 2 Cor. 8:19, 23). This is ample authority for organizing and managing efficiently such bodies as missionary societies, church schools, publishing plants, and the like, for which a denominational organization is usually considered essential. But one can search in vain for any evidence that the apostolic church was organized as a human corporation in the sense that denominations are organized today.

Step Three

The apostolic church was organized by the inward urge of the Spirit of God, which led men to undertake the work of preaching and the like, and led the believers to recognize and encourage their call. Where believers could not sense the existence of the call by the instinct of the indwelling Spirit, there was not much danger involved in allowing such a person to exercise himself in some other way till his calling became manifest to the sanctified judgment of the assembly of believers.

The church can only regain her lost visible unity by rallying around our Lord Jesus Christ. In the past there have been cries to rally around this doctrine or that creed, or to rally to this or that battle-cry. Now the call is to come alone to Jesus Christ. "The scepter shall not depart from Judah, nor a law-giver from between his feet, until Shiloh come; and unto him shall the gathering of the people be" (Gen. 49:10).

Doctrine is very important; but more important it is to get back to the supreme Person, who is the source of all true doctrine. He has said, "I am the way, the truth, and the life." When all Christendom gets back to him it will be one. There will then be plenty of time to compare and study doctrines, when the clamor of debate has given place to the silence of the humble and earnest pupils in the school of Christ.

179. Establishment of a Commission on Christian Unity

Editor's Note: See entry 14. While Christian unity always has been a central concern of the Church of God movement, by 1965 most leaders realized that there was need for a representative group from the movement that was empowered to make ecumenical contacts, hold conversations, and help develop lines of ministry cooperation with Christians not associated with the movement. This became the Commission on Christian Unity which functioned for thirty-four years until it and other commissions were disbanded in 1998 as part of the reorganization of the national ministries.

180. Schismatic and Accommodationist

Excerpted from Val Clear, *Where the Saints Have Trod* (Chesterfield, IN.: Midwest Publications, 1977, based on his 1953 doctoral dissertation). Even a movement on behalf of Christian unity occasionally suffers from its own internal disunity and the eventual dissipation of its reformation impulse. The prophetic voice can itself grow silent and religious movements can (usually do) go through common sociological stages of development.

The first sizeable division in the history of the Church of God movement came in 1899. Data for analysis are weak and sparse. It was defined as a doctrinal dispute over the nature of sanctification, whether it could occur simultaneously with regeneration. Because the rejected view was earlier taught by Count Zinzendorf and the Moravians, the heretical doctrine was termed Zinzendorfism, and was officially repudiated in 1899 by the annual assembly. The senior historiographer of the movement (Charles E. Brown), who was a minister at that time, estimates that half of the ministers left, but by 1906 most of them had returned. No permanent group developed from the break.

Shortly thereafter another period of unrest developed, aimed primarily at liberalizing practices in dress and diet. Christians were clearly told to "lay aside all filthiness and superfluity of naughtiness" (James 1:21)...but many leaders were weakening by wearing neckties, lace collars, dresses with unnecessary gatherings, showy combs, and gaudy print. The editor of the *Gospel Trumpet* tended to side with the conservatives, and most of what was published was critical of the liberals. Even so, one article did appear in which the writer observes: "In some localities a preacher is not of much use unless he says much about the 'old paths'.... If the old paths are construed to mean merely what we preached ten or fifteen years ago regardless of the gospel, then they are nearly 2,000 years too young to be binding on the consciences of men.... Above all things, holy brethren, let us not judge one another nor find fault with one another...."The issue finally centered around neckties and the editor reported that "a few ministers...have but little if anything more than 'necktie' religion.... On the other hand, some have 'anti-necktie' religion." The editor apparently sided with the "anti-necktie" faction, but their opponents subsequently prevailed. As a result of the 1913 camp meeting in Anderson, the anti-necktie group began to publish a periodical, *The Herald of Truth*, which is still being published in Guthrie, Oklahoma, under the title *Faith and Victory*. This group persists, but in an extremely stunted form. It is likely that not one percent of today's members of the Church of God movement are aware that the schism ever occurred or that this schismatic group exists.

About a decade later, rumblings of unrest were heard again. The spokesmen were a missionary, G. P. Tasker, and a pastor, Fred Bruffett. Both of these men had been "highly esteemed in the past. . .still loved by practically all who know them." Tasker had developed doctrinal views at variance with the consensus of the church at home, and had mailed booklets in large numbers from India to laymen and ministers in the States. Bruffett's attack was on a broad front, but particularly focused on centralization of authority in the central boards and the growth of power in the ministerial assembly. A small circle of supporters gathered about Bruffett and Tasker, but no permanent conflict group persisted.

There have been other occasional local eruptions of protest limited to a few leaders, most of which never became a separate protest group. One, however, started in Indiana in 1943, and snowballed until it became a major threat to the central organization, which spent virtually all its efforts for several years in defending itself against the onslaughts of the "Watchman-on-the-Wall" controversy.

Literally tons of material were circulated and accusations were myriad, but most protests centered around two general complaints: (1) Anderson leaders were relaxing personal, moral, ethical, and religious standards; and (2) the organization of the Church of God movement in Anderson had reconstructed the evils of organized Protestantism from which it originally withdrew. It was accused of being an "ecclesiastical octopus" with a voracious appetite for power.

The General Ministerial Assembly appointed a committee to investigate the charges. When it presented its inconclusive report, both sides claimed vindication. The agitation continued. At one time there were reportedly 1,100 names on the schismatic mailing list and several hundred congregations. The new group sent its own foreign missionaries, set up its own school, and organized administrative boards.

The General Assembly finally did take official action and withdrew recognition of the protesting leaders as ministers of the Church of God movement. These disfellowshipped leaders promptly interpreted this as proof that their claims were accurate, that the parent body was apostate, and that the new group was really the remnant of the original movement, now preserved in freedom and truth. The new group continued to call itself "Church of God." One interesting comment by its leader is very pertinent to this discussion. He said: "It was a mistake ever to declare a *last reformation*. While the truth that was brought out in 1880 must never be lost, yet the people who embraced the truth, most of them have today forgotten it. . .have repudiated it. It remains therefore for God to sound out clearly and distinctly a clarion call...." Later in his life this leader relaxed his criticism and was reinstated in the parent body.

At the present time [1977] there are only undercurrents of dissension in the Church of God movement. A few ministers have joined counterparts in traditionally non-charismatic denominations such as the Presbyterian and Episcopal Churches in experimentation with *glossalalia*. For the most part, these have found it difficult or impossible to continue in the Church of God ministry [see entry 123 on glossalalia]. A larger minority has clustered around the conservative group publishing the *Reformation Witness*. Some distance appears to be developing between Gulf-Coast Bible College and the liberal arts colleges. But all of these tensions appear to be only eddies in the onflowing stream. The Church of God movement has reached the quietude of middle age and is busily engaged in building new churches, in educating young people to occupy pews and pulpits, and in trying to find a *raison d'etre* for itself in a world that has changed rapidly while the movement has been growing to maturity.

Editor's Note: In July, 1989, Dr. Clear circulated among a circle of friends his late-life reflections on the Church of God. In part, he said the following:

What has happened, it seems to me, is that the Church of God has allowed the drive for respectability. . .to inundate its traditional and historical drive. In the late 1980s, completely gone is the impulse to challenge tradition in the Warner sense, and totally dominating is the impulse to look "good" in the view of the mainstream Christian denominations. This is respectability come full flower. The ancient Romans conquered the Greeks politically but the Greeks conquered the Romans culturally from within. In a strange reverse relationship, the mainline denominations have conquered the Church of God Reformation Movement from without....

I have no reluctance to concede that the message of D. S. Warner was timely and functional at the time he appeared on the scene. It is true that the organized Christian church needed a revitalization and he came along with the right gifts at the right tine in history. There were, however, a number of other individuals who had a somewhat similar message that was also successfully pronounced at about the same time. Most of those moved rapidly toward institutionalization, whereas Warner and his successors moved reluctantly, although inevitably, toward institutionalization, followed by the drive for respectability.... So it appears to me that the future holds an indefinite period of continuing attempts at sophistication, at enhancing ecumenical respectability.

> *Editor's Note*: See also the 1957 masters thesis by Cecil Watson titled "Schismatic Tendencies in the Church of God Reformation Movement" (Anderson School of Theology). Note this expression of concern by W. Dale Oldham in the special centennial issue of *Vital Christianity* (June 22, 1980, 28): "Our own reform movement is at a dangerous crossroads today. We have moved in from the back streets to occupy million-dollar edifices. We have changed from the simple to the complex, from ignorance to learning. Now comes the question: Will we hold to the basic spirit and the fundamental truths for which Christ, his disciples, and some of our own fathers gave their lives? Or will we drift down the slow-moving stream of history into oblivion? Our preachers, teachers, church musicians and educational institutions hold in their collective hands and hearts the answer to this frightening question."

181. Options for the Movement's Future

Excerpts from John W. V. Smith's *The Quest for Holiness and Unity* (Anderson, Ind.: Warner Press, 1980), 439-443.

One item with major unresolved issues for the future of the Church of God movement comes under the general heading of relationships. In light of the movement's central emphasis on Christian unity, these issues become particularly important. It must be remembered that despite, its strong irenic focus, the Church of God was born and developed in a very polemic atmosphere. Enemies were readily and specifically identified—even invited. Attacks by and on these adversaries were vigorous and frequent. If, as many sociologists affirm, a certain degree of conflict is essential to group formation and growth, then the early Church of God movement had the basic ingredients for a solid self-identity and rapid expansion. Unity as a doctrine or an ideal for the church was itself a source of conflict because it was opposed by loyal "sectarians" who were offended by the call to "come-out" of their denominations and stand together in an open fellowship of the Spirit. In this context the message of Christian unity was a call to action and combat.

Then the religious climate began to change after 1910 when the glow of ecumenism sparked by the Edinburgh Missionary Conference began to grow brighter and burst into a light by 1948 with the formation of the World Council of Churches—a development in which the Church of God had been totally uninvolved. For this movement it might have been thought of as having won a war without having been in a single battle, but that was not the case. The launching of a worldwide ecumenical movement was not regarded as a victory, and there was not rejoicing over the fact that a great segment of Christendom had come to the point of openly questing for the same goal the Church of God had upheld for two-thirds of a century. Instead, the changing external climate sparked the beginning of a time of internal assessment within the movement itself.

The Church of God movement had lost its enemies and with their passing came a sense of wonderment resulting from the erosion of a sharp definition of identity and purpose. This condition set off an avalanche of self-analysis studies by young Church of God scholars. The popular response to what was happening outside the Church of God was for it to become critical of the ecumenical movement regarding its methodology, for its truncated view of union rather than unity, and, along with other conservative evangelicals, for its involvement in social and political issues. In the ultimate sense, however, there could be no denying that the Church of God and the cooperating "sinful sectarians" were aiming at the same target.

To complicate the situation, the non-cooperative stance of the Church of God led it to a position of relative aloneness in the Christian world. At the same time that the movement was losing its enemies, it was not cultivating many close friends.... There were no real allies to join forces with in doing battle with the major evils of the world. So at its first century's end [1980] the movement found itself with a rather fuzzy identity as related to the rest of Christianity, without specifically identified enemies, and without any formally declared friends. In this uncomfortable context it is difficult to find exciting ways to give emphasis to the doctrine of Christian unity.

317

In facing this situation the Church of God movement has several options. At least four possible courses regarding its unity stance seem to be open to the movement as it looks toward the future.

Option One

The first option is simply to continue as in the past—preach unity vigorously, get emotional about the biblical vision of the one holy church, write articles and books about it, tell others that "we believe in it," and then wait for it to happen, taking little or no responsibility to implement it or further its achievement. Stated this way, such a position appears idealistic, even dreamy and unrealistic. This, many would quickly say, is the best way to insure that Christian unity will never be realized. The voice of practicality would say that such a stance should be altered and that the movement should quickly find ways to become involved in the multitude of opportunities to further the cause of unity.

On the other hand, there still is the possibility that there may be some validity to what Church of God leaders have been saying for many years about being "leaven in the lump," about being dedicated to a "unity of the Spirit" approach, and about the inadequacies inherent in the federation or council-of- churches path to unity. It could be that the non-joining stance might be, in the long run, a greater witness to real unity than to be linked on a marginal basis with many other groups. Careful scrutiny and evaluation might determine that the historic stance is an option that is both tenable and defensible or that only slight modifications need to be made.

Option Two

The second option would be to seek out compatible allies and work with them in all ways that would enhance the spread of the gospel and increase the impact of the church's mission in the world. This is already being done in selected areas such as curriculum, foreign missions, and stewardship education. The possibilities for enlarging these cooperative arrangements are almost infinite. Such a posture allows a high degree of selectivity regarding both what and with whom such relationships are established. Probably it would cut costs and increase overall effectiveness in the cooperative areas. If this option were selected, the movement's aloneness would be mitigated. It would be possible to do this without violating the non-joining principle. It is a viable option, but obviously not a major step on the road to Christian unity. Such arrangements are nice, but they really do little to solve the deep problem of Christian disunity. [See entries 142-147 for a brief overview of the recent Church of God dialogues with the Churches of God: General Conference and the Christian Churches/Churches of Christ.]

318

Option Three

Another option would be to reassess the historic non-joining stance and to affiliate with selected interdenominational organizations with which the movement could feel comfortable. The long and often advanced argument, that the Church of God cannot join any organization because its polity does not provide for any corporate body which has authority over the various congregations, would need to be dealt with in such a manner that it would be clear to all just what commitments were being made. The General Assembly itself could join any of these ecumenical organizations, and it is true that this would not obligate any congregation to any greater extent than it desired— a condition which is true for any action of the Assembly. This would pose no problem for any of the ecumenical organizations, for they would simply list the General Assembly of the Church of God as a member rather than the Church of God. Properly understood, it should pose no problem for the movement either.

Once this hurdle was passed, the next big question would be which interdenominational group(s) to join. Unfortunately, there are competitive and rival councils and associations. Theologically, the Church of God movement would find greater affinity with groups such as the National Association of Evangelicals and the Christian Holiness Association, and there has been considerable involvement of Church of God persons in the meetings and continuing programs of groups like these. On the other hand, there has been an even longer involvement in program departments, divisions, commissions, and committees of the National Council of Churches. Recent restructuring within this body has eroded the opportunities for non-members to be included, so that participation there has been considerably lessened in recent years. Even so, relationships have been good and the spirit of openness and freedom of expression have created good feelings on the part of participants, even though there might be strong disagreement with some National Council pronouncements and programs....

Option Four

There is one other possible option. Being a Christian unity movement, the Church of God could enter the ecumenical arena "full blast"—joining *all* interdenominational organizations whose "basis" would not require a compromise of cardinal biblical teachings. Standing where it does in the theological spectrum, and with relatively wide acquaintance already in the various camps, the Church of God may be in the unique position of serving as a bridge across the wide chasms created by these polarized clusters in national and world Christianity. The full implications of such a move are difficult even to imagine, but it is an option and all the avenues of reformation have not yet been traveled. It would take a great deal of finesse—and courage— to make this choice and act upon it.

182. Where Do We Go From Here?

Excerpts of "A Statement of Concern and Guidance to the Church of God (Anderson, IN) from this movement's Commission on Christian Unity," published by the Commission, June, 1983.

This statement grows out of a necessary assessment of where we are in fulfilling our voiced concern to foster and assist Christian unity. It is issued after considerable study and in the spirit of responsible love.

For the greater part of our history as a reform movement, our people took pride in the comfort and security of being "all just alike." We dressed alike, talked alike, lived alike, learned alike, prayed alike, and worshipped alike. Patience was limited toward any who dared to differ, because to tolerate differences was like drifting from the moorings or "letting down the standard." But as more and more believers were attracted to our fellowship, and more and more instances of difference were evidenced, the church had to begin dealing with backgrounds and theological positions that were not all alike. The church became painfully aware of groupings to the left and right on what had been the acknowledged center in worship style, prayer manner, musical expressiveness, dress code, social class, and educational concerns. Again and again our seriousness about Christian unity was being tested.

It is time to deal seriously with our concern to relate to other believers and exemplify unity. We must learn how to implement our concern in the midst of different doctrinal emphases, patterns of race and ethnic expectation, different educational levels and intellectual concerns, different income groups, age differences, and orders of worship. The need before us is to work toward an intentional togetherness, to exercise a "willed movement toward each other." We must seek to understand each other in order to relate with greater creativity.

We must work deliberately to remove any barriers which separate us from other confessed Christians, and we must do so both as individuals and congregations. God intended that his people be one in fellowship and we must do this by bypassing all structures of our organizationally diverse group traditions. The boundaries of God's revealed truth about Christian unity have not been reached. All who have "light" are under mandate to share it with others—and to receive "light" from them as well, offering and receiving more in the spirit of love.

The willingness to recognize every true believer as belonging to God's church is a must. So is the need for us all to remain open to the Scriptures, studying what is taught there with eyes that look beyond our own tradition and group background. True believers have a common participation in the grace of God and are under the guidance of the one Spirit. All are blessed by the overarching will and love of a common Lord. To recognize this will help us overcome denominational differences and flow together with a concern for the will of the Lord. Separated believers lack the unity needed to take the good news of salvation to all nations. As individual Christians and local congregations, we must search for productive ways to experience oneness with other confessed Christians; only thus can we visibly show what it means to *be* the church and serve to the glory of God and the good of the world.

The church has benefited from the enthusiastic preaching and inspirational singing and courageous approach to mission long associated with the Black congregations. The church has benefited from the vision and tested operational skills of its White majority. The church has benefited from the work stamina of the Women of the Church of God, the outreach of the Men of the Church of God, and the experimental ministries of the para-mission groups. The church has profited from the intercultural sensitivity and theological insights of the Church of God in other countries, the questing spirit of its many minorities, and the heritage concern often associated with fellowship groups. It has been enriched by the excitement of the newly-converted and the wisdom of experienced believers. We can have a fresh life and a contagious witness at such a time as this, if we are willing to live and learn together, searching the Scriptures anew to be guided by what the Lord is saying to us all.

Our movement traditionally has considered itself as being a non-structured reform movement, and the very words "sect" and "denomination" have been so abhorrent that there is an evident reluctance to consider any formalized relationship with any other church group. For many, the thought of relating ourselves with other groups in any formal way seems foreign to our historic self-image and what we believe our group represents as a reform movement.

The question is: How can our group that seeks to epitomize the whole church dare to identify with one or more of the "fragments" of the church without denying the vision we hold of the true church? This has been and is a very real obstacle to any consideration of our formal togetherness with other church groups. To seek to work cooperatively with any group which we have previously regarded as a "sect" has been viewed as a compromise of our own idealized self-image, a reduction of the Church of God to being only one among other "man-made organizations," and thus to sell short the concept of the church presented by the New Testament writers. So there has been a strong theological and psychological resistance against even considering the possibilities open to us to pursue or accept more formal relations with other Christians in life and work for Christ.

Practically and functionally, then, all of our presently authorized agencies can participate in cooperative work with other church groups. The fact is that all of our agencies have long done so. In curriculum preparation, in facilitating missionary assignments both at home and abroad, in higher education endeavors, in missionary education, in stewardship education, to name only a few areas, our agencies have entered into working agreements and participated in cooperative programs on a rather wide basis and at very significant levels across many years.

Without question, these contacts have been our most immediate ways to relate with other Christian groups so far, and these contacts have done more to make us and our work and witness known nationally and internationally than any other single activity in which we have engaged.

The Commission calls the Church of God movement to recognize that at many points we are indebted to others beyond our fellowship. We have benefited from our sharing with them. The time has come to state this plainly, and to rejoice over opportunities to experience unity in working with other believers in some of the causes listed above.

It is time for us to think soberly and respond creatively as we face God's call for his people to be one. As contacts continue to be sustained and initiated with other church groups, and as our basic togetherness of faith and love is clearly seen and experienced, *we must be ready to do what agape love demands and what unity inspires.*

God has chosen to use us as a particular people within both the wider church and world at this time. God is still guiding, but we must follow. The challenge is still "holiness and unity," not just the one or the other, but both. We are called to model them so that the church which is seen by the world will be an effective representative of Christ. Such is the challenge and opportunity confronting the Church of God movement in its second century of ministry.

183. Acceptable Inter-Church Cooperation.

Editor's Note: For the content of this action of the General Assembly regarding relationships to other church bodies (June, 1985), see entry 25. An early action in this regard was in 1944 in relation to the Federal Council of Churches (see Entry 48).

184. The Wisdom of Fraternal Guests

Samuel G. Hines, with Clyde Van Valin, Bishop of the Free Methodist Church

Editor's Note: Between 1987 and 1994 the officers of the General Assembly took initiative to bring some ecumenical perspective to its annual meetings. They invited a series of "fraternal guests" to observe, evaluate, and then address the Assembly, with their addresses then published in the *Yearbook of the Church of God*. These guests were Clyde VanValin, Bishop of the Free Methodist Church (1987), Myron Augsburger, Mennonite college president and theologian (1988), Billy Melvin, Executive Director of the National Association of Evangelicals (1990), David McCord, pastor and president of the North American Christian Convention (1991), B. Edgar Johnson, retired General Secretary, Church of the Nazarene (1993), and Dennis Kinlaw, Old Testament scholar and past president of Asbury College (1994). The following is a condensed presentation by Barry Callen of the perspectives of these Christian leaders on the General Assembly of the Church of God, and of the movement itself.

Humorously, David McCord reported that, "as one of our great American philosophers, Yogi Berra, has said, 'You can observe a lot just by looking.' " The observation most commonly made by these fraternal guests might be described as the "enthusiastic ethos" of the Assembly. McCord, for example, reported: "I like the enthusiasm of your singing and worship. I appreciate very much the fervency of your prayers and the joyous fraternal spirit that I have discovered here." Clyde VanValin spoke of a "winsome style" by which "you celebrate easily and joyfully" with a distinctive "unity within diversity." He said that "you are an anointed people of God" who appear to feature "a trust in the integrity of each other without the need of an authoritarian hierarchy."

Myron Augsburger reported observing "the spirit of praise and joy" functioning with a "spirit of freedom and openness" and a special "sense of community." B. Edgar Johnson noted the role of music in strengthening this community. He referred to the song "O Church of God" as the movement's "national anthem." When he first heard it sung by the Assembly, "I couldn't help but feel enthused.... I've since had the opportunity to read the words and I enjoyed and appreciated them very, very much." Dennis Kinlaw observed that "wherever God is among his people, music develops.... There is within you a sense of loyalty to your tradition.... Pay any price to keep it, not to sanctify the past, but don't you lose those roots."

Kinlaw, however, issued an important caution along with his observation about roots. He called on the Assembly to develop further its sense of church history before Daniel Warner in the late nineteenth century. In the body of Christ "we've got four thousand years of history and if you are a part of that kingdom, all of that history at its essence belongs to you.... Any denomination that is less than a hundred years old is a sect by definition."

Affirmations of distinctive emphases of the Church of God movement were common in the statements of these ecumenical guests. VanValin, for example, spoke of the movement's focus on Christian unity as "a message that we all need to hear expounded and demonstrated." Augsburger characterized this unity emphasis as something "the Christian world needs to understand because it is far more biblical and far more dynamic than an organizational ecumenicity. It is an ecumenical spirit." With this affirmation, however, there also came a challenge.

VanValin put the challenge in question form: "What if you exported more frequently and fervently your message, your music, your vision of the body of Christ throughout the whole evangelical movement? We need that message and we welcome it." Billy Melvin was direct and specific: "I wonder why I have not seen more involvement by the Church of God in the community I represent—the National Association of Evangelicals. I believe with all my heart that the Church of God has something to share with those larger bodies of Christ. You have some great rootage and great fruitage in your fellowship." Beyond sharing, Melvin noted, "I believe you could also learn from this experience as you would share in the larger body of Christ."

Other affirmations clustered around the subject of holiness. As a Mennonite, Myron Augsburger wanted to be sure that "we are not just talking about whether I smoke or drink; we are also talking about how I feel toward the poor and the dispossessed and the issue of violence." Melvin warned similarly that the world today "is not so much interested in our *talk* as our *walk*. He affirmed the longstanding emphasis of the Church of God movement on holy living, noting that "few evangelical denominations that I know have done as beautiful a job in involving our Black brothers and sisters and other ethnics and minorities as you have in your [Church of God] fellowship."

A final affirmation centered around the concept of "movement" that is highlighted by the Church of God tradition. VanValin called for a retaining of this focus and pointed with admiration to the International Convention of the Church of God that convenes annually in Anderson, Indiana—of which the General Assembly is a part. He observed: "The Convention and the Assembly, the camp meeting, this week-long annual event...is the glue that holds the Church of God together. You do not depend on structures and processes, form and legislation to make you who you are so much as you depend on this gathering." Added Kinlaw:

> I love the vision that brought you [Church of God movement] into existence, the one that transcends denominational lines, but, more than that, the one that champions the unity of the body of Christ. I think what promoted this was a deep sense of "seek ye first the Kingdom of God and His righteousness" in which Kingdom loyalties were put ahead of all other loyalties. You've got an organization now, but don't lose that trans-organizational vision. You must lead the way in sharing it so that the rest of us that are trapped can see somebody who cares more about the Kingdom of God than they care about their own organization. The Kingdom is first. Now, that's part of who you are.

Kinlaw warned the movement never to lose the heart of its heritage: "Don't let anything stop within you that hunger for the Spirit to work in your midst."

There were other observations and cautions in the area of the church organization. Augsburger observed that the Church of God movement is "wrestling, as we [Mennonites] are, with what it means to be persons who have a polity of order without selling oneself out to institutionalization." Melvin openly wondered "if perhaps so much emphasis in the Church of God movement has been placed on independence of the local church that there has not been sufficient emphasis on the interdependence of the whole church. You are moving to a point in time when you are going to have to work harder with what it means to interrelate one with the other as local churches." Edgar Johnson offered this advice:

> If we depend on organization for success, we may fail; but if we don't organize we may fail too.... There is a problem with lack of structure. It could be like a body without a skeleton, lacking direction. Probably some of your expressed fears about structure in the church's life may be carried over from a long-ago problem—maybe a problem in the thinking of the early founders of the Church of God movement that may not exist today.

Perhaps the observation and caution of Myron Augsburger serves best as a general summary. To the Assembly of 1988 he said:

> You use *movement* language; I like that. Movement means something that is dynamic, something that is happening. The risen Christ is moving among us, the Holy Spirit is doing

325

something. That also means that I (we) have to become flexible and be willing to be vulnerable—not act as though I (we) have captured the Kingdom. To date, the Church of God movement has visioned rightly and worked diligently in this regard.

185. Women of the Church of God

by Kay Shively

Linda Mason
National Coordinator
Women of the
Church of God

"Women of the Church of God" is an organization within the life of the Church of God movement that began with a picture of a wheat field. One day in 1930, Nora Siens Hunter sat looking at a magazine cover which pictured a combine cutting a wide swath through a wheat field. Since her heart had just been sensitized by a five-month mission trip to Europe, North Africa, and Syria, she was struck by the analogy of that picture to the "broader fields" of human potential she had seen on her trip. The United States was in the throes of the Great Depression. The Church of God had forty-seven missionaries on the field, missionaries who managed on inadequate salaries which had been cut repeatedly as the church struggled to stay alive. But Nora Hunter could think of only one thing—those broad fields waiting to be harvested.

A verse from the Bible impressed itself deeply on her: "The Lord gave the word; the company of women that published the tidings are as a great host" (Psalm 68:11 ARV). The two impressions—"the broader fields" and "the company of women that published the tidings"—merged in her consciousness until the picture was clear: the women of the Church of God could spread the Word of God across those unharvested fields! Thus was born the vision of the National Woman's Home and Foreign Missionary Society. During the following months, Mrs. Hunter corresponded with the Rev. H. M. Riggle, Secretary of the Foreign Missionary Board, and met with committees of women, ministers, and gospel workers to assure a broad base of support for her idea.

During the 1932 Anderson Camp Meeting, the society was organized; bylaws were adopted and officers were chosen. The women marched from the tabernacle to the auditorium singing "Onward, Christian Soldiers," led by Rachel Lord. Fifty-eight women signed as members that day. By the next camp meeting, the society had 948 members and a budget of $1,000. The society's first national officers were Nora Hunter, president; Inez Bright, recording secretary; Frances Tallen, treasurer; Grace Henry, historian; Lucena Byrum, director of prayer services; Zuda Rothman, director of program services and missionary education; Anna Blewitt, director of music and young people's and children's work; and Mrs. C. R. Brial, director of sewing circles. Eventually, state and local units were organized.

From the beginning of its ministry, the society's objectives covered a wide variety of concerns, as follows.

> To cooperate with all recognized agencies of the Church of God in promoting missionary work at home and abroad; to make the cause of missions a heart interest rather than a passing fancy; to study the spiritual, moral and social needs of the world; to educate the children and young people of the church in home and foreign missions; to train leaders to carry the gospel of Christ to all people at home and abroad; to encourage liberality and wisdom in the stewardship of prayer, the stewardship of personality, and the stewardship of possessions; to fulfill the scripture, "The Lord gave the word; the company of women that published the tidings are as a great host."

One of the more important of the early goals was to keep the missionaries on full salary, and the women's organization has continued its concern for the material and spiritual needs of the missionaries through the years.

The basic principle of fund-raising was, from the first, that any money raised was to be over and above the tithe so as not to rob from other ministries of the church. The women often spoke of "gleaning" and "gathering up the fragments," using what might otherwise have been considered worthless. A great emphasis was placed on each woman contributing out of the richness of her own talent—baking, cooking, sewing, whatever her gift. Even in the Depression years, thousands of dollars were raised in this way and put to work for missions.

Today, nearly seventy years later, the organization, now known as WOMEN OF THE CHURCH OF GOD, has more than 30,000 members. Fund-raising remains a major focus, amounting to nearly $2,000,000 annually (including the Christ's Birthday Offering) for ministries of the Church of God. However, the organization also seeks to challenge and inspire women to a variety of ministries as reflected by its motto, "United in Mission, Friendship, Personal Growth and Service," and by its mission statement:

> The mission of WOMEN OF THE CHURCH OF GOD is to extend the gospel of Jesus Christ, promote spiritual and personal growth, build friendship and interdependence, widen

mental horizons and enlarge vision, encourage the stewardship of all of life, and support the united ministries and beliefs of the Church of God through gifts of finance and leadership.

Local groups are encouraged to organize around the needs and interests of their members. Executive leaders have been:

Nora Hunter	1932–1948
Hallie Patterson	1948–1970
Nellie Snowden	1970–1981
Doris J. Dale	1981–1998
Linda Mason	1998 to present

Editor's Note: In recognition of their superb leadership, Anderson University awarded honorary doctorates to Nellie Snowden (1973) and Doris J. Dale (1988).

Editor's Note: For an extensive discussion of issues related to women in the life of the Church of God movement, see Juanita Evans Leonard, ed., *Called To Minister, Empowered to Serve.* Also note the significant involvement of Susie Cunningham Stanley and other Church of God women in the series of International Wesleyan/Holiness Women Clergy Conferences (the fourth convening in Jacksonville, Florida, in April, 2000). The web homepage of these conferences is *www.messiah.edu/WHWC.*

186. Hispanic, Native American, and African-American Beginnings in the Church of God

Excerpts from David A. Telfer, *Red and Yellow, Black and White and Brown: Ministry and Evangelism in Ethnic Communities, Home Missions in the Church of God Reformation Movement* (Anderson, Ind.: Warner Press, 1981), pages 10-11, 32-33, 46-47. Also see David Telfer's "Sociological and Theological Foundations for Church of God Ministry in Ethnic Minority Communities in the United States" (Iliff School of Theology, 1975).

Hispanic Ministry

The first Hispanic Church of God congregation in the United States was started in San Antonio, Texas, in 1921 by the Reverend M. F. Tafolla, a Mexican-American minister who came in touch with the Church of God through reading a *Gospel Trumpet* presented to him by a Mr. L. Ball. An Anglo layperson, Ball invited Tafolla to preach to Mexican-Americans on his farm near Buda, Texas. Later, Brother Tafolla conducted camp meetings on property along the Medina River near the town of Somerset ten miles southwest of San Antonio. This summer camp meeting continued for over twenty years under Tafolla's leadership. The meeting predated the founding of the congregation in San Antonio and later helped plant the Hispanic church in Somerset.... Ernie Lopez was a small boy in the Somerset church when the building was dedicated [1950]. He was nurtured and grew up in the congregation. After ministerial training he returned to his home area to pastor the church at Somerset and later at San Antonio, and to give significant leadership in the Spanish-American Concilio.

> *Editor's Note*: The Church of God now includes "Hispanic Council of the Church of God" (United States and Canada).

Native American Ministry

God's Spirit broke through in an amazing way in leading the Church of God reformation movement to begin evangelizing in native American communities in 1939.... Amazingly, on the same Sunday in March 1939, the first native American worship services were held on two reservations twelve hundred miles apart: on the Tulalip Reservation in northwestern Washington State and the Pine Ridge Reservation in South Dakota.... The pioneer of the Tulalip ministry was J. Frank Shaw, who had been the pastor at the neighboring Everett congregation. Rollo Maulsby, a layperson who had leased land on the reservation, invited Shaw to the reservation to survey the needs of the people and consider starting a church.... The Church of God witness on the Pine Ridge Reservation began in the Robert Fast Horse home near Porcupine Butte.... A group of students from Gordon Bible School, an institution sponsored by the Gordon, Nebraska, Church of God, led a prayer service in the Fast Horse home and were invited to return.... The first pastor of the Church of God ministry on the Pine Ridge Reservation was Herbert Peterson, who served from 1940 to 1949.

> *Editor's Note:* Today Church of God ministries incluede the "American Indian Council of the Church of God."

African-American Ministry

Jane Williams is the first known black leader in the Church of God. In 1886 she established a congregation in Charleston, South Carolina. This state became an important center for the southern blacks in the Church of God during this early period of development in the reformation movement. In these beginning years blacks were included in the movement's traveling evangelistic teams and were recognized as ministers in the church. The first predominantly black congregation in the South to own property was located at Augusta, Georgia, in 1893.

Initial efforts of evangelism by the Church of God among blacks in the South were carried out by mutual cooperation of black and white leaders. The 1897 Alabama State Camp Meeting was held a few miles out of Hartselle, Alabama, and was attended by both blacks and whites. The services were held in a tent that had a rope stretched down the middle of the audience as a recognition of segregation [required by local law]. During the meeting, Lena Shoffner preached a sermon about tearing down the middle wall of partition. The rope was taken down while whites and blacks knelt at the altar and prayed together. That night a mob threw dynamite under the boarding house and other camp buildings. Several ministers escaped during the night.... In 1890 D. S. Warner was the target of a violent attack in Mississippi because of his preaching, which was contrary to accepted customs of racial separation.

Editor's Note: See the next entry about the "National Association of the Church of God" for more on the development and organization of Black identity and ministry within the Church of God movement.

187. The National Association: A Positive Force

Timothy J. Clark,
President
National Association
of the Church of God

Editor's Note: This is an excerpt of a chapter by James Earl Massey in *National Association of the Church of God: Diamond Jubilee*, Wilfred Jordan and Richard Willowby, co-editors (Warner Press, 1991), 3-5. For an insightful interview with Dr. Massey in which he comments on his life in and valuing of the Church of God movement, see Barry L. Callen, ed., *Sharing Heaven's Music: The Heart of Christian Preaching*, Essays in Honor of James Earl Massey (Nashville: Abingdon Press, 1995), 203-219.

It is a fact of more than passing significance that the Church of God has long had the active presence of a larger number of African-Americans within its life than any of the holiness-oriented church bodies, and, in addition, a larger number than any of the mainline denominations reporting a black constituency. Why? First, some statistics are in order.

Among the holiness denominations which have had primary contact with African-Americans are the Christian and Missionary Alliance Church, the Church of the Nazarene, the Pilgrim Holiness Church, the Holiness Christian Church, the Salvation Army, and the Church of God (Anderson).

Although the separate history of any one of these groups has not always reflected the best social arrangement with their black members, it is interesting that blacks did not break away from any of these church groups to form independent organizations—as was the case with segregated blacks in the Methodist Church, for example. Part of the reason for not separating might lie in the fact that most of the named groups have had so few black members in comparison with the white majority.

The holiness body that has had the most fruitful results for its message among African-Americans is the Church of God. Although its black constituency has experienced social trauma at critical stages of wider social strain in the nation, there has not been any widespread interest on the part of blacks in breaking away from the larger group. In fact, the relationship between African-Americans and the Church of God movement as a whole has been remarkably stable, with an obvious pattern of calculated responsiveness in the midst of threatening strain. It is important to understand what stands behind this result. One of the reasons for this continued involvement of blacks in the life and work of the Church of God is the appealing and promising ideal of the unity of believers. This message has kept thoughtful members, both black and white, mindful of the need to keep working at reducing the points of tension and strain as they have arisen.

Early on, the unity emphasis in the message of the Church of God appealed strongly to African-Americans who were otherwise beset by restrictive segregation patterns in the land. The message of unity provided promise for needed affirmation of self-worth, on the one hand, and needed social togetherness, on the other. Unlike other church groups whose doctrinal positions accented non-relational themes and teachings, the central theme of the Church of God movement was a relational one, the unity of believers. When social relations within this movement have been under strain, the challenge of the unity ideal has always been present as a prodding factor toward correction and reform. To be sure, the sad fact of race distancing and polarization in Church of God history can be documented as readily as that result in other church groups; but the unity ideal never has allowed that separateness to stand unchallenged. Rather, the announced ideal has stirred the most thoughtful to seek a remedy for the problem and to bridge the distances that have developed.

But there is another reason why African-Americans within the Church of God have remained openly relational despite times of racial tension in the larger body. That reason is the organizational entity known as the National Association of the Church of God (West Middlesex, Pennsylvania, initially formed as a camp meeting organization in 1916).

331

The National Association has been a social means for black assertiveness and black group pride. The National Association has at times functioned as an active witness against racist influences at work in the church; it has been the social entity to protest when the church was not as socially responsible and active as the unity ideal seemed to demand. It is not too much to say that, at nearly every time when social and racial awareness needed to be increased within the Church of God, the National Association helped to effect this result, sometimes offering distinct strategies for dealing with race issues, always involving persons who were interested in making needed changes.

That the Church of God has both gained and held African-Americans within its communal life has been duly noted by other church bodies, but the reason for such sustained togetherness is more than doctrinal; it is based in part upon a system of relating that includes recognition of voluntary associations within the church that nurture ethnic identity and group pride and grant opportunities for training and enrichment. It is in these areas of benefit that the National Association of the Church of God has historically shown a strategic influence during its eighty years of existence.

Across the years the National Association has continued to play a major role in helping to effect many changes and developments in both the African-American congregations that support and depend upon its ministries and the Church of God movement generally, within which it remains one of the most vital and vibrant voluntary associations. Aware that the Church of God has been like most of the other religious groups in America in having to deal with the sad influences imposed by conditions of faulty social customs and limiting stereotypes, the National Association has worked steadily to help the whole church deal with its deficiencies and challenges at the point of race and develop a sustainable fellowship in keeping with the social implications in the Church of God message about the holiness of life and the intended unity of believers.

Editor's Note: Dr. Massey wrote the article "Race Relations and the American Holiness Movement" for the *Wesleyan Theological Journal* (Spring 1996). He reported the following in this article, having made clear that the movement's message of the unity of all believers implies that a strong interracial stance is inherent in the message itself.

The message voiced by the Church of God about the unity of believers appealed strongly to African Americans who were otherwise restricted and segregated in a racist society. The message of unity provided promise for a needed affirmation of self-worth, on the one hand, and for needed social togetherness, on the other. Unlike other church groups whose doctrinal positions accented non-relational themes, the central theme of the Church of God was, and remains, a relational one: believers belong together, united by love. Although social relations within the Church of God have witnessed the same problems and stresses all other church bodies have faced, the challenge of the biblical insistence on unity has always been present in the group's heritage and message as a prodding factor toward freeing its life from racist concerns in the national environment and toward reform of its life as people of God called to practice holiness. To be sure, evidences that some persons within its congregations have yielded to prevailing social patterns of race distancing and polarization can be documented in the history of the Church of God, just as in the history of other church groups in America. Nevertheless, the unity ideal central to its heritage and reason for being has never allowed such lapses from the ideal to stand unchallenged.

Editor's Note: The National Association of the Church of God has existed for nearly a century as a visible expression of racial openness and togetherness, an organizational expression within the Church of God that seeks to foster Christian unity and be sure that lapses from the unity ideal never go unchallenged. A listing of the Chairs of the General Ministerial Assembly of the National Association document a few of the outstanding African-American leaders who have enriched the life of the Church of God generally. The Chairs have been:

Marcus H. Morgan

Rufus J. Smith	1917–1923
George R. Dixon, Sr.	1923–1930
Samuel J. Taylor	1930–1936
Charles A. White	1936–1943
Raymond S. Jackson	1943–1955
Clifton M. Morgan	1955–1957
Marcus H. Morgan	1957–1965
Leonard E. Roache	1965–1973
Lawrence P. Wyatt	1973–1989
Ronald J. Fowler	1989–1991
Marcus H. Morgan	1991–1996
Benjamin F. Reid	1996–1999
Timothy J. Clarke	1999 to present

In addition, two other African-American pastors, Samuel G. Hines and Robert A. Culp, provided distinguished service as Chair of the movement's

General Assembly (USA and Canada) See Entry 44. Rev. Marcus H. Morgan, a 1952 Anderson University graduate, pastored one congregation in Chicago for forty-two years and chaired the Leadership Council of the Church of God from 1970-1981. Edward L. Foggs served with distinction as the General Secretary of the Leadership Council of the Church of God from 1988 to 1999 (received an honorary Doctor of Humane Letters degree from Warner Pacific College on his retirement in 1999).

For another brief history of the National Association of the Church of God, see Sanders', *Saints In Exile.* For an excellent source of information and inspiration, particularly regarding the African-American community in the Church of God, see the periodical *The Shining Light* edited by Wilfred Jordan (who received an honorary Doctor of Divinity degree from Warner Pacific College in 1992).

In recent decades a major annual event within the African-American community of the Church of God has been the Inspirational Youth Convention. See the 1981 thesis of Diana Cook titled "A Study of the Historical Development and Current Perspectives of the Inspirational Youth Convention of the National Association of the Church of God, West Middlesex, Pennsylvania" (Anderson University School of Theology). The first of these significant conventions to convene apart from the West Middlesex Campmeeting was in Chicago in 1938 under the leadership of Gabriel P. Dixon. There were about 600 delegates. The Inspirational Youth Convention grew rapidly in the 1940s and 1950s, in part because of superb new leaders like James Earl Massey—to be followed in later years by Edward L. Foggs, Richard Goode, Ronald J. Fowler, and others. For detail, see Diana Swoope, "The National Inspirational Youth Convention, 1938-1990," in Jordan and Willowby, eds., *National Association of the Church of God: Diamond Jubilee.*

Why should there be particular focus on the Black experience within the Church of God movement? A "caucus" of African-American leaders in the Church of God gathered in Cleveland, Ohio, in April, 1970, to address this question. This was a time of social turmoil in the United States. The published proceedings of this meeting (*The Church of God in Black Perspective*, was introduced by Rev. Ronald J. Fowler. He wrote: "There has developed an increasing credibility gap between the church and Christ. The church's pronouncements are yet well ahead of her performances.... A 'united church for a divided world' continues to be a vision awaiting birth" (iii). Rev. Fowler, a 1966 graduate of Anderson University's School of Theology and Chair of the University's Board of Trustees from 1981-1991, was awarded an honorary doctorate by the University in 1986.

188. Gospel of Unity in Diversity

Editor's Note: Curtiss Paul DeYoung was reared in the Church of God, a movement that he appreciatively recalls has taught that unity is a concern at the very heart of the Christian gospel. Following his college days at Anderson University and numerous subsequent involvements in ecumencial settings, he wrote his book *Coming Together: The Bible's Message in an Age of Diversity* (Judson Press, 1995). Dedicated to his two Church of God mentors in the ministry of reconciliation, Samuel G. Hines and James Earl Massey, and endorsed by Cheryl J. Sanders, a Church of God pastor and professor at Howard University, DeYoung affirms:

> "One human family, many cultural expressions" is a biblical truth that needs to be reclaimed and proclaimed in this age of diversity. The Bible is a multicultural document. The Hebrew Bible proclaims God's universal love for humanity from the very beginning. This message of oneness keeps emerging even in the midst of Israel's ethnocentrism. The New Testament declares a faith initiated by Jesus that was truly multicultural at its core.... We must not let that powerful flame of unity and reconciliation, set ablaze by the hope of the 1950s and 1960s, become an intermittent flicker as we enter the twenty-first century. The Bible's message, in this age of diversity, is an invitation to come together at God's table of fellowship and to go forth into all the world as God's artisans of reconciliation (28, 187-188).

Editor's Note: From its earliest years there was considerable ethnic diversity in the Church of God movement in addition to the substantial African-American presence. For example, see Merle D. Strege's 1982 dissertation done at the Graduate Theological Union at Berkeley and titled "Where Scandinavian Is Spoken: Ethnic Identity and Assimilation Among Scandinavian Immigrants in the Church of God (Anderson, Indiana)."

189. Christian Unity: A Statement About Its Meaning and Expressions

This is an excerpt of a paper given by James Earl Massey to the Doctrinal Dialogue Task Force (Christian Churches/Churches of Christ and the Church of God), Cincinnati, Ohio, May, 1993.

Two things are central in the Christian experience of unity: first, the awareness that we belong together, and second, the spirit to fulfill what belonging together requires. The whole matter is summed up in this expression: "a shared life." This is the ideal that was given to guide us, and it also argues for a function to which we must remain actively open.

The concept of unity is, in my opinion, best expressed in our time as community. The word "community" can keep us moderns from thinking singly about an institutional form or our organizational structures. "Community" immediately reminds us that unity is more than a theological concern and a spiritual given, that ii also is a social result dependent upon our personal and willing involvement.

This fact of denominational families and denominated organizational forms is one of the most familiar facts in contemporary religious life. It is also, however, one of the most problematic facts in light of the biblical mandate for Christian unity. We all know that there is something essentially problematic about the boundaries our institutional differences and loyalties have made between us. Some formally-fixed boundaries (doctrinal and otherwise) are so delimiting that they hinder a holistic view of the universal Church, while some others are more loosely structured because of a wider perspective generated by the biblical ideal of unity.

Denominated organized forms can be honorable and effective, but only if these are not honored as ends in themselves. If fellowship and mission are given prior place in the organizational life and purpose, with the group's work being more basic than the group's structure, then that denominated group need not be a barrier to unity. Whether any denominated group is a barrier to or an agency of the biblical unity ideal depends largely upon how and why the group began, what it teaches and promotes, and the spirit that characterizes its life. If that spirit is one of openness and cooperativeness with respect to other believers, then the group can serve the purpose and spirit of the wider Church. But if the spirit of a denominated group is closed, competitive, and argumentative, then that group—whatever its beginnings and orthodoxy—is in need of renewal and reform.

Separately structured group life is not necessarily schismatic. The human family involves multifaceted forms and varieties of cultures, so it is only natural that the richness expressed in creation would be seen as well in the variety of responses humans make in organizing to promote the gospel and its claims. Diversity is not evil, only the spirit of divisiveness is. As Paul pointed out in First Corinthians 12:12-27, diversity of members in the body is not incompatible with the unity of the body.

Three attitudes are necessary on our part if we are to make Christian unity visible. The first attitude is one of *acknowledgment*: Since the New Testament tells us that all true believers belong to the Church, we must refuse to see other believers through eyes clouded by discriminating categories of placement. Ours must be an attitude that accepts all other believers despite the "historical accident" of their differing denominational backgrounds. The second attitude is one of *affirmation*: We must promote an atmosphere of participation and belonging. Every Christian believer has a legacy in every other Christian believer. The third attitude is one of *participation*: We must make common cause with each other. Any lingering and understood loyalty to tradition notwithstanding, the relational imperative of *agape*-love is set for sharing and cooperative mission. Christian love never stops prodding us to transcend what is parochial and local; it works ever and always to help us think and pray and plan and work with the wider world in view.

There is far more to Christian unity than meets the eye, much more than we experienced at first or have experienced since we believed. There are deeper levels in fellowship than we have dared to open ourselves to experience. We need to take another look at the concept of unity, and then take still another look. The seeing will search us, stir our hunger for more, and test our openness to venture. There is more in the doctrine and experience of Christian unity than we have yet seen or lived. May God grant us the wisdom and courage *to go on and live it.*

Editor's Note: For an extended treatment of Christian unity by Dr. Massey, see his 1979 book *Concerning Christian Unity.*

190. Celebrating Christian Unity Today

Following is an edited digest of the presentation made by Gilbert Stafford to the World Forum of the Church of God, Sydney, Australia, July, 1995.

What are the things that bind us together? We have a common Bible, a common Lord, a common commitment to making disciples, a common desire to be people of the Spirit, a common urgency about living the holy life, a common desire to be church together. We agree that the Bible is the book of God's revelation in written form, that Jesus is the Lord and Savior, that disciple-making is the church's mission, that the Holy Spirit is the church's source of power, that holiness of life is the church's mode of life, and that believers only are the true church.

I am convinced that we need to return to the study, preaching, and teaching of the Bible's message on unity. The New Testament has no dearth of passages setting forth Christian unity as part and parcel of the divine will for the church. By regularly preaching and teaching from them, we emphasize again and again that unity is a biblical mandate, and not simply the idealism of the early leaders of the Church of God movement or of contemporary ecumenists. Since Christian unity is a New Testament theme, it is a subject with which Christians as Christians need to wrestle.

337

By definition, unity of any kind presupposes diversity. If there were no diversity, we would not have unity, but sameness. The key question has to do with the limits of diversity. The short answer is that the limits are transgressed whenever the church ceases being the church. Any diversity which contradicts the essential nature of the church is unacceptable.

The most basic understanding of the church is that it is the circle of Christ's disciples (see Matt. 28:19-20). Furthermore, it is the fellowship of those who both believe in the atoning death and resurrection of Jesus Christ and live dead to sin and alive to Christ (see Rom. 6). The church, then, is the universal circle of those who have a personal relationship to the risen and living Lord Jesus Christ, believe that he died for our salvation and rose again, and are committed to the life of Christian holiness (i.e., dead to sin and alive to Christ). These are the biblical tests of fellowship.

In the course of time, however, the church had to identify itself in opposition to heresies. In doing so it fleshed out these basics in terms of formalized understandings about Jesus' relationship to his heavenly Father and to the Holy Spirit, resulting in Christian trinitarian thought, and about Jesus' personhood, that he is fully human and fully divine, yet one person. So, for us to be the church which continues to stand against these ancient and contemporary heresies, we must affirm the Trinity and the two natures of Christ.

What I have said to this point has to do with the church as Christian church. But what about our particular fellowship of the Church of God (Anderson)? What theological diversity can we tolerate? In order to answer this question I believe that we need to make a distinction between the *teaching ministry* of the church and the *general fellowship* of the church. What I have said up to this point applies to the general fellowship of the church as Christian church. That means that within the general membership of a local congregation, we cannot allow for a diversity which denies any one of the following: our call to Christian discipleship, Christ's atoning death and resurrection, Christian holiness, the Trinity, or the two natures of Christ.

The question is whether agreeing on these fundamental matters is sufficient for being involved in the *teaching ministry of the Church of God (Anderson).* I think not. As a particular fellowship of Christians we have doctrinal understandings which are part and parcel of who we are as a church. To disagree about these "Church of God" perspectives does not mean that one is not a Christian, as is the case of the matters mentioned above. It simply means that these are matters about which equally devoted Christians may disagree. I have in mind such widely held understandings of the Church of God as: salvation is synonymous with membership in God's one church; it is God's will to do a perfecting work in the lives of believers prior to death; the kingdom of God was inaugurated by Jesus Christ, is manifested in hearts made pure by faith, and will be brought to consummation at the return of Christ when world history will end and the saints will be gathered into heaven; and believers' baptism by immersion, the Lord's supper, and feet washing constitute the basic ordinances of the church.

These matters are deeply rooted in our history. If we are to continue being a distinctive tradition of Christians, our teaching ministry needs to be broadly united regarding these issues. But what about *participation* in the life of the church? Should all members of local congregations be required to adhere to this broad consensus? I answer No, because it is not these matters which determine whether one is a Christian in a biblical and historical sense. These matters do not have to do with the *essential being* of the church, but they do have to do, we believe, with the *well-being* of the church. If this is the case, and I believe it is, then these must not be tests of Christian fellowship in the same sense that the matters mentioned earlier are. Rather, Church of God perspectives are matters for which we are called to be good stewards in the interest of the *well-being*—not the *essential being*—of the whole church. If, then, we are divinely called to be good stewards of these perspectives, our teaching ministry needs to have enough unanimity about these matters to enable us both to share them with others and be agents of orderly thought in our own churches.

How can the Church of God cooperate with others without losing its distinctiveness? This is where we need to plow some new ground. Originally we were a come-out group in that we called those who had seen the light regarding the church to "come out from among them, and be ye separate, saith the Lord." Consequently, deeply ingrained in our historical life is not only a passive distrust of other church groups, but an overt war against them. However, in the course of time another stream of thought developed among us which is much more appreciative of the broader Christian world.

The Church of God (Anderson) ought to be making itself available to other church groups for the purpose of asking the following question both of them and of ourselves: What changes do all of us need to make in order to be the one church which is pleasing to God? Others can see things in us which need to be changed, things which we cannot see in ourselves. They have contributions to make to us, and we have contributions to make to them which in God's spiritual economy perhaps only they can make to us and only we can make to them.

Involvement with other Christians does not rob us of our identity; it enhances it. Cooperation with other believers does not destroy our distinctiveness; it expresses it. Participation with others of like precious faith does not endanger our tradition; it enriches it. Interaction with other church groups is not dangerous to our spiritual health; it nourishes it. The Christian mission is too important for any of us to be satisfied with the perpetuation of our own little slice of church life without being willing to become deeply involved with the whole cause and people of Christ. Unity is a *biblical mandate*, not a Church of God relic.

191. Together We Go

This doctrinal essay by Barry L. Callen appeared in
Vital Christianity, November, 1995.

This key entry appears in the personal journal of Daniel Warner on March 7, 1878: "On the 31st of last January the Lord showed me that holiness could never prosper upon sectarian soil encumbered by human creeds and party names, and he gave me a new commission to join holiness and all truth together and build up the apostolic church of the living God. Praise his name! I will obey him." Warner wrote a year later that "the God of all grace has most emphatically taught us in his word that his church is one, as the Father and Son are one, and that a manifestation of this unity is to be the world-saving salt of the church."

With these motivating insights, Warner became the primary pioneer of the movement of the Church of God, a gathering among God's people of some believers who know that they belong together by God's grace and that their obvious togetherness in the Spirit is crucial to effective Christian mission. In the early years of this movement this holiness-unity vision challenged many human compromises in the church and determined to find a better way to be God's people in the world. It still is the case that unity is a biblical mandate, not simply the idealism of our early leaders or of contemporary ecumenicists.

In the twentieth century the Christian community has given dramatic new attention to the problems of a divided Christian church. The Church of God movement has chosen not be involved for the most part. Why? Unfortunately, there has been at least a trace of arrogance by some of us who have felt that we already represent adequately what ought to be. There has been occasional fear that the movement might become contaminated by public association with Christians who represent differing traditions of belief and practice. There has been much insistence that the movement not support any preoccupation of Christians with solving the disunity problem the wrong way (theological compromises and denominational mergers).

But now the time for such criticizing of others is mostly past. Warner's was a prophetic voice that now must be translated into constructive action. We are both to tear down old obstructing walls and build new relationship bridges. For this movement of the Church of God, the need now is to develop its particular gifts to the glory of God, while respecting and benefiting from the divine gifts of other Christians. After all, every Christian has a legacy in every other Christian. We experience that legacy only as we receive each other and move eagerly beyond our group boundaries.

Believers who choose to be isolated from other believers get stunted by their isolation and soon are open to idolatries of their own making. Even a movement dedicated to Christian unity can destroy its own genius by failing to move creatively within the larger body. It is time for this movement to do more moving. Christian unity is first a gift of God and then the achievement of those committed to its fullest realization. True oneness comes only as the Spirit breathes the new life of holiness *and* as disciples dare to take appropriate uniting actions as inspired by the Spirit.

The unity of the earliest Christian churches was a unity of spirit which grew out of the shared experience of God's Spirit. Christians are to have the one Spirit poured out on them (Rom. 5:5), making them members together of the one body of Christ. This oneness of the body is a consequence of sharing the one Spirit (1 Cor. 12.13).

Today individual congregations of Christians should act as representatives of all of God's people. Evangelizing should be done *as the church* (the whole body of Christ) and for the church. New believers belong first and foremost to the church and not to a denomination that may recruit and nurture them. When a congregation baptizes a new believer, that baptism should be into the *whole church*, not merely a sectarian piece of it. The invitation to the Lord's supper should be issued as representatives of the whole body to any in the body wishing to participate—after all, it is the *Lord's* table, not *ours!*

A united church, living in creative togetherness, is a sign of the already coming Kingdom of God. The church is to be a united community of faith in a very divided world of unfaith. Christian mission is so important that none of us should get stuck in protecting our own little group at the expense of being involved deeply in the whole cause of Christ. There is a place for church structures; but that place is not for them to lead lives of their own.

Dating back to the vision of pioneers like Daniel Warner, this simple line of thought should still lead us forward. The center is Christian mission. Holiness enables authentic unity, which in turn increases a credible witness to the world. The authority and power all belong to God. In fact, it's God's Church!

192. Position Statements from Within the Recent Life of the Movement

Editor's Note: At the request of the Commission on Christian Unity, Barry L. Callen compiled this list of eleven recent statements about Christian unity emerging from within the life of the Church of God movement.

1. 1963. *All-Boards Congress and Planning Council*: "We need a strong emphasis on redemptive fellowship in the

church. Often our acceptance of other denominations and even members of our own congregations has been conditional, based on whether or not they agreed with 'Church of God' thinking. Perhaps we have forgotten the great inclusiveness of 'being in Christ'" [from the final report to the General Assembly of the Findings Committee, June, 1963].

2. 1970. *Consultation of the Church of God*: "Consensus: (1) Polarities recognized were: inclusive vs. exclusive fellowship; social concerns vs. evangelism; 'come-outism' vs. cooperative involvement; cardinal beliefs vs. tradition; diversity vs. uniformity; delegated assembly vs. general assembly. (2) Recognition of racial divisiveness and need to press for the removal of it. (3) Need to rethink sainthood and servanthood. (4) Find ways to utilize a larger variety of ministries. (5) Remain a non-joiner but initiate more conversations with other groups. (6) Clarify responsibilities of the Committee on Christian Unity. (7) Officially endorse cooperative endeavors overseas. (8) Share insights on unity wherever doors are open" [report to the General Assembly, June, 1970].

3. 1974. *Consultation on Doctrine*: "As we have examined the theological and historical root system which has produced the movement, we have recognized the humanness of the pioneers of the past, while, at the same time, recognizing the rightness of direction which they gave to the movement. A reexamination of their posture regarding the nature of the church and the role of the Church of God as a reforming movement has given additional evidence that the Church is of God and that God is still working in his church to call sinners to repentance, *Christians to unity*, and the world to judgment." See the significant section "The Unity of the Church" in this Consultation's printed report to the General Assembly, [June, 1974, 23-29].

4. 1974. *Yokefellow Statement*: "It is our belief that the New Testament sets forth the ideal that all Christians, operating in true humanity, should be able to learn from one another. We maintain, moreover, the conviction that this movement represents a force of reformation leadership within Christendom with its emphasis on ecumenicity based on unity rather than on union. To this end, therefore, we

encourage through every means possible the establishing and maintaining of work relationships with other like-minded groups on the national, state, and local levels" [report to the General Assembly, June, 1974].

5. 1979. The *WE BELIEVE* statement of the School of Theology, Anderson University: "The dividedness among Christian people today is not just unfortunate; it is inappropriate and wholly unacceptable. Unity is clearly God's will for the church.... The goal is less a contrived peace treaty among deeply divided church organizations and more a radical reconsideration of what is an appropriate network of relationships among brothers and sisters in Christ."

6. 1983. *Commission on Christian Unity*: "Where Do We Go From Here?", a printed booklet presented to the General Assembly as "a statement of concern and guidance to the Church of God (Anderson, Ind.) from the Commission on Christian Unity," June, 1983 [see entry 133].

7. 1984. *Consultation on Mission and Ministry of the Church of God*. This Consultation established as one of its priority areas of concern the task of the church to really function as the church. One stated goal for the movement to the end of the twentieth century is "to expand ministries through voluntary relationships with Christian groups outside the Church of God Reformation Movement and seek to live out the vision of unity through broader interdependent relationships that serve mutual needs for training, fellowship, and witness" (Indianapolis, April, 1984, see entry 122).

8. 1985. *Committee on Long Range Planning and Executive Council* presented the following "for information and guidance" to the June, 1985, General Assembly: ". . .supports the historical stance of the Church of God Reformation Movement to seek intentional inter-church relationships through which its own ministries are strengthened and which provide opportunity for the Church of God Reformation Movement to live out its message of Christian unity through enriching the entire Body of Christ."

9. 1988. The *General Assembly* adopted the resolution, "Inter-Church Cooperation," June, 1988. It reads in part: "Inter-church relationships should be seen as opportunities to serve and witness in light of the distinctive heritage of

343

the Church of God reformation movement. We have something important to share as well as receive in any such relationship." (See Entry 25.)

10. 1988. *Mission Statement for the Church of God Movement*. The General Assembly endorsed a mission statement for the Church of God in June, 1988. It includes: "To build up the whole body of Christ *in unity*." (See Entry 125).

11. 1995. *Leaders' Visioning Retreat*. See entry 115. This retreat of leaders of the Church of God (Jan. 1995) affirmed that the Church of God exists, among other things, to *"Celebrate the Unity of the Body of Christ."*

---

193. Conversations in Recent Decades: Church of God (Anderson) and Churches of God (Winebrennerian)

Editor's Note: Within the evolution of the Commission on Christian Unity (see Entry 179), several "ecumenical" contacts were pursued, at least at the getting acquainted level. Included were meetings of Church of God leaders with leaders of the Church of the Brethren, the Evangelical Covenant Church of America, and especially the Churches of God (Winebrennerian). In this latter case there was recognition of "major commonalities and heritage," acknowledgment of some difference in polity and doctrine (especially on the subject of "sanctification"), and by 1969 serious discussion about the practicalities of "flowing together." Following is a brief summary by Barry L. Callen concerning the conversations with the Churches of God: General Conference. For more on the influence of John Winebrenner on Daniel Warner, see Entry 3.

Daniel Warner, primary pioneer of the Church of God movement, originally was a minister of the Churches of God (Winebrennerian). His experiences with and final break from this body are detailed in Barry Callen's book, *It's God's Church*. The resulting separation of these bodies, both committed to Christian unity, has continued for over a century, although a series of events from 1941-1977 renewed a considerable lever of constructive contact between them.

In 1941 the Churches of God: General Conference formed a Committee on Christian Unity for the purpose of seeking "close cooperation or definite organic unity" with selected other church bodies. That same year the Gospel Trumpet Company (Church of God) began customizing its Sunday school

344

literature for use by the Churches of God. This publishing relationship lasted about thirty years.

During the years 1955-1959 the young School of Theology in Anderson (founded in 1950) initiated faculty/student dialogue with the Churches of God seminary in Findlay, Ohio. By 1960 the Executive Council of the Church of God had formed a Committee on Conversations that met with its counterpart to explore the possibilities of even closer cooperation. Several joint ministry opportunities were pursued. In 1964 the dialogue was expanded to include the Brethren Church and the Church of the Brethren. Particularly between the Church of God and the Churches of God there were joint conferences, exchanges at the General Assembly and General Conference level, discussion of a joint hymnal, a merger of two congregations (Auburn, Indiana), discussions at the state level in Michigan and Pennsylvania, and even consideration of the seminary in Findlay closing and opening a foundation on the Anderson campus of the Church of God. There was the evident hope that at least these two bodies might "flow together."

For whatever reasons, little such functional flowing together actually occurred in the following years. Priorities tended to keep the paths of these two church bodies largely separate. The most recent meeting was at Anderson College in 1977 with about ten leaders from each group present. There was no talk of "merger," but tentative plans were made for a "Consultation on the Holy Spirit" (which never convened). Despite the considerable commonality of heritage, various experiments in joint ministries, etc., only a few mutually appreciative personal acquaintances (e.g., church historians Harvey Gossard and John W. V. Smith) has kept a certain warmth in this marginal relationship.

In 1995 two books by Barry Callen (*It's God's Church!* and *Contours of a Cause*) drew upon certain Churches of God (Winebrennarian) published sources, sought the critical perspective of Harvey Gossard of the Findlay seminary, and sought to present a fair assessment of the historic relationship between these two church bodies. Callen's earlier history of Anderson University (*Guide of Soul and Mind*, 1992) relied in part on consultation with Richard Kern who earlier had written the history of the University of Findlay. Also in 1995, Donald Dennison, pastor of the Indian Village Church in Auburn, Indiana, was named "Associate in Cross-Cultural Ministries," a Church of God (Anderson) minister called to administer the missions work of the Churches of God: General Conference.

Currently there are no unity dialogues between these two historically related bodies. Occasionally greetings are brought to each others assemblies and seminaries, keeping alive at least congenial contact in the relative absence of significant relationships and cooperative ministries.

345

194. Open Forum: Church of God In Dialogue with the Christian Churches/Churches of Christ

Editor's Note: This news release was published both in *Vital Christianity* and *Christian Standard* in February, 1993, seeking to inform wider circles in both movements of this Open Forum dialogue to that date. It was co-authored by Barry L. Callen and James B. North (a historian of the Christian Churches).

In the nineteenth century two different Christian movements began that had a common dream. They hoped that all children of God would come together in unity and work for the perfection and mission of God's people under the authority and guidance of biblical teaching.

These two reforming movements—one symbolized by the leadership of Alexander Campbell, the other inspired by pioneers such as Daniel S. Warner—became significant bodies of believers as they grew and matured. Congregations of the Christian Churches/Churches of Christ and the Church of God (Anderson) soon dotted the entire American landscape as well as spreading to many other countries. Leaders such as Campbell and Warner shared a similar vision of Christian unity, but the two movements they represented have remained apart.

Recently that awkward separation has been changing. For the last year, ministers of these two movements have been meeting together in Cincinnati, Ohio, to share their vision of the church, talk about mutual problems of local ministry, and learn about each other's strengths and idiosyncrasies. They have eaten together, prayed, joined in fellowship, and even argued together, and have planned joint worship times. The goal of all this has been to bring to fuller realization the prayer of Jesus that "they all may be one" (John 17:21).

In 1989, national meetings began to occur between leaders of the Christian Churches/Churches of Christ and the Church of God (Anderson). These meetings became known as the "Open Forum." The Open Forum actually began in 1984 as a brainstorming effort within the Christian Churches/Churches of Christ about how to get their congregations out of a lethargic plateau they were then experiencing. A number of individuals decided to call for a meeting of representative key leaders in the Christian Churches/Churches of Christ to probe ways to restore real "movement" into what is fondly called the "Restoration Movement"—a movement to restore New Testament Christianity to today's splintered denominational world.

After several successful meetings where issues of importance were discussed, members of the Church of God (Anderson) were invited in 1989 to come to Traders Point Christian Church in Indianapolis to worship together and discuss issues of common interest in church history, theology, practice, and the ordinances. What emerged from this first meeting was the realization that both groups have an overwhelming number of essential elements in common. Additional meetings involving hundreds of persons now have convened in Anderson, Indiana, in 1990 and in Lexington, Kentucky, in 1991. These friendly meetings have not been shallow and nonconfrontive, however. In spite of the numerous similarities acknowledged by the Christian Churches/Church of God (Anderson), there are still some significant differences between them.

Because of the differences, leaders in the national gatherings decided in 1991 that provision should be made for the scholarly, in-depth discussion of these issues, getting beyond the exploratory conversations held in the much larger Open Forum meetings. In August of that year, a Task Force on Doctrinal Dialogue gathered in Cincinnati, composed of equal numbers of individuals from the two groups. Formal papers were presented from both groups in this and subsequent meetings.

Beyond abstract discussion of theological issues, however, these Task Force meetings have manifested a concern for the evangelistic mission of the church. In what ways can these two movements join together in common work for the advancement of the kingdom of God on earth?

Editor's Note: For a full accounting of the process and results of this multi-year dialogue, along with extensive appendixes of classic unity documents emerging from these two traditions, see Barry Callen and James North, *Coming Together In Christ.*

195. What We Have Learned

Editor's Note: What follows are excerpts of a paper delivered by Barry Callen to the Central States Ministers' Meeting of the Church of God, St. Joseph, Michigan, March, 1993 (also appears in edited form in Callen and North, *Coming Together In Christ*). It highlights eleven lessons being learned by Church of God participants in the "Open Forum" process with the Christian Churches/Churches of Christ. This paper attempts to represent the thinking of the Church of God participants, the most active being Barry Callen, Keith Huttenlocker, Kenneth Jones, David Lawson, Vernon Maddox, Arlo Newell, Spencer Spaulding, and Gilbert Stafford.

    1. *This Process Is Worth the Time*. The last thing any of us needs is more busywork, more routine and maybe unnecessary tending to organizational machinery. All of us are busy people and have to be convinced that such a new venture as this multi-year "Open Forum" process with the Christian Churches/Churches of Christ is not just more meetings and

endless talk. Dialogue participants have dealt directly with the question, "Is it all really worthwhile?" Although the final verdict is not in, most of the participants have developed a growing conviction that this process may be ordered of God for some important ends. We judge it most worthwhile, even though many specifics of potential outcomes still are seen only dimly, if at all.

2. *Historical Perspective Increases One's Humility.* The Church of God movement, especially in its early decades, tended to dismiss as without value much of Christian church history. That history was seen mostly as centuries of apostasy now about to end with the gathering of God's true church and the return of Christ. In the train of bold reformers like Martin Luther and John Wesley, movement leaders rejoiced in the belief that God was introducing again the "early morning light." We saw ourselves being called to "cleanse the sanctuary" in a full and final way as the age was coming to a close. So it has been easy for us as a movement to value A.D. 50 and A.D. 1880, while generally lamenting most in between as a sorry state of affairs.

There now is a growing realization of the loss we have sustained by devaluing the long and rich "restorationist" tradition of which the movement is a part. Particularly in the United States, the Stone/Campbell tradition predated the Church of God movement and is full of common cause with it. There are some differences, to be sure. Some of these differences can be an enrichment to the movement. Why? In part because, in addition to any distinctiveness granted the Church of God movement by divine grace, the movement also is a product of a given time and place in church history. That time and place inevitably have had a significant shaping influence, an influence we have only begun to understand. Sharing with a dialogue partner who has so much in common with us sharpens our historical perspective and thereby enhances our self-understanding.

3. *We Too Have Some Walls.* Church of God participants in the Open Forum have learned that the structural and non-structural obstacles to real Christian unity are more subtle and complex than sometimes we have assumed. We all live in a day when traditional denominational walls are eroding rapidly. Nevertheless, even free-church "restorationist"

bodies that champion non-creedalism and Christian unity visions often themselves develop significant and stubborn "denominational" characteristics (products of humanity and history). For idealists like us, that is a hard lesson to accept.

4. *We Need To Practice What We Preach.* Why did some Church of God leaders become involved in this particular dialogue process? The answer is more than the fact that there was an opportunity and a direct invitation from leaders of the Christian Churches/Churches of Christ. For many decades our movement has set forth what we have judged to be the New Testament vision of Christian unity. We have declared our willingness to "reach our hands in fellowship to every bloodwashed one." Sometimes over the decades we have been accused of being sectish ourselves, not living up to our proclaimed ideal. In fact, we have not always modeled clearly what we have announced with the best of intentions. At first it was natural for our movement to focus on being critical of the obvious wrongs seen all across the denominationalized and demoralized Christian community. The positive building of a viable alternative, however, always is more difficult than the negative judging of what is so wrong. Some of us in the movement have learned only slowly that it is difficult to preach convincingly a commitment-based and fellowship-based vision of Christian unity without being intentional about seeking its actualization.

5. *Both Groups Resist the "M" Word.* Participants in this dialogue process have reminded each other over these last years that the "M" word, *merger*, is not on the Open Forum agenda. A structural uniting of our two church bodies is not our priority goal. We all know that immediate mistrust and spirited opposition would arise from within each of our constituencies if it were perceived that these dialogues were exploring seriously anything like a "denominational" merger. Neither body envisions such a union outcome as the way to achieve Christian unity. Neither body has a structure to make such a thing possible even if it were desirable. We have learned, nonetheless, that a certain "flowing together" is a possibility, probably even in some sense a divinely guided goal. Such meshing should focus on building relationships, enriching understandings, and discovering cooperative ministry opportunities.

We have become convinced that there are many important things that we and the Christian Churches/Churches of Christ can do to help each other in church life and mission. Without raising the specter of a "merger mentality," we can do much together to further the Kingdom's cause. We have learned, however, that moving over this fruitful frontier, whatever its components might turn out to be, will require a selfless attitude, and certainly an avoidance of "turf protection" by our several church institutions. History teaches that, right as it may be, this cooperative path is narrow and traveled successfully only by a few.

6. *Mission Is the Motive That Inspires our Dialogue.* Merger is not the goal, and a bad conscience about poor performance in past unity efforts did play a key role in beginning this dialogue process. The primary motive driving and sustaining this dialogue, however, has been a mutual concern for the better accomplishment of Christian mission. Mission is the motive. Mission is accomplished best in cooperation with brothers and sisters in Christ. The church is bigger than "us." Its mission will get done best when we decide to do it together.

7. *We Have Much To Learn If We Remain Open.* Driven by our commitment to accomplishing the church's mission, the Church of God participants in this dialogue have tended to learn one or two theological lessons in the process. One is that the movement should take more seriously its own stance of non-creedalism. The challenge for us is not to protect our current perceptions of truth (one way to define denominationalism) so much as it is to continue seeking the most adequate possible apprehension of truth in an open fellowship of maturing believers. Openness and maturing does not survive well in a context of defensiveness and suspicion. It is enabled by widening the circle of disciples who are searching for all that God intends for the whole church to know and be and do. Much overblown has been our movement's historic fear of theological contamination if we should involve ourselves seriously with Christians whose perspectives differ at points from our own. Some of us now are learning that we ought to believe more strongly that truth is not that fragile and that God still superintends the life of his faithful people. In the end, it is not light that yields to darkness, but darkness to light.

350

8. *Baptism: Study of an Apparent Doctrinal Difference.*
Neither body involved in this Open Forum process is
creedal in nature, nor by tradition is either "fundamentalist"
in the rigid, doctrinaire sense of this term. Doctrinal
positions, nonetheless, have been explored in considerable
detail, with only a few found to be stubbornly troublesome
between us. Theological "style" and emphasis occasionally
vary between our groups, mostly products of our differing
histories of origin. A key reason appears to be the impact
of aspects of the "Enlightenment" on one group and the
more experience-oriented impact of American revivalism
on the other.

The doctrinal dialogue portion of the Open Forum often
has focused its attention on the subject of Christian baptism. Both groups believe baptism to be a biblical mandate
and best administered by immersion. We agree that genuine
repentance of sin is required prior to baptism, thus making
this sacred practice not appropriate for infants. We agree
further that there is no merit leading to salvation in the
baptismal mechanics themselves—baptism is not what
saves. With all this agreement, however, one key area
related to baptism remains unresolved. Our dialogue
partner tends to see the phrase "for the remission of sins"
necessarily related closely to baptism, although by this
association not meaning "baptismal regeneration." We have
explored why the retention of this phrase with baptism is
seen as so crucial by one group and why it is a matter of
substantial concern for the other. Language certainly is one
problem. Time and patient listenings are required to really
hear and understand each other here. But language is not all
of the problem.

One insight we have gained has been of some help. Our
differing approaches to baptism and "the remission of sins,"
obviously a biblical phrase, can be explained in part by the
differing "enemies" each group has been fighting over the
decades. The Christian Churches/Churches of Christ is a
movement that has been resisting "faith-only" revivalism
and "liberalism" as represented to them by the Disciples of
Christ wing of the restorationist movement. "For the remission of sins" has become a touchstone in their eyes for strict
biblical obedience. The Church of God, on the other hand,
has been resisting Roman Catholicism and her "Protestant
daughters." Our movement has been very sensitive about

anything that appears to retain for establishment Christianity a control over the dispensing of God's grace through given church rites, including baptism.

9. *We Suffer a Common Dilemma.* Both dialogue bodies have the dilemma of freedom-spontaneity versus efficiency-accountability in church life. Both groups resist a denominationalizing trend, but also seek some path to more efficiency and mutual accountability. Here is a central dilemma we share, one not easily resolved. While neither of us wants any more church structure, both are searching for better ways to be accountable and effective. No one has yet arrived at the ideal place. Are there ways that we can assist each other along this uncharted path? We are learning that there are.

10. *Testimony Is a Good Strategy.* A productive way to proceed in demonstrating the potential meaningfulness of this Open Forum is to take local and practical action. In Cincinnati, Ohio, for instance, pastors and spouses from each of these church groups now have become acquainted and mutually supportive. Professors and administrators from some Church of God schools have met some of their counterparts. Visits and guest lectures across group lines have begun. Such developments are encouraging and might be repeated elsewhere with good benefit. All of these Open Forum meetings and talk are helpful only when real relationships evolve and prove productive for the Kingdom of God. Some good things have happened and need to be told widely.

11. *Each Group Is Challenged To Widen the Dialogue Circle.* More dialogue participants are invited and more wisdom is needed. The bottom line is this—two similar groups of God's children have begun an honest quest for a fuller realization of the divine will for our day. The goal is elusive, but since it seems divinely motivated, the quest goes on.

Editor's Note: For a full accounting of the process and results of this multi-year dialogue, along with extensive appendixes of classic unity documents emerging from these two traditions, see Barry Callen and James North, *Coming Together In Christ (1997)*.

196. The Faith and Order Movement: Holiness Church Participation

Editor's Note: This essay by Gilbert W. Stafford was published in 1997 both in the *Wesleyan Theological Journal* (Spring 1997) and as Appendix H in the Barry Callen/James North book *Coming Together In Christ*. Beginning in 1984 Dr. Stafford represented the Commission on Christian Unity of the Church of God (Anderson) at meetings of Faith and Order. Early in the article he provides a good history of Faith and Order and then offers his view of the several reasons why holiness bodies like the Church of God should participate actively in such an ecumenical body. His reasons are reproduced below.

1. Participation is **an opportunity to learn *about* other traditions in a dialogical setting**. One of the more rewarding intellectual experiences of my life was my sub-group's discussion in an earlier triennium (as it was then) of our several understandings of apostolic faith. The fact that each Christian tradition makes claims of being apostolic in its faith provided a basis for vigorous discussion. In our extended deliberations we learned enough about each other's traditions to be able to identify points both of agreement and of divergence. We came to appreciate that all of us agree that being a church of apostolic faith includes at least these basic components: the confession that Jesus Christ is God and Savior; the guidance and inspiration of the Holy Spirit; the authoritative witness of the Scriptures; and the church as the community of faithful worship, witness, and service in the world. But we differ when it comes to other characteristics of what it means to be apostolic. Some traditions emphasize normative creedal and confessional statements; others emphasize normative teaching offices and polities; and others emphasize normative experiences of conversion, sanctification, holiness, and liberation.[1]

2. Faith and Order is an opportunity **to learn *from* other traditions**. Other traditions of the faith ask questions about one's own tradition that insiders tend not to ask. Once in a discussion about creeds, I explained that traditionally my

---

1. See Thaddeus D. Horgam (ed.), *Apostolic Faith in America* (Grand Rapids: Eerdmans, 1988), 60-66.

own church (Church of God, Anderson) has been anti-creedalistic and that we even have a song one stanza of which begins: "The day of sects and creeds for us forever-more is past."[2] "What!" an Orthodox priest exclaimed, "how can you be Christian if you don't believe something?" He asked the right question and pressed the right issues for a tradition that has perhaps been too unreflective in its anti-creed rhetoric.

3. Faith and Order provides **an arena of discussion with a wide spectrum of Christian traditions**. This arena is wider than any other I know. Obviously, wide spectrums can be found in seminaries, theological forums, the acade-my, and in informal conversations. That which makes Faith and Order distinct from these, however, is that its members are, for the most part, chosen in some official way to represent their respective churches or organizations. In my case, I am elected by the Commission on Christian Unity of the Church of God, a commission made up both of representatives from our several national agencies and persons elected by the General Assembly of the Church of God.

The role of a participant is not that of setting forth his or her own personal theological positions, but those of the church being represented. Faith and Order participants are, in a sense, personifications of the differing traditions of Christian faith. For instance, when in my own sub-group Samuel Nafzger of the Lutheran Church—Missouri Synod speaks, we want him to give voice to the Missouri Synod. The assignment is not "Tell us what you personally think about this issue," but "Tell us, to the best of your ability, what you believe your church tradition holds concerning this matter." That goes even for the most overtly independent participants. When Doug Foster, a member of the Churches of Christ (non-instrumental), speaks, he, true to his tradi-tion, makes it clear that he speaks only as Doug Foster, but we push him to represent to us, to the best of his ability, the Church of Christ tradition, not the Doug Foster view.

Where else can one find such a wide spectrum of thought being expressed by those who seek earnestly to speak for

2. Charles W. Naylor, "The Church's Jubilee,"*Worship the Lord: Hymnal of the Church of God* (Anderson: Warner Press, 1989), 312.

the respective traditions out of which they come? In my sub-group this quadrennium are representatives from churches as diverse as United Methodist, Orthodox, Roman Catholic, Churches of Christ (non-instrumental), Quaker, Evangelical Lutheran, Reformed Church in America, Assemblies of God, Presbyterian, United Church of Christ, National Baptist, and Church of God (Anderson).

4. Faith and Order provides each participant the opportunity **to teach other traditions about one's own tradition**. It is as though each tradition has the opportunity to bring other Christian traditions into its classroom for a short while for the purpose of teaching something about the Christian faith which it believes God has entrusted to it. Over the course of several years, for example, I have had the opportunity to present to my colleagues in Faith and Order several short papers: two on "The Apostolic Faith" as understood by the Church of God (Anderson), another titled "The Holy Spirit and the Experience of Church," and two papers on authority: "Authority in the Church of God (Anderson...)" and "Authorities for Making Decisions in the Church of God...". Also, I prepared a paper in answer to the question: "What would be the prerequisites for the Church of God (Anderson) to become a part of a Christian organization which is inclusive of Christian faith in its widest possible spectrum?" Another paper was prepared under the title, "Visioning for Koinonia in the Life of the Church." All of these were opportunities to teach others about matters which my church believes are crucial if the church at large is to be in health.

More recently, my papers have centered especially on our identification as a holiness church. I presented a paper titled: "The Nineteenth Century Holiness Movement and Christian Unity." At the time of this writing, I am working with two other colleagues on presentations for an upcoming meeting in New Orleans. The first project has to do with "The Unitive Power of Holiness." The sub-group will consider my paper from the holiness perspective and that of Father Kevin McMorrow, editor of *Ecumenical Trends*, from the Roman Catholic perspective. Upon exchanging papers, each of us will write a response that will include three components: points of resonance with each other, differences, and points at which we simply do not understand the other. These four papers, then, will be presented to our sub-group for discussion.

The second project will use the same dialogical method on the subject of "The Hermeneutics of Reconciliation in Worship." My partner is John Erickson, professor of theology at St. Vladimir's Orthodox Theological Seminary in Crestwood, New York. In preparation for this assignment, Professor Erickson told me that since he had never worshipped in a holiness church, he would like to have that experience. I put him in touch with a Church of God congregation which, without my knowing it, turned out to be close to St. Vladimir's. He has already worshipped there and has invited the Church of God to be guests at St. Vladimir's. In New Orleans, he and I will present our papers to the plenary, which we hope will be enriched both by holiness and orthodox insights.

5. Faith and Order work is the opportunity for one's own tradition to **recognize in other traditions dimensions of the apostolic faith which lie dormant in one's own**. While for one Christian tradition verbal confession about the person and work of Christ may be very much alive, an emphasis on the converting ministry of Christ in the here and now may lie dormant. In another tradition the enlivening presence of the Holy Spirit may be very much front and center, but the hard sayings about Kingdom life may lie dormant. For still another tradition an emphasis on personal conversion may be alive, but communal confession of the faith may be dormant. And for another tradition Kingdom teachings may be considered with great seriousness, but the joy of the risen Christ may be dormant. Faith and Order provides an ecclesial opportunity for each tradition of the faith to feed into the bloodstream of other traditions. It is in this kind of setting that the emphasis on personal sanctification, which holiness churches are convinced is part and parcel of the apostolic faith, can be fed into the bloodstream of a wide spectrum of other Christian traditions.

An example of how this happens is reflected in the following segment of the summary report of the last quadrennium:

At Newark the Episcopal representative was inspired by what the Church of God (Anderson) representative had said about. . .join[ing] his church. When

356

asked how people become members, he replied: "The process would be similar to the acceptance around this table. None of us has been formally 'checked out.' We sense some basic assumptions as we talk with each other. We share. It's not legalistic...." As the representative of the Church of God (Cleveland) said in response to the information about the lack of formal joining in the Church of God (Anderson): "You are probably providing a model for the future, where things aren't so sharply defined as [they are] by organizational entities."[3]

Whether one agrees with the subject mentioned in this excerpt is not the point. It is simply an illustration of how one tradition can feed into the bloodstream of other traditions. In this instance an anabaptist-holiness tradition, a pentecostal-holiness tradition, and a mainline-anglican tradition were engaged in conversation about a new paradigm never before considered by some.

I cherish the possibility of the Church of the Nazarene, the Wesleyan Church, the Free Methodist Church, the Salvation Army, and others, *as churches*, taking advantage of the Faith and Order opportunity to feed their own rich understandings of the apostolic faith into the bloodstream of the wider church.

6. Faith and Order is the opportunity **to develop a deeper understanding and appreciation of one's own tradition**. It is both refreshing and challenging to explain one's tradition to those who may be learning about it for the first time. As we are pressed to explain the meaning of a particular aspect of our tradition, we are required to rethink the dynamics of it. That which within the circles of the tradition itself is dealt with in a shorthand way has to be written out in longhand, so to speak, for those unacquainted with it. The end result is that one's understanding of one's own tradition matures.

7. Faith and Order work is the opportunity for churches **to guard against becoming root bound** within their own

---

3. O. C. Edwards in "Faith and Order Reports 1992-1995" (New York: The National Council of the Churches of Christ in the U.S.A. 1995), 21.

narrower tradition. Just as root-bound plants eventually die, so do Christian traditions that limit themselves to their own little bit of Christian soil. Doctrinal development in controlled theological hot houses may lead to only superficially healthy churches. In order to be in health, all churches need to develop in the open spaces of doctrinal discussions in the church at large.

8. Faith and Order is the **opportunity for a wide spectrum of ecclesial bodies to work together** in theological endeavors. In 1982 at a Faith and Order meeting in Lima, Peru, over one hundred theologians unanimously agreed to present a statement for common study by and official responses from any and all churches willing to do so. Published under the title "Baptism, Eucharist and Ministry" (BEM), it is the product of some fifty years of study and consultation representing Orthodox, Catholic, Lutheran, Anglican, Reformed, Methodist, Disciples, Methodist, Adventist, and Pentecostal traditions. BEM has become one of the more widely discussed theological documents in the church's history.

In 1984, the Believers Church Conference (consisting of churches that stress believer's baptism) was hosted by Anderson School of Theology for the purpose of discussing the baptism section of BEM. Participants included Brethren, Mennonite, Church of God (Anderson), Adventist, Churches of Christ, Disciples, and Baptist theologians and church historians. But also present were scholars from infant baptism churches, including the associate director of Faith and Order (NCCC), Brother Jeffrey Gros, a Roman Catholic. On the basis of four days of papers and discussion, the conference affirmed eight points of agreement with BEM on baptism, stated six points of disagreement, listed two consequences that so-called believers churches can draw from BEM for their relationships and dialogues with other churches, and stated four contributions that BEM can make to them as believer-baptism churches. The report concludes by giving three suggestions for the ongoing work of Faith and Order, which included the view of some in the conference that "Scripture. . .[should] be regarded as the sole source and criterion of Christian belief, standing as the authoritative corrective to our various traditions."[4]

My only reason for lifting up this last issue is not to emphasize the "Bible only" position, but to use it as an illustration of the opportunity that Faith and Order both provides and promotes for a wide spectrum of ecclesial traditions to be heard as they work together in theological endeavors.

One of John Wesley's well-known sermons is on the "Catholic Spirit." His text is 2 Kings 10:15, "Is thine heart right, as my heart is with thy heart: And Jehonadab answered, It is. If it be, give me thine hand." In the sermon, Wesley spells out what he has in mind by one's heart being right: it is right with God; it believes in the Lord Jesus Christ; it is "filled with the energy of love"; it is doing the will of God; it serves the Lord with reverence; it is right toward one's neighbor; and it shows love by what it does.

This "catholic spirit" is to be expressed both towards those outside the faith and within. Regarding those outside the faith, Wesley says that the person with a catholic spirit "embraces with strong and cordial affection neighbors and strangers, friends and enemies. This is catholic or universal love. And he that has this is of a catholic spirit. For love alone gives the title to this character: catholic love is a catholic spirit" (III.4).

Following this consideration, Wesley then deals with the catholic spirit in relation to fellow believers. He refers to love for all "whatever opinion or worship or congregation, who believe in the Lord Jesus Christ, who love God and man, who, rejoicing to please and fearing to offend God, are careful to abstain from evil and zealous of good works." Continuing, Wesley says that the one who is of a truly catholic spirit, "having an unspeakable tenderness for their persons and longing for their welfare, does not cease to commend them to God in prayer as well as to plead their cause before men; who speaks comfortably to them and labours by all his words to strengthen their hands in God. He assists them to the uttermost of his power in all things, spiritual and temporal. He is ready 'to spend and be spent for them' [cf. 2 Cor. 12:15], yea, 'to lay down his life for' their sake [Jn. 15:13]" [III.5].[5]

---

4. Merle Strege (ed.), *Baptism and Church; A Believers' Church Vision* (Grand Rapids: Sagamore, 1986), 201.
5. See Johh Wesley, ed. Albert C. Outler (New York: Oxford University Press, 1964), 91-104.

9. Faith and Order provides the opportunity for us to become **interpreters of other traditions at points where they may be misunderstood**. A personal example of this is Cecil Robeck's information about the traditional pentecostal understanding regarding the distinction between tongues as the initial evidence of baptism in the Holy Spirit and the gift of tongues. Robeck, professor at Fuller and a representative of the Assemblies of God, taught all of us in that particular discussion that the classical pentecostal position is not, as some non-pentecostals think, that all Spirit-baptized persons have the gift of tongues. Rather, tongues speaking is simply an initial evidence of the baptism. Consequently, a person baptized in the Holy Spirit may initially speak in tongues but never again do so because they do not have the gift.

As a result of that Faith and Order "lecture," I, as a non-pentecostal, have been able to teach others about a pentecostal understanding and to correct a widespread misunderstanding in my own church that pentecostals believe that all should have the gift of tongues. Many among us point to 1 Corinthians 12:30 which asks rhetorically, "Do all speak in tongues?" and has the implied answer that not all do. Why, then, they want to know, can't pentecostal people see the error of their ways? But that is to misunderstand the pentecostal position. Robeck has helped me as a seminary teacher, preacher, and writer to fulfill an important role of clarifying the pentecostal position among my own people, not so that they will become pentecostals, but so that they will relate to others of "like precious faith" on the basis of accurate information instead of misinformation. Christian charity demands no less. In like manner, would it not be helpful to have more people in non-holiness churches *clarifying* for those traditions holiness terminology such as "Christian perfection" and "entire sanctification"?

Faith and Order is certainly no panacea for the dividedness of Christ's church, but it is an opportunity for that dividedness to be addressed within the context of a broad spectrum of Christian faith traditions. Many have been the times when I have been thoroughly frustrated in the meetings and by the process. There have been times when I have wondered whether it was worthwhile. But the benefits far outweigh the liabilities.

360

At Faith and Order meetings (twice a year), I often desire the participation of more of my holiness colleagues in the faith. By participating, a church has much to gain. Not only may it feed into the bloodstream of the wider Christian community its own treasures of the apostolic faith, but also it can be immeasurably enriched by the treasures of the same faith which others feed into the bloodstream. But of greatest importance is this: Faith and Order is one additional small step toward the fulfillment of our Lord's prayer in John 17:21-22 that we "may all be one," to the end "that the world may believe." It is one additional feeble attempt toward responding positively to Paul's plea in Ephesians 4:1-3 for us "to lead a life worthy of the calling to which [we]. . .have been called. . .making every effort to maintain the unity of the Spirit in the bond of peace."

Part Five:
SPREADING THE LIGHT
INTERNATIONAL VISION, INITIATIVES, PARTNERSHIPS

Editor's Note: From the earliest years of the Church of God movement, the leaders saw their mission as global in scope. Their vision was to get a vital message out to the whole world. The presses of the Gospel Trumpet Company turned out tons of gospel literature that found their way to country after country. God was believed to be renewing the church, the whole church, beyond the restrictions of all human boundaries. The might be limited before Christ would return. The story had to be told! A key vehicle for the early years of telling was the periodical the *Gospel Trumpet*.

197. Early Efforts Toward a World Vision

Editor's Note: The following are excerpts from chapter six of John W. V. Smith's *The Quest for Holiness and Unity* (Warner Press, 1980).

As would be expected, the initial thrust of evangelistic efforts by the "flying ministry" was concentrated in the United States. The calls for meetings were so numerous. . .that every available worker was traveling constantly in response to requests. There was little time to sit and dream of new worlds to conquer. It needs to be noted, however, that even during the first decade of the movement's history [1880s] there were several contacts and some overt efforts to extend the reform work beyond the national borders. By the turn of the [twentieth] century the international activity was extensive, and by the time of the first organization of any planned effort through the creation of a "missionary committee" in 1909 the work was global. This chapter will review the highlights of this period of spontaneous, unstructured expansion of the movement to worldwide proportions.

Since a great deal of the activity of the publishing work and the itinerant ministry was centered in the upper Middle West, it was only natural that the first international extension of the message was to Canada. The first contact made by the movement to this northern neighbor of the United States was through the printed pages of the *Gospel Trumpet.*

The first extension of the Church of God reformation movement beyond the southern border of the United States was initiated by Benjamin F. Elliott (1859-1926). In 1889 Elliott, a former Methodist preacher, began preaching in the streets of Santa Barbara, California. Around 1891 he became impressed with the need to spread the gospel to the Spanish-speaking people. In the fall of 1891 Elliott was led to go into Lower California (Baja Calif.), Mexico.[1]

In addition to its extension to these North American neighbor countries of Canada and Mexico, the Church of God, by the time of the formation of the Missionary Committee in 1909, had spread to or had significant contacts in at least seventeen other countries. In the British Isles the movement was functioning in England, Scotland, and Ireland. On the European continent there were congregations or known adherents in Germany, Switzerland, Denmark, Sweden, Poland, and Russia. In Asia there were either missionaries or native pastors in China and Japan, and in India there was significant work developing from four widely separated geographic centers. Egypt was the only African nation represented. The continent of Australia also had been reached and there were congregations on at least three islands in the West Indies: Jamaica, Trinidad, and Bermuda.

Focus on giving for world mission,
Anderson Camp Meeting, 1947

In reviewing this world-wide expansion without benefit of a sending agency or any other method of assuring the underwriting of travel expense and support, one cannot help being struck with some sense of amazement that such could happen. While it is true that there was a certain "naturalness" about much of the international activity—German immigrants went to Germany, Scots to Scotland, Swedes to Sweden—there was more than the desire to share a good thing with kith and kin. The same spirit which drove the "flying messengers" to crisscross the North American continent also motivated these global itinerants. They were in possession of a message which they believed all the people in the world ought to hear. Any place on the earth was a potential "field" for witness and evangelization simply because the people there had

---

1. For biographical and ministry detail about this first Church of God missionary, including his meeting D. S. Warner in Los Angeles in 1892, see Maurice Caldwell in *Church of God Missions* (June, 1992), 2-3.

not yet heard. While being "burdened for" or "led to" a given place often was related to previous contacts or information, the "call" was considered to be God-sent and there was a willingness to respond with faith that the means would be provided. By 1909 [when the Missionary Board in the United States was first being formed] more than two dozen people were "out there," by faith, sharing the message in at least twenty countries of the world.

198. Waking Sounds in Western Canada

Walter Froese, *Sounding Forth the Gospel on the Prairies*
(Camrose, Alberta: Gospel Contact Press, 1982).

The beginnings of the Church of God reformation movement in western Canada is closely connected with a religious journal called the *Gospel Trumpet*. This weekly periodical was the mouthpiece of some enthusiastic people who wanted to spread the good news of salvation to sinners, sanctification to the redeemed, divine healing to the bodily sick, and Christian unity to all true believers.

The *Gospel Trumpet* began in 1881 with a relatively unknown middle-aged preacher, Daniel S. Warner, in the state of Indiana. Due to the fiery enthusiasm of Warner and the devout dedication of his fellow workers, the circulation of the journal grew quickly. In 1895, a German language edition of the paper, called the *Evangeliums Posaune*, started to appear so that the great truths of the budding movement could spread among the many Americans of German descent. A few years later, a Dano-Norwegian and even a Swedish version of the *Trumpet* found numerous avid readers.

These various versions of the *Gospel Trumpet* were sent to subscribers in diverse corners of the globe. A note in the *Gospel Trumpet* of 1882 suggests that the paper was greatly appreciated in eastern Canada at that early date, but it is not known when the *Trumpet* found its first readers on the Canadian prairies. Many dedicated workers were needed for the ever increasing tasks related to publishing the periodical and around the turn of the century even Canadians—as many as thirteen at one time—had joined the "Trumpet Family" as helpers at the place where the English and German *Gospel Trumpets* were edited and printed.

During the first decade of the twentieth century the literary "Trumpets" that came into Canada were augmented by human messengers who ventured into the vast northwest. In 1905, William Ebel, a man who had helped in the publication of the *Evangeliums Posaune* for many years, came to Winnipeg and gathered a small group of German Church of God saints. On April 28, 1906, William H. Smith, a young black minister from Colorado, arrived in Edmonton and immediately began to "preach the gospel on the streets and from house to house and distribute *Trumpets* and tracts" (*Gospel Trumpet*, 1909, p. 620). And in 1907, Gottlieb Butgereit, a pastor from North Dakota who was fluent in both English and German, came to southeastern Alberta and established a work near Irvine. Thus the truth became accepted and grew in western Canada (9-10).

Editor's Note: In 1888 the Daniel Warner evangelistic company had responded to an invitation and journeyed to Ontario, Canada. They found several groups of believers who knew the teachings of the Church of God movement through the preaching of Mrs. Eliza White who had subscribed to the *Gospel Trumpet* since 1882. The company stayed four months and established three congregations and gathered forty new subscribers to the *Trumpet*. See Beverley Anderson's master's thesis, "A History of the Church of God in Ontario, 1882-1955."

199. Rise of the Church of God in Europe

Excerpted from *Church of God in Europe, 1902-1973*, ed. by Willi Krenz (European Committee, 1973).

Willi Krenz
Germany

George Vielguth from the United States came to Germany in 1901 to proclaim the truth of the gospel, which he had learned to love in America. He began to distribute Christian literature in Hamburg. While doing so he met a Christian lady, Mrs. Niemann, who helped to make other contacts. It did not take long until a small congregation was formed which became very active. One day George Vielguth got a newspaper in his hands in which he found an advertisement of a Christian music shop in Herne, Ruhrvaley. To this address he mailed an American-German *Gospel Trumpet*. In reply, the owner, Mr. Gabel, extended an invitation to Vielguth with the request that hold meetings in his place. Very soon connections were made in Essen.

In 1903, Karl Arbeiter from the United States came and continued the work while George Vielguth left for Russia to spread the gospel there, and then go back to the United States. The first conference of the Church of God in Germany was held in Gelsenkirchen-Horst during the Christmas season in 1906. Vielguth had been invited from the United States to be the guest speaker. According to the proposal of George Vielguth, a Missionary Home was established in a rented house at Essen in 1907, which became a missions and Bible training center. Otto Doebert came from America and was entrusted

365

with the management of the Missionary Home after he had gone on a missionary trip to Russia. The annual Conference held at Essen on Christmas developed into a camp meeting. In the Ruhr area the work was extended to several cities owing to the influence of the Missionary Home. In Recklinghausen there lived some Dutch people who came to the services, among them the brothers Jeeninga, who got converted to the Lord and started meeting places in Holland. From Germany many missionary efforts were made into Russia, Latvia, Poland, Ukraine, Hungary, Rumania, Bulgaria, and Switzerland.

In 1922 a decision was made to issue the first *Gospel Trumpet* in Essen, Germany. World War II destroyed most of the work. Church buildings were demolished and church members were scattered. It had to be started again literally among the ruins. Very many persons and families emigrated to the United States or Canada. The first church building after World War II was built by the church in Essen and was dedicated in 1949. Gerhard Klabunde did not only serve as pastor of the Essen church, but founded the printing shop "Wickenburg" in the basement of the new building in 1952. At Frizlar, Ernst Kersten began the new Bible School in 1948. Three World Conferences of the Church of God have convened in Germany. The first was held in 1955 at Fritzlar, the second in 1959 at Essen, the third in 1963 at Bochum [and now a fourth, convened in Wiesbaden in 1991—see Entry 205 on the history of World Conferences].

Editor's Note: In 1994 the churches in Germany convened in Hamburg, in part to celebrate a century of the work of the Church of God in Germany. Barry L. Callen from Anderson University in the United States was the invited guest speaker.

200. Establishing the North American Missionary Board

Editor's Note: For detail on the initial establishing of a missionary board in Anderson, Indiana, see entry 26 and chapter two of Lester Crose's *Passport for a Reformation* (Anderson, Ind.: Warner Press, 1981). Long before there was such a board, however, there was cross-cultural missionary outreach in the Church of God. A key year was 1892.

. . .a former Methodist minister and professor of Greek at the University of Southern California, Benjamin F. Elliott, felt a call to preach to the Spanish-speaking people who lived near Santa Barbara, California.... Elliott had cast his lot with the Church of God movement in the mid-1880s.... By the end of the year [1892] he and his young son were in

San Diego, awaiting the financial means that would open the way for them to sail to Ensenada, on the Baja Peninsula of Mexico. Who should they encounter during their wait but D. S. Warner, then on a preaching tour through the far west. As Elliott, his son, and their co-worker S. C. Shaw waited on the dock, Warner pressed into Elliott's hand the money necessary to purchase their passage to Mexico. In that moment cross-cultural mission was born among Church of God people. While the Elliott missionary party laid plans for Mexico, J. H. Rupert and W. J. Henry sailed across the Atlantic and opened a mission in England (23-24).

201. Circling the Globe: Beginnings in the Near East, Far East, Latin America, and East Africa

by Lester A. Crose,
Passport for a Reformation (1981),
33-35, 46, 70-71, 77-78

THE NEAR EAST: EGYPT AND SYRIA

When E. E. Byrum and company were on their way to India in 1904 they stopped for several days in Egypt, visiting both Alexandria and Cairo. They went on the streets distributing literature but had no particular results. But through reading his Bible, an Armenian medical doctor named G. K. Ouzounian, in Alexandria, received the light the following year calling him out of Babylon (denominations) into the unity of the people of God. Two years later, at the invitation of Hanna Arsanious, an Egyptian Christian who had read some Church of God literature and had written to America for someone to come to Egypt to help, George P. Tasker and Hiram A. Brooks stopped in Egypt for an extended visit on their way to India. This was a good opening. They were permitted to distribute literature and to conduct evangelistic services.

Meetings were conducted primarily in Alexandria and Assiut in Upper Egypt. There appeared to be real potential, but both the visitors, and the few Egyptians felt the need for a missionary to come immediately. E. A. Reardon left the missionary home in Chicago at once and arrived in Egypt before Tasker and Brooks went on to India. Reardon remained in Egypt for only seven months, living in Assiut, but he helped build a foundation for the work in Assiut under the leadership of Mossad Armanious and in Alexandria under G. K. Ouzounian. The seed had been planted and was beginning to bear fruit, but after Reardon returned to America no resident missionaries of the Church of God were sent to Egypt until 1923, even though a request for missionaries from the saints in Egypt was frequent. Contacts were maintained through correspondence and occasional visits by missionaries passing through Egypt.

A kind of historical accident occurred one day in 1907 on a street in downtown Cairo. Tasker, Brooks, and Reardon met Vartan Atchinak and his wife who, along with her sister Asma Trad, had started the Bible Lands Gospel Mission in Schweifat, a village on the Lebanese hillside just out of Beirut. The Atchinaks were on their way to America to find teachers for the school. They would prefer Church of God teachers. Even though the response was not immediate, Church of God missionary teachers did arrive later in Syria.

THE FAR EAST: JAPAN AND CHINA

Crossing the bay between San Francisco and Oakland on a train ferry, A. U. Yajima, a young Japanese Presbyterian minister from Hawaii, picked up and read a copy of the *Gospel Trumpet*. His heart was touched with the truth contained therein. Later, in response to a letter he wrote to E. E. Byrum, Yajima was told to contact J. D. Hatch in Los Angeles. Hatch took Yajima to the Lodi Camp Meeting in central California, which was the main camp meeting in California at the time. During that meeting Yajima was impressed to seek conversion, which he had never experienced, and to ask for more light on the truth of God's Word. My father, John D. Crose, then a young minister, gathered along with others around A. U. Yajima as he knelt at the altar

After working briefly in the Gospel Trumpet office in Moundsville, West Virginia, Yajima felt called of God to return to his homeland, Japan, and take the Good News to his own people. Arriving in Tokyo in 1908, he started a work of the Church of God by doing personal visitation, conducting meetings and having a paper printed called *Pure Gospel*. He felt the need for assistance, and so he wrote to America for missionaries. The response was almost immediate. J. D. Hatch and W. G. and Josie Alexander, along with their daughter Grace, sailed for Japan in 1909. The Alexanders had been impressed by Yajima at the Lodi Camp Meeting and had felt the call to Japan at that time.

William J. Hunnex, his wife, and their two sons survived the Boxer Rebellion in China. During 1904 the parents sent William and Charles to America for higher education. Soon after their arrival both came into contact with the movement, but in different places. By 1905 both young men were at Moundsville working in the Gospel Trumpet office, and they generated considerable enthusiasm regarding missionary work in China. Both of them wanted to be missionaries to China. Having grown up there, they knew the language and the culture. William A. Hunnex married Gloria Hale and they left for China in 1909 to begin a work in Chinkiang. Charles waited another year before he was ready to go.

KENYA, EAST AFRICA

Byrum Makokha
Kenya

In Kenya, East Africa, there was preparation for Church of God entry into that country. By 1901 the railroad from Mombasa and Nairobi had reached Kisumu on Lake Victoria. This opened up the Western Province. American Quakers from Richmond, Indiana, settled at Kaimosi in 1902 and the Church Missionary Society of the Church of England at Maseno in 1908. A. W. Baker, a Christian British attorney in Johannesburg, South Africa, and founder of the South African Compounds and Interior Mission, sent Robert Wilson north to Kenya to establish a mission in the interior among primitive African tribes. Following some exploration Wilson decided on a large piece of land given by Chief Otieno in Bunyore, situated between Kaimosi and Maseno. In 1905 this new mission was started and named Kima, Wilson's nickname for his wife. In the local vernacular "Kima" meant "anything with life having a healthy condition." How appropriate for what Kima was destined to become in terms of Christian life and witness.

H. C. and Gertrude Kramer had been in Kenya for several years as American Quaker missionaries working with the South Africa Compound and Interior Mission and were due a furlough. By then A. W. Baker in South Africa felt he could no longer sponsor and support his mission in Kenya, and so he asked the Kramers to seek out a church in America that would be willing to assume responsibility for the mission in Kenya. Baker said that mission should (1) not stress "the speaking in tongues"; (2) teach the Bible as the Word of God; and (3) teach the unity of God's people.

The Kramers had been receiving the *Gospel Trumpet* literature irregularly for several years, and they had come to appreciate its teachings. So during their furlough in the spring of 1921, while visiting their sponsoring family in Pomona, California, they became acquainted with Abram and William Bixler, two brothers in the Church of God congregation there. Through the Bixlers' influence and that of the congregation, the Kramers embraced the truth. Upon hearing of the offer being made by A. W. Baker, William Bixler felt strongly that the Kramers should present the opportunity in Kenya to the Missionary Board. Correspondence with the Board took place, and the congregation in Pomona paid the train fare for the Kramers to be in Anderson for the camp meeting and the meeting of the Missionary Board. Baker's offer was presented to the Board, including what it would cost. The price was fifteen hundred dollars plus the cost of Mabel Baker's residence and a residence for another missionary family. Board members were obviously interested in this opportunity to enter East Africa. But before a final decision could be made, some investigation was necessary. Since Sam Joiner and his wife had expressed an earlier interest in Africa, the Board sent them to Kenya. Together with W. J. Bailey they looked into the condition of the mission at Kima and sent back a favorable report to the Board. Transfer of the mission was negotiated and completed. In the end Baker turned over everything without cost to the Missionary Board. He was well pleased with the attitude of the Board and the beliefs of the Church of God. During the meeting of the Board, Henry and Gertrude Kramer were appointed as missionaries of the Church of God, as were the Joiners. Also, Mable Baker was accepted as a Church of God missionary. Ruth Fisher was appointed as a missionary to Kenya to teach the missionaries' children, and she went to Kenya with the Kramers.

LATIN AMERICA: BRAZIL AND ARGENTINA

Mario Hort
Brazil

Victor Ruzak
Argentina

To escape the results of the 1917 communist take-over in Russia, Adolf Weidman and twenty-two families went first to Germany and then on to Brazil in 1923. This colony of German Church of God refugees settled in Santa Catarina. They formed a congregation and kept in touch with the German work in America centered in York, Nebraska. More German Christians, led by Edward Wagner, fled Poland and settled in Rio Das Antas in Brazil. Others took up residence in the state of Sao Paulo, while the Koenig family found a home in the city of Curitiba.

The first Church of God camp meeting in Brazil was held by the German believers at Nova Esperanza in 1929. By 1931 the Church of God in Brazil became officially registered. David Meier, a German American, and his family felt called to missionary service among the German immigrants in Brazil and arrived there in 1935. For some time he was forced to teach school to provide food for his family. Meier was the first evangelist to go to Argentina, holding meetings in Alem in Misiones Province. His work was also among German immigrants. Solomon Weissburger, his son Heinrich, and their families fled Germany as Hitler began to persecute the Jews. They settled in Rio Das Antas in Brazil. During World War II all these colonies of German Church of God Christians had to remain quiet. For a time the German language was forbidden in Brazil, and on occasion some people endured imprisonment just because they were Germans.

In Argentina, Adolf Weidmann became the strong leader at Alam. Under capable leadership the work among these German-speaking people grew slowly but surely. And they were very German, reflecting their culture in almost every aspect of their lives. There were only rare attempts to do any evangelizing among the Portuguese-speaking people in Brazil or the Spanish-speaking people in Argentina.

> *Editor's Note*: Also see: (1) Raymond Hastings, "The Church of God in Jamaica," a 1959 masters thesis at Anderson University School of Theology; (2) James Royster, "A History of the Church of God in South India, 1897-1960," a 1967 dissertation, Hartford Seminary Foundation.

202. On the Air! CBH

Christian Brotherhood Hour—Christians Broadcasting Hope

by Barry L. Callen

W. Dale Oldham

Two of God's chosen servants dreamed together about a broadcasting ministry of the Church of God. Each one had expertise in his own field—one the outstanding preacher, the other a competent producer and announcer. In the hearts of W. Dale Oldham and Richard Lee Meischke, the basic plan was born. The Brotherhood—now the Men of the Church of God—also caught the vision and launched "The National Radio Project." This new venture was under the care of the Board of Church Extension and Home Missions. In January, 1947, the program started on nineteen stations. The original flagship station was KGGF in Coffeyville, Kansas.

In the sanctuary of the old Park Place Church at Eighth Street and College Avenue, Anderson, Indiana, with recording equipment and engineer in the nursery adjacent to the sanctuary, the first Christian Brotherhood Hour programs were recorded on acetate discs. With Richard Meischke announcing, a quartet joined the Anderson College Choir under the direction of Dr. Robert A. Nicholson. Dr. Oldham, already a veteran broadcaster, was the dynamic speaker on the CBH program. Fred Shackleton arranged music and served as a featured soloist. The gracious Cynthia Kane charmed listeners with her all-girl choir. One of the early quartets was composed of Homer Schauer, Gene Dyer, Doug Oldham, and Lowell Williamson.

By the end of 1949, CHB was being heard over 128 stations in the United States and had moved south into Panama. In 1952 a studio was set up on South Meridian in Anderson. Soon production activities moved to Chicago. In 1955 a Radio and Television Commission was established formally under the Executive Council of the Church of God. Beloved was the Christian Brothers Quartet comprised of Paul Clausen, Ernie Gross, Doug Oldham, and Ronald Patty.

In 1961, Dr. Oldham, radio speaker, resigned as the pastor of Park Place Church of God in Anderson to devote fulltime to the Christian Brotherhood Hour (later renamed "Christians Broadcasting Hope," keeping the "CBH," but avoiding the sexist overtones of "brotherhood"). Soon he called on Paul E. Yerden to be his assistant in charge of promotion. By 1964 CBH aired from Alaska to Australia, from California to the Caribbean on 294 stations. In 1965 CBH was launched in Spanish and began reaching deep into the Latin American world. Fidel Zamorano was the original Spanish speaker and would serve in that role for thirty years.

When Dr. Oldham approached retirement age, the Radio and Television Commission sought for a new speaker to represent the church in its now worldwide ministry. R. Eugene Sterner, who had been associated with the work as director from 1954–1961, was asked to return as both director and speaker in 1968. With the return of J. Richard Lee (Richard Lee Meischke) in 1971 as producer and announcer, CBH took on a new sound, "The Sound

of the 70's." It now was reaching nearly every continent over 370 stations. The Gaither Trio and Doug Oldham became regular features on the program. Barbara Creager was deeply appreciated as a regular artist, and Imodean Lister brought her own unique style. Becoming widely recognized radio singing voices were those of the Leppien Sisters, the Singing Servants led by Dean Schield, and Sandi Patty.

Sandi and Ronald Patty

In 1974 the Radio and Television Commission made the decision to separate the two assignments of speaker and director to allow for more ministries by mass media and to make the speaker more available across the field. Phil M. Fair was named executive director. R. Eugene Sterner continued as the speaker. The Mass Communication Board of the Church of God, Inc., became an agency under the General Assembly in 1976, replacing the former Radio and Television Commission. Thus the scope of assignment was expanded for an even greater ministry. In June, 1976, the General Assembly approved the appointment of Dr. James Earl Massey as speaker-elect for the Christian Brotherhood Hour. His voice was heard regularly beginning July 1, 1977, when R. Eugene Sterner retired. Mort Crim became CBH-English announcer in 1978. Others were to follow.

Jim Lyon interviewing Martha McFadden for CBH "Viewpoint" broadcast.

The CBH-English speakers, then, have been W. Dale Oldham (1947–1968), R. Eugene Sterner (1968–1977), James Earl Massey (1977–1982), David Grubbs (1982–1986), Gilbert W. Stafford (1986–1996), and Jim Lyon (1996 to the present)—with the program now known as "Viewpoint." At the beginning of the twenty-first century, the CBH broadcasts cover nearly the whole world, going out in eight languages, including James Lyon (English), Gilbert Davila (Spanish), Daniel Mdobi (S wahili), Mario Hort (Portuguese), Asim Das (Oriya-India), Walentin Schule (Russian), Adel Masri and Riyal Hayek (Arabic), and an unnamed—for security reasons—Pastor X (Mandarin-China).

203. Organizational Restructuring: Key To Growth

by Robert W. Pearson

Who we are often determines what we see. This timeless principle is vividly illustrated in the made-for-television movie "The Great Outdoors." In the movie, John Candy plays Chet, a man vacationing with his family in a small lake community in the northern woods of Wisconsin. He and his family are surprised when his sister-in-law and her husband Roman drop by for an unexpected visit. Dan Ackroyd plays the part of Roman, who is cast as an entrepreneur known for shady business deals. As the two men sit on the porch of their cabin overlooking the lake, they start to talk. Roman, who sees himself as a wheeler-dealer, shares his vision with Chet. "I'll tell you what I see when I look out there. . .a mining operation, a green belt between the condos on the lake, and a waste management facility.... Now I ask you, Chet, what do you see?" "I, uh, I just see trees." "Well," replies Roman, "nobody ever accused you of having a grand vision!"[1] Chet saw trees because he was there to enjoy the breathtaking views. Roman saw business opportunity because he was an entrepreneur on the lookout for ways to make money. Who we are often determines how we see the world around us.

---

1. John Maxwell, *The 21 Irrefutable Laws of Leadership* (Nashville TN: Thomas Nelson Publishers, 1998), 84.

Growth Through the Struggle

The same identity and vision issues exist as sweeping changes take place in the Church of God Reformation Movement at the end of the twentieth and the beginning of the twenty-first centuries. There is in process a major restructuring of many of the North American and international ministries. We tend to view and evaluate these changes through the lenses of our generational, cultural, theological, and even geographical backgrounds and perspectives.

For instance, there were two very different responses to Leith Anderson's major report delivered in the June 1996 General Assembly of the Church of God meeting in Anderson Indiana [see Entries 65, 71].[2] As a formal consultant, Anderson had developed a proposed plan for restructuring the national ministries of the Church of God and had presented it to the Assembly. One of the more distinguished of the elder statespersons of the Church of God then stood before the Assembly and passionately spoke in opposition to the Assembly prematurely adopting these recommendations. He feared the possibility that the Church of God would leave behind its movemental roots and cement itself in new denominational trappings. The next person who approached the microphone was a young pastor of a large church who represented a new generation moving into national leadership. While this individual was sensitive to the fear represented by the former speaker, he expressed the view that the significant changes being proposed would give the Church of God the urgently needed opportunity to put real "move" back into the Movement.

When this second speaker sat down, the formal vote was taken. The General Assembly approved the consultant's recommendations in concept, and by a very large margin. Later, the consultant remarked to several Church of God national agency leaders that, with these two speakers and the subsequent vote, the mantle of the Movement's leadership had passed from one generation to another.

The Church of God has often wrestled with the tension of being movemental versus being denominational. This has been particularly evident during those periods in the Movement's history when the lack of dynamic and sustained growth has caused the church to examine how it is organized for ministry. At each one of these historic crossroads, church leaders have struggled to find ways to organize for more effective ministry, while not betraying the theological vision that brought the Movement into being. As a

---

2. Dr. Leith Anderson was retained as a consultant by the Leadership Council of the Church of God following the 1995 General Assembly when it was determined that the church was floundering in its attempts to change its structure to meet the needs of a new century and millennium. For one year he studied the history and theology of the Church of God, conducted extensive interviews with church leaders, and presented his recommendations to the 1996 General Assembly in a paper titled "Movement for the 21st Century."

result of the struggle during these pivotal times and the resulting restructuring actions, the church has been renewed and has enjoyed fresh bursts of growth.

It is my intention to identify a series of such key transitional periods in the history of the Church of God Reformation Movement, periods when organizational structures have been reexamined and reshaped for more effective ministry. I do so for the purpose of demonstrating why church leaders now have reason to be optimistic about the future growth of the Movement as we stand at the beginning of a new century and millennium.

1. Charismatic Leadership Launched a Cause

Consider the Movement's beginnings [see Entries 1-2]. During the month of October in 1881, two small groups of people separated themselves from the church fellowships of which they were a part. The first group, led by Daniel S. Warner, walked out of a meeting of the Northern Indiana Eldership of the Churches of God held in a small country church in north central Indiana at a place called Beaver Dam.. Two weeks later, about 160 miles north of Beaver Dam, a second group in Carson City Michigan disengaged themselves from the Northern Michigan Eldership of the Churches of God [see Entry 4]. The Carson City group was led by Joseph and Allie Fisher, friends of Warner.

Three distinctives characterized these two groups according to Church of God historian John W. V. Smith. First, they rejected the denominational system representative of the two elderships. Second, they intentionally avoided creating a new organizational hierarchy and declared themselves an open fellowship of "all truly regenerated and sincere saints who worship God in all the light they possess." Third, they were not willing to define their identity by a creedal statement, which in their view would separate themselves from other Christians. Reliance upon the Word of God and the leading of the Holy Spirit was sufficient [see Entry 6].[3]

The Movement flourished during its early years with very little organization. The *Gospel Trumpet*, first published by D. S. Warner and later by Enoch E. Byrum, served as the theological voice of the Movement. These two early editors of the *Gospel Trumpet* propelled the Movement forward by the force of their personalities and the power of their position. While the *Gospel Trumpet* changed publishing locations six times in its first seven years of existence, the magazine largely defined the Movement's message and kept its traveling evangelists in touch with each other.[4] Known as the "flying messenger" period of Church of God history, these evangelists

---

3. John W. V. Smith, *The Quest for Holiness and Unity* (Anderson IN: Warner Press, 1980), 47.
4. Ibid., 59-60.

traveled extensively across North America calling people out of denominationalism and into the "light" of the one true church. They were so driven by
the urgency of Christ's second coming that little emphasis was placed on
organizing anything, including local congregations. These ministers were
even warned not to stay too long in any one place and congregations were
exhorted not to tempt them to stay.

In an 1892 editorial, Daniel Warner admonished local groups of saints
not to entice preachers to stay by building homes for them. "Beware," said
Warner, "how you through selfish motives of having frequent preaching lay
a snare to entangle God's flying messengers.... This is the time of the end,
and God's messengers must run to and fro."[5] As a result, flying messengers
covered a great expanse of territory but didn't always leave lasting results.
H. M. Riggle, one of the more effective of the flying messengers, once
observed: "One of the greatest mistakes of my early ministry was to open up
new fields of work and then rush of and leave them."[6] Subsequently, flying
messengers often revisited areas several times to restart congregations
before a permanent fellowship was established.

As the twentieth century unfolded, tensions mounted and challenged old
paradigms and traditions. John W. V. Smith observes:

> The inevitable alterations of perspective which accompany
> growth, frustrations with the inadequacies of the old pattern
> of non-organization, and new problems with the increasing
> variety and expansion of work of the Gospel Trumpet
> Company permitted and compelled consideration of organi-
> zational structures that unquestioably would have been
> rejected in Warner's time.[7]

Warner, remember, was adamantly opposed to any form of human ecclesiastical organization. He often spoke out against all sorts of human rule—
committees, bylaws, officers, creeds—anything that resembled a denominational system. Warner was primarily concerned with preserving biblical
truth. As the editor-in-chief of the *Gospel Trumpet*, he was the central theological voice of the Movement. Smith notes that "almost everyone who
remained prominent in the Movement very long agreed with him on major
issues or else said very little about any area of disagreement"[8] [see Entry 27].
After Warner's death in 1895, E. E. Byrum became the editor-in-chief of the
Gospel Trumpet and, as a result, became the theological spokesperson for
the Movement.

---

5. Ibid., 124.
6. Ibid., 80.
7. Ibid., 205-206
8. Ibid., 206.

2. Broadening the Leadership Base

As the Movement continued its growth and expansion, however, church leaders began to realize that organizational changes were needed to facilitate additional growth and expansion. In a twelve-year period, between the years 1916-1928, a number of significant organizational decisions occurred which greatly altered the way the Movement organized for ministry. The General Ministerial Assembly was organized with a written constitution and by-laws [see Entry 42]. The corporate structure of the Gospel Trumpet Company was changed to include a president and an editor-in-chief. Byrum was not encouraged to continue in both roles. He therefore resigned his role as editor-in-chief to assume the presidency of the company. The Company also came under the jurisdiction of the General Ministerial Assembly and was governed by a Publication Board approved by the Assembly.

The National Association of the Church of God came into being in 1917. Also, Anderson Bible Training School was launched in 1917, amid great concerns from the field over the need for higher education [see Entry 80]. In the same year, the *Yearbook of the Church of God* was published for the first time. Some feared that this decision would promote "ecclesiasticism" by determining who was an official Church of God minister and congregation, and who was not. The period also saw the establishment of various boards to facilitate the work of foreign missions [see Entry 28], church extension, and Christian education. It was also during this period that the concept of Associated Budgets [see Entry 77] was introduced to help the five existing church agencies cooperate instead of compete with one another for funding from local congregations.

In 1920 the General Ministerial Assembly officially declared an "organization as needed" policy.[9] Reflecting on these twelve years, Smith notes that "the organizational changes which developed were made to extend decision-making control to a larger part of the church and to enhance the growth of a movement which was changing its perspective in regard to its own mission and role in Christian history."[10] Commenting again, Smith writes: "The power structure shifted from Holy Spirit leadership with only minimal informal organization to what was hoped to be Holy Spirit leadership with formal organization."[11]

Did these dramatic organizational changes enhance further Kingdom growth through the Church of God? Apparently so. Membership totals for the next ten years, as recorded in the Church of God *Yearbooks* from 1926

---

9. Marvin J. Hartman, "The Origin and Development of the General Ministerial Assembly of the Church of God, 1917-1950," unpublished B.D. thesis (Indianapolis, IN: Butler University, 1958), 21

10. Smith, *The Quest for Holiness and Unity*, 206.

11. Ibid., 223.

to 1935, show a dramatic increase from 27,771 to 59,799. This represents a 115 percent gain during a time when overall Protestant membership growth during this decade was around fifteen percent. Smith observes: "During these years one heard references to the Church of God as 'the fastest growing religious movement in America.'"[12] The growth continued during the decade of 1936-1946, in spite of the rigors of the Great Depression and the Second World War. The movement's membership almost doubled. Smith notes, "There was a significant increase in the number of congregations, in the number and size of Sunday schools, in the number of ministers, and in the number of church buildings."[13]

3. Democratization Continues

Another significant period of organizational evaluation and change followed World War II. While there were a number of issues that fueled a growing unrest, one of the key components was the sense that Anderson agency leaders were in charge of the decision-making processes of the church. The launching of the General Ministerial Assembly in 1917 had placed the control of the national agencies under the oversight of the Assembly. However, this action had apparently not changed the earlier patterns of relegating the decision-making of the church into the hands of an influential few. John Smith comments: "Before 1917 they had simply assumed leadership; after 1917 they were nominated and elected to leadership."[14] However, these nominated and elected leaders of the Anderson ministry agencies were often appointed by each other to one another's boards. As this trend became increasingly obvious to church leaders across the country, a growing sense of frustration and powerlessness grew among a number of ministers who saw themselves as pawns on a church chessboard. As the level of dissatisfaction increased, a number of ministerial leaders were willing to participate in criticizing the national organizational structures and the leaders nominated and elected by the Assembly to lead them.

Chief among these critics was L. Earl Slacum, an Indiana Church of God minister who preached a message titled "Watchmen on the Wall" to ministers gathered in an Indiana Ministerial Assembly meeting in Terre Haute on September 19, 1944. He was particularly concerned about signs of worldliness evident in the lives of Anderson agency leaders, a failure to preach important historic doctrines of the Church of God, and the perception of the growing power of the Anderson agencies. Slacum's writings in a periodical he produced called "The Watchmen on the Walls" triggered a

---

12. Ibid., 258. Also see Merle Strege's essay "New Wine and Old Skins" in his *Tell Me Another Tale* (Warner Press, 1993), 75-80.

13. Ibid., 320.

14. Ibid., 327.

considerable amount of support from "hundreds" of ministers across the country [see Entry 34].

In 1945 the General Ministerial Assembly appointed the Committee on Research and Improvement to investigate Slacum's charges. It reported to the 1947 Assembly that Anderson agency leaders had not been guilty of any of the charges or practices raised by Slacum and others [see Entry 49]. It did, however, recommend that the Assembly continue to examine agency structures. Slacum was not satisfied with this report. After a protracted discussion the Assembly reaffirmed its faith in the Anderson agencies and condemned Slacum for his actions. Over the next few months, a number of ministers and congregations withdrew from Anderson and formed a reformation which came to be known as the Watchman movement. It should be noted that in May 1951, Slacum wrote a letter to the Watchman movement in which he indicated that the new movement had developed more structure in five years than Anderson had in twenty-five. He then resigned from all boards of the Watchman movement and later was reinstated in 1953 as a minister-in-good-standing with the Indiana Ministerial Assembly of the Church of God.

One of the by-products of the Slacum years was a thorough evaluation of the national organization of the Church of God. Following the investigation and report to the Assembly of the Committee on Research and Improvement, the Assembly renamed it the Committee on Revision and Planning. This Committee was charged with the task of studying the church's national organization and suggesting possible changes. In a report to the 1948 Assembly the Committee identified three desires of ministers generally:

1. The desire for more direct rights and privileges on the part of the ministry in the making of nominations to the general boards.
2. The desire for more direct control of the boards and their policies by the ministry.
3. The desire for a more representative General Ministerial Assembly.[15]

By 1954 the General Ministerial Assembly approved a design for restructure that addressed the above-mentioned desires. The design called for an enlarged and reorganized Executive Council that had previously been founded in 1932 to serve as a legal entity for the General Ministerial Assembly [see Entry 47]. The World Service Commission, established in 1945, became a division under the Council. The Clergy Bureau became another division and was called Church Service. A third division was created, called General

---

15. Ibid., 337.

Service, and charged with the task of planning and public relations. The design of the Executive Council called for the election of more ministers and laypersons than Anderson agency leaders. Subsequently, the "power bloc" of Anderson agency personnel was severely reduced.

Did the further democratization of Anderson agencies contribute to further kingdom growth? Again, one could build such a case. In 1950, estimated membership in the Church of God *Yearbook* was listed at 96,749 persons in 1,932 congregations. The 1955 *Yearbook* listing shows 121,655 members in 2,141 congregations. Total membership increased during these five years by twenty-five percent and the number of congregations rose over ten percent. The Movement's growth rate during these years is not as large as the previous growth rates of the 1920s and 1930s. It is a very significant increase, however, when one understands the internal issues facing the Movement during these years.[16]

4. Visionary Leadership and Participatory Democracy

Since 1975 the number of congregations of the Church of God in the United States has hovered between a low of 2,239 in 1975 and a high of 2,350 in 1992. Church membership stood at 139,539 in 1965 and was registered at 221,346 in 1995, the last year the *Yearbook* of the Church of God recorded membership figures. However, in the decade of the 1990s, average weekend worship attendance increased from 192,578 in 1991 to 230,549 in 1999.

Part of the reason why the Church of God has experienced dramatic growth during this period is because of Vision-2-Grow, an intentional effort by the Church to win people to Jesus Christ and to disciple them in the Christian faith [see Entry 164]. Vision-2-Grow was conceived in a national Visioning Retreat in the early 1990s. Designed as a ten-year intensive effort from 1992 to 2002, its purpose is to promote spiritual and numerical growth and to enhance leadership development in the Church of God. Vision-2-Grow has served as a catalyst in bringing together independent national agencies, providing them with a common focus that has promoted dialogue and cooperation. Certainly Vision-2-Grow has fostered an increased sense of grassroots ownership in the national ministries of the Church of God. One might even say that Vision-2-Grow has helped to create an environment that has given birth to the most recent restructuring of our national agencies.[17]

During this same period, Church of God leaders grappled with the urgent need to equip and resource local congregations for more effective

---

16. Ibid., 345.

17. Robert W. Pearson, 1999 *Yearbook* of the Church of God (Church & Ministry Service: A ministry of the Leadership Council of the Church of God and Church of God Ministries, Inc.), 15.

ministry and mission. In 1987 the General Assembly of the Church of God established a Task Force on Governance and Polity [see Entry 173] to analyze the church's governance and polity structures and to make recommendations for change that would enhance ministry and mission. In 1995 Leith Anderson was hired as a consultant by the General Assembly's Leadership Council to assist in bringing further clarity to these recommendations. Anderson's proposals were approved in concept by the General Assembly in June 1996. An Implementation Task Force was then established to develop a strategy on how to proceed. The General Assembly approved the Task Force's recommendations in its June 1997 meeting. The Task Force became an Implementation Transition Team to facilitate the approved strategy.

The result of these years of reflection and retooling has been the creation of a new structure called Church of God Ministries, Inc., which is directly accountable to the General Assembly. On December 31, 1998, the following ministry functions merged into Church of God Ministries: the Board of Christian Education, the Mass Communications Board, the Missionary Board, the Home Missions and Church Growth components of the Board of Church Extension, Vision-2-Grow, and the curriculum and book/periodical publishing functions of Warner Press. The Church Resources division of Warner Press is now a subsidiary organization of Church of God Ministries, Inc. For the last few months these ministries have been in the process of being organized into three Ministry Teams—the Congregational Ministries Team, the Resource and Linking Ministries Team, and the Outreach Ministries Team. Each of these Ministry Teams and their respective ministries will operate under the supervision of the Ministries Council of Church of God Ministries and its General Director.

Two directives have been given in this restructuring effort. First, the church is calling the General Director to be a visionary leader. In the past the role of the General Secretary has been one of coordinating and facilitating the work of the various national church agencies. However, each national agency was accountable to its own Board of Directors, and through its Board to the Leadership Council and the General Assembly. Cooperation with the General Secretary occurred voluntarily; it wasn't built into the national structure as part of the natural process. Consequently, duplication and overlapping of ministries were perceived to be occurring. Under the new structure each of the program ministries of the church is part of Church of God Ministries, Inc., and is directly accountable to the General Director. The General Director, in turn, is accountable to the Ministries Council of Church of God Ministries and the General Assembly of the Church of God. The opportunity for the General Director to provide visionary leadership has been built into the new national structure.

At the same time, the church is calling for more grassroots involvement and ownership in the national, North American, and international ministries of the Church of God. This will happen in the following ways. First, the constituency of the Ministries Council is reflective of the generational, geographical, gender, and cultural diversity of the Movement in North America. Twenty of the twenty-three members are chosen from five geographical regions of North America, four from each area. A pool of names is developed by recommendations intentionally generated from state, regional, and cultural assemblies in each of these regions. The General Assembly's Business and Leadership Resource Committee is then charged with the task of choosing nominees from this pool, reflective of the skills and diversity needed to ensure that the Council remains representative of the entire church.

Second, the new structure calls for a Triennial Visioning Conference. The first was held September 29-October 1, 1998 in Colorado Springs, Colorado [see Entry 177]. Approximately 250 individuals from across North America, including global missionary presence, came together to discuss the state of the church and to determine where the Church of God should head in the future. Much of this work has greatly influenced the ministry priorities of Church of God Ministries, Inc. Future Visioning Conferences will occur every three years. Third, and certainly not least, every licensed and ordained minister in the Church of God is entitled to participate in annual General Assembly meetings of the Church of God held in Anderson, Indiana, during the International Convention of the Church of God. In addition, each congregation of the Church of God is privileged to appoint delegates to the General Assembly in proportion to its size.

As one surveys the historic path the Church of God has taken regarding the organizational structure of national, North American, and international ministries of the Church of God, one notices that the new structure is reflective of lessons learned from the past. For instance, in the early days of the Movement, visionary leadership was centralized without participatory accountability to the larger body. D. S. Warner and E. E. Byrum led in their role as editor-in-chief of the *Gospel Trumpet*. As the Movement progressed, decision-making leadership was expanded to include the General Ministerial Assembly in 1917 and extensive field representation on Anderson agency boards and commissions in 1954. Over the years, however, participatory democracy has made it more difficult for visionary leadership to focus the church in a particular direction. The new structure allows for the possibility of the General Director to lead the Movement, while accountability is ensured through the participatory involvement and ownership of the diverse constituencies of the church in the field.

Will the Church of God flourish because of the new organizational structure? While nothing is guaranteed, the possibilities are incredibly bright. Anticipation from a variety of constituencies is at an all-time high as we enter the twenty-first century. The decade of the 1990s witnessed great growth for the Church of God, and organizational changes should facilitate and accelerate this growth. The most encouraging sign, however, is that significant growth has followed each of the major Church of God restructuring efforts in the past. We have every reason to believe that this trend will continue.

204. Anderson University Nurtures and Honors the Church's Mission

by Barry L. Callen

Founded in 1917 as Anderson Bible Training School, Anderson University is the oldest and largest of the institutions of higher education related to the Church of God movement. For decades it has been crucial for the life of the Church of God, including the church's missionary thrust to the world. A few examples follow.

Through the lives of its many graduates and by the granting of honorary doctorates, the University has educated and then later honored several of its own who distinguished themselves in the service of the church's mission. Two of the earliest honorary doctorates ever granted by the University went to John D. Crose (Doctor of Divinity, 1939) and Adam W. Miller (Doctor of Divinity, 1940), missionary pioneers of the Church of God. A son of John Crose, Lester, was an Anderson graduate in 1945 and received its honorary Doctor of Divinity degree in 1959. Lester was the executive leader of the Missionary Board of the Church of God for many years and wrote the history of Church of God missions titled *Passport for a Reformation* (1981). Several senior missionaries of the Church of God have been so honored, including 1943 Anderson graduate Arthur R. Eikamp (Doctor of Letters, 1985), 1958 graduate Ann Espey Smith (Doctor of Divinity, 1977), 1952 and 1955 graduate Sidney M. Johnson (Doctor of Divinity, 1989), 1952 and 1955 graduate Phillip L. Kinley (Doctor of Divinity, 1999), and 1952 graduate Phyllis Gillespie Kinley (Doctor of Divinity, 1999). Following a long missionary career with her husband Nathan in Japan and South Korea, the Smiths returned home and Ann served her alma mater as a trustee and Director of Church Relations. Phillip Kinley taught Christian mission part-time on the Anderson campus. Sidney Johnson still joins his wife Jean in giving leadership to the international "Children of Promise" program of the Church of God.

In 1976 Lester Crose became the founding director of the missions program in the University's School of Theology, to be followed by Douglas E. Welch who came to the campus after long missionary service in Kenya, East Africa, to teach Christian mission. As the twentieth-first century began, Dr. Welch was Archivist of the Church of God historical collection housed by the University. The Director of Overseas Ministries for Church of God Ministries was Michael D. Curry (Anderson graduate, 1978 and 1983), with the following regional missionary directors for the Church of God all graduates of the Anderson campus: Robert E. Edwards, Middle East/Europe; Michael D. Kinner, Asia/Pacific; Donald C. Riley, Africa; and Johnny L. Snyder, Latin America.

Anderson University has served the mission of the church in other ways, including gospel music and the international education of hundreds of its students. Heralded worldwide for spreading the Christian gospel through music are these three Anderson graduates, who also have been honored by their alma mater with honorary doctorates: 1959 graduate William J. Gaither (Doctor of Music, 1973); 1965 graduate Gloria Sickal Gaither (Doctor of Letters, 1989); and 1979 graduate Sandi Patty (Doctor of Music, 1991). The international education program, known as TRI-S (study, serve, share) and designed originally as a Christian version of President John Kennedy's Peace Corps, began in 1964 and was led from 1964-1998 by Norman Beard and since 1998 by Willi Kant. Every year hundreds of Anderson students have gone around the world for cross-cultural exposure and hands-on Christian ministry. Many of them have found this experience life-changing and have dedicated their lives to the mission of the church.

205. History of World Conferences and World Forums, 1955-2000

by Barry L. Callen

Editor's Note: Since the 1920s the Church of God movement in North America has convened International Youth Conventions every other year. They all have met somewhere in Canada or the United States. The first to be convened apart from the Anderson Campmeeting was in 1930 in South Bend, Indiana. The most recent is the 2000 Convention in Orlando, Florida. Only more recently have there been regularized gatherings of world leaders of the Church of God movement. Following is a brief history of these World Conferences and World Forums.

Only in recent decades has the Church of God movement established formal international settings for cooperative dialogue and ministry. The first and most prominent of these is the World Conference that to date has convened as follows:

1955 Fritzlar, Germany
1959 Essen, Germany
1963 Bochum, Germany
1967 Zurich, Switzerland
1971 Oaxtepec, Mexico
1975 [Beruit, Lebanon—canceled because of war]
1980 Anderson, Indiana, U.S.A.
1983 Nairobi, Kenya
1987 Seoul, South Korea
1991 Wiesbaden, Germany
1995 Sydney, Australia
1999 Birmingham, England
[2003 Latin America—projected]

A particularly historic convening was the 1980 World Conference in Anderson, Indiana. This was a celebration of the centennial of the Church of God movement and saw the first convenings of the World Forum and the International Dialogue on Doctrine (both meeting immediately prior to the World Conference itself.)

The quadrennial event of World Conferences began in 1955 when the Church of God movement was active in only thirty-five nations. T. Franklin Miller, then the executive of the Board of Christian Education in the United States, provided much of the initial vision and leadership.

Shortly after World War II, during an International Youth Convention in Miami, Florida, the Church of God in North America was invited to hold in Europe a world meeting of the church's youth. The resulting meeting was in Fritzlar, Germany, in the summer of 1955. Fritzlar was and still is the home of the Bible Training School in Germany. Dr. Miller named Tom A. Smith, national youth director in the United States, to carry major planning responsibilities. His young counterpart in Germany was Willi Krenz, a ministerial student at Fritzlar.

Dr. Miller continued giving executive direction during the decade of the 1950s through sponsorship of the national Board of Christian Education in the United States. Financial assistance came largely from the national ministry agencies of the North American church. Leadership and financial responsibility for the conferences was turned over to the Executive (Leadership) Council in 1960. The Executive Secretary of the Council became the chief coordinator for these events. Charles Weber was director of all conferences in the decade of the 1960s. T. Franklin Miller continued to make many of the arrangements during that decade. William Reed directed the conferences in the 1970s, Paul Tanner in the 1980s, and Edward Foggs during the final decade of this century, all from their leadership posts in Anderson, Indiana.

World Conferences have been scheduled at four-year intervals, with the exception of 1980 when the meeting was scheduled at a five-year interval to coincide with the centennial celebration of the Church of God movement's beginning. In the Tenth World Conference (Australia, 1995), special recognition was given to Willi Krenz of Germany, participant in all Conferences and planning leader of most.

Dr. Miller reports concerning that first meeting in 1955: "Deep emotional and spiritual tides flowed freely at Fritzlar. It was not only the first world meeting of Church of God people, but it was the first meeting of its kind to be held following World War II. Youth were present who had only recently fought on opposing sides. Leaders from seventeen countries gathered to build bridges of redemptive Christian love and to give themselves again to the supremacy of Jesus Christ. Friendships were begun there which have lasted across the years." One friendship was that of youth leaders Willi Krenz (Germany) and Norman Beard (United States). Together they would contribute much to future Conferences and to TRI-S, the international education program of Anderson University in Europe and elsewhere.

Following an evaluation of the 1955 event, it was agreed that this type of international fellowship and dialogue was needed and should continue. Essen, Germany, was selected as the site for a 1959 World Conference. The theme for the Essen meeting was "Jesus Christ Is The Lord." Eighteen nations were represented. All program materials were prepared in both the English and German languages. There were 212 registered delegates, with over 1,000 persons attending general services.

The stirring procession of national flags, which has characterized the opening and closing of all subsequent Conferences, first occurred at the Essen meeting. In those days commercial flags were not available, so they were hand-made by the women of the Essen congregation. Essen was also the first occasion to feature the graphic arts with an impressive backdrop to highlight the Conference theme. Essen also was the longest of the World Conferences to date, lasting over two weekends. All meal functions were held in the Handleshof Hotel and Sunday services were held in the town hall. Conferences were planned during the daytime hours, with buses transporting the entire delegation to churches in neighboring cities for mass meetings. The bonding that resulted in these eight days of preaching, singing, sharing, and fellowship impacted the delegates greatly.

The 1963 World Conference in Bochum, Germany, was especially noteworthy for two significant reasons. First, sponsorship changed from the Board of Christian Education to the Executive Council in the United States. Second, this turned out to be the last World Conference to be held in Germany for nearly three decades. The trend was toward a widening international focus. Since the Conference now was more an "all church" meeting than principally the gathering of the church's youth, it was judged by the

Board of Christian Education that an agency more representative of the church's total constituency and concerns should assume responsibility. Since the Executive Council was now a staffed office of the General Assembly in North America, it was agreed that the Council should accept this assignment.

Twenty nations were represented in Bochum, Germany, in 1963. The 600 delegates gathered to discuss the theme, "One Lord, One Faith, One Task." Weekend attendance swelled to more than 1,000. This Conference was scheduled for Wednesday through Sunday, the pattern for all succeeding conferences except Seoul, Korea, which was Wednesday through Friday to accommodate the specific needs of the Korean church. Like the Conference in Essen, the Bochum meeting was held in an auditorium during the day and moved to the churches for evening services.

The World Conference moved to Zurich, Switzerland, in 1967. Said Harold Phillips: "This was quite a setting in which to explore the topic 'The Church: Her Nature and Mission,' for just a few blocks away stood the church in which Zwingli lit reformation fires in the sixteenth century and not a few gave their lives as Christian martyrs." About six hundred delegates from eighteen countries explored the meaning of this theme. The program was built around the New Testament metaphors of salt, light, soldier, and servant. R. Eugene Sterner, program chair, said in his welcome to the delegates: "We come from every continent, from climates tropical and frigid, from both eastern and western hemispheres, to beautiful Switzerland, with its towering Alps and its peace-loving people. We come because we want to be together and because one overarching purpose dominates our lives—to make Christ known, and to become, in this troubled world, the penetrating, proclaiming, marching, serving church."

It was agreed in Zurich that four years hence another Conference should be held, this time in the western hemisphere. Thus the 1971 World Conference convened outside Mexico City in Oaxtepec, the beautiful site of earlier Pan American Games. Housing and meals were provided in the sports complex so that opportunity for fellowship and dialogue could be enhanced. The theme, "Called To Serve the Present Age," directed the 496 registered delegates in their thinking for the four conference days. A new record of international involvement was set with twenty-seven different countries represented. This was also a landmark meeting in that for the first time representative delegates from the various nations participated in the World Conference planning. This was a new plateau in internationalizing this worldwide event.

Franco and Bea
Santonocito
Italy

Fouad Melki
Lebanon and Syria

The planning committee elected in 1971 convened in 1973 to make preparations for the 1975 Conference. The site for the Conference was to be the city of Beruit, Lebanon, located on the eastern coast of the Mediterranean. To the great disappointment of all who were planning to attend, the meeting had to be canceled because of the outbreak of war in the Mideast.

According to T. Franklin Miller, "The most significant gathering in regard to planning since 1955 was the next meeting of the planning committee in 1977." It convened as the Worldwide Strategy and Planning Consultation and met in a conference center about 100 miles outside Nairobi, Kenya. For ten days the members listened to various points of view, took time for reflection, and sought the will of the Holy Spirit. It was in this 1977 meeting that world leaders of the Church of God movement drafted a design and further nurtured the growing idea that soon would become the World Forum.

The first World Forum met in Anderson, Indiana, in 1980 preceding the sixth World Conference. In this inaugural Forum major papers were delivered by Donald Johnson and Douglas Welch on the theme "International Partnership In Mission." It was unanimously agreed to continue the World Forum on a regular basis. It has preceded each World Conference since that time. Another first for 1980 was the convening of the International Dialogue on Doctrine hosted by the Anderson School of Theology (the Dialogue's history is told briefly in entry 149). The 1980 Conference set all records for Church of God international participation to that date.

Laura Withrow was chair of the program committee for the 1980 annual campmeeting held in Anderson. Barry Callen preached the keynote sermon for the World Conference and T. Franklin Miller acted as overall coordinator for the Conference, Forum, and Dialogue. More than 250 overseas guests from most of the countries where the Church of God was at work participated in this sixth World Conference. Willi Krenz of Germany and Carlton Cumberbatch of Trinidad were co-chairs of the planning committee for this historic event. Three thousand registered delegates attended the Conference to discuss the theme "Let the World Know." About seven thousand were present at general services, with an estimated 30,000 different persons attending at least one service of the eight-day event (including the annual Anderson International Convention). Simultaneous interpretation was utilized, translating all services into English, Japanese, German, and Spanish.

Nairobi, Kenya, was selected as the site of the 1983 World Conference. It was held in the beautiful Kenyatta Conference Center in the heart of downtown Nairobi. Twenty-four countries were represented, with four hundred and thirty delegates from the United States. Because the Church of God in Kenya had about 100,000 members, delegates and guests from Africa swelled the attendance at general services to approximately 4,000 persons.

The World Forum in 1983 addressed the subject of "Strategies for Interdependence in Mission." Subjects for the sessions included: "A Biblical Basis for Interdependence in Mission," "How Do We Evangelize Together?," "How Do We Respond To Personal Needs Cooperatively?," and "How Do We Relate to Persons or Groups Seeking Affiliation With the Church of God?" Excerpts from the paper delivered by Douglas Welch are found in Entry 150. The planning committee, chaired by Isai Calderon of Guatemala, had set the Conference theme "Partners in God's Action." The keynote sermon was delivered by Edward Foggs following an opening address and greeting to the Conference by the President of Kenya, Daniel Moi. The African choirs were a great blessing. Planned visits to African villages were a highlight for international guests. The Conference ended with a candlelight service.

A new planning committee chaired by Victor Babb of Barbados was named to prepare for the 1987 Conference scheduled for Seoul, South Korea. Represented on the committee were leaders from South Korea, Tanzania, Singapore, Germany, and the United States. The theme chosen for the World Forum was "Unity With Diversity." The World Conference theme was "Arise My People."

Church of God leaders from 52 nations gathered in Seoul, South Korea, in the summer of 1987, with all conferences, rallies, lodging, and food services under one roof, the Seoul Hilton International Hotel. Never before had so many nations been represented in a world gathering of Church of God people. The great increase, from 24 countries represented in Nairobi to 52, was due in part to a strategic decision by the Executive Council of the Church of God in the United States. Since this event was becoming more significant to the life and work of the Church of God all around the world, it was agreed that a way must be found to avoid lack of representation from any nation because of lack of funds.

Budgetary means were appropriated through allocation of World Service funds (United States) on an annual basis and from a premium registration charged North American delegates. Assemblies in every country were invited to send at least one delegate, with some subsidy provided as necessary for travel, food, and lodging. Most nations now not sending delegates were deterred for personal or political reasons, not financial. There were 700 United States delegates in South Korea and 300 registered delegates from other countries. About 2,000 persons were in attendance at the mass evening rallies to celebrate the theme "Strengthening Our Unity." Excerpts of the paper delivered by Donald Johnson to the World Forum are found in entry 151. Many of the Americans present were pastors and laypersons who came in tour groups. All travel arrangements were made by Norman Beard of Anderson University. To the South Korean experience were added tours to China, Japan, and Hong Kong before or after the Conference.

Program highlights included a footwashing service in the World Forum and the Lord's Supper in the World Conference. The same persons who carried flags in the opening pageantry wore banners and national costumes as they distributed the elements for the communion service. A 5:00 a.m. morning prayer service was led by members to the Korean church, where such services are traditional and contribute to much of the Church's fervor and growth. The Korean Children's Choir of World Vision sang in one event and put on a cultural performance in another. They won the hearts of the delegates. The meeting closed with 2,000 delegates holding their candles high and pledging themselves to go back into their world of influence to more effectively share the gospel of Jesus Christ.

The year 1991 saw the World Conference return to Germany for the first time since 1963. The very first Conference had been in Fritzlar when the devastation of World War II was still very visible. Now the large gathering in Wiesbaden came soon after the infamous Berlin Wall had been torn down. The nation finally was united again—a fitting symbol for the goal of the international work of the Church of God.

The titles of the presentations in the 1991 World Forum reflected the global perspective and practical purposes of the Forum. They were: "Exploring Strategies for Mission in the 21st Century (Edward Foggs, USA); "Biblical Strategies for Mission" (Arturo Schultz, Argentina); "Understanding Our World" (Eckhard Bewernick, Germany); "Exploring Mission Strategies for the Local Church" (Fouad Melki, Lebanon); and "Partners in Mission" (Leaderwell Pohsngap, India). Norman Beard again arranged all travel, sending hundreds of the delegates across Germany and into neighboring European countries either before or after the Wiesbaden gathering.

The tenth World Conference and the fifth World Forum and International Dialogue on Doctrine were convened in 1995 in Sydney, Australia. The World Forum convened from July 18-20 in the Sydney Hilton Hotel with the theme "Learning to Celebrate." Delegates were present from forty-eight countries. Major papers were "We Celebrate Our Heritage" (Barry Callen, United States), "We Celebrate Our Message" (Nelson Junges, Brazil), "We Celebrate Our Mission" (Borman Roy Sohkhia, India), "We Celebrate Our Ministry" (regional reports from around the world), and "We Celebrate Our Unity" (Gilbert Stafford, United States). Edward Foggs, Forum coordinator, thanked regional assemblies for their efforts to help fund their own delegates and emphasized the importance of effective communication between the Leadership Council in the United States and the several assemblies in the matter of expediting Forum arrangements.

The half-day International Dialogue on Doctrine then was convened by Barry Callen of the United States. It again was sponsored by the School of Theology of Anderson University. About sixty world leaders explored the theme "Christian Unity: God's Will and Our Role." Immediately following, in the convention center at Darling Harbor near downtown Sydney, convened the World Conference itself. Australian pastor Leonard Bradley brought greetings on behalf of the host country. Cleve Grant of Jamaica delivered a stirring keynote sermon, with Diana Swoope of the United States delivering a powerful closing message. Willi Krenz of Germany had chaired the planning committee's work for this Conference. One program highlight was a special offering taken to assist the Australian church in planting a new congregation in nearby Auckland, New Zealand, to be led by a young family commissioned from the Australian church.

The eleventh World Conference and sixth World Forum of the Church of God convened in July, 1999, at the International Convention Centre in Birmingham, England. The Conference Director was Edward Foggs of the United States and the Co-Chairs of the Planning Committee were Asim Das (India) and Victor Babb (Barbados). With the theme "Jesus Is Lord" and Barry L. Callen functioning as Recording Secretary, the Forum convened first and focused on the issues of integrity in leadership (paper by Norman Patton, USA), biblical principles for the family (paper by Helmut Krenz, Switzerland), and challenges confronting the church in the twenty-first century (paper by Edward Foggs, USA). In the business session the Forum named Robert W. Pearson (USA) as the 2003 Conference Director and identified the future location as somewhere in the southern cone of Latin America. Reasoning for this choice included the facts that only the 1971 World Conference (Mexico) had ever convened in Latin America and that there were in Latin America some 570 congregations and 34,000 constituents of the Church of God who could be effective hosts and benefit greatly from the worldwide exposure of a Conference. The southern cone includes Argentina, Brazil, Paraguay, and Uruguay.

The Conference itself involved some 1,500 international participants and was both educational and inspirational. Ministry reports were given by six leaders from various sections of the world. Sermons at the general worship services were delivered by Walentine Schule (Russia), Cheryl Sanders (USA), Cyrill Pillay (South Africa), Norberto Hort (Brazil), and Vernon Lambe (Bermuda). Special recognition was given to T. Franklin Miller (USA), who played a significant role in the earliest years of the World Conferences, and to Norman Beard (USA) and Willi Krenz (Germany) who had attended all of the Conferences since the first in 1955.

From their beginning, the World Conferences have been international gatherings of the church, ministers, laypersons, and youth. The main purposes have been to network, instruct, and inspire all participants. Since 1980, however, the World Forums have supplemented the Conferences with much smaller, delegated, task-oriented gatherings.

As revised in Seoul in 1987 and reaffirmed in the subsequent 1991 and 1995 meetings, the objectives of the Forums are:

1. To foster acquaintance and fellowship with Church of God leaders from around the world;

2. To share the good news of what God is doing in the world through his faithful servants, but not to become authoritarian or elitist as to what others should do;

3. To experience the oneness and unity which exists interculturally within the Church of God;

4. To discuss needs and concerns as well as solutions and resources for fulfilling our ministry;

5. To consult with one another on doctrinal and theological issues, with the awareness that it shall not function as a supreme authority in these matters;

6. To provide opportunity for national Boards of Missions to seek harmonious working relationships in countries where work overlaps;

7. To arrange for future World Conferences through the selection of a Conference coordinator, a planning committee, and a location for the next Conference;

8. To think strategically regarding the work of the Church of God around the world.

At the Seoul meeting of the World Forum (1987), Donald Johnson, former executive secretary of the Missionary Board in the United States, presented the paper "Affirming Our Diversity" (see entry 152). This paper highlighted the maturing purpose of the Forum itself. Said Johnson: "It is right and proper for us to affirm our variety. Rather than *conformity*, we desire *multiformity*. The variety of resources, emphases, contributions, and of theological awareness is staggering. Our purpose is to identify our diversities and maximize them." Beginning with that first gathering in Fritzlar, Germany, in 1955, these many world meetings of Church of God people certainly have enhanced acquaintances, appreciations, and cooperative ministries.

Editor's Note: At times the international spirit of acquaintance and reconciliation was best lived out by prominent individuals. There is no better example in the recent history of the Church of God (Anderson) than that of Samuel G. Hines (1929-1995). This native of Jamaica believed that dogmas divide and ministry unites, that the purpose of the gospel of Christ is to reconcile people to God and each other. Hines pastored during the final years of his life in Washington, D. C. He chaired the General Assembly of the Church of God (1983-1989) and worked for years in South Africa to help demolish apartheid. He was a global ambassador for Christ, a worldwide peacemaker, a living, preaching, serving model of the Church of God at its best.

206. History of the International Dialogues on Doctrine, 1980-1995

by Barry L. Callen

Barry L. Callen
Anderson University

The General Assembly of the Church of God in the United States and Canada recognized in 1970 that there were "theological and doctrinal problems that need to be openly and honestly faced by this Assembly." Since those problems, it was assumed, "grew out of evidently changing patterns of our preaching, teaching and publications across sev-

Gilbert W. Stafford
Anderson School
of Theology

eral decades," the Assembly acted in June, 1970, to call a major "Consultation on Doctrine." Its stated purpose was to enable "a serious restudy of the theological and doctrinal message of our movement" and "mutual discussion among us as leaders in faith and practice." Soon a design committee had adopted the following formal statement of purpose for the Consultation:

> To explore biblically and historically the church's nature, mission, polity, and unity in order to find a common ground for the commitment of old and the nurturing of newer members of our churches.

The intent did *not* include any attempt to develop "a creed or definitive statement of our position."

Four papers were written and distributed widely, papers on the nature, mission, polity, and unity of the church. By 1974 about thirty area assemblies, involving a total of some 2,200 church leaders, had participated in dialogue on the substance and implications of these papers. A final report given to the 1974 General Assembly detailed five areas in which the Consultation was seen as having served a useful purpose. One was having provided a vehicle for the encouragement of persons of differing points of view "to sit together and discuss these differences without fear of judgment or ostracization."

If no adequate standing vehicle existed in North America for broadly representative, disciplined dialogue on doctrinal issues of common concern (thus such an *ad hoc* consultation process), neither did one exist in the international arena of the life of the Church of God. As a sense of need evolved for such serious dialogue internationally, the North American Consultation of the early 1970s was one available model, even a stimulus for launching the first International Dialogue on Doctrinal Issues in 1980 in Anderson, Indiana. This was a natural time and place because of the celebration of the centennial of the beginning of the Church of God movement and the convening of a World Conference (and the first World Forum). Anderson University, through its graduate School of Theology, committed itself to sponsoring this first and subsequent doctrinal dialogues as a service to the church worldwide. Drs. T. Franklin Miller, Barry Callen, and Gilbert Stafford of the School of Theology were instrumental in the Dialogue's beginning.

The faculty of the School of Theology developed during 1979-1980 a booklet titled "WE BELIEVE" for use by the Church of God on the occasion of its centennial celebration. It sought to state central theological burdens which for a century had been at the heart of this movement's theological tradition. The decision was made to use this booklet as a means of focusing discussion as the first International Dialogue on Doctrine convened in Anderson in June, 1980. Gilbert Stafford of the School of Theology acted as convenor and began the dialogue by telling the participants: "Just because the Church of God has no written creedal statement does not mean that we do not believe much. We have thought very carefully about our doctrinal life. However, our idea of arriving at doctrinal consensus will not work unless there is doctrinal dialogue.... That is what this meeting is all about." Then the group heard and reacted to four papers which had been prepared in relation to various sections of the "WE BELIEVE" booklet. They were written by P. V. Jacob of India on "Salvation," Carlton Cumberbatch of Trinidad/Tobago on "The Church," Franco Santonocito of Italy on "Mission," and Byrum Makokha of Kenya on "Unity."

The 1980 Dialogue participants proceeded to share their perceptions of the most pressing doctrinal issues in their respective countries at the time. As a group they then prioritized these issues for future consideration. The general issue of greatest common concern internationally was "Pentecost and the Church." Thus, this issue was chosen as the subject for the second International Dialogue to convene in Nairobi, Kenya, in 1983. In August, 1982, in preparation for Nairobi, Koesuke Nishitani of Japan wrote a paper titled "What Does the Pentecostal Experience of the Holy Spirit as Reflected in Acts 2 Mean for the Life of the Church Today?" All expected participants received in advance from the School of Theology of Anderson University (1) the Nishitani paper, (2) a guide to it prepared by Dr. Stafford, and (3) three formal responses to it prepared by Nelson Junges of Brazil, Martin Goodridge of England, and R. Eugene Sterner of the United States. When the Nairobi Dialogue had concluded, it was clear that there was need and desire to continue pursuing dimensions of these concerns, now in the third International Dialogue set to convene in Seoul, South Korea, in July, 1987.

In Seoul, Dr. Stafford, again serving as convenor, clarified that the purpose was not to seek common agreement on an issue so that such an agreement could be considered standard worldwide in the Church of God. Rather, the purpose was said to be taking advantage of the meeting of so many church leaders in order to facilitate the sensitizing of each other to the thinking of the church around the world. The subjects under consideration in Seoul centered in the "gifts of the Spirit," with four thoughtful monographs written, sent, and studied by all in advance. They were: (1) "The Concepts of Gifts in the Letters of Paul" by Leaderwell Pohsngap of India; (2) "Tongues in the New Testament" by Franco Santonocito of Italy; (3) "Doctrine of Sanctification" by Eckhard Bewernick of Germany, and (4) the "Report of the Study Committee on Glossolalia" by the General Assembly of the Church of God in the United States and Canada. Dr. Barry Callen (U. S. A.) recorded highlights of the subsequent discussion focused around these four documents. This printed record was sent to all participants by the School of Theology.

Through a steering committee, Dialogue participants determined the desired focus of the next meeting, this time to convene as the Fourth International Dialogue on Doctrine in Wiesbaden, Germany, in July, 1991. That focus was to be "Sanctification." A four-year plan of preparation was laid, including (1) the writing, publishing, and mailing of key papers on this subject, (2) the gathering of responses to the papers by leaders from around the world, and then (3) the writing by Barry Callen of a paper reflecting the status of the discussion and suggesting aspects of the subject of sanctification which appear desirable for particular attention in the Wiesbaden Dialogue. On-site leadership was provided by James Earl Massey, dean of the sponsoring Anderson University School of Theology in the United States. A very stimulating and insightful discussion was launched by Fouad Melki of Lebanon who highlighted the paper he had written in the study booklet sent in advance to participants.

The fifth International Dialogue was convened in Sydney, Australia, in July, 1995, again immediately prior to the opening of the tenth World Conference. Barry Callen acted as coordinator and discussion leader. Two of his related works *It's God's Church!: Life and Legacy of Daniel Warner* and *Contours of a Cause: The Theological Vision of the Church of God Movement* had been sent to participants in advance in order to stimulate reflections on the

Dialogue theme, "Christian Unity: God's Will and Our Role Today." Jeannette Flynn of the United States served as recording secretary.

The half-day dialogue process in Sydney focused on five prepared reflection presentations, one each by Nelson Junges of Brazil, Willi Krenz of Germany, Bassem Malek of Lebanon, Leaderwell Pohsngap of India, and Gilbert Stafford of the United States. About sixty persons participated in exploring this topic so central to the heritage of the Church of God movement. It was clear that much about the issue of Christian unity had changed in the movement and in the Christian community generally since the movement's nineteenth-century beginnings. New challenges and opportunities lie ahead.

The World Conference that convened in Birmingham, England, in July, 1999, did not include the scheduling of a Dialogue on Doctrine (lack of adequate advance planning and appropriate facility availability). However, an informal gathering of a few leaders present in Birmingham and convened by Eckhard Bewernick (Germany) and Barry Callen (United States) explored the continuing need of serious international exchanges on theological topics of mutual concern. The need was reaffirmed and the group looked to the possibility of a strategy meeting to be hosted by Fritzlar Bible College in Germany in 2000. At such a meeting, plans could be laid for a Dialogue to be convened at the 2003 World Conference in Latin America.

Consistent with the non-creedal and "movement" nature of the Church of God, these Dialogues have been times of serious theological study and interaction among interested leaders from around the world. They have not been intended to work toward formalized positions on given topics, positions to be thought of as "official" and urged on others. Rather, they have sought to be ad hoc settings in which the Spirit of God could better inform and inspire the teaching ministry of the church around the world.

---

207. International Partnership in Mission (1983)

by Douglas E. Welch

Editor's Note: In the 1980 World Forum of the Church of God convened in Anderson, Indiana, Donald Johnson and Douglas Welch attempted to initiate a serious dialogue on the concept of international partnership in mission. Welch later described the problem this way, speaking of North American Church of God leaders: "We have called the plays for so long that some of us cannot conceive of not continuing to do so. We have determined for the whole world community [of the Church of God] what is theological orthodoxy. . .what is missionally appropriate. . .and what is structurally acceptable" (16). The following are excerpts of a presentation then made by Douglas Welch to the World Forum of the Church of God meeting in Nairobi, Kenya, in July, 1983.

396

I will touch briefly on four areas which I see the Bible addressing in relation to the Church of God movement as a world body. How do these areas affect our common life? What changes in our interrelationships do they call on us to make? What new forms of obedience do they demand of us in our various contexts? Perhaps these areas of concern can become an integral part of our dialogue from this point on, both in this Forum and in other settings.

Selfhood

In the first place, there is the area of *selfhood*. It may seem that Paul was being self-contradictory when he insisted that "there is neither Jew nor Gentile," that there is only one body, not many, and then judged that Gentiles do not have to think and behave like Jews. But interdependence does not demand *uniformity*. It begins rather with *diversity*. If the whole body were only one part and functioned only as the one part functions, there would be no body. This diversity is to be recognized and celebrated.

Interdependence begins with the recognition of selfhood. Selfhood does not mean *independence*, for each part needs the whole to be truly itself. Nor does it mean *self-sufficiency*. No part can say to another, "So who needs you?" True selfhood has to do with full self-acceptance, with the recognition of the gifts one has to give. It has to do with being set free from the imprisonment of inherited structures, of church polity or organization, of theology, structures of domination and dependence. It is being set free from the need to dominate, to be preeminent, to maintain control, and to think and speak for others.

A part of the world community of faith, acting as if it can by itself represent the whole, that is, speak for it, speak to it, and speak of it, is a distortion of selfhood—both of its own and that of others. This includes the doing of theology. As Orlando Costas argues in *The Integrity of Mission,* theology is not something we simply memorize and repeat. Theology is something we *do*. It is not equivalent to faith; it relates faith to the context of life (50).

For the spiritual wholeness and theological health of every part of the body, it is necessary that it have the benefit of the theological reflection, the doing of theology, of every other part of the believing community. If the doing of theology is relating faith to the contexts of life, then we shall all be vastly enriched by the diversity of theologies among us. All theologies will be accepted as pilgrim statements arising from differing socio-cultural and historical contexts, but all speaking of our *one faith* and of our *one Lord*. For Africa or India or Japan simply to parrot the conclusions of American theological reflection is a denial of the selfhood which the Bible insists upon.

Community Building

A second area which the biblical material addresses by implication is that of *community building* among us. Our special problem in the West is our lack of a sense of world community. Very many of us have little knowledge of the world church and little inspiration to seek that knowledge. Ours is the problem of self-sufficiency. There is a strong, scarcely-realized feeling that we really do not need anyone else. We have it all; we know it all; and we understand it all. Our responsibility is simply to take it to the rest of the world.

It is urgent that, at this juncture in our history, we sit down together and discuss ways and means of informing ourselves more fully about each other. We must find ways of building community among us—*koinonia*. We need to build mutual acceptance and trust. We must be willing to be vulnerable with each other. We must allow each other the freedom to make our own mistakes.

Structuring for Missions

Thirdly, there is the area of *structuring for missions*. It is to be accepted as a biblical "given" that missions are a necessary part of our total mission as the People of God, a necessary part of our missionary obedience in Christ. But no longer can this missionary obedience be largely a movement from North America to the rest of the world. Geopolitical reality, if nothing else, makes that impossible in many areas of the world, particularly in Asia. It is not possible to send Western personnel to a growing number of nations. Even when it is possible, it is not always desirable. Such sending may violate the selfhood of other parts of the community.

Decisions which affect the whole community should not be made *unilaterally*. This is especially true in the area of missions. Every segment of the community is charged with the missionary mandate. And every segment is responsible for its own obedience to that mandate, both within its own borders and beyond them. Particularly in those efforts which take a part of the community beyond its own borders, there is need for consultation, coordination, and cooperation with other parts of the community. One segment of the community is violating the selfhood of all other segments when it acts unilaterally, both in decision-making and in missionary sending. No one part can take upon itself that right and that obligation on behalf of all the other parts.

Resource Sharing

Fourth, there is the very sensitive area of *resource sharing*. Here we refer to the total resources of the church: spiritual resources; human resources; and financial resources. It is in this area that the principle of *reciprocity* applies. We do not share the same things with each other. As Paul remarks in 2 Corinthians 8, it is fitting that we also should share our material resources with the churches elsewhere, for they have shared their spiritual resources with us. While we do not give and receive the same things, we must all both give and receive. But our philosophies and structures of resource sharing have made it impossible for some of us to give and for others of us to receive. Some of us feel we have nothing to give, and others of us feel we have nothing we need to receive.

We in the West have great spiritual problems with our affluence. Rather than enhancing the spiritual and numerical growth of our congregations, it seems to be doing quite the opposite. We can no longer say, "Silver and gold have we none." Neither can we say, "In the name of Christ, rise up and walk." We need non-Western believers to sit down with us and help us deal *spiritually* with our affluence. They must help us know how to *share* our human and financial resources in ways which do not create dependence, which do not stifle local initiative, and which do not violate selfhood. We all need to learn how to be servants.

Conclusion

The church desperately needs biblical renewal. But this does not mean simply reaffirming and enhancing our traditional ways of thinking and doing. It means reaffirming our *obedience* to the normative principles of Scripture. We speak much of the authority of Scripture, but waffle at the point of obedience. That is the ideal, we seem to say. But we must be practical. Things will not change overnight. Church people will not give to support programs not in keeping with their traditional views and practices. What the Scriptures infer is the ideal, and we affirm that. But much of it is simply not expedient, which is what we generally mean by practical. I ask then: Where is the authority of Scripture? Do we live only by that which is expedient?

Why is it that I get the uncomfortable feeling that what we usually mean by the authority of Scripture is that it is authoritative in the formulation of our doctrinal beliefs, rather than in the living of our life as a People of God? Our boast is that we teach only what the Bible teaches. But do we intentionally seek to live by the principles revealed in Scripture, principles such as those we have discussed here? It is at this point that we are too often guilty of bowing before the idol of expediency. For our Lord, right doing was always primary in relation to right doctrine. He did not say, "Affirm this and you will live." What he said was, "Do this and you will live."

The Scriptures challenge us to take seriously the total interdependence of the community of faith. This is not optional. It is therefore urgent that we sit down together, intentionally and as immediately as possible, to discover new wineskins for the new wine of the Spirit flowing in this age.

Editor's Note: One of the most successful programs of international partnership in the Church of God has been the TRI-S program of international education maintained by Anderson University since 1964. Norman Beard was the prominent program leader for over three decades, followed in the 1990s by Willi Kant who brought to the campus significant experience with the international mission work of the Church of God.

208. Affirming Our Diversity (1987)

by Donald D. Johnson

Editor's Note: This is an excerpt of the address by Donald D. Johnson to the World Forum of the Church of God, Seoul, South Korea, 1987.

Church of God missions throughout most of its 100 years plus has affirmed and rewarded *unity*, not *diversity*. The sending church in North America has responded best to the establishment of look-alike churches. It has been the similarities reported in the younger churches which have prompted us [in the U. S.] to believe we were doing mission properly. The supporting church has responded with its dollars when both missionaries and Missionary Board reported on and pictured people around the world who sounded like, looked like, were structured like, and believed like its missionaries and the "home" church. It is not overly critical to observe that producing North American Christians has seemed at least as important as producing biblical Christians. This is part of the confessing we now need to do as North Americans.

The very fact that we are coming now to recognize and value our diversities, rather than only our similarities, is a quantum leap forward. It has not come about easily or quickly. As early as the middle 1950s, both missionary and national church leadership of the Church of God in the U. S. were talking about the "indigenous church." Paternalism and colonialism were labels being dealt with by missions around the world. The Missionary Board of the Church of God responded by moving to "turn the church over" to local leadership. Missionary personnel decreased in numbers. Emphasis increasingly was placed on the education of local leadership. Encouragement was given to the development of locally written material. The Missionary Board dissolved its legal entities as national churches became incorporated in order to hold their own property. Mistakes were made, but the movement was in the right direction.

Two additional sets of circumstances began to emerge through the 1960s and into the 1970s. National assemblies were developing, strengthening and taking greater local leadership. As these assemblies emerged, the North American missionaries had to find a new identity. Their role changed from that of being supervisory to that of being colleagues in mission. Obviously, this did not happen with the same speed or to the same degree in each country, but the trend now was clear. Things finally were changing, and rightly so.

As National Assemblies with integrity and recognition emerged, the need of communicating with area neighbors followed close behind. It was time for the Church of God in one country to begin to be aware of others around them. Multi-national assemblies began to be emerge [see entry 158]. The Missionary Board in North America was asked to help facilitate international gatherings of the Church of God. Planning sessions and strategy sessions were undertaken. Lester Crose describes these as "orbits of influence" in his book, *Passport For A Reformation* (1981). So, what had been the rather exclusive responsibility of the Missionary Board of the Church of God to be the coordinative clearing house for missions and the one entity relating to all countries in which a mission existed, now became the work, interest, and prerogative of various assemblies.

When the World Forum first convened in Anderson, Indiana, U.S.A. in 1980 [see entry 151], Douglas Welch and Donald Johnson were asked to write a paper addressing "International Partnership in Mission: A Missiologist's View and a Mission Administrator's View." In that paper a concept of *interdependence* emerged for the Church of God which has been enlarged, tested, and widely practiced since. The term interdependence implies that there are differences in our churches. Each has its own unique strengths to contribute to a truly international partnership. It is proper for us to *affirm* our variety. Rather than *conformity*, we desire *multiformity*. The variety of resources, of emphases, of contributions and theological awareness is staggering.

Our churches are an expression of our story. No one of us has the right to deprive others of us of our histories. We do not always think logically or theologically about our responses to the gospel; they are a part of our community life. I urge considerable tolerance as we open up to each other in the midst of our diversity.

209. The Three Frontiers (1992)

by Louis P. Meyer

Excerpt from Louis Meyer, *Pioneering New Frontiers in North America: A Historical Overview of the Board of Church Extension and Home Missions of the Church of God, 1921-1991* (1992), 257-260.

The tasks assigned by the General Assembly to the Board of Church Extension and Home Missions in its original charter were clear, and in many ways timeless. Seventy years later, congregations still need assistance with building needs; new congregations still need to be developed; people still need to be confronted with the claims of the gospel and invited to claim their inheritance in Christ; and the church still needs to be challenged to reach out to hurting and forgotten people in the United States and Canada.

This is an agency of the church seasoned in living on the frontier. It has served the church well on many social, ethnic, programmatic, and mission frontiers. This rich heritage should serve it well as it continues to help the church be effective in the twenty-first century, where new frontiers will abound. With a clear sense of its assignment, with commitment and resolve, the uncharted waters ahead should be welcomed as a gift from God.

I have been asked to conclude this writing with a suggestion of some possible trends and frontiers I see facing the church and all its agencies in this, the last decade of this century, and in the coming century. What I have listed below is not a full treatment or development of any trend or coming event. It is simply a hint of what might be ahead, an arrow pointing in the direction of a possible future.

To serve effectively in the century ahead, the church must become far more proactive and less reactive. This Christian belief that God is the God of the future as well as of the past, brings liberation. The desire to return to the past fades, while faith and confidence increase and enable believers to join with God, who is still creating and making all persons and all things new.

The Global Frontier. In June, 1989, the world watched as a Chinese university student, alone, stood before an army tank in Tianamen Square, challenging its repressive mission. Because of instant satellite coverage, it was as riveting as though one were viewing the event in his or her own neighborhood. Indeed, it was in our neighborhood, our global neighborhood.

A key shortcoming in much thinking today is in the way the world is perceived. Many have not acquired the global neighborhood perspective. This is a challenging frontier for all individuals, institutions, religions, nations, and governments. Whether the world's critical need is environmental restoration, ecological balance, food production and distribution, peace and reconciliation, or meeting human spiritual needs, solutions based on a global perspective will bring more lasting and satisfying solutions.

To be effective in the twenty-first century, the Church of God also needs this enlarged perception of reality—the global community perspective. Proposals, plans, and strategies based exclusively on parochial or national boundaries will not suffice. This frontier will exact the creative energies and skills of all agencies of the church. Perceiving our mission as one to a global community will position the church for a positive and effective ministry in the decades ahead.

The Multicultural Frontier. Diversity is God's plan. This is evident in the changing seasons, the mountains and valleys, and in the people of the globe. Yet, human beings have not fully appreciated or come to terms with God's pluralistic creation.

Based on the 1990 census and other demographic studies, if current trends continue, by the decade 2040 European Americans will comprise less than half of the United States population. This country will be a nation of ethnic minorities with no single group as a majority. Such a frontier will challenge the church and all institutions of society. Those who begin now to access the information, assimilate it, and accept the multicultural realities as within God's plan will be far more effective in the twenty-first century. Anything done to promote and encourage cross-cultural understanding will help lay the foundation for a peaceful, reconciling world.

The Religious Frontier. There can be no true understanding of the causes of the world's wars, nor of finding paths to peace without taking into account the religious factor. Peace between the world's peoples will never be realized unless there is better understanding and peace between the religions of the world. Far too often, religion makes people fanatical, angular, and exclusive, rather than cooperative, understanding, and reconciling.

This will be an even more critical frontier in the next century. As the world's population increases, as nationalism continues to rise in many countries, as the United States and other nations become even more multicultural, the religious bodies and their leaders must play a greater role in developing the conditions for peace and justice. To do the work required of the church universal in the twenty-first century, all religions must endeavor, not to form a syncretistic faith, but to understand one another and discover how to work together. New roads must be built for joining ministries to alleviate some of the world's pain, suffering, and misunderstanding. The Church of God, with its enduring belief in Christian unity, could carve out an exciting niche for its work and mission on this frontier.

These frontiers are but examples of what appear to be exhilarating and challenging decades ahead. The Board of Church Extension and Home Missions has had enough experience in vanguard and frontier life to be of help to the Church of God as it pioneers this intriguing future (257-260).

210. Honoring the Six "R's" of Heritage Celebration

by Barry L. Callen

Excerpt from the keynote address delivered by Barry L. Callen to the Fifth World Forum of the Church of God, July, 1995, Sydney, Australia.

Why should we celebrate the heritage of the Church of God movement on the occasion of this Fifth World Forum? There are at least six reasons, six "R's", six dimensions of true celebration.

1. We should celebrate by **Remembering** our heritage. Israel's identity was preserved in its remembering. God is known by what God does. To forget the history of God's actions is to fail to be God's people. The words of the Psalmist express generations of the faithful who determine not to forget: "I will call to mind the deeds of the Lord; I will remember your wonders of old" (Ps. 77:11 NRSV). The Church of God movement, like ancient Israel, is a "testifying" people. We are intentional *re-callers* and grateful *re-tellers* of what God has done *in* Christ, *for* us, and *among* us as a movement of God's people.

   The Church of God movement has been a people who seek to *come-out* of what now is wrong with the church because of a vision of what once was and again should be right with the church. We remember and honor the church's *apostolic beginnings* and seek to represent now that "early morning light."[1] True identity relies on effective memory. Unfortunately, many people associated today with congregations of the Church of God do not know the historic vision and reforming burden of this movement.[2] One essential for moving forward is intentionally staying rooted in the right past. When we stop to remember, we realize anew that there is much to celebrate. We must not forget!

2. We should celebrate by **Reassessing** our past. All that we remember is not worth repeating. According to one movement historian: "Tradition is important, but we are under no divine obligation to blindly accept a belief or a method simply because it is what has been said or done in the past. A Reformation Movement cannot reject the principle of continuing reform."[3] According to another of our movement historians, the title "reformation people" cannot be inherited, "cannot be passed on from generation to generation like the family Bible." Any legitimate claim to be a reformation people "must be made by each generation for itself."[4]

---

1. See Robert H. Reardon, *The Early Morning Light* (Anderson, Ind.: Warner Press, 1979).
2. See Barry Callen, *Contours of a Cause: The Theological Vision of the Church of God Movement* (Anderson, Ind.: Anderson University School of Theology, 1995).
3. John W. V. Smith, in Barry Callen, the *First Century,* vol. 2 (Anderson, Ind.: Warner Press, 1979), 826.
4. Merle D. Strege, in Barry Callen, ed. the *First Century,* vol. 2 (Anderson, Ind.: Warner Press, 1979), 830.

We are to remember gratefully; but we remember adequately only when our remembering is accompanied by a Spirit-enabled *discrimination* of our memories. We celebrate not merely a proud past, but the presence of God's Spirit with us now, the Spirit who helps us evaluate what has been and apply what now should be. We are to be rooted in a remembered past, but not captured by it. The goal is effective mission *now*.

3. We should celebrate by **Reaffirming** our central convictions.[5] Remembering and reassessing our movement's past will reveal much that is worth reaffirming. We should recognize that, if today we are tall, it is because we are standing on the shoulders of many great souls who have gone before us in the life of this Church of God movement. For instance, let us remember and reaffirm with joy the first world gathering of the Church of God movement. It convened in 1955 in war-torn Germany. Dr. T. Franklin Miller and Dr. Thomas Smith of the United States carried major planning responsibility, with youth leaders Norman Beard (U.S.) and Willi Krenz (Germany) leading then and leading still. We celebrate these men of God!

There is a vision given to us by our movement pioneers that yet has power to send us on mission to a still divided church and a still unholy world.[6] What, for instance, in the following should still inspire and motivate us as we remember, with discrimination, and with an eye to reaffirming what still should be? ...

> Free from babel, in the Spirit,
> Free to worship God aright;
> Joy and gladness we're receiving,
> O how sweet this evening light![7]

4. We should celebrate by **Reuniting** ourselves in thought and action. If *together* we will remember, reassess, and reaffirm, then *together* we can be effective in our current mission opportunities (thus the great importance of the World

---

5. One important attempt to do this was the "WE BELIEVE" booklet published by the administration and faculty of Anderson University School of Theology on the occasion of the 1980 celebration of the centennial of the church of God movement (see Entry 9).

6. See especially Barry Callen, *Contours of a Cause: The Theological Vision of the Church of God Movement* (Anderson, Ind.: Anderson University School of Theology, 1995).

7. Verse 4 of "The Evening Light" hymn, lyrics of Daniel Warner, based on Zech. 14:7, as in *The Evening Light and Salvation Echoes* (Moundsville, W.V.: Gospel Trumpet Co., 1897), 3.

Forums, International Dialogues on Doctrine, etc.). Says historian John Smith: "As a movement grows and expands to many countries and cultures, there are inevitable tendencies toward the formation of definable, internal groupings built around special doctrinal interests, variant methodologies, racial and cultural differences, or certain leaders with particular appeal. These tendencies are not necessarily divisive, but they are potentially so."[8] The more we focus on the vision the less we will "fuss" with each other.

The Church of God now is a worldwide movement that must learn increasingly to profit from its diversity, not be paralyzed by it. We always have said that unity does not mean that we all will look, act, and think exactly alike. Instead of being threatened by diversity among us, may God help us to celebrate it and channel it for God's glory. God's call is that we be *united*, not *uniform*. We represent differing cultures and God gives us differing gifts; but we are to be *one people* by the power of the Spirit.

5. We should celebrate by **Reaching Out**. Celebration is more than remembering, reassessing, reaffirming, and reuniting. To truly celebrate God's good news is to break free of *self-preoccupation*. This movement does not exist for itself, but as a witness to holiness and unity, and as an instrument of God's healing work in the church and the world. To date, the Church of God movement has kept too much *to itself*, thus risking self-preoccupation. Fearing the contamination of our doctrinal understandings, and thinking it wrong to look and act like the denominations, we have been too much *isolationists* with our unity witness. The irony of this now is quite apparent, and should end.[9] It is time for this

---

8. Smith, *op. cit.,* 826.

9. This self-imposed isolationism persists even in relation to "holiness" people with whom the Church of God movement has so much in common. Such is changing slowly, in part because the Editor of the *Wesleyan Theological Journal* now is a Church of God person (Barry Callen) and there are recent articles in this *Journal* by Church of God authors (Barry Callen, Timothy Dwyer, James Massey, Sharon Pearson, John Smith, John Stanley, and Susie Stanley).

movement to take more risks and be more humble about the finality of its own wisdom apart from the wisdom of the whole Body of Christ. Let us celebrate the whole church!

We leaders in this movement should do more than just keep saying that "we reach our hands in fellowship to every bloodwashed one." We should actually reach out, build ministry bridges, celebrate our God-given solidarity with all our brothers and sisters in the faith, regardless of church labels and honest differences in biblical understanding. The 1984 "Consultation on Mission and Ministry of the Church of God" (United States/Canada) wisely set this as one key goal for today's movement:

> To determine and develop the structures that best express interdependence and enable ministry and mission in the Church of God throughout the world.... To expand ministries through voluntary relationships with church groups outside the Church of God Reformation Movement.... Through voluntary relationships we often can achieve our mission more effectively and expand our ministries.[10]

Within the Church of God movement, this goal highlights the importance of the World Forum, World Conference, and International Dialogue on Doctrine. Outside the movement, this goal calls for creative and courageous new relationships on behalf of Christian mission. Let us celebrate the many opportunities before us! Let us celebrate visionary souls who have walked among us as ministers of reconciliation. One was Samuel G. Hines, recently deceased, whose bridge-building ministry was felt from the islands of the Caribbean to the world power center of Washington, D.C., to the racially torn nation of South Africa.

6. We should celebrate by **Rejoicing**! We celebrate the God who is, who comes in Jesus, and who forms the church, a new community of the Kingdom of God. This Kingdom community, this Pentecost people is not a place of restrictive law and arrogant creed, not a place of authoritarian priests and mandatory cultic practices. The church is the family of the Spirit, a house of prayer for all the nations

10. As in Barry Callen, compiler and editor, *Thinking and Acting Together* (Anderson, Ind.: Leadership Council and Warner Press, 1992), 107.

(Mk. 11:17). It is the "eschatological" community of Christ. This does not mean that the church should be a hotbed of rash speculation about the details of God's future. It does mean that in the church there should be an unbounded and thrilling belief that:

1. God's future is already here in Jesus Christ (Mk. 1:15);
2. What now is important is preaching the good news to all the nations (Mk. 13:10);
3. What is required is being willing to leave all for the sake of Jesus and the gospel (Mk. 10:28-30);
4. God will be with us in the face of all obstacles, even to the end of the age (Matt. 28:20). Therefore, rejoice!!

So, let's celebrate! How? We celebrate best by remembering, reassessing, reaffirming, reuniting, reaching out, and rejoicing in the gospel of Christ, in the reality of the church, and in our movement's heritage and mission responsibility within the church. These things should be done together with all of God's people, in humble recognition of the Kingdom's presence and power. All of this can bring so much joy and hope—if *together* we will be *holy*, living in the *unity* Christ gives, sharing with the *church* Christ forms, and serving the *mission* Christ brings.

211. Development of Regional Assemblies

Editor's Note: Although there was an international dimension of the work of the Church of God movement from almost its beginning, formalized international mission structures developed very slowly. In the most recent decades, however, assemblies of the world's regions have evolved and become significant. A brief overview of them follows. The regional directors named are employees of Global Missions, the Outreach Ministries division of Church of God Ministries in North America. Typical purposes of these regional assemblies (fellowships) are: (1) to facilitate effective communication; (2) to promote fellowship and unity; (3) to facilitate cooperative ministry partnerships; and (4) to offer educational opportunities for church leaders.

Year Estab.	Regional Organization	Basic Information
1960	**European Ministers' Conference**	
	Countries	17
	School	Fritzlar Bible College (Germany)
	Publication	*German Gospel Trumpet*
	Regional Director	Robert Edwards
1962	**Inter-American Conference**	
	Countries	19
	School	La Buena Tierra (Mexico)
	Publication	*LaTrompeta*
	Regional Director	Johnny Snyder
1980	**Mediterranean Area Fellowship**	
	Countries	9
	School	Mediterranean Bible College (Lebanon)
	Publication	*Arabic Gospel Trumpet*
	Regional Director	Robert Edwards
1981	**Caribbean/Atlantic Assembly**	
	Countries	14
	School	West Indies Theological College (Trinidad)
	Publication	*Cross Talk*
	Regional Director	Victor Babb
1982	**Asia/Pacific Church of God Conference**	
	Countries	19
	Schools	Asia Bible College (India) Nichols-Roy Bible College (India) Han Yang Seminary (South Korea)
	Publication	*Asian Church of God Magazine*
	Regional Director	Michael Kinner

For the spiritual wholeness and theological health of every part of the body, it is necessary that it have the benefit of the theological reflection, the doing of theology, of every other part of the believing community. If the doing of theology is relating faith to the contexts of life, then we shall all be vastly enriched by the diversity of theologies among us. All theologies will be accepted as pilgrim statements arising from differing socio-cultural and historical contexts, but all speaking of our *one faith* and of our *one Lord*. For Africa or India or Japan simply to parrot the conclusions of American theological reflection is a denial of the selfhood which the Bible insists upon.

Community Building

A second area which the biblical material addresses by implication is that of *community building* among us. Our special problem in the West is our

Victor and Yvonne Babb
Regional Directors
Caribbean/Atlantic Assembly

Gilbert and Melba Davila
Regional Directors
United States and Canada

Michael and Debra Kinner
Regional Directors
Asia/Pacific Conference

lack of a sense of world community. Very many of us have little knowledge

Donald and Paula Riley
Regional Directors
Executive Committee
for Africa

Robert and Janet Edwards
Regional Directors
Europe and Mediterranean
Conference

Johnny and Paula Snyder
Regional Directors
Latin America

212. Church of God Movement in the World Today: Countries and Totals of Congregations and Believers (as of 1999)

AFRICA

Countries
Cote d'Ivoire
Congo
Ghana
Kenya
Malawai
Mozambique
Rwanda
South Africa
Tanzania
Uganda
Zambia
Zimbabwe

Regional Totals:
12 Countries
2,156 Churches
231,857 Believers

Edward Nkansah
Ghana

ASIA/PACIFIC

Countries
Australia
Bangladesh
Bhutan
China
Guam
India
Indonesia
Japan
Malaysia
Myanmar
Nepal
New Zealand
Philippines
Saipan
Singapore
South Korea
Sri Lanka
Taiwan
Thailand

Regional Totals:
19 Countries
965 Churches
91,640 Believers

Borman Roy Sohkhia
India

CARIBBEAN/ATLANTIC

Countries

Antigua
Barbados
Bermuda
Cayman
Curacao
Grenada
Guyana
Haiti
Jamaica
Nevis
St. Kitts
St. Thomas
St. Vincent
Trinidad/Tobago

Regional Totals:

14 Countries
334 Churches
39,205 Believers

Carlton Cumberbatch
Trinidad/Tobago

LATIN AMERICA

Countries

Argentina
Belize
Bolivia
Brazil
Chile
Colombia
Costa Rica
Cuba
Dominican Republic
Ecuador
Guatemala
Honduras
Mexico
Panama
Paraguay
Peru
Puerto Rico
Uruguay
Venezuela

Regional Totals:

19 Countries
573 Churches
34,095 Believers

Tom and Jean McCracken
Brazil

412

MIDDLE EAST/EUROPE

Countries	Regional Totals:
Bulgaria	19 Countries
Cyprus	90 Churches
Denmark	7,940 Believers
Egypt	
France	
Germany	
Great Britain	
Greece	
Holland	
Hungary	
Italy	
Lebanon	
Russia	
Serbia	
Spain	
Switzerland	
Syria	
Turkey	
Ukraine	

**Martin Goodridge
England, Barbados**

NORTH AMERICA

Countries	Regional Totals:
Canada	2 Countries
United States	2,353 Churches
	234,311 Believers

TOTAL NATIONS, CONGREGATIONS, AND BELIEVERS IN THE CHURCH OF GOD AROUND THE WORLD

Countries	Congregations	Believers
85	**6,471**	**639,038**

SELECT BIBLIOGRAPHY

**Life, Thought, and Work of the
Church of God Movement (Anderson, Indiana)**

Editor's Note: This extensive bibliography of the heritage of the Church of God movement is divided into the following categories: **A**. Autobiographies; **B**. Biographies; **C**. Histories and Studies of the Church and the Church of God movement; **D**. Theological and Biblical Works; **E**. Songbooks and Hymnals; **F**. Institutional Histories; **G**. The Periodical and Church Curriculum; and **H**. Web Sites. Numerous academic theses and dissertations are identified throughout these sections by their subjects rather that being grouped together.

A. AUTOBIOGRAPHIES

Byrum, Enoch E. 1905. *Travels and Experiences in Other Lands*. Moundsville, W. Va.: Gospel Trumpet Company.

——— 1928. *Life Experiences*. Anderson, Ind.: Gospel Trumpet Co.

Cole, Mary. 1914. *Trials and Triumphs of Faith*. Anderson, Ind.: Gospel Trumpet Co.

Germany, J. Horace. 2000. *At Any Cost*. Anderson, Ind.: Warner Press.

Gray, Albert F. 1966. *Time and Tides on the Western Shore*. Pub. privately.

Khan, A. D. 1954. *From Darkness to Light: The Testimony of A. D. Khan*. Anderson, Ind.: Board of Christian Education.

Massey, James Earl. 2001 (forthcoming). *Aspects of My Pilgrimage*. Anderson, Ind.: Anderson University Press.

Morrison, John A. 1962. *As the River Flows*. Anderson, Ind.: Anderson College Press.

Newberry, Gene W. 2000. *A Boy from Lewis County*. Published privately.

Oldham, Dale. 1973. *Giants Along My Path*. Anderson, Ind.: Warner Press.

Reardon, Robert H. 1991. *This Is the Way It Was: Growing Up in the Church of God*. Anderson, Ind.: Warner Press.

Riggle, Herbert M. 1924. *Pioneer Evangelism*. Anderson, Ind.: Gospel Trumpet Company.

Smith, Frederick G. 1915. *Missionary Journeys Through Bible Lands*. Anderson, Ind.: Gospel Trumpet Co.

Strawn, Lucille A. 1999. *I've Been There*. Anderson, Indiana: published privately.

Warner, Daniel S. 1872-1879. *Journal of Daniel S. Warner*. Reprint 1993. Springfield, OH: Reformation Publishers.

B. BIOGRAPHIES

Bolitho, Axchie. 1942. *To the Chief Singer: A Brief Story of the Work and Influence of Barney E. Warren*. Anderson, Ind.: Gospel Trumpet Co.

Buehler, Kathleen. 1993. *Heavenly Song: Stories of Church of God Song Writers and Their Songs*. Anderson, Ind.: Warner Press.

———— 1996. *They Answered God's Call: Stories of Faith from Early Church of God Days*. Anderson, Ind.: Warner Press.

Byers, Andrew L. 1921. *Birth of a Reformation: Life and Labors of D. S. Warner*. Anderson, Ind.: Gospel Trumpet Company.

Byrum, Noah. 1902. *Familiar Names and Faces*. Moundsville, W.Va.: Gospel Trumpet Co.

Callen, Barry L., ed. 1990. *Listening to the Word of God*. Anderson, Ind.: Anderson University and Warner Press. Includes a major biographical tribute to Boyce W. Blackwelder.

———— 1992. *She Came Preaching: Life and Ministry of Lillie S. McCutcheon*. Anderson, Ind.: Warner Press.

———— 1995. *It's God's Church! Life and Legacy of Daniel S. Warner*. Anderson, Ind.: Warner Press.

———— ed. 1995. *Sharing Heaven's Music: The Heart of Christian Preaching*. Essays in Honor of James Earl Massey. Nashville: Abingdon Press. Includes a biographical interview with Massey.

Fudge, Thomas A. 1998. *Daniel Warner and the Paradox of Religious Democracy in Nineteenth-Century America*. Lewiston, NY: Edwin Mellen Press.

Kern, Richard. 1974. *John Winebrenner: Nineteenth Century Reformer*. Harrisburg, Pa.: Central Publishing House.

Ludwig, Charles. 1994. *A Dangerous Obedience: Life and Ministry of J. Horace Germany*. Anderson, Ind.: Warner Press.

Massey, James Earl. 1967. *Raymond S. Jackson: A Portrait*. Anderson, Ind.: Church Service Printing/Warner Press.

Neal, Hazel, and Axchie Bolitho (revised by Marie Meyer). 1982. *Madam President: The Story of Nora Hunter*. Anderson, Ind.: Warner Press.

Newell, Arlo F. 1995. *A Servant in God's Kingdom: Story of Max Gaulke's Life*. Anderson, Ind.: Warner Press.

Preston, Lee. 1969. "Charles E. Brown: His Life and Influence as Editor-in-Chief of the Gospel Trumpet Company on the Organization of the Life and Work of the Church of God." S.T.M. thesis, Iliff School of Theology.

Smith, John W. V. 1955. *Heralds of a Brighter Day*. Anderson, Ind.: Gospel Trumpet Company. Brief biographies of Daniel Warner, Enoch Byrum, Herbert Riggle, Frederick Smith, and Nora Hunter.

C. HISTORIES AND STUDIES OF THE CHURCH
AND OF THE CHURCH OF GOD MOVEMENT

Adams, Robert. 1980. "The Hymnody of the Church of God (1885-1980) as a Reflection of That Church's Theological and Cultural Changes." Diss., Southwestern Baptist Theological Seminary.

Anderson, Beverley C. 1955. "A History of the Church of God in Ontario, 1882-1955." Thesis, Anderson School of Theology.

Berry, Robert L. 1931. *Golden Jubilee Book.* Anderson, Ind.: Gospel Trumpet Company.

Blumenberg, Rick. 1997. *Standing with the Saints: A History of Yellow Creek Lake, Camp/Ministry Center and Congregations of the Church of God in Northern Indiana.* Bridgman, Mich.: FlowerMountain Publishers.

Brown, Charles E. 1951. *When the Trumpet Sounded.* Anderson, Ind: Warner Press.

Callen, Barry L. 1979. *The First Century.* Vols. I & II. Anderson, Ind: Warner Press.

——— 1992. *Thinking and Acting Together.* Anderson, Ind.: Warner Press. Revised and expanded under the new title *Journeying Together,* 1996.

——— ed. 1995. *Sharing Heaven's Music: The Heart of Christian Preaching,* Essays in Honor of James Earl Massey. Includes a biographical interview with Massey. Nashville: Abingdon Press.

——— 1999. *Radical Christianity: The Believers' Church in Christianity's History and Future.* Nappanee, Ind.: Evangel Publishing House.

——— 2000. *Following the Light: A Documentary History of the Church of God Movement.* Anderson, Ind.: Church of God Ministries, Inc.

Church of God Heritage: Reformation Reflections (set of audio taped lectures, Anderson School of Theology, February 5-8, 1980, on the occasion of the movement's centennial celebration). Included:
1. Robert H. Reardon, "Much Ado About Heritage"
2. John W. V. Smith, "Historical Heritage"
3. Gene W. Newberry, "Theological Heritage"
4. Val B. Clear, "Sociological Heritage"
5. T. Franklin Miller, "Reflections on the Day"
6. Harold L. Phillips, "The Miracle of Survival" (publishing history)
7. John W. V. Smith, "National Church Structure for Ministry"
8. F. Dale Bengtson, "We Sing Our Heritage"

Clear, Valorous B. 1953. "The Church of God: A Study in Social Adaptation." Diss., University of Chicago Divinity School. Published in 1977 as *Where the Saints Have Trod.*

Clear, Valorous B. 1963 (Jan. 16). "Reflections of a Postsectarian," *The Christian Century.*

Confer, Robert L. 1992. *Remembering, Reflecting, Renewing: A Look at the Historical Developments of the Church of God In and Around Grand Junction, Michigan.* Grand Junction: Warner Camp.

Cook, Diana L. 1981. "A Study of the Historical Development and Current Perspectives of the Inspirational Youth Convention of the National Association of the Church of God, West Middlesex, Pa." Anderson University School of Theology.

Courtney, Donald A. 1954. "A Study of the Development of the Sunday School in the Church of God." Anderson University School of Theology.

Dye, Dwight. 1963. "Asceticism in the Church of God Reformation Movement from 1880 to 1913. University of Tulsa.

Fowler, Ronald J., ed. 1970. *The Church of God in Black Perspective.* Proceedings of the Caucus of Black Churchmen, Cleveland, Ohio, April, 1970. Shining Light Survey Press.

Hall, Kenneth F. 1954. "A History of Curricular Materials in the Church of God." Butler University School of Religion.

Hartman, Marvin. 1958. "The Origin and Development of the General Ministerial Assembly of the Church of God, 1917-1950." Thesis, Butler University.

Hastings, Raymond E. 1958. "The Church of God in Jamaica: A Critical Study of its Structure and Work." Anderson University School of Theology.

Hayes, Sherrill D. 1962. "Concerns for Christian Education in the Church of God as Expressed by the Program of the National Board of Christian Education." Anderson University School of Theology.

Heffren, H. C. 1970. *Voices of the Pioneers: Early Years of the Church of God in Western Canada* (Camrose, Alberta: The Camrose Canadian).

Hetrick, Gale. 1980. *Laughter Among the Trumpets: A History of the Church of God in Michigan.* Lansing, Mich.: The Church of God in Michigan.

Hughes, Richard T., and C. Leonard Allen. 1988. *Illusions of Innocence: Protestant Primitivism in America, 1630-1875.* Chicago: University of Chicago Press.

———— 1996. *Reviving the Ancient Faith: The Story of Churches of Christ in America.* Grand Rapids: Eerdmans.

Forrest, Aubrey. 1948. "A Study of the Development of the Basic Doctrines and Institutional Patterns in the Church of God." Diss., University of Southern California Graduate School of Religion.

417

Froese, Walter. 1982. *Sounding Forth the Gospel on the Prairies: A History of the Church of God Reformation Movement in Western Canada.* Camrose, Alberta: Gospel Contact Press.

Johnson, Donald D. 1955. "An Historical Survey of the Church of God in the Pacific Northwest." Thesis, Anderson School of Theology.

Jordan, Wilfred, and Richard Willowby. 1991. *Diamond Jubilee: National Association of the Church of God.* Anderson, Ind.: Warner Press.

Koeth, Robert E. 1983. "A History of Anti-Catholicism in the Church of God Reformation Movement." Anderson University School of Theology.

Leonard, Juanita Evans, ed. 1989. *Called To Minister, Empowered To Serve: Women In Ministry.* Anderson, Ind.: Warner Press.

Long, L. Leon. 1958. "Pacifism and War Participation in the Church of God." Graduate School, University of Illinois.

Massey, James Earl. 1957. *An Introduction to the Negro Churches in the Church of God Reformation Movement.* N.Y.: Shining Light Survey Press.

Meeds, Wilfred V. 1996. "The Hymnody of Barney Elliot Warren." Claremont Graduate School, California.

Miller, Holly G. "The Church with a Mind of its Own," *The Saturday Evening Post* (November 1985).

North, James B. 1994. *Union in Truth: An Interpretive History of the Restoration Movement.*Cincinnati: Standard Publishing.

Reardon, Robert H. 1979. *The Early Morning Light.* Anderson, Ind.: Warner Press.

Riggle, Herbert M. 1912. *The Christian Church: Its Rise and Progress.* Anderson, Ind.: Gospel Trumpet Company.

——— 1924. *Pioneer Evangelism.* Anderson, Ind.: Gospel Trumpet Company.

Royster, James E. 1967. "A History of the Church of God in South India, 1897-1960." Dissertation, Hartford Seminary Foundation.

Sanders, Cheryl J. 1996. *Saints In Exile: The Holiness-Pentecostal Experience in African American Religion and Culture.* N.Y.: Oxford University Press.

Schell, William. 1893. *Biblical Trace of the Church.* Grand Junction, Mich.: Gospel Trumpet Company.

Schultz, David C. 1980. *Church of God Missions: The First 100 Years.* Anderson, Ind.: Missionary Board of the Church of God.

Smith, Frederick G. 1911. *The Evolution of Christianity.* Anderson, Ind.: Gospel Trumpet Company.

Smith, John W. V. 1956. *Truth Marches On: A Brief Study of the History of the Church of God Reformation Movement.* Anderson, Ind.: Warner Press. Rev. ed., *A Brief History of the Church of God Reformation Movement* (1976).

Smith, John W. V. 1967. "The Church of God at Eighty-Six," in *The School of Theology Bulletin* (Anderson, Ind., Spring 1967), 3-10.

——— 1980. *The Quest for Holiness and Unity*. Anderson, Ind: Warner Press.

Strege, Merle D. 1982. "Where Scandinavian Is Spoken: Ethnic Identity and Assimilation Among Scandinavian Immigrants in the Church of God (Anderson, Indiana). Berkeley:The Graduate Theological Union.

——— (2 vols.). 1987, 1989. *A Look At the Church of God for Children*. Anderson, Ind.: Warner Press.

——— 1991. *Tell Me the Tale: Historical Reflections on the Church of God*. Anderson, Ind.: Warner Press.

——— 1993. *Tell Me Another Tale: Further Reflections on the Church of God*. Anderson, Ind.: Warner Press.

Sterner, R. Eugene. 1960. *We Reach Our Hands in Fellowship: An Introduction to the Church of God*. Anderson, Ind.: Warner Press.

Telfer, David A. 1975. "Sociological and Theological Foundations for Church of God Ministry in Ethnic Minority Communities in the United States." Iliff School of Theology.

——— 1981. *Red, Yellow, Black, White, and Brown*: Ministry and Evangelism in Ethnic Communities, Home Missions in the Church of God Reformation Movement. Anderson, Ind.: Warner Press.

Warner, Daniel, and H. M. Riggle. 1903. *The Cleansing of the Sanctuary*. Moundsville, W.Va.: Gospel Trumpet Co.

Wickersham, Henry C. 1900. *A History of the Church*. Moundsville, W.Va.: Gospel Trumpet Co.

Williams, Lima Lehmer. 1986. *Walking in Missionary Shoes: A History of the Church of God in East Africa*. Anderson, Ind.: Warner Press.

Church of God Publications

419

Willowby, Richard. 1986. *Family Reunion: A Century of Camp Meetings.* Anderson, Ind.: Warner Press.

Vital Christianity. 1980 (June 22, vol. 100, number 12). Special historical issue of this Periodical, celebrating the first century of the Church of God movement.

D. THEOLOGICAL AND BIBLICAL WORKS

Blackwelder, Boyce W. 1958. *Light from the Greek New Testament.* Anderson, Ind.: Gospel Trumpet Co. Reprinted 1976, Baker Book House.

Boyer, Harold W. 1960. *The Apostolic Church and the Apostasy.* Anderson, Ind.: Gospel Trumpet Co.

Brown, Charles E. 1931. *A New Approach to Christian Unity.* Anderson, Ind.: Gospel Trumpet Co. Reprinted in the mid-1990s by Warner Press as part of the "Church of God Classic Collection."

———— 1939. *The Church Beyond Division.* Anderson, Ind.: Gospel Trumpet Co.

———— 1944. *The Meaning of Salvation.* Anderson, Ind.: Warner Press.

———— 1945. *The Meaning of Sanctification.* Anderson, Ind.: Warner Press. Reprinted in the mid-1990s by Warner Press as part of the "Church of God Classic Collection."

———— 1947. *The Apostolic Church: A Study in Historical Theology.* Anderson, Ind.: Gospel Trumpet Company.

———— 1954. *When Souls Awaken: An Interpretation of Radical Christianity.* Anderson, Ind.: Gospel Trumpet Co.

Byers, J. W. 1899. *The Grace of Healing or Christ Our Physician.* Moundsville, W. Va.: Gospel Trumpet Co.

Byrum, Enoch E. 1919. *Miracles and Healing.* Anderson, Ind.: Gospel Trumpet Co. Reprinted in the mid-1990s by Warner Press as part of the "Church of God Classic Collection."

Byrum, Russell R. 1925. *Christian Theology.* Anderson, Ind.: Gospel Trumpet Co. Revised by others, 1982.

Callen, Barry. 1969. "Church of God Reformation Movement: A Study in Ecumenical Idealism." Thesis, Asbury Theological Seminary.

———— 1978. *A Time To Remember: Teachings.* Anderson, Ind.: Warner Press.

———— ed. 1990. *Listening to the Word of God.* Anderson, Ind.: Anderson University and Warner Press. Includes a major biographical tribute to Boyce W. Blackwelder.

———— 1995. *Contours of a Cause: The Theological Vision of the Church of God Movement (Anderson).* Anderson, Ind.: Anderson School of Theology.

Callen, Barry L. 1996. *God As Loving Grace*. Nappanee, Ind.: Evangel
　　Publishing House.

───── 1997. *Faithful In The Meantime: A Biblical View of Final Things and
　　Present Responsibilities*. Nappanee, Ind.: Evangel Publishing
　　House.

─────, and James North. 1997. *Coming Together In Christ: Pioneering A
　　New Testament Way to Christian Unity*. Joplin, MO: College Press.

───── 1999. *Radical Christianity*: The Believers Church Tradition in
　　Christianity's History and Future. Nappanee, Ind.: Evangel
　　Publishing House.

Camp-Meeting Sermons, June 6-15, 1913. Anderson, Ind.: Gospel Trumpet Co.

DeYoung, Curtiss Paul. 1995. *Coming Together: The Bible's Message in an
　　Age of Diversity*. Valley Forge, Pa.: Judson Press.

Forrest, Aubrey L. 1948. "A Study of the Development of the Basic
　　Doctrines and Institutional Patterns in the Church of God
　　(Anderson, Indiana)." Dissertation, University of Southern
　　California Graduate School of Religion.

Gaulke, Max R. 1959. *May Thy Kingdom Come—Now!* Anderson, Ind.:
　　Warner Press.

Gray, Albert F. 1944, 1946, 2 vols. *Christian Theology*. Anderson, Ind.:
　　Warner Press. Reprinted in the mid-1990s by Warner Press as part
　　of the "Church of God Classic Collection."

Jones, Kenneth. 1980. *The Word of God*. Anderson, Ind.: Warner Press.

───── 1985. *Commitment to Holiness*. Anderson, Ind.: Warner Press.

───── 1995. *Theology of Holiness and Love*. University Press of America.

Linn, Otto F. 1941-42. *Studies in the New Testament* (3 vols.). Anderson,
　　Ind.: Gospel Trumpet Co. (vol. 3 does not carry the company
　　name—offered a controversial view of the Book of Revelation dif-
　　ferent from the "standard" F. G. Smith view).Volume 3 reprinted
　　in the mid-1990s by Warner Press as part of the "Church of God
　　Classic Collection."

McCutcheon, Lillie S. 1964. *The Symbols Speak*. Published privately. Rev.
　　ed., Jackson, KY: Reformation Publishers, 1999.

Massey, James Earl. 1979. *Concerning Christian Unity*. Anderson, Ind.:
　　Warner Press.

Martin, Earl L. 1942. *Toward Understanding God*. Anderson, Ind.: Gospel
　　Trumpet Co.

───── 1946. *The Wondrous Cross*. Anderson, Ind.: Warner Press. Reprinted
　　in the mid-1990s by Warner Press as part of the "Church of God
　　Classic Collection."

───── 1952. *This We Believe, This We Proclaim.* Anderson, Ind.: Gospel
　　Trumpet Co.

Miller, Gene, ed. 1972. *Dynamics of the Faith: Evangelical Christian
　　Foundations*. Houston, TX: Gulf-Coast Bible College.

Newell, Arlo F. 1978. *Receive the Holy Spirit*. Anderson, Ind.: Warner Press.

Reardon, Robert H. 1943. "The Doctrine of the Church and the Christian Life in the Church of God Reformation Movement." Thesis, Oberlin School of Theology.

Riggle, Herbert M. 1899. *The Kingdom of God and the One Thousand Years' Reign*. Moundsville, W.Va.: Gospel Trumpet Co. Reprinted in the mid-1990s by Warner Press as part of the "Church of God Classic Collection."

——— 1909. *Christian Baptism, The Lord's Supper, and Feet Washing*. Anderson, Ind.: Gospel Trumpet Publishing Co. Reprinted in the mid-1990s by Warner Press as part of the "Church of God Classic Collection."

——— 1918. *Christ's Kingdom and Reign*. Anderson, Ind.: Gospel Trumpet Publishing Co.

——— 1919. *Christ's Second Coming and What Will Follow*. Anderson, Ind.: Gospel Trumpet Publishing Co.

Royster, James. 1958. "Historical and Analytical Survey of Anderson, Indiana, Camp Meeting Preaching in the Church of God, 1907-1957." Thesis, Anderson University School of Theology.

Schell, William G. 1899. *The Better Testament or The Two Testaments Compared*. Moundsville,W. Va.: Gospel Trumpet Co.

——— 1922. *Sanctification and Holiness: The False and the True*. Chicago: Herald Publishing Company.

Select Camp-Meeting Sermons, June 16-24, 1928. Anderson, Ind.: Gospel Trumpet Co.

Smith, Frederick G. 1908. *The Revelation Explained*. Anderson, Ind.: Gospel Trumpet Co. Reissued through the 1940s in numerous editions. Reprinted in the mid-1990s by Warner Press as part of the "Church of God Classic Collection."

——— 1914. *What the Bible Teaches*. Anderson, Ind.: Gospel Trumpet Co. Condensed by Kenneth E. Jones (Anderson, Ind.: Warner Press, 1955, 1999).

——— 1919. *The Last Reformation*. Anderson, Ind.: Gospel Trumpet Co.

Smith, John W. V. 1954. "The Approach of the Church of God and Comparable Groups to the Problem of Christian Unity." Dissertation, University of Southern California Graduate School of Religion.

——— 1985. *I Will Build My Church: Biblical Insights on Distinguishing Doctrines of the Church of God*. Anderson, Ind.: Warner Press.

Stafford, Gilbert. 1973. "Experiential Salvation and Christian Unity in the Thought of Seven Theologians of the Church of God (Anderson)." Dissertation, Boston University School of Theology.

——— 1996. *Theology for Disciples*. Anderson, Ind.: Warner Press.

Stanley, John E. 1990. "Unity and Diversity: Interpreting the Book of Revelation in the Church of God (Anderson)," *Wesleyan Theological Journal* (Fall 1990), 74-98.

Sterner, R. Eugene. 1978. *Healing & Wholeness*. Anderson, Ind.: Warner Press.

Strege, Merle D., ed. 1986. *Baptism and Church: A Believers' Church Vision*. Grand Rapids, Mich.: Sagamore Books.

————— 1991 (April). "Demise (?) of a Peace Church: The Church of God (Anderson), Pacifism, and Civil Religion," *Mennonite Quarterly Review*, 128-140.

—————, and Richard Willowby. 1996. *God's Redeeming: Story: A Theological Primer*. Anderson, Ind.: Warner Press.

Strong, Marie. 1980. *Basic Teachings from Patmos: A Guide to the Basic Message of the Book of Revelation*. Anderson, Ind.: Warner Press. Revised 1995,

Sharon Clark Pearson, ed., with the new title *A Common Sense Approach to the Book of Revelation* (Warner Press).

Tasker, George P. 1924. *An Appeal to the Free and Autonomous Churches of Christ in the Fellowship of the Evening Light*. Calcutta, India: published privately.

Teasley, D. O. 1918. *The Bible and How To Interpret It*. Anderson, Ind.: Gospel Trumpet Co.Reprinted in the mid-1990s by Warner Press as part of the "Church of God Classic Collection."

Warner, Daniel S. 1880. *Bible Proofs of the Second Work of Grace*. Goshen, Ind.: E. U. Mennonite Pub. Society. Reprinted 2000 by Reformation Publishers with an Introduction by Barry L. Callen.

E. SONGBOOKS AND HYMNALS

Adams, Robert A. 1980. Doctoral dissertation, "The Hymnody of the Church of God (1885-1980) as a Reflection of That Church's Theological and Cultural Changes," Southwestern Baptist Theological Seminary, Fort Worth, Texas.

Major Songbooks

Title	Editor(s)	Date
Songs of Victory	Joseph Fischer	1885
Anthems from the Throne	D. S. Warner, B. E. Warren	1888
Echoes from Glory	B. E. Warren, D. S. Warner	1893
Songs of the Evening Light	B. E. Warren, A. L. Byers	1897

Salvation Echoes	B. E. Warren, A. L. Byers,	
	C. E. Hunter, D. O. Teasley	1900
Truth In Song	B. E. Warren, A. L. Byers,	
	C. E. Hunter, D. O. Teasley	1907
Songs of Grace and Glory	A. L. Byers, D. O. Teasley,	
	N. C. Clausen	1918
Reformation Glory	A. L. Byers, B. E. Warren	1923

Major Hymnals

Title	Editor(s)	Date
Select Hymns	B. E. Warren, A. L. Byer	
	Clara M. Brooks, D. O. Teasley	1911
Hymns and Spiritual Songs	A. L. Byers, B. E. Warren	1930
Hymnal of the Church of God	Robert A. Nicholson	1953
Hymnal of the Church of God	Robert A. Nicholson	1971
Worship the Lord: Hymnal of		
The Church of God	Lloyd A. Larson, Frank K. Poncé	1989

Presentation at the 1953 Anderson Camp Meeting of the new 1953 Hymnal.
L. to R.: Harold L. Phillips, Editor in Chief;
Robert A. Nicholson, Hymnal Editor; Lottie M. Franklin, Book Editor.

F. INSTITUTIONAL HISTORIES

Byers, Andrew L. 1907. *The Gospel Trumpet Publishing Work.* Gospel Trumpet Company.

Callen, Barry L. 1988. *Preparing For Service: A History of Higher Education in the Church of God.* Anderson, Ind.: Warner Press.

——— 1992. *Guide of Soul and Mind: The Story of Anderson University.* Anderson, Ind.: Anderson University and Warner Press.

Crose, Lester A. 1981. *Passport for a Reformation.* Anderson, Ind.: Warner Press. [Mission endeavors outside North America.]

Meyer, Louis. 1992. *Pioneering New Frontiers in North America.* Anderson, Ind.: Board of Church Extension and Home Missions and Warner Press.

Phillips, Harold L. 1979. *Miracle of Survival.* Anderson, Ind.: Warner Press. [History of the Gospel Trumpet Company/Warner Press]

G. THE PERIODICAL AND CHURCH CURRICULUM

Nearly all of the issues of the Church of God movement's periodical, first known as the *Gospel Trumpet* and later as *Vital Christianity*, published between January, 1881, and September, 1996, are available in hardcopy, on microfilm, and soon in digital format.

Warner Press publishes a church curriculum know as "*Bridges.*" Its materials are designed for all ages and are supported by an eleven-volume series of books designed to invite persons ever deeper into the responsibilities and joys of discipleship.

H. WEB SITES

Church of God, General:	www.chog.org
Archives—by way of the Anderson University Library Site:	bones.anderson.edu
Christians Broadcasting Hope:	www.cbhviewpoint.org
Church of God Colleges/University/Seminary	
Anderson University	
General:	www.anderson.edu
School of Theology, via.	www.anderson.edu
TRI-S:	www.anderson.edu/tri-s
Mid-America Bible College	www.mabc.edu

Warner Pacific College:	www.warnerpacific.edu
Warner Southern College:	www.warner.edu

Board of Pensions: www.cogpension.org
Credit Union: www.cogcu.org
Discussion Group:
                    http://chogtalk@onelist.com/community/chogtalk
International Youth Conventions   www.IYC2000.org
Wesleyan/Holiness Women Clergy Conferences
                                www.messiah.edu/WHWC